# The Book of
# CHEESE

ALSO BY LIZ THORPE:

*THE CHEESE CHRONICLES*

# The Book of
# CHEESE

## THE ESSENTIAL GUIDE TO DISCOVERING CHEESES YOU'LL LOVE

## LIZ THORPE

### PHOTOGRAPHY BY ELLEN SILVERMAN

FLATIRON
BOOKS
NEW YORK

THE BOOK OF CHEESE.

Copyright © 2017
by Elizabeth Thorpe.
All rights reserved.
Printed in China.
For information, address
Flatiron Books
175 Fifth Avenue
New York, N.Y. 10010.

www.flatironbooks.com

Photographer: Ellen Silverman
Food stylist: Eugene Jho
Prop stylist: Bette Blau
Book design: William van Roden
Production manager: Adriana Coada

The Library of Congress
Cataloging-in-Publication Data
is available upon request.

ISBN 978-1-250-06345-8
(hardcover)

ISBN 978-1-250-06346-5
(e-book)

Our books may be purchased
in bulk for promotional,
educational, or business use.
Please contact your local
bookseller or the Macmillan
Corporate and Premium
Sales Department at
1-800- 221-7945,
extension 5442,
or by e-mail at
MacmillanSpecialMarkets
@macmillan.com.

First Edition: September 2017

10 9 8 7 6 5 4 3

FOR ALL THE MAKERS AND
ALL THE MONGERS.
WITHOUT YOU, THERE WOULD
BE NO CHEESE
FOR THE REST OF US.

# CONTENTS

# The Book of
# CHEESE

# INTRODUCTION

# I walked into a small Brooklyn butcher shop one afternoon in 2000, having recently been laid off from my dot-com job, and found myself lulled by

the siren call of a cheese case. The meat guys stood behind the counter while I ogled what seemed like an impossible number of cheeses. There were maybe twenty, of which I was familiar with four or five. Those in the counter crew were veritably bouncing on their tiptoes, asking politely, if somewhat urgently, what they could get for me. They wanted to sell me something, but I just wanted to sample all those cheeses. After that, I wanted an explanation for how so many existed in the first place. I remember one with a murky black line through the center, like a teacher's pen slash. Several reminded me of rock slabs, their bases littered with little crumbs and flecks. A few oozed silently. I don't recall exactly when I went from staring at them to buying and eating them, but I remember feeling intensely curious as to where they came from, and also mildly shocked that a food I had known my whole life—cheese—was actually hundreds of different foods.

Being the consummate good student with an unexpected amount of free time, I took the only step I could think of. I bought a book about cheese. It was a revelation, a guide called *Cheese Primer*, written by a man named Steven Jenkins. I recall diving into this book, organized by country, and expecting to master French cheese. And then the bizarre sensation of looking down at the book and seeing I'd turned many pages but hadn't retained anything. The cheeses all slipped past me, a parade of names in a language I didn't speak and a slew of facts that quickly jumbled in my (usually stellar) memory. It was all so abstract. I wanted to know these cheeses, to understand them in reference to one another. I wanted to walk into that butcher shop, point to a cheese, and confidently say, "I'd like that one" (while knowing that I really would like it). After several cover-to-cover reads of *Cheese Primer*, I concluded that I was more literal than I realized, and my only recourse should I wish to understand cheese was to go find Mr. Jenkins and get him to hire me. Together, we could taste and travel and maybe then I'd master the world of cheese.

Luckily, Jenkins was the cheese guru of Harlem's Fairway Market, and he not only took my call but offered to meet me in his store. Happily, he confirmed that my literalism was the best way to learn cheese. He suggested that I take a job at the Fairway counter, where I would cut, wrap, and sell cheese all day. His counter, by the way, probably had 300 cheeses. Talking cheese while scrambling back and forth behind forty linear feet of it would, he assured me, make it stick in my brain. Unhappily, he did not offer me a travel pass to Europe or an assistantship doing rarefied things like research and blind cheese-tasting. And there were no women working at his counter. Heck, there was no one under forty-five at his counter. The pay was, I think, minimum wage. And, to tell the truth, I was just plain scared. My fledgling cheese curiosity was threatening to tank my boring, predictable, post-collegiate life. I thanked Steve, declined the job, and vowed to keep cheese as my weekend hobby.

But I still thought about it. I'd graduated from reading about cheese to reading about cheese while tasting it. I'd buy small wedges of a few things and write down what they reminded me of. Then I'd bone up on the facts. What I began to notice was that my tasting notes were all about my memories. I had no idea what the soft, silken cheese Reblochon was supposed to taste like. But it felt like my mom's scrambled eggs (she still makes them better than anyone), slightly wobbly, knitted together with a tongue-coating skim of butter. Unwrapping a triangular wedge of Reblochon, and again after swallowing some, I could close my eyes and feel my-self next to D.W., the chestnut quarter horse I rode in middle school. I could smell what for me had been the soothing intoxication of equine perspiration, fresh hay, leather saddles, and—hanging in the background—manure. I was dimly aware that telling my friends that a cheese tasted like poop wasn't going to make them try it, but I could tell them that eating a bite transported me to a place where I had been supremely happy.

My efforts to keep cheese a weekend hobby were steadily failing. I spent my days at a job that I didn't particularly care about and pondered how adults spent their entire lives at work when they kind of hated their work. The cubicle was killing me. I wondered if I could invent a career out of cheese. So I started looking around again, and my cold calling brought me to the New York City institution Murray's Cheese. Once again, I was given the advice that I'd have to work the counter if I really wanted to learn the cheese. This time I was ready, and I said yes. I gave myself a year to see if cheese and I could really be something and got behind the counter a few weeks later. At first, working the cheese counter was terrifying. I lived in low-grade panic that a customer would ask for something that I'd never heard of (a likely scenario as I hadn't heard of much), and when they inevitably did, I scrambled to fill time while I scanned 200 cheeses looking for the handwritten sign that most closely approximated what I thought they'd said. To appear conversational, I asked what they liked about that cheese. Usually, they told me how it reminded them of another cheese but it was better. Happily, that other cheese was often one I knew. Cheddar, say. Or maybe Brie.

As the months passed and I began to master Murray's offerings, I was able to use this trick with the customers who walked in and didn't know what they wanted. I'd start by asking them what basic cheeses they did or did not enjoy. Knowing that they liked Blue told me they were open to stronger flavors; they weren't afraid of salt; they were likely to be more adventurous. Hearing that Havarti with dill was one of their favorites told me they preferred more approachable flavor; that a cheese with a moldy rind might turn them off; that rich, fatty cheese would make them happy. It gave me a jumping-off point. Within a few months, I stopped asking if they wanted an English cheese or an Italian cheese because most people had no idea what that might entail. And, over the years as the cheese choices multiplied exponentially, being English wasn't likely to entail much at all. Suddenly, the English were making every style of cheese imaginable.

I never asked customers what kind of milk they liked. To most, that implied whole, 2 percent, or skim. That one might milk a goat or sheep and make cheese hadn't occurred to a lot of people, or, even worse, they had an immediate and negative reaction to what goat cheese was like based on one crappy salad they'd been served in a restaurant. I had learned that how a cheese is made has a huge impact on how it tastes, so an unaged sheep cheese and a two-year aged sheep cheese might as well be different milk types, so dramatic is the flavor difference.

The fun of the cheese counter became the detective work of figuring out what customers thought they liked and then getting them to try something new inspired by their preferences. I gave myself bonus points when that something new was enthusiastically received, despite previous assurances that they hated all goat cheese, or whatever it was.

As Jenkins had promised, the cheese counter taught me cheese, but after nearly a year I was feeling the itch for something new. Around this time, New York's better chefs (most of whom were European, usually French) had begun coming to Murray's to buy cheese for their restaurants. They wanted to offer a cheese course after dinner, and they needed a dealer. I made my pitch to take over Murray's fledgling wholesale business, and within weeks was running around Manhattan with a bag of samples. It wasn't long before chefs in Atlanta, Chicago, and San Francisco began calling. Every week, I'd speak to the team behind Thomas Keller, a chef people were whispering might be the best in America. The chefs, it turned out, were touchingly nostalgic about cheese-tasting; their memories were of their grandmother's farm in Gascony or the gleefully insistent reek of farmers' market cheeses in Alsace. Mainly, they talked about the cheese they were given when they came home from school each day. Some woman—a mother or aunt or neighbor—would ceremoniously present them with a piece of cheese each afternoon, and this was the food of their childhoods.

The chefs came to me for one course of the four-star meals they served, and because of them a whole bevy of exotic and previously unfamiliar cheeses started to infiltrate the lives of America's cities. The chefs' demands sent me, and Murray's, all over Europe finding and securing exactly the right Manchego or Comté. Their willingness offered the first significant sales outlet for fledgling American cheese makers striving to produce handcrafted food that could rival the best of the imports. Food TV started to gain momentum as American entertainment, and overnight these chefs morphed into rock stars. Thanks to these proselytizers, cheese was becoming big business, and I got to stand beside them, finding what they needed and advising on what they should serve next. In return, they showed me a new possibility, of which their restaurants were only the first step. It was the picture of their childhoods—of daily life when cheese was an essential and constant component. Cheese wasn't rarefied and mysterious; it was sustenance and comfort. Cheese was a snack. It was good, everyday food.

As America's interest in and appreciation for food grew, so did our businesses at Murray's. We opened an education center in 2004 and began teaching our customers about cheese. As I worked on curriculum and prepared lectures for the weekend-long Boot Camp series, I thought more about my own struggles to master cheese. Most people weren't going to quit their jobs and go work at a counter to learn cheese. How could I translate my experience into a classroom? Those weekend-long classes included incessant tasting—usually seventy-five to eighty cheeses over two and a half days. My biggest challenge was getting people to talk about their impressions. Just as I felt when I first tasted Reblochon, they were interested but completely intimidated. They didn't want to be wrong or look stupid. They were all wondering what they were *supposed* to be tasting. It was one of these first students who had the courage to raise his hand one Sunday afternoon as I talked about Loire Valley goat cheese tasting like wet rock. He looked a little uncomfortable, cleared his throat, and said, "But, um. What does wet rock taste like?" And I paused, immediately realizing that I was contributing to everyone's fear of not getting it right. That's because I had failed to establish a clear connection between smell and taste. Not only was there no common language for talking about cheese—no agreements about what Swiss cheese was and wasn't supposed to taste like—but no one had mapped out what cheese was supposed to smell like. No one was helping everyday cheese eaters recognize that their smell impressions were going to inform their taste impressions as much as (or even more than) what was happening on their tongues. It was a major awakening for me. I had experienced it myself back when I first served my friends Reblochon and tried to tell them how the cheese could taste like poop, and have that be a good thing.

It wasn't more than a few years later that Big Retail came walking through the door of little Murray's Cheese. We were approached by the country's largest traditional supermarket about opening Murray's Cheese counters in their stores across the nation. This was 2007, and food hipsterdom was blowing up. Brooklyn was fast becoming the epicenter of all things artisanal. New Yorkers were fermenting for fun in their apartments. I was still racing around trying to ensure that Murray's cheese selection included the newest and smallest and greatest cheese makers from around the world, and increasingly from across the United States. And here was a giant supermarket, wanting to bring us in to improve their cheese selection and their customers' experience. A lot of people (truth be told, most everybody in the business, some to my face and many more behind my back) questioned why I would be excited about trying to sell ordinary cheese in Dayton, Ohio; Marietta, Georgia; and Fort Worth, Texas. I went to these places and wandered through massive supermarkets, some so big that locals walked around them for exercise when the weather was bad. I talked to people pushing carts through the deli department, people who cast a glance at the cheese counter, paused, and then picked up some prepackaged thing they'd bought a dozen times before. I trotted out my old counter pickup line: "Tell me what kind of cheese you like, and I'll help you find something new that you'll love." They usually looked wary, a little relieved, and then maybe they'd apologize because they only knew a few cheeses. But, they'd say, "I really like Cheddar. Or Brie. Or Blue. Or Havarti (with dill)." Times had changed since I started at the Murray's counter, and in only a few years Food Network and cooking magazines and Emeril Lagasse had penetrated the national consciousness and left in their wake some cheeses that, back when I started, were still exotics: Taleggio, say, or Manchego. People knew a handful of cheeses but had no idea where to go from there. Standing in those supermarkets, talking with all those people who were excited about cheese, but a little afraid of it, made me believe that the picture my fancy New York chef friends had painted was possible. We could be more than a nation of eaters gobbling down bad cheese pizza. We could be a nation of cheese eaters, and our kids could enjoy a small piece of something delicious and wholesome just by opening the refrigerator. That was why I wanted to open hundreds of satellite cheese counters. The consumers were there and they were willing. They just needed a guide.

When I left Murray's in 2012, after a decade of leading and managing all these cheese-focused businesses, I started a consulting company. Sometimes my clients were producers of cheese trying to grow their business across the United States, or in the case of the Europeans, struggling to understand the American market. Other times, my clients were retailers: big and little guys wanting to improve their selection, or train their employees, or become leaders in the cheese category. Always, for both kinds of clients, there was the desire to sell more cheese. Everyone kept butting up against the same problems: how could they help customers branch out, buy more, and come back again? I think all the time about the chats I had in the supermarket aisles back in 2007. If I could have those conversations everywhere, my clients would sell a lot more cheese. But I've realized that I don't have to be there—I just have to take what I've learned in the past fifteen years and give people a road map to follow. *The Book of Cheese* is that road map.

## HERE'S WHAT I'VE LEARNED SINCE MAKING CHEESE MY LIFE'S WORK:

- It doesn't matter where cheese is made.
- Or what kind of milk it's from.
- Or the technical classification I or any other expert would give it.

### WHAT MATTERS IS:

- Starting with general, universally understood cheese-reference points.
- Using them to establish what kind of cheese you like.
- Having guidelines so you know what kind of flavors that jumping-off point will lead to.
- Embracing the awesome miracle that your own memories and experiences—their smell and texture and temperature—inform your impressions of what's good.

### AND, THEN, MOST IMPORTANT:

- Venturing out with these guides to discover other cheeses that you are going to love.

## HOW THE BOOK OF CHEESE IS ORGANIZED
### THE GATEWAY CHEESE

For years, I've struggled to organize the world of cheese for people. The typical classifications of country, milk type, and style (pressed or bloomy) are deeply problematic. Organizing by country assumes that all French cheese is the same (it's not). Milk type assumes that how a cheese is made has less influence on flavor and texture than the animal the cheese started with (it doesn't). Style will tell you about flavor and texture commonalities, but it's so technical and, honestly, kind of boring. All of these traditional classifications presuppose just enough knowledge that they're nearly useless for someone just getting into cheese, and none of them take into account our personal preferences. Just because I say a cheese is good doesn't mean you're going to like it. Aren't you ultimately interested in finding more cheese you're going to like?

All those cheese-counter customers and supermarket shoppers led me to the approach of organizing cheese by gateway. That, plus every person at every party I've ever brought cheese to. When I arrive with cheese, everyone gathers around excitedly and a few brave souls ask me, "Is this a Cheddar? Swiss? A Brie?" And I answer, "Well, not technically. But it's like a Brie. If you like Brie, you're gonna lose your mind over this cheese." The gateways are a handful of cheeses you've likely heard of, that you might even have eaten as a kid, and that you've almost certainly eaten as a grown-up. And you know what? Nearly the entire world of cheese can be mapped out from these gateways. There are some cheeses that I still find so weird, or so much a part of two worlds, that linking them to a single gateway would be forced. Those outliers are the misfits, and they're grouped together in the book's final chapter.

Each gateway cheese is a jumping-off point. It's a cheese with specific flavor and texture associations, and it leads you to a group of cheeses that share these qualities. Like many other foods (and drinks), however, that group of cheese exists along a spectrum of flavor. There are milder, more approachable examples and stronger, more intense examples. It's worth noting that, for me, *intense* flavor doesn't imply off-putting or alienating, just bigger and more concentrated. It's like the difference between a Ruby Red grapefruit and a lemon, or ground chuck and dry-aged sirloin steak. Citrus or beef flavors are gateways into a group, but that doesn't mean you're going to like every single member of that group. You may, you may not, but the gateway cheese and its flavor spectrum help you narrow down the options and figure out your preferences. And these preferences are likely to hold true across gateways. You may find that the Mozzarella Gateway leads you to an entire flavor spectrum you love—approachable, intermediate, and intense. But the Blue Gateway introduces a group of cheeses that on the intense end of the flavor spectrum may be too much for you, although you find the approachable end revelatory. The takeaway: you don't care for persistent, peppery, fermented flavors in your cheese. That's good to know, because the flavor spectrum of other gateways may contain persistent, peppery, fermented-tasting cheeses. They're not Blues, but chances are you won't care for them, either.

The gateways are your cheeses of departure. They'll introduce you to a larger group, arranged along a spectrum of increasing flavor intensity, so you can confirm what you like, branch out across gateways with confidence, and avoid the cheeses that, for you, just don't taste good.

## MOZZARELLA IS THE GATEWAY TO:

Unaged and rindless (aka "fresh") cheeses, all about the flavor of the milk from which they're made, becoming increasingly intense thanks to salt.

**APPROACHABLE:** Milk

**INTERMEDIATE:** Yogurt

**INTENSE:** Milky brine

## BRIE IS THE GATEWAY TO:

Soft, smearable, white-rinded cheeses that embrace cream, butter, and yogurt, becoming increasingly intense with flavors of cooked vegetables.

BRIE FLAVOR SPECTRUM

**APPROACHABLE:** Cream

**INTERMEDIATE:** Crème fraîche

**INTENSE:** Cooked mushroom and cruciferous veggies (broccoli/cauliflower), bitter greens

## HAVARTI IS THE GATEWAY TO:

The consummate everyday eating cheeses (the Europeans call them table cheeses), plush and springy in texture, with milky flavors that move from tangy to sweet to seriously earthy.

HAVARTI FLAVOR SPECTRUM

**APPROACHABLE:** Barely tangy milk

**INTERMEDIATE:** Sweet, cooked milk

**INTENSE:** Bitter greens, soil and hay aromas

## TALEGGIO IS THE GATEWAY TO:

The world of stinky cheese. Soft and sticky, with a pungent aroma if not necessarily strong flavor. The first time I used the phrase "gateway cheese," I was working at the Murray's counter, and this was the cheese it applied to. When customers came in saying they liked soft cheese but wanted something stronger, I recommended Taleggio.

TALEGGIO FLAVOR SPECTRUM

**APPROACHABLE:** Yeasty pizza dough

**INTERMEDIATE:** Cured meat

**INTENSE:** Beef bouillon, smells of the body

## MANCHEGO IS THE GATEWAY TO:

The cheeses you're least likely to have heard of, and most likely to enjoy. Aged sheep and goat cheeses start with subtle, outdoorsy associations and progress into caramel, piquant, and downright gamy concentration.

MANCHEGO FLAVOR SPECTRUM

**APPROACHABLE:** Subtly herbaceous and nutty; soft, gentle flavor

**INTERMEDIATE:** Caramel edging into butterscotch

**INTENSE:** Piquant and gamy, like rare meat

## CHEDDAR IS THE GATEWAY TO:

Firm, chunky, and crumbly cheeses beyond the world of mild, medium, and sharp. These cheeses begin milky and lactic, progressing to sweet buttered toast and, ultimately, sour, wild intensity.

**CHEDDAR FLAVOR SPECTRUM**

**APPROACHABLE:** Cultured butter

**INTERMEDIATE:** Buttered toast

**INTENSE:** Wet soil, game

## SWISS IS THE GATEWAY TO:

A bevy of smooth, pliable, brilliant melters with sweet (as in not sharp) flavor that becomes increasingly toasty and roasty, culminating in caramelized onion and beef bouillon. The one with holes is the first we all met, but chances are you'll find several that are better.

**SWISS FLAVOR SPECTRUM**

**APPROACHABLE:** Swissy, cooked milk

**INTERMEDIATE:** Toasted/roasted nuts, meaty

**INTENSE:** Tropical fruit, caramelized onion

## PARMESAN IS THE GATEWAY TO:

Hard, grainy cheeses with nutty character, these guys start sweet and candied and wind up savory and acidic. It's where aged Gouda shows up, so radically different from its moist, red-wax–covered little brother, and where I break down the merits and distinctions between American Parmesan and Italian Parmigiano-Reggiano.

**PARMESAN FLAVOR SPECTRUM**

**APPROACHABLE:** Candied nuts

**INTERMEDIATE:** Bourbon and butterscotch

**INTENSE:** Kombucha

## BLUE IS THE GATEWAY TO:

Cheeses with interior mold, and generally higher salt, but still a radically diverse group ranging from soft, sweet, and buttery, to savory and fudgy, to smoky, acidic, and crumbly.

**BLUE FLAVOR SPECTRUM**

**APPROACHABLE:** Salt, Blue Brie

**INTERMEDIATE:** Toasted nuts, licorice

**INTENSE:** Fermented fruit, black pepper

## THE MISFITS:

Even cheese has a category for The Ones That Don't Fit Anywhere Else. The misfits include goat cheeses betwixt Mozzarella and Brie, scoopable specimens made with plants, and cheeses made and aged in such specific ways that they require a chapter category unto themselves.

## THE MAP

I've mapped out each chapter's cheeses according to flavor (on a spectrum of 1 to 10, approachable to intense) and availability (on a spectrum of 1 to 3, from likely available in your supermarket cheese department to single-source, mail-order obscure). When you reach the cheeses, entries begin with those most approachable in flavor and end with those that are most intense.

## THE TEXTURES

The cheeses of each gateway have shared textures. Knowing what's typical will help you recognize what's *not* typical. You may want a waxy, granular texture from the cheeses in the Parmesan Gateway, but definitely not from those in the Havarti Gateway.

## THE FLAVOR & AROMA WHEEL

Part of what makes cheese (and wine, and beer) intimidating is that experts toss out descriptions like mustardy, lactic, and floral all the time. This language can feel both overwhelming and random, and it doesn't help you find other cheeses you're likely to enjoy.

The flavor and aroma wheel shows you the smells and tastes you should expect to find in cheeses of the chapter (as well as those you *don't* want to find). These are grouped into the following flavor/aroma categories:

| | | |
|---|---|---|
| LACTIC (MEANING, DAIRY-RELATED) | FUNGUS | OTHER FOOD |
| | HERB | SPICES |
| FRUIT | PLANT | ATMOSPHERICS |
| VEGETABLE | ANIMAL | FLAWS |

**FLAVOR AND AROMA WILL HELP YOU IN SEVERAL WAYS:**

• By developing a common language of smell and taste across a related group of cheeses, you can better learn what you like (and what you don't), and how to describe it.

• Aroma and flavor preferences transcend the confines of each gateway cheese. So, if you really like the caramelized onion flavors of intense Taleggio types, you're probably going to like the caramelized-onion flavors of intense Swiss types.

• Cheese is tricky—flavors that are typical and desirable in the cheeses of one gateway (say, bitter greens in the Brie types) may be undesirable flaws in the cheeses of another gateway (like the Taleggio types).

# DESCRIBING CHEESE FROM THE OUTSIDE IN

You'll hear me describe cheese with the following words:

**RIND:** The exterior skin or crust of a cheese. Cheese makers can develop a specific kind of rind by adding mold (as in Brie) or washing the exterior of the cheese with salt water/brine (as in Taleggio). A cheese that's aged in the open air grows layers of ambient mold and yeasts and bacteria that, over time, become what's called a natural rind (like the Blue cheese Stilton). Some rinds are made of wax (as in Manchego) and others are cloth (as in clothbound or bandaged Cheddar). The rind is the barrier between a cheese's inside and its environment and, like our skin, it gets weathered over time. Young cheese is plump and moist with tight, soft skin. Aged cheese doesn't get wrinkly; it gets dried out, the rind becoming harder, crustier, and generally less desirable for eating.

Each Chapter Guide will give you tips about the edibility of those cheeses' rinds.

**CREAMLINE:** My word for the gooey layer (paper-thin to as much as half an inch) that develops between a soft, edible rind and the interior of a cheese. Flavors concentrate as you move from the inside to the outside of a cheese, so the taste of the creamline will be more intense than the cheese's center, and most influenced by the aroma and flavor of the rind. You may find a creamline on Brie and Taleggio types, but not on dry, aged cheeses like Manchego, Cheddar, Swiss, or Parmesan types.

**PASTE OR PÂTÉ:** The edible interior of a cheese, no matter how gnarly the rind may be.

**HOLES:** Described interchangeably as holes, eyes, or openings, these are small, round pockmarks in the paste of a cheese. A closed cheese is one with a firm, tight, evenly knitted texture, whereas an open cheese will be airier, squishier, and punctuated by holes that can be as small as a sesame seed or as large as a grape.

## INTRODUCTORY ESSAY

You've likely heard of the gateway cheeses and have eaten them too. But food is also deeply personal. My experiences and assumptions led me to choose the gateway cheeses that I did. The introductory essay will tell you more about the gateway, the group of cheeses you can expect to be led to, and why I've put them there. Sometimes cheese-making technique is the driving unifier; other times it's a certain mold or a shared lack of age. At the end of the day, what matters is that the group of cheeses share flavors. It's why there's no Goat Cheese Gateway. Goat cheese can taste like fifty different things.

## CHAPTER GUIDE

The basic terms and facts relevant to all cheese (like what's the deal with pasteurization, or some cheese-making basics that will help you understand flavor and texture) can be found throughout this book's Introduction (see pages 2–27). But the technical nitty-gritty of each gateway cheese can be found in the Chapter Guide. Look for:

- What to know

- What to avoid

- Storage and shelf life

## THE CHEESES

Each chapter's cheeses are presented in order from approachable to intense in flavor (in accordance with the map at the gateway opening). Each entry includes:

### ➺ BASIC FACTS

- **NAME**

- **COUNTRY OF ORIGIN**

- **MILK TYPE**

- **PASTEURIZATION:** A cheese is either pasteurized, unpasteurized, or (un)pasteurized—the latter meaning it can be found in both states.

## ➤ MAKERS AND BRANDS

The way cheeses are named might be the most complicated thing about them and the biggest barrier to buying something new. Generally speaking, American and European makers approach naming differently.

> • Americans typically make singular cheeses under one specific name, and present their cheese name along with their producer name (for example, Bayley Hazen Blue from Jasper Hill Farm).

> • Europeans typically adopt general names for their cheese, with dozens or hundreds of makers producing the same cheese (for example, feta or Brie or Appenzeller). For this reason, I provide recommended brand(s) where needed. Then you can look for specific names that I associate with superior cheese.

> **THERE ARE EXCEPTIONS TO BOTH OF THESE GENERALIZATIONS:**

> • There are American makers producing cheese with a general name (such as Monterey Jack or Gouda or Cheddar). The best of these will be included in my recommended brand(s).

> • Some Europeans are making singular cheeses that are sold under a specific name or brand, although these are not often marketed with the producer name as with American cheeses. Accordingly, I've presented these as they are likely to be sold (for example, Montgomery's Cheddar or Challerhocker).

And finally, it's important to know that the Europeans have a system of name protection (Protected Designation of Origin, called the PDO system) that defines which standards must be met to call a cheese by a certain name. When a general name qualifies for PDO status (as in Comté), the PDO appears as part of the name. Again, these are going to be general types and so I have also included my recommend brand(s).

## ➤ ABOUT THE CHEESE

Each entry includes what I think of as essential knowledge. This might include stories about history, important suggestions about use, and always the 411 on the cheese's flavor. Each entry is summarized with Aroma, Texture, and Flavor notes. Finally, there's In Short, a quick summary of a cheese that I give at my parties when people don't want to be hammered with a ten-minute monologue about what's on the coffee table.

# NAME PROTECTION DECODER

In 2014, *The Guardian* asked me to weigh in on an international furor developing between the European Union and the United States. As part of trade negotiations, the European Union wanted U.S. food makers to be restricted from using names with historical ties to Europe. Several of my gateway cheeses (Cheddar and Parmesan) were included in the list. My position? Some cheeses and their particular production methods are so specific as to warrant protecting their names. Others (most of my gateways!) have become general types so popularized in the United States that it's too late for Europe to take their names back as singular and unique.

Parmesan is not the same as Parmigiano-Reggiano. Parmesan leads you to the ballpark of hard, aged, granular cheese with nutty or caramel flavor. Parmigiano-Reggiano is a singular cheese, made in a limited region of Italy, following strict production and aging criteria, just as Champagne is a unique wine made in a given region of France.

European countries have established regulated naming structures to protect their Parmigiano-Reggiano equivalents—traditionally produced foods, tied to specific geographic areas. Most commonly seen in cheese are:

**(FRANCE) AOC = APPELLATION D'ORIGINE CONTRÔLÉE**

**(ITALY) DOP = DENOMINAZIONE DI ORIGINE PROTETTA**

**(SPAIN) DO[P] = DENOMINACIÓN DE ORIGEN (PROTEGIDA)**

**(SWITZERLAND) AOP = APPELLATION D'ORIGINE PROTÉGÉE**

In 1992, the European Union introduced the PDO, or Protected Designation of Origin, intended to gather multiple countries' protections under one cohesive label. PDO status is granted only after country-level protection has been approved.

Some cheeses carry the PGI, or Protected Geographical Indication, meaning that at least one of the stages of production, processing, or preparation takes places in a specific geographic area.

These name protections are recognized within the European Union, while expanding over time through bilateral agreements with non-EU countries. In other words, outside of the European Union, countries (such as the United States) may or may not agree to honor these protected names.

Throughout this book, I've used PDO to designate any cheese granted protection under its country's specific regulation. And remember, Switzerland isn't part of the EU so protected Swiss cheeses will be identified only as AOP.

## SIDEBARS

Throughout the chapter, look for sidebars containing nonessential but neat, weird, and intriguing bits of information related to the cheeses and makers in a given chapter.

## MY PICKS

Pretty self-explanatory, and ideal for the days you don't feel like cheese adventuring, My Picks will give you my favorites in each chapter. Arranged into two groups, My Picks is grouped into the approachable half of the flavor spectrum and the intense half. Tasting a few of these will also give you a quick read on how much of a gateway's flavor spectrum you dig.

## VERTICAL TASTINGS

While working on this book, I gathered a small group of cheese advisors—people whose palates and knowledge I respect, and whose humor keeps my brain sharp. I was nervous about asking these folks, who eat cheese all the time, to join me for intentionally repetitive cheese-tastings. Really!? Taste four different Bries side by side? What we all found was that our assumptions about what Brie meant were blown to bits when we considered them in a group. Hence, my advocacy for vertical tasting. Pick three cheeses across a gateway's flavor spectrum (even easier, use my Vertical Tastings in each chapter). Line them up and take a moment to notice how varied they are. (White is not white, is it? It might be bone or snow or almond milk—enough shades of white to make a book of paint chips.) Then taste the cheeses, moving from the mildest, most approachable flavors that a gateway offers to its most intense conclusion. Notice what you like—what compels you, and perhaps what repels you. You'll notice that although entries for the cheeses often include my recommended brands, the Vertical Tastings do not. What's important here is the exercise of tasting comparatively within a specified theme or group. If you can't find my favorite brand of triple crème cheese, I'd still like you to try some brand of triple crème next to some brand of double crème Brie. The point is to feel and taste the differences to better understand what you like.

The flavor wheels in this book evolved from vertical tastings during which a buttery Brie unfolded 360 degrees to become yogurt-like, or doughy, or reminiscent of sweet cream ice cream.

## PAIRINGS

The landscape of food and beverage pairing is littered with adages meant to make things easier: What grows together goes together. Or, likes with likes and opposites attract. Although I've spent the last fifteen years immersed in the cheese world, even I get nervous when it comes to proper pairing. Good cheese is expensive. What if I mess it up?

**HERE'S WHAT I'VE LEARNED:**

• If you like it, it's a good pairing.

• For me, cheese is an everyday eating food. As such, I tend to serve it with other everyday eating foods. It is a rare occasion indeed where I'm making special recipes to serve with my cheese. Because of this, my guidelines lean heavily on foods and drinks that are readily available at the grocery store.

• It's more useful to have general guidelines rather than prescriptive pairings. My goal is not to tell you a ten- to twelve-month aged Manchego should be paired with Willamette Valley Pinot Noir (ideally from Evening Land Vineyards, 2012 vintage). What if you don't know the age profile of your Manchego, or you don't want to spend $70-plus on your bottle of wine?

• The pairings wrap up each chapter with a summary of the flavors you're likely to find therein, and take you through my tasting notes about what foods and drinks work generally well with the cheeses of the chapter.

**SO, WHAT MATTERS WHEN YOU'RE PAIRING CHEESE WITH OTHER STUFF? A FEW THINGS:**

**1. BALANCE:** Classic pairings are all about balance. Blue cheese with dessert wine, for example, takes a typically salty, spicy cheese and puts it next to a sweet, viscous drink. The opposing flavors and textures balance one another–they smooth the rough edges, so to speak. Ask yourself: What qualities does the cheese have? What flavors or textures will balance those qualities? The goal is to harmonize, not to bury the cheese under other foods or drinks.

**2. TEXTURE:** A seriously understated element of successful pairing is texture, and I think that's especially true for a fat- and protein-rich food like cheese. Soft, slippery cheese paired with oily foods feels greasy rather than good. Introducing some crunch preserves balance. Pairing isn't just about flavor, it's also about mouthfeel.

**3. SUGAR AND SPICE AND EVERYTHING ACIDIC:** Let's be real. Cheese is deliciously salty (and fatty). My strategy for balancing these qualities is to pair them with something sweet: fruit or (dessert) wine or, more recently, chocolate. Acidic (and sometimes spicy) foods and drinks are another tack to cutting a cheese's density. I rely on sugar and acid to balance salt, fat, and protein.

**4. TRUST AND MEMORY:** We all have a lifetime of food memories to draw on: what was your favorite sandwich when you were a kid? What did you crave when you were pregnant? What is your number-one guilty eating pleasure? These are all clues to your preferences—your creature comforts. Use them to guide your explorations of pairing and trust yourself. When I eat Manchego and quince paste (two foods I had never heard of fifteen years ago, although they now fall into the classic pairing camp), I immediately think of canned cranberry sauce on Thanksgiving turkey. That's a combo I've loved for as long as I can remember, although I eat it only once a year. Manchego and quince paste gives me the same insta-satisfaction without needing to roast anything.

Because each chapter is based on shared flavors and textures, it's relatively easy to generalize. You'll notice recommended pairings that repeat from chapter to chapter, usually with the exact same language and rationale for the pairing. This isn't accidental (or lazy!); it's intended to help you see the commonalities of flavor across gateway cheeses and their chapters. For example, coffee or chocolate-covered coffee beans are a recommended pairing with cheeses on the approachable end of Mozzarella's flavor spectrum. Those cheeses boast sweet, milky flavors, and the pairing is not unlike pouring cream in your cup of coffee. Coffee shows up again with approachable Brie types, where the cheese is akin to butter. Chances are, if you like the approachable end of Mozzarella's flavor spectrum, you'll be similarly pleased with the milder cheeses of the Brie Gateway. And it's entirely possible that you won't care for the intense cheeses of either chapter with their salty, vegetal, or slightly bitter notes. Shared pairings are an ideal way to branch out from cheeses that you know you like to those you might like, even when the gateway cheese differs.

# WHAT YOU NEED TO KNOW BEFORE READING THIS BOOK
## WHAT'S THE DEAL WITH RAW MILK CHEESE?

Some of the most common questions I'm asked are about raw milk cheeses—are they legal? Are they safe? Do cheeses made with raw milk taste better than those made with pasteurized? What is pasteurization, anyway?

**LET ME START TO ANSWER THESE QUESTIONS WITH A FEW BASIC FACTS:**

• Pasteurization refers to the heating of milk, at set temperatures, for designated periods of time, which (if it's going to occur) happens prior to cheese making.

• Raw milk and unpasteurized milk are terms that tend to be used interchangeably when discussing cheese, although raw milk technically has never been cooled and then reheated, and unpasteurized milk may have been.

• U.S. law requires that all cheese aged for less than sixty days be made of pasteurized milk. This is true for both imported and domestically produced cheeses. As a result, buttery, creamy Brie types and young, rindless cheeses will always be pasteurized in the States.

• The reason for mandatory pasteurization is to destroy potentially harmful pathogens that could be living in raw milk; for now, the U.S. Food and Drug Administration posits that these pathogens won't survive in cheese after sixty days of aging (hence the sixty-day minimum).

• Regarding the pasteurization of milk for cheese, some countries have more relaxed laws (in Europe, any cheese can be made of unpasteurized milk, regardless of age) and some countries have stricter laws (in Australia, all but half a dozen cheeses must be made of pasteurized milk).

• The laws about raw milk are different from the laws about cheese made from raw milk. In the United States, it's possible to buy raw milk in certain states, but you cannot (legally) buy raw milk cheese less than sixty days old in any state.

• As a result, many of Europe's classic cheeses are not available in the United States, or are available in modified form.

The question of whether or not all this matters is much more subjective. To quote an e-mail that my friend and American cheese-making luminary Mateo Kehler of Vermont's Jasper Hill Farm sent me: "The microbial ecology of raw milk is the sum of the practices on a farm. How you bed, feed, milk, and clean all contribute selective pressures that define the potential of a cheese by steering microbiology in particular ways. That's why a great raw milk cheese is so much more than a piece of cheese. It is the sum of a production system and the design, philosophy, and people behind it."

**IN OTHER WORDS, IT MATTERS. I WOULD FURTHER ELABORATE:**

• Cheese is the sum of its parts. Unpasteurized milk handled responsibly, in a clean, controlled environment of healthy animals and traceable production methods, is not only safe, but can be more flavorful, more complex-tasting, and healthier for your body than pasteurized milk. Any milk, pasteurized or otherwise, handled carelessly in a dirty, uncontrolled environment of unhealthy animals, is not safe, not tasty, and not good for you or the environment. Sure, it's possible to sterilize dirty milk by pasteurizing it, making it (technically) safe for consumption. But that doesn't mean the milk or the system that produced it is a good one. These are the main reasons that I refuse to agree with the U.S. Food and Drug Administration that young cheese must be made of pasteurized milk to be safe. It's also why the sixty-day rule is problematic. It suggests that time is the only factor that determines safety. There have been numerous recalls of contaminated cheese made from pasteurized milk. And, two months' aging won't magically repair a cheese produced from an unsanitary or unregulated environment. What determines safety, and quality, in any cheese are the responsible, traceable, clean inputs from animal to milk to curd to cheese.

• This being said, I don't believe pasteurized cheese tastes inherently inferior to raw milk cheese. Over the years, I've noticed that American cheese makers have gotten especially skilled at making excellent younger pasteurized cheeses. I think this is because it's a confine they've always had to deal with. I've also noticed that when a cheese is made in two versions, unpasteurized and pasteurized, the unpasteurized version almost always offers a greater (if sometimes more elusive) complexity and depth of flavor. An example of this is the classic English Blue Stilton (always pasteurized) and the relatively new cheese Stichelton (only unpasteurized). The best Stiltons are very fine cheeses, but they don't capture the layers of flavor that Stichelton will give you (see pages 349 and 350 for more on those cheeses).

For more technicalities on pasteurization, see Appendix 1: The Nitty-Gritty on Pasteurization (page 388).

## "I WANT TO EAT CHEESE. I DON'T WANT TO MAKE IT."
## STILL . . . UNDERSTANDING THE BASICS IS HELPFUL

When I wrote my book *The Cheese Chronicles*, I began by telling the story of the first time I made cheese. I have never wanted to be a cheese maker, and entering a small, closed room that reeked of steaming, woolly sheep milk while deathly hungover (as I was that fateful day at Vermont Shepherd) only confirmed my suspicions that making cheese was not for me. Despite this relatively traumatic initiation, I have returned to the cheese-making vat in half a dozen countries, often in the predawn hours, sometimes after hiking for several miles into abandoned, mountainous terrain, for the opportunity to (quite literally) watch milk curdle. Understanding the basics of cheese making is incredibly helpful for understanding why a certain cheese turns out the way it does. Standing next to a small Swiss man who is pantomiming the steps of cheese making, because he doesn't speak English and I don't speak French, and smelling the aroma of milk cooking in a copper vat, is to lock in the essential flavor backbone of Gruyère: the cheese tastes like the skin atop a mug of hot milk—lightly golden, nutty, and sweet—because that's how it began as much as a year before anyone ever tasted it as a sliver of cheese.

Cheese making can explain how the same basic ingredients yield thousands of different cheeses: Why some are spillingly creamy while others are rock hard and waxy. Why one hard cheese melts beautifully while another goes greasy. Even how it's possible that one Cheddar costs $5 per pound while another costs $30. I'm not saying you have to become a super-technical cheese geek to enjoy eating the stuff, but understanding the basic steps of cheese making will help you know why your cheese is the way it is and how to get more you'll love to eat.

Cheese begins its life as milk. The liquid part of milk, known as whey, is mainly water and milk sugar (lactose). For cheese, you need the solids: fat and protein that can be made into curd. Removing the water and manipulating the solids are the fundamentals of the cheese-making process.

**ACIDIFICATION** is the first step in gathering solids. This is the conversion of milk sugar (lactose) into lactic acid. Long, slow acidification yields a more crumbly texture and tart flavor (as in unaged goat cheese logs), whereas brief acidification followed by stronger coagulation yields a smooth, pliable texture and sweeter taste (as in Swiss types). Acidification is determined by temperature (lower = slower, higher = faster) and cultures.

**BACTERIA, OR CULTURES,** are added to the milk to convert sugar into acid. Cultures are also added to produce flavor over time. Some cultures work immediately, whereas others (adjunct cultures) lie dormant in a cheese until—after weeks or even months—the moisture, salt, and acidity levels are just right and the cultures activate. They break down fats and proteins, which can cause changes to texture, or the emergence of specific flavors.

**MOLD OR YEAST** (in powder or liquid form) may be added to the milk, as in Brie and Blue. These microbes will grow later, after the cheese is shaped into a wheel, with exposure to oxygen. The most commonly used molds are *Penicillium candidum, Penicillium camemberti,* and *Geotrichum candidum* (Brie types) and *Penicillium roqueforti* and *Penicillium glaucum* (Blue types).

**COAGULATION** is the visible conversion of liquid milk to solid curd. Adding coagulant makes milk's protein chains form a web and traps fat and water. That web is curd—a gelatinous substance that can be cut or scooped. Cheese makers can coagulate milk using rennet (an enzyme derived from an unweaned animal's stomach lining); microbial rennet derived from molds or yeasts, and thus vegetarian (otherwise known as enzymes); or vegetable rennet, derived from a plant such as the thistle.

The more the curd is **CUT**, the more whey it releases. Big, spongy, uncut hunks of curd will make a creamy, buttery cheese like Brie. Tiny curds cut to the size of rice grains are the first step to making a long-aging, hard cheese like Parmigiano-Reggiano.

In addition to cutting, the curd may be **HEATED OR COOKED**. With added heat comes added moisture expulsion. To remove the maximum amount of whey, curd is cooked to a high temperature and cut into tiny pieces, yielding small, dry pieces suitable for aging (and eventually a dense, hard-textured cheese). Cooking the curd impacts the flavor of the final cheese—imparting sweet flavors of cooked or scalded milk, with toast and marshmallow undertones.

Once a cheese maker coagulates the milk (possibly cutting and/or cooking it as well), whey is drained off and the remaining curd is removed from the vat to be formed into rounds, wheels, pyramids, or whatever shape the cheese will take. Those curds can be **PRESSED** on (gently, slightly, by hand; or heavily, repeatedly, and mechanically by hydraulic machine). Once again, pressing will impact how much moisture is left in the cheese, and how creamy or hard its final texture. Pressing may also be a time for the curd to continue sitting out at room temperature, allowing acidity to increase. An acidic cheese is often described as tasting sharp.

Wheels are **SALTED**, sometimes with dry salt, sometimes with brine—possibly by machine, possibly by hand. Some cheeses are salted as curd, still in the vat, before wheel formation occurs. Salt is a critical ingredient in cheese and impacts everything from what bacteria or mold can grow to how much moisture is further expelled to how acidic a cheese can be. Salt changes everything.

**AGING OR RIPENING** isn't technically part of the cheese-making process, but it can make or break a cheese. Cheeses might age for a day or for several years. Those aged in an open-air environment (called a cave or a cellar) have to be turned, brushed, washed, and monitored. Those vacuum-sealed in plastic can be basically forgotten about so long as they're refrigerated. An open-air environment that's too dry will crack and break the wheels. One that's too moist might harbor unintended bacteria or mold. What grows on one style of cheese isn't ideal for another style of cheese, so different styles must be aged separately. In Europe, there is a tradition of *affinage*: a cheese ager (*affineur*) buys very young cheese from a maker and takes over its ripening.

For more detail on cheese making, see Appendix 2: The Steps of Cheese Making (see page 388).

## TIPS FOR TASTING

Tasting cheese with a group of friends is an amazing social experiment (especially if alcohol is involved). This is different from putting out some cheese for your holiday cocktail party. In that context it's food. People eat it, and maybe they talk about how much they like it. Mindful tasting requires a group of people to sit down and share their impressions of appearance, aroma, and flavor. What's incredibly enlightening (and often hilarious, and occasionally kind of gross-out) are the associations your loved ones have with food. During the first year of writing this book, I conducted regular tastings with a small advisory group, and in many cases the In Short summary section that I've assigned each cheese was a direct outcome of those tastings.

There was the tasting of Havarti types, which led to a heated debate about whether or not young, waxed Gouda was a lame-o or lay-low cheese: the first meaning predictably lame (and not worth eating); the second meaning the ultimate brainless (but delicious) snacking cheese. (We agreed, finally, on the latter.)

On another evening, we tasted something like a dozen Cheddars, and the non-cheese professional in the group reminded us of Liz Lemon singing "Night Cheese" on *30 Rock*. You know: the cheese you eat all of, after dark, alone in your house, wearing a Snuggie, because it's so damn good. Suddenly every Cheddar was some variant on Night Cheese: the Basic Night Cheese; the Ulterior Motive Night Cheese (what you give your date to get in their pants); the Guilty Night Cheese (because you'd eat it all and then beat yourself up because it cost $25 per pound). I will share that those Cheddars failing to receive some classification of Night Cheese didn't make this book, because everyone agreed they just weren't tasty enough.

More than perhaps any other food, cheese has personality. There are punk cheeses and boring cheeses, surprising cheeses and essential comfort cheeses. Tasting cheese carefully, in a group, becomes the platform for articulating that personality. It also helps tremendously with understanding fundamentals like flavor and quality. It cements in your mind what you do and don't like, and why. And, hearing other people describe what they're experiencing can fill in a lot of blanks about tastes and textures that are eluding you.

**FIRST, TASTE WITH YOUR EYES.** Taking a moment to really look at a cheese will give you many clues about milk type, animal feed, edibility of rind, and age. If you keep this book's Chapter Guides handy, you can also determine if a cheese appears to be of good quality or not.

**SECOND, TASTE WITH YOUR NOSE.** Under many circumstances, smelling the food on the end of your fork may be considered rude. Under cheese-tasting circumstances, it's essential. So much of our impression of flavor comes from our noses, not our mouths! That's how we wind up with cheese or wine reminiscent of wet stone, or grass, or cat pee. None of these are things you eat (I hope), but they're probably things you've smelled. And when you taste a food that makes a retronasal impression, your first association may be of something totally inedible but profoundly familiar. This is a place where tasting with friends can quickly become intimate, hysterical, and deeply moving.

Smelling your cheese will familiarize you with what's normal (some bad smells are appropriate) as opposed to what's spoiled. It will also help you lock into your brain associations that mean something to you—you will remember the cheeses that you have a smell memory for, even if that association is meaningless to everyone else.

**ONLY THEN, TASTE WITH YOUR TONGUE.** Your mouth and tongue can detect sweetness; saltiness; bitterness; acidity, and the fifth taste sensation, umami, a satiating, savory essence. It's only in conjunction with your nose that these materialize as being like porcini mushroom, or grapefruit, or seawater. In addition to flavor impression, your mouth is the tool for gauging precise texture. A cheese isn't just soft or even buttery. It may be like frozen butter, cold butter, tempered butter, or melted butter. Remember to approach tasting from milder to stronger, (as the cheeses in each chapter are listed) or creamier to harder—those big, long-lasting flavors will overwhelm the delicate, fleeting quality of younger cheeses.

# TASTE CAREFULLY AND YOU WILL FIND . . .

• Goat milk is whiter than cow or sheep milk because it lacks beta-carotene, which gives milk (and cheese) a yellow color.

• A buttercup yellow interior is usually a sign of grass-fed cow milk (super beta-carotene).

• Orange paste is a giveaway that the cheese was colored with annatto, a flavorless plant-derived coloring.

• A soft white or yellowish rind is made of mold or yeast and is totally edible.

• A soft orange rind will be saltier, stinkier, and totally edible.

• A hard, thick, crusty, or sharp-edged rind is not likely to taste good (although it won't hurt you if you eat it).

• Wax and cloth rinds are not recommended for eating.

• Runny, drippy, or creamy cheeses contain more water and are usually younger cheeses with a shorter shelf life.

• Firm-to-hard cheeses contain less water and are usually more aged cheeses with a longer shelf life.

• Signs of spoilage (or perfect ripeness)—see Chapter Guides for help.

## TASTE WITH YOUR NOSE AND YOU WILL FIND . . .

• Differences between the rind and the paste.

• Smell memories of things you might not eat (like my cheese student and the wet rock) that help you remember cheeses you love (or hate).

• Signs of spoilage (or perfect ripeness)—see the Chapter Guides for help.

## TASTE WITH YOUR MOUTH AND YOU WILL FIND . . .

• Sharp cheese is higher in acid, and makes the sides of your mouth water.

• Sweet cheese is lower in acid, and won't make your mouth water.

• Bitter flavors catch you in the back of the throat.

• Cheeses with tropical fruit flavors are often accompanied by a hairy tongue feeling, similar to eating pineapple.

• Younger/higher moisture cheeses often have a shorter finish—the flavors fade quickly after you swallow.

• Aged/lower moisture cheeses often have a longer finish—the flavors last (and, ideally, evolve and unfold) long after you swallow.

## STORING AND EATING CHEESE AT HOME

Each chapter guide includes storage and shelf-life guidelines most relevant to the cheeses of that gateway. A few general notes:

• I keep cheese in the crisper drawer of my fridge. It can be set with higher humidity and there's less chance of the cheese picking up other food smells (or other foods picking up cheese smells).

• Special cheese paper can be purchased for storage, and it will buy you a few extra days' shelf life.

• My favorite storage method (for all cheeses) is a small zip-top plastic bag that allows you to suck the air out before closing. It keeps cheeses separate, the delicate ones don't get smothered, and I've never had problems rinsing, air-drying, and reusing the plastic bags.

• Cheese should always be eaten at room temperature, so take it out an hour before you plan to serve it.

• Never freeze cheese. It kills the flavor and imparts a mealy texture.

• The semiexception is moist, pliable cheese that you plan to grate. Cheeses like Havarti, Monterey Jack, and young Gouda will gum up your grater. Give them twenty minutes in the freezer to firm up and grating will be easier, with much less cheese loss.

• When I'm serving a bunch of cheeses, I provide a knife for each. You don't want the intense flavors of Blue cheese being dragged through something mild, milky, and delicate.

• Avoid cheese planes—those triangular-shaped tools with a slit across the middle intended for shaving cheese. They're great if you're garnishing salad plates, but what are people supposed to do with the one on your coffee table? Cheese planes are useless unless you pick up the entire wedge, which is greasy and potentially smelly for your guests.

FETA

HALLOUMI

BURRATA

FRESH GOAT CHEESE

# Mozzarella

OVOLINE

CILIEGINE

RICOTTA

MASCARPONE

## MOZZARELLA: THE GATEWAY TO . . .

**Driftless**
PAGE 50

**Paneer**
PAGE 40

**Bread Cheese**
PAGE 45

**Oaxaca**
PAGE 50

**Halloumi**
PAGE 53

**Cheese Curds**
PAGE 40

**Queso Fresco**
PAGE 45

**Ricotta Salata**
PAGE 53

**Quark**
PAGE 41

**Ricotta**
PAGE 45

**Burrata**
PAGE 49

**Buffalo Mozzarella**
PAGE 54

**Mascarpone**
PAGE 44

**Petite Breakfast**
PAGE 49

**Mozzarella**
PAGE 43

AVAILABILITY SUPERMARKET → SPECIALTY SHOP

**FLAVOR** APPROACHABLE →

1 MILK
2 COOKED MILK
3 SALTY MILK
4 MORE SALT THAN MILK
5 GAMY MILK

**Crescenza/Stracchino**
PAGE 55

**Teleme**
PAGE 54

**Banon PDO**
PAGE 57

**O'Banon**
PAGE 57

**Fromage Blanc**
PAGE 56

**Feta (PDO)**
PAGE 58

**Fresh Goat Cheese,
or Chèvre**
PAGE 56

**Smoked
Mozzarella**
PAGE 43

**INTENSE**

| **6** | **7** | **8** | **9** | **10** |
|---|---|---|---|---|
| YOGURTY WHIFF | CITRUS TANG | LEMONY | TANNIC | ALL THAT, PLUS BRINE |

# Despite growing up in a Connecticut town that was 95 percent Italian American, located outside the town where they say American pizza was

invented; despite little shops that sold freshly baked stuffed broccoli breads and hand-filled cannoli; despite my less-than-ten-mile-proximity to two of the finest ricotta and Mozzarella makers in the entire country; despite all this, as a teenager I was suckered in by Polly-O Fat Free Mozzarella Cheese. Like many well-meaning but not terribly informed teenage girls, I went through a diet phase where I committed myself to eating absolutely no fat. Ironically, it was this fervent dedication that led me to cooking. The first recipe I mastered was a vegetable lasagna made with fat-free ricotta and fat-free Mozzarella. Because the cheeses were fat-free, I piled the lasagna high using an entire doorstopper-like block of low-moisture, vacuum-packed, anemic-looking Polly-O from the supermarket dairy case. I grated it and layered it and watched it through the oven door—softening, melting, bubbling, and browning. It wasn't unusual for me to sit down and eat half of the pan of lasagna because it didn't taste like much, and it never really satisfied. Luckily, I got over this phase by college, but while I kept the cooking habit, I also kept my assumptions about Mozzarella. I always bought fat-free or low-fat, and I took it as a given that the cheese didn't have any flavor. No wonder everyone liked it! There was no way it could offend.

Fast-forward several years past college graduation, when I found myself once again in a neighborhood that was 95 percent Italian American, with all the same breads and cannoli but with a new local cheese on the block. The Mozzarella came from Joe's Dairy or the Lioni Brothers. These fat, almost gelatinous balls were all that was available. They didn't have nutrition facts or ingredients listed on the plastic packaging—they looked like they'd been wrapped by the hairy-armed guys behind the counter. One evening I bought one, because what else was there? At home, ravenous after work and unwrapping my packages in the tiny kitchen, I sliced off a fat round of the Mozzarella ball. Eating it straight out of the plastic with my fingers, I was blown away by how delicious it was: sweet and milky but well salted and wet, slippery on the outside but shredding in the center like a gently poached chicken breast. This Mozzarella was the first time I comprehended the sublimity of simplicity that real food offers. Real Mozzarella was like my first ripe summer peach or my first morsel of Copper River salmon.

When I talk about Mozzarella, I mean real or traditional Mozzarella: freshly pulled cheese curd that is stretched into a smooth, snow-white ball sold in a cup or container, bobbing in a light brine that tastes of sea spray on your lips. Or perhaps that ball is tightly hand-wrapped, the cheese gently weeping a milky juice when you press the blade of your serrated knife against it. In either form, real Mozzarella is the epitome of what cheese folk call fresh cheese. By fresh, we mean: White. High moisture. No rind. Ideally, recently made. Unaged. Terribly perishable. And, when you get a good one, the purest vehicle for communicating the flavors of the milk from which it was made. Most of us know the taste of cow milk; fresh cow milk cheeses tend to be accordingly approachable in flavor. They're simple, sweet, and clean. Goat and sheep milk are less familiar, and their accompanying grassy tang tastes stronger than what many think of as milky. They are also more likely to be turned into cheeses that are essentially pickled (think feta), so intense saltiness can contribute additional flavor intensity. Along this spectrum of possible flavor, Mozzarella extends a gentle invitation to step through the gateway of fresh cheese and really explore what milk of all kinds is about.

More than a few folks I know in the cheese world claim Mozzarella or burrata as their number-one favorite cheese. Often, they get a lot of grief from other cheese people for touting a cheese that the critics say is pedestrian. Boring. Plain. But the good stuff isn't! Mozzarella and other fresh cheeses, because they're unaged, are incredibly hard to make well. There's nothing to hide behind in a fresh cheese. One needs good milk and proper technique, and the resulting cheese must be sold and consumed in very little time. Texture becomes profoundly important: you're more likely to notice gritty or gummy or pasty glop if the accompanying flavors are subtle and soft-spoken. Small flavor imbalances are suddenly immense: a bit of extra acidity that goes unnoticed in a dense, nutty Cheddar renders a fresh goat cheese inedibly sour. As is true with a glass of milk, my knee-jerk reaction is always to sniff suspiciously lest I start my day with a swallow of something gone rancid.

Fresh cheeses are simple, but the good ones are never boring. They're amazing foils for other flavors, cheeses to be eaten instead of meat—sauced with pesto, oil, or roasted red pepper puree. Sliced and layered with tomatoes. Cubed on a kebab and grilled. Chunked with olives (or watermelon, if you have a sweet tooth). Or, as

I once did in my Brooklyn apartment and still do today with my daughters, eaten in shreds with bare fingers while the rest of the meal is being chopped and cooked.

Fresh cheeses are often dismissed as cooking cheeses, as if being integral to key dishes in dozens of cultures was lesser or inconsequential. Every cheese-making country has a fresh cheese that's its signature, if not only, important cheese: from ricotta and Mozzarella in Italy to fresh chèvre (goat cheese) in France to queso fresco in Mexico, paneer in India, and feta in Greece. Sadly, many of these have been bastardized by shoddy imitators. If there's one style where buying authentic or, conversely, buying local is likely to make a meaningfully tastier difference, it's here in the world of fresh cheeses. Across the board, these are cheeses made to be eaten quickly rather than to travel long distances, and by their very nature they are cheeses meant to be eaten as part of everyday life. They are also, fundamentally and critically, cheeses about milk. When you take an unaged cheese that for centuries was made from sheep and goat milk and start cranking it out of cow milk, it's not the same cheese. And it's just not as good. Fresh cheeses may not seem sexy, but they're fundamental. It's time to give them their due and acknowledge the wondrous flavors of milk.

# Chapter Guide

Welcome to the world of fresh cheeses. An acquaintance new to cheese pointed out to me how confusing the phrase "fresh cheese" is. Shouldn't all cheese be fresh, she asked? Don't I want to avoid cheese that's old? Yes. You do. But by fresh cheese, I mean unaged as opposed to not-old cheese. Cheese has been famously described as milk's great leap into immortality; fresh cheeses are the first possible stop on that journey.

## WHAT TO KNOW

➤ **EAT IMMEDIATELY:** These cheeses lack a rind to protect them. Those that are brined (submerged in salt water) are the most durable, but once exposed to air even they will sour or mold quickly. This is the only group of cheeses that should be categorically free of color. You want bright, snowy white cheese. Any spots or specks of anything are a sign of spoilage.

## WHAT TO AVOID

➤ **COLOR:** These cheeses are white and should stay that way. Spots or patches of blue, brown, green, gray, pink, or yellow are all signs of spoilage.

➤ **AROMA:** Ideally and typically, these cheeses smell like almost nothing. If you've a keen nose, you might say they smell like milk or maybe vaguely oceanic. Concentrated sour, sharp, or pungent smells are all signs of old cheese.

➤ **FLAVOR:** Sour, spoiled, and sharp flavors (basically, the off qualities you'd associate with a sip of milk gone bad).

➤ **EVERLASTING CHEESE:** Many of these cheeses are vacuum-packed, with the air removed before they are sealed. This creates an inert environment, protected from the elements, where the cheese can last happily for weeks or even several months (that's how it's possible for a log of goat cheese to have a sell-by date of two months from now). Once this seal is broken, however, the clock starts ticking. Rapidly. Be suspicious of fresh cheeses that claim, once open, they'll be spoil-free for weeks. If they are, they aren't going to taste like anything to begin with and are likely enhanced with preservatives.

## STORAGE AND SHELF LIFE

In the village dairies of Italy's Campania and Puglia regions, Mozzarella di Bufala PDO and burrata are famously sold for only a few hours each morning. It's made. It's sold. It's eaten. Obviously we don't all have a *latteria* down the road from our kitchen, but take a page from this tradition.

Eat the cheeses as quickly as possible. Their essence is subtle and fleeting, even if a week may pass before they go bad.

Wrap tightly in plastic wrap to keep air out. If you purchase a fresh cheese in brine (such as Mozzarella or feta), ask to have it packaged in the brine and store it that way at home.

Ideally, consume immediately upon opening and plan to store leftovers no longer than three to five days.

### IN A WORD: MOIST

**LIGHT AND AIRY**
AIRY   CREAMY   CRUMBLY   CURDY
FLUFFY   SILKY   SLIPPERY   VELVETY
WHIPPED

**SMOOTH AND/OR SPRINGY**
BOUNCY   BULGING   CHEWY
DOUGHY   ELASTIC   EVEN   PLIABLE
SMOOTH   SPRINGY   SQUEAKY
STICKY   STRETCHY   STRINGY   TENDER

**HEAVY AND/OR WET**
CLAY   COLD BUTTER   FUDGE
HEAVY   MOIST   PUDDING   YIELDING

**LIQUESCENT**
SCOOPABLE   SMEARABLE

**FLAWS**
GLUEY   GRAINY   MUSHY

## WHY ARE MOZZARELLA TYPES ALWAYS PASTEURIZED?

While some of the cheeses in this chapter may keep, unopened, for weeks or months, thanks to the wonders of vacuum-packaging or salt brine as pickling liquid, they are, at their core, fresh cheeses. They are meant to be consumed immediately after production and have the shortest of shelf lives once open to the air. Because U.S. law prohibits raw milk or unpasteurized cheeses aged less than sixty days, you can expect every cheese in this chapter, and in this style, to be made of pasteurized milk. If it's legal, that is.

## ATMOSPHERICS
SMOKE · BURNT WOOD · PETROL · WOODSY · BRINE / SEAWATER · (WET) SOIL · POWDER · MINERAL · PUTRID · ACETONE (NAIL POLISH REMOVER) · METALLIC · SULFUR (ROTTEN EGG) · FISHY · AMMONIA · FISHY · PUTRID · BITTER

## FLAWS
ACRID · EXCESSIVE SOURNESS · RANCID

## LACTIC
FRESH ➤ GOAT MILK · COW MILK · SHEEP MILK · BUFFALO MILK · CREAM · BUTTER · CULTURED ➤ CULTURED BUTTER · GAMY BUTTER · CRÈME FRAÎCHE · YOGURT · BUTTERMILK · SOUR CREAM · COOKED ➤ COOKED MILK / MILK SKIN · MELTED BUTTER · BROWNED BUTTER · CHEESE-Y (MAC-AND-CHEESE POWDER)

## FRUIT
STONE FRUIT ➤ APRICOT · PEACH · PLUM · GREEN OLIVE · BLACK OLIVE · BERRIES ➤ STRAWBERRY · BLUEBERRY · RED CURRANT · CITRUS ➤ ORANGE · GRAPEFRUIT · LEMON · TROPICAL FRUIT ➤ PAPAYA · PASSION FRUIT · PINEAPPLE · COOKED FRUIT · PICKLED FRUIT · FERMENTED FRUIT

## VEGETABLE
AROMATICS ➤ (COOKED) CELERY (ROOT) · (COOKED) TURNIP · (COOKED) LEEK · (CARAMELIZED) ONION · (ROASTED) GARLIC · OTHER ➤ BAKED POTATO · CORN · NORI · CRUCIFEROUS ➤ (COOKED) CABBAGE · (COOKED) CAULIFLOWER · (COOKED) BROCCOLI · BROCCOLI RABE · SPICY ➤ MUSTARD GREENS · BITTER ➤ ENDIVE · ARUGULA · HORSERADISH · DANDELION

## FUNGUS
MOLD/MILDEW · WHITE MOLD · BLUE MOLD · SHIITAKE MUSHROOM · PORCINI MUSHROOM · TRUFFLE · BUTTON MUSHROOM · YEAST · BREAD DOUGH · (COOKED) MUSHROOM

## HERBS & PLANTS
HERBS ➤ THYME · HERBACEOUS · ROSEMARY · MINT · PLANT MATTER ➤ (MOWN) GRASS · FLORAL · HAY · TOBACCO · PINE · EUCALYPTUS

## ANIMAL
BODILY ➤ MUSK · SWEAT · UNWASHED SOCKS · (WET) WOOL · LEATHER · MANURE · BARNYARD · FERMENTED / CURED ➤ SERRANO · JERKY · SAUCISSON SEC · PAN DRIPPINGS · LAMB FAT · GAMY · OFFAL · BEEF BOUILLON · MEATY · GRILLED · COOKED ➤ CHICKEN BROTH · BEEF BROTH

## OTHER FOOD
FERMENTED FOODS ➤ WHITE WINE · COFFEE · RED WINE · MILK CHOCOLATE · COCOA · BOURBON · DARK CHOCOLATE · DULCE DE LECHE · WERTHER'S ORIGINALS (CARAMEL HARD CANDY) · LEMON CURD · CARAMEL · BUTTERSCOTCH · SWEETS ➤ CHOCOLATE-DIPPED ORANGE · COCONUT (OIL) · (TOASTED) HAZELNUT · WALNUT · (BOILED) PEANUT · PECAN · (TOASTED) ALMOND · PINE NUT · MACADAMIA NUT · NUT SKIN · NUTS ➤ POLENTA · COOKED PASTA · (BUTTERED) TOAST · BISCUIT · BLACK PEPPER · LICORICE · CLOVE

## SPICES
ANISE · WHITE PEPPER · VANILLA · NUTMEG

# Paneer

INDIA/CANADA | COW

PASTEURIZED

**RECOMMENDED BRAND:**
Nanak

**AROMA:** None

**TEXTURE:** Spongy curd bits

**FLAVOR:** Room-temperature milk

**IN SHORT:** The extra-firm tofu of cheese

The fresh cheese of South Asia (notably India and Nepal) is paneer. It's quite difficult to find in the United States unless you have ready access to the Little Indias of Jackson Heights, Chicago, Berkeley, Raleigh, and so on. Made like most ricotta today (from acid-coagulated milk, not whey), paneer is then drained and pressed for several hours, after which it is bathed in cold water. For the adventurous, paneer can be made at home following my ricotta recipe, with the additional steps of draining, pressing, and cold water bathing. These steps result in a firmer, smoother fresh cheese than the fluffy curds we associate with ricotta, but notably it's often made without salt. Accordingly, it's like biting into a spongy milk patty. As with Halloumi, bread cheese, and frying queso fresco, the cheese is nonmelting and holds its shape in dishes like spinach stew (saag).

# Cheese Curds

UNITED STATES | COW

PASTEURIZED

**RECOMMENDED BRANDS:**
Beecher's Handmade Cheese, Ellsworth Creamery, your local farmers' market maker

**AROMA:** None

**TEXTURE:** Squeaky chew

**FLAVOR:** String cheese

**IN SHORT:** Snackable by the bowlful

Cheese curds are the building blocks that get pressed and manipulated into other cheeses. Usually curds sold for eating are those that didn't become Cheddar, and they bear a strong resemblance to Silly Putty. They're a regional specialty of Wisconsin (where they're usually battered and deep-fried to make something akin to but far greater than a Mozzarella stick) and Quebec (where they top french fries and are blanketed with gravy to make the late-night drunkard's friend poutine). If you've never made cheese, it's kind of cool to eat a curd because you can experience what Cheddar is before it ages and becomes Cheddar as you know it. Curds are a simple delight—what string cheese wants to be, a food that anyone can happily, mindlessly eat from a bag, and a blank slate for tossing with all kinds of seasonings (sriracha, buffalo sauce, and curry powder are a few of my faves). Ideally, get 'em fresh (within a day or two of production) when they still have the weird appeal of being squeaky as you bite down (as described by Louisa Kamps at the *New York Times*, they sound like balloons trying to neck).

# ARE YOU PULLING MY CURD?

Taking a ball of fresh Mozzarella and leaving it around for a few months won't produce an aged cheese; it will produce a spoiled one. That's because Mozzarella is so high in moisture. But the *pasta filata* (spun curd or pulled curd) technique of cheese making that produces Mozzarella can also be used to make drier cheeses that age for several weeks or even many months. The curds of *pasta filata* cheeses are steeped in hot water (or whey) and then kneaded and pulled until a fibrous, stretchy texture develops. The resulting exterior is smooth and glossy, with an interior texture reminiscent of poached chicken breast.

Several of the best-known aged *pasta filata* cheeses share the mellow, approachable flavor of cheese curds or string cheese, although they're not fresh cheeses. Dense and chewy, but ultimately tasting of milk and salt, these are the aged cheeses that eat like freshies:

YOUNG OR MILD PROVOLONE: By young, I mean deli-slicing Provolone, which is most often made in the United States from pasteurized cow's milk. As a kid I preferred it to American cheese, which, even then, struck me as artificial and weirdly sweet. Mild Provolone is similar to string cheese: off-white and smooth, with a mellow, salty, reaching-toward-savory flavor.

SCAMORZA: A charming Italian cheese traditional to Puglia and Calabria and unlikely to be found in all but the best cheese and Italian specialty shops, scamorza is sold in shiny yellow, pear-shaped knobs, often hung by rustic ropes. Imagine a dried, slightly tangy Mozzarella ball. I'm especially partial to the smoked version, although both melt and grill beautifully.

CACIOCAVALLO (SILANO PDO): While the cheese dates back to ancient Greece and is traditional in southern Italy, if you ate a piece and didn't know it was caciocavallo you'd likely think it was a dried-out hunk of deli Provolone. I don't say this in a critical way: it's tasty and noshable in the way Mozzarella is. You eat without thinking too much, although it's got a lot more salt than fresh *pasta filata* cheeses.

# Quark

Although quark (fresh curd) is common food in Germany, German-speaking nations, and northern Europe, I've never seen imported quark in the States—only domestically produced. The closest American equivalent is cottage cheese, although this is a chunky, curdy paste often clotted up with gums and stabilizers, especially when purchased as a fat-free diet food. Quark is simply milk that coagulates overnight into curd, which is then slightly drained and whipped for a smooth, airy texture. It's a naturally lower fat alternative for cheesecakes and baking, or just for topping fruit. Because it's made of milk, the flavor tends to be leaner and ever so slightly more tart than fresh cheeses made of cream.

UNITED STATES | COW
PASTEURIZED

RECOMMENDED BRAND: Vermont Creamery

AROMA: None

TEXTURE: Depending on the producer, curdy (like cottage cheese) to whipped

FLAVOR: Mild and milky

IN SHORT: Milk cloud

MOZZARELLA

APPROACHABLE

# Mozzarella

As America has started making more and better cheese in the past 30 years, there is greater opportunity to buy freshly made fresh cheeses. It's less likely that you will be restricted to a low-moisture, tasteless block of Mozzarella, and more likely that you'll instead find freshly pulled or water-packed versions made within a few hours of your home market. These are often marketed under the Italian phrase *fior di latte*, or "flower of the milk." Mozzarella is also a common cheese for small farms to start out on, so your local farmers' market is likely to yield all kinds of newbies. Look for a smooth, glossy ball that is both springy and tender, and pulls apart like poached chicken breast. Avoid gluey, tough, or sticky offerings. Many supermarkets now pull their own mozz. Although they're buying rather than making the curd, they're doing the hot water dip and stretching, as well as controlling the salt. Raw material matters but so does technique, the mismanagement of which leaves you with dull flavor and the texture of prechewed gum. So this kind of Mozzarella is high risk and potentially high reward. If it's well done, it will be vastly superior to brands that are already packaged. Good to know about, but harder to find, is smoked Mozzarella, which should be flavored by real smoke rather than liquid additives. It is a phenomenally compelling cooking cheese, especially with hearty bedfellows like eggs, cauliflower, broccoli, and leafy greens.

**UNITED STATES | COW PASTEURIZED**

**RECOMMENDED BRANDS:** Belfiore, Di Bruno Bros., DiStefano, Lioni Latticini, Liuzzi Angeloni Cheese, Maplebrook Fine Cheese

**AROMA:** Minimal, fresh milk

**TEXTURE:** Moist, tender, springy

**FLAVOR:** Clean and milky with briny restraint

**IN SHORT:** Eminently snackable

## LITTLE MOZZARELLA

If you have the chance to shop in Italy, or at a traditional Italian *latteria* in the States, you may come across the delight that is fresh Mozzarella in dozens of shapes and sizes. Typically packed in water, you can look for:

**PERLINE:** little pearl-sized, or little perle

**PERLE:** technically pearl-sized, but I think of these as gumdrop-sized

**NOCCIOLINE:** nut-sized (think almonds, in the shell)

**CILIEGINE:** cherry-sized

**BOCCONCINI:** morsel-sized or bite-sized (but a big bite, to be sure)

**OVOLINE:** egg-sized

# Mascarpone

**ITALY/UNITED STATES**

COW

**PASTEURIZED**

**RECOMMENDED BRANDS:**
Bel Gioioso, Ciresa, Vermont
Creamery

**AROMA:** Cooked milk

**TEXTURE:** Smooth,
grain-free fluff

**FLAVOR:** Sweet cream

**IN SHORT:** Room-temperature
sweet-cream ice cream

I feel I'm doing mascarpone a great disservice if I tell you it's cream cheese. That conjures up pleasantly bland, somewhat gummy blocks of Philadelphia, which is nothing at all like this fresh cheese made from cultured cream, native to the northern Italian region of Lombardy. Rather than beginning with milk, mascarpone starts with full-fat cream. This is gently acidified and cooked at a high temperature, which results in a markedly sweet taste and voluminous, fluffy texture. In my early twenties I worked with a pastry chef who offered to help me overcome my terror of baking and dessert making. She asked me to pick five desserts I wanted to be proficient in. Tiramisu was one of the five—the Italian confection of espresso-soaked ladyfingers and eggy, booze-laced cream. That's when I first got down with mascarpone and found that while you can make tiramisu with it, you can also eat it straight from the container, or sprinkle some berries on it and call that dessert. Technically it has savory applications, but the cooking of the cream imparts a nearly candied sweetness that keeps this cheese all about breakfast and sweets, at least in my book.

# Queso Fresco

Queso fresco is the ubiquitous fresh cheese made across Mexico, as well as in the United States. Queso blanco is the name indicating Central or South American origins. I've known it as the nonmelting flecks of cheese atop enchiladas, but eaten alone it's an entirely different proposition. Often milled and then pressed back into a round, different regions of Mexico wrap queso fresco in various leaves: corn husk in the South, banana on the Coasts, no wrapper in Central Mexico. The flavor of good queso fresco is remarkably sweet, like a ricotta that's cooked and recooked, but the texture is firm and springy and crumbles in the mouth. Also look for frying queso fresco, which is smooth and pressed and holds its shape against heat. For those familiar with ricotta salata, imagine a younger, wetter, and less salty version.

**MEXICO/UNITED STATES**
COW
**PASTEURIZED**
**AROMA:** Cooked milk
**TEXTURE:** Springy, squeaky
**FLAVOR:** Heated milk
**IN SHORT:** The nonmelting cooking cheese

# Bread Cheese

The American-made derivative of Finnish Leipäjuusto is, I am convinced, bound to capture our national fancy soon enough. It's like a cheese curd mated with a grilled cheese sandwich, all in sliceable, dippable format. Fresh, pressed cow milk cheese is oven-baked (the Finns would also flambé or grill it) to develop a sweet, brown, crusty exterior. The interior paste is springy and squeaky, and the whole thing can be popped into a toaster oven or microwave to warm and soften without turning into molten goo. Traditionally, the cheese would be aged until dry, when it was pocketed for hiking and skiing, resuscitated over a fire, and dipped into cups of coffee. Sweet, mild, and extremely buttery, bread cheese reminds me of a diner sandwich: American cheese on Wonder Bread, grilled with plenty of butter, minus the actual bread.

**UNITED STATES | COW**
**PASTEURIZED**
**RECOMMENDED BRAND:** Carr Valley Cheese
**AROMA:** None until cooked, then it becomes toasty
**TEXTURE:** Bouncy until softened with heat
**FLAVOR:** Toasted marshmallow with sea salt
**IN SHORT:** Brown bread without the bread

# Ricotta

Like my first encounter with real Mozzarella, my first taste of full-fat, high-moisture ricotta was a game changer. Ricotta had previously occupied the space of the pasty layer in dishes like lasagna and eggplant Parm, its texture somewhere between grainy and weepy. Good ricotta is light and fluffy and noticeably sweet. That sweetness comes from the traditional process of (re)cooking whey, from which ricotta gets its name. This is one of the original examples of food recycling: liquid whey left over from cheese making (originally, Italian Romano) was cooked and recooked at high enough temperatures to separate

UNITED STATES/ITALY

COW, SHEEP, OR BLEND

PASTEURIZED

**RECOMMENDED BRANDS:**
Calabro, Bellwether Farm,
Sierra Cheese

**AROMA:** Cooked milk

**TEXTURE:** Fluffy curds—what
cottage cheese wants to be

**FLAVOR:** Sweet, cooked milk

**IN SHORT:** Versatile—it can go
savory or sweet

any remaining solids (fat and protein) from water; those curds were then skimmed off the top. Most producers now make ricotta from a blend of milk and whey, and the high temperature cooking transforms already sweet lactic milk into practically candied fluff. Many ricottas include vinegar, which is used to accelerate acidification but contributes a sharp edge to flavor. Bellwether Farm, in San Andreas, California, makes ricotta without any vinegar, adding starter bacteria to the milk and allowing it to develop natural acidity over time before cooking. Their whey ricotta, using whey from cow and sheep cheese production, is also a revelation. Good ricotta is so simple and satisfying that we serve it at my house for Easter dessert, piled high in bowls and drizzled with brackish buckwheat honey. When in doubt, read labels and avoid ricotta made with gums and stabilizers. These lock in moisture and guarantee you a watery mess of whatever dish you're cooking.

# THE ONLY CHEESE WORTH MAKING AT HOME

I'm often asked to recommend books for home cheese making. My honest opinion is: Why make cheese at home when purchased will inevitably be better? I've never encountered a homemade Cheddar or Parmesan that held a candle to the most basic options available in any supermarket.

The exception to my rule is ricotta. Most ricotta that's available on supermarket shelves is industrially produced, grainy-textured and bland, thickened and stabilized with various gums. True, authentic ricotta is recooked whey, but most of what's sold in the United States is made from milk. You can make the same at home in fifteen minutes, and you are guaranteed impeccably fresh, creamy clouds of caramel-scented curd.

**2 CUPS WHOLE MILK**
(Ideally, use organic and unhomogenized and not UHT—ultrapasteurized. If you must choose, prioritize the absence of UHT and homogenization over organic certification. )

**1/4 TEASPOON SALT**

**2 TABLESPOONS DISTILLED WHITE VINEGAR**
(It's possible to use lemon juice or buttermilk, but I don't recommend them for their more noticeable impact on flavor and curd structure.)

❶ Heat milk and salt over medium-high heat. Scrape and stir while the milk is heating to avoid a cooked milk layer on the bottom of your pot.

❷ When milk begins to simmer (or registers 165°F/74°C to 185°F/85°C on an instant-read thermometer), add vinegar, turn heat to low, and stir constantly for 1 to 2 minutes until curds rise and separate from liquid whey. If using raw milk, be sure to heat to 180°F/82°C.

❸ Remove pot from heat and spoon (don't pour) curds into a double-paper-towel–lined sieve and drain to desired consistency. Expect draining to take 5 minutes to 2 hours, depending on the desired texture.

*Note: Steps 1 and 2 can be completed in a microwave. Add all ingredients to a glass bowl and cook on high for two to four minutes, until mixture bubbles. Remove from microwave and stir. This may save your pots, but I swear the flavor isn't as sweet and deep as stove-top ricotta.*

BURRATA

# Petite Breakfast FROM MARIN FRENCH CHEESE

These 4-ounce nuggets are essentially tiny, unripened Bries. They are cream-enriched, sharing the same recipe as Marin French's Triple Crème Brie, but because they are unripened there is no edible white rind. In fact, they have no rind at all to inhibit their gentle smell of warm milk with a whiff of caramel. Marin French uses primarily Jersey and Guernsey cow milk, which is higher in fat than the typical Holstein. That fat is best showcased here, in fresh rounds that are dense and sticky rather than stretchy like typical Brie types. I also appreciate Marin French's unflinching use of salt. A lot of fresh cheeses are undersalted, making them weak and watery. With so little to contribute to the flavor (no fancy rind, no months of aging), firm salting pushes forward the round sweetness of fresh milk. These guys also melt beautifully, making them happy companions with eggs and toast.

# Burrata

This bulging, bursting bomb of lactic decadence is like Mozzarella's souped-up and much sexier cousin. It looks like a solid ball of Mozzarella, but the interior is filled with a spillingly creamy mixture of milk, cream, and scraps or strands of Mozzarella. Producers call this center *stracciatella* or *panne di latte* interchangeably. It's delectable and simply the most perishable cheese you can import; in Italy it's traditionally eaten on the morning of its production. You can push its life span to several weeks, enough time to get it here on a plane and sell it in a few days before it sours, but this is challenging under the best circumstances. Accordingly, I look to several American producers who are making respectable and sometimes deliriously good approximations. The best burrata are so tender and moist, with such a thin exterior skin, that handling them is risky because they're likely to burst milky rivers down your arm. There is no cheese more dependent on youth than burrata, lest it lose its most seductive traits: sweet, clean milk and a slight briny finish. Nothing more, nothing less, nothing to hide behind.

**UNITED STATES | COW**

**PASTEURIZED**

**AROMA:** Warmed milk

**TEXTURE:** Dense, sticky, and wet

**FLAVOR:** Salty-sweet

**IN SHORT:** (I mean this as a compliment) like Polly-O string cheese, but better

**ITALY/UNITED STATES**

**COW**

**PASTEURIZED**

**RECOMMENDED BRANDS:** Bel Gioioso, Di Bruno Bros., DiStefano, Gioia Cheese, Lioni Latticini, Liuzzi Angeloni Cheese, Maplebrook Fine Cheese

**AROMA:** A glass of cold, fresh milk

**TEXTURE:** Tender and spillingly creamy

**FLAVOR:** Lush milk, grassy, briny

**IN SHORT:** The cheese to bathe in

## STRING CHEESE BEYOND THE STICK

In the States, string cheese refers to low-moisture Mozzarella in sticks. During manufacture, the proteins are aligned so they can be pulled off in strings or strips. It's typically flavorless, if inoffensive. If I'm going to buy it I reach for organic brands based solely on their milk sourcing, but truth be told I don't subscribe to the belief that kids require bland food (they do like de-stringing it, though).

In other countries, string cheese can refer to more complex or handmade offerings, such as Armenian string cheese, made of goat or sheep milk and pulled so as to develop strings, or Mexican Oaxaca (see below).

# Oaxaca

**MEXICO/UNITED STATES**

COW

**PASTEURIZED**

**RECOMMENDED BRANDS:**
Look for house-made, cut-to-order Oaxaca in Mexican specialty stores

**AROMA:** Very little—a whiff of milk

**TEXTURE:** Elastic, stringy

**FLAVOR:** Fresh milk, seawater

**IN SHORT:** Shred-arific

Traditional Mexican cheeses are a new group for me, and proof that delving into the unknown is the best way to defy preconceptions about food. I once thought Oaxaca was a bland block of gummy cheese. But just as boring dairy-case Mozzarella bears little resemblance to freshly pulled, high-moisture, or water-packed Mozzarella, authentic Oaxaca can be a revelation. It's packaged in giant ropes that look like snow-white taffy, requiring someone to slice off a run for you and coil it into a bag for transport home. Oaxaca is more akin to Armenian string cheese than Italian-style Mozzarella—pulling apart in thick, distinctive ropes the texture of overboiled chicken breast that are typically shredded into quesadillas before melting. Although prepackaged Oaxaca is bland and not especially interesting, cut-to-order Oaxaca is milky and simply delicious. When I first tasted it, I imagined serving shreds in a bowl, dressed with olive oil, parsley, and red pepper as a sublime no-veggie salad.

# Driftless FROM HIDDEN SPRINGS CREAMERY

**UNITED STATES | SHEEP**

**PASTEURIZED**

**AROMA:** Very little—a breath of mown grass

**TEXTURE:** Fluffy, spreadable

**FLAVOR:** Lemon meringue

**IN SHORT:** What cheese people mean when they say sheepy

It's rare to find fresh sheep milk cheeses; without a rind or the layered flavors that aging imparts, you can really savor the full fattiness that sheep milk offers. I find the taste of fresh sheep cheese in Europe (and this superlative one made in the Driftless Area of Wisconsin) to be immediately transportive to freshly mown summer lawns, green and full. They are milky and fresh, often pleasantly lemony, but where I catch the essence of the animal (the sheepiness) is in the incredible heaviness of the milk and a complex vegetal note that tastes like breathing in an open field. The creamery also produces Driftless in a number of flavored varieties, the best of which is Maple.

APPROACHABLE

Milk pails drying

Homemade rennet

Coagulation

Curd cutting

# MY WINTER GAME CHANGER

Long before kale became the new It Vegetable, I fell in love with this incredibly simple but utterly addictive salad at (still, after all these years) the best Italian restaurant in New York: Lupa. They serve it as an antipasto, and it's proof that four perfectly melded ingredients can carry you through the darkest, coldest, and longest of winters. When we lived in Brooklyn and there were no local vegetables to speak of for months on end, we ate this salad four or five times a week. The combo of citrus, kale, and olive oil tastes vaguely green banana-ish; the Ricotta Salata is nearly squeaky, briny, and rich yet neutral in flavor.

**1 BUNCH LACINATO (TUSCAN) KALE**

**1 LEMON, JUICED**

**⅓ CUP EXTRA VIRGIN OLIVE OIL** (splurge on Frankie's 457)

**2 TO 4 OUNCES RICOTTA SALATA,** broken into bits with your fingers

**KOSHER SALT**

**BLACK PEPPER,** freshly ground

**❶** Derib the kale, fold the leaves in half lengthwise, and roll them up like a joint. Cut into thin strips with a big knife for long, thin ribbons of veg.

**❷** Mix the juice of ½ to 1 lemon with the olive oil, 2 hefty pinches of salt, and several grindings of pepper until blended. Pour half of the dressing over the kale and toss with your hands until lightly coated. Taste and increase dressing to your taste. Toss with your hands. Add niblets of ricotta salata. I go for the full 4 ounces, but you may be more restrained.

# Ricotta Salata

Before we get anywhere, let me reveal: Ricotta Salata isn't technically a cheese, as it's made from whey rather than milk. But it's sold and used like a cheese, and I love it, so there you go. The white, crumbly wheels are produced from the residual whey of sheep cheese production, which is recooked until the solids can be skimmed off, pressed, salted, and aged for roughly three months. Some American producers make it from cow milk, but that's not the tradition, and you miss the rich fat solids from sheep milk when this money-saving approach is used. Even though real Ricotta Salata is crumbly, it manages to be moist when you bite into it. I find the round, moderately salty flavor an ideal addition to dark leafy greens (cooked or raw) and surprisingly delicious alongside the acidic sweetness of citrus fruit.

# Halloumi

If I had a top ten list of cheeses everyone should know about, Halloumi would probably be number one. Most are the size and shape of a man's wallet (although I've seen half-moons as well), and boast uncommon durability. Sold in vacuum packaging, it's the only cheese I've encountered that can be frozen and thawed with no ill effects. Although Halloumi is traditionally made from a blend of sheep and goat milk, many producers now add cow milk; disagreement over the exact ingredients has kept the cheese from receiving PDO status as milk farmers fight over the right to be included in the recipe. Cooked, Halloumi is the love child of fried cheese curds and Mozzarella sticks, except no breading is required and frying is optional. It's typically grilled (my preference); the firm, salty block holds its shape under extreme heat and takes lovingly to a squeeze of lemon and showering of whatever fresh herbs you've got lying around. Or do like the Cypriots and toss with watermelon and olive oil. Some Halloumi is speckled with bits of mint, a holdover from the days when herb-wrapped blocks kept better and longer than those without. Opt for a plain Halloumi if you can get it so there's nothing to distract from the squeaky, layered chew and universally likable briny flavor.

**ITALY** | SHEEP (WHEY)
PASTEURIZED
**RECOMMENDED BRAND:** Mitica
**AROMA:** Very little
**TEXTURE:** Mealy but moist
**FLAVOR:** Salt and sheep fat
**IN SHORT:** The most underrated cheese for cooking

**CYPRUS**
SHEEP/GOAT/COW
PASTEURIZED
**RECOMMENDED BRAND:** Mt. Vikos
**AROMA:** Salt water
**TEXTURE:** Springy and squeaky
**FLAVOR:** Briny
**IN SHORT:** Cheese curds meet Mozzarella sticks

# Buffalo Mozzarella

ITALY: MOZZARELLA DI
BUFALA CAMPANA PDO

COLOMBIA/UNITED STATES

WATER BUFFALO

PASTEURIZED

**RECOMMENDED BRANDS:**
Annabella Creamery, BUF
Creamery

**AROMA:** Grassy

**TEXTURE:** Bouncy but
succulent and fatty

**FLAVOR:** Slightly gamy,
grassy, and rich

**IN SHORT:** What Mozzarella
wishes it could be

Not unlike burrata (see page 49), buffalo Mozzarella is a case of a classic and highly perishable cheese finding new incarnations outside its traditional southern Italian region of production. Notably, some of the best options are now being made in South America. Italian Mozzarella di Bufala Campana is a protected cheese made in parts of Campania, Lazio, Puglia, and Molise. What I've found is that the minimum transport time from Italy is often too great for such a delicate cheese; so much of the buffalo Mozzarella that's available in American stores is already going downhill: mushy, watery, and exceedingly gamy—or more likely, sour. Fresh buffalo mozz should be plump and tight, although rich and fatty, and while the milk is grassier tasting and ever so slightly muskier than cow milk, it shouldn't be harsh or acidic. Recently, several quality producers have emerged from Colombia. Their water buffalo herds are grass-fed, and cheese can be air-shipped from Colombia to Miami, often clearing customs with forty-eight hours of production. That means the cheese can reach your plate within a week and retain its original charm. As is true with all high-moisture fresh cheeses, the preferred scenario is eating it at the source, ideally still warm and within hours of its production.

# Teleme

UNITED STATES | COW

PASTEURIZED

**RECOMMENDED BRAND:**
Franklin's/Mid Coast Cheese
Company

**AROMA:** Dough and sour cream

**TEXTURE:** Sticky bounce
softening to scoopable

**FLAVOR:** Milky and tart

**IN SHORT:** Lactic comfort

Teleme is an especially important cheese in the context of California's dairy industry. Invented in the 1930s by Giovanni Peluso and his son Frank, the soft, milky wobble was dusted with rice flour and proved a huge hit with the Italian immigrant population south of Paso Robles. Giovanni's grandson Franklin resurrected the family recipe in the early 1980s but sold the Peluso Cheese Company in 2005. Around that time, under new management, what Teleme you could find had turned bland and rubbery, the flour dusting a gritty coat. Franklin started a second company under his first name and is again making the doughy-looking cheese, with its yellow, lactic paste and slightly tangy, lemony flavor. Given several weeks of aging, the cheese softens into an oozy spread. My cheese colleague, Gordon Edgar, describes it as "Taleggio without the washed rind," which makes me think of treating it as a real Italian might, and generously layering it atop polenta before broiling for an untouchable blanket of molten goodness.

# Crescenza/Stracchino

The story goes that in the northern Italian regions of Piedmont, Lombardy, and Veneto, cows whose milk was made into Gorgonzola and Taleggio were herded up to mountainous fields for summer grazing. At the beginning of autumn, the tired cows (*vacca stracca*) returned to the valley floor, their udders heavy with fatty milk. In fact, it was the end of their lactation cycle that accounted for the richer milk rather than their wandering summers, but the story stuck as this tired cow milk was made into the blob-like, rindless cheese known as stracchino or crescenza. Golden white, not unlike a thick pudding, the cheese manages to be mild and essentially lactic in flavor while delivering the slightest of tangs on the finish. Its high moisture content makes it instantly meltable, smearable, and layerable, ideally with acidic counterparts like ratatouille.

**ITALY/UNITED STATES**
COW
**PASTEURIZED**
**AROMA:** Faint hint of yogurt
**TEXTURE:** Sticky pudding
**FLAVOR:** Fatty and slightly yogurty
**IN SHORT:** Cheese dough

## CHEESE FOR THE LACTOSE INTOLERANT

I can't tell you the number of woeful, sad-eyed people who've told me that, unfortunately, they can't eat cheese because they're lactose intolerant. I'm here to tell you that unlike milk, most cheese has only low to trace levels of lactose.

During the acidification stage of cheese making, the lactose (sugar) in milk is converted to lactic acid. Residual lactose continues to convert over time. This means that younger, fresher, and less aged cheeses will have more lactose than hard, dry aged cheeses. While these fresh cheeses may also have milk or cream added to them, as in ricotta, they still have markedly less lactose than fluid milk.

**1 CUP OF MILK CONTAINS 11 GRAMS OF LACTOSE.**

**1 CUP OF RICOTTA CONTAINS 6 TO 12 GRAMS OF LACTOSE.**

**1 OUNCE OF MOZZARELLA WILL TAKE YOU DOWN TO .8 GRAMS OF LACTOSE**

**1 OUNCE OF SWISS, CHEDDAR, OR PARMESAN COMES IN AT .5 GRAMS OF LACTOSE OR LESS**

Although each person's lactose intolerance varies, many find that they can regularly enjoy cheese, yet a bowl of ice cream might be tantamount to gastrointestinal torment. In light of all this hopeful news, consult your doctor if eating dairy has made you miserable in the past.

# Fromage Blanc

FRANCE/UNITED STATES

COW OR GOAT

PASTEURIZED

**RECOMMENDED BRAND:**
Vermont Creamery

**AROMA:** Very little, yogurt

**TEXTURE:** Thick yogurt

**FLAVOR:** Clean, tangy, milky

**IN SHORT:** The blank slate for
your spooning pleasure

Native to northwestern France, this fresh cheese (literally "white cheese") is traditionally made from skimmed cow milk after the cream has gone to butter production. These days, however, cream is often added back in to improve flavor and increase richness. Folks liken fromage blanc to yogurt, but it is actually a cheese. The cultures do their work of acidification while the cheese is being made, whereas yogurt is teeming with a cocktail of live cultures onto the supermarket shelf. Good fromage blanc is allowed to acidify overnight. Although many cheeses undergo the same process in minutes, the long, slow approach for fromage blanc ensures a tart and bracing tang to offset the natural sweetness of milk. Fromage blanc made with goat milk only amplifies this quality. The French often serve it for dessert, with sweetener or fruit, but I like it as a yogurt-replacing base for savory dips. What you want to avoid is fromage blanc that is in any way gritty. It should be airy and smooth, begging to be eaten with a spoon.

# Fresh Goat Cheese, or Chèvre

UNITED STATES / FRANCE

GOAT

PASTEURIZED

**RECOMMENDED BRANDS
(NATIONAL):** Chavrie, Laura
Chenel's Chèvre, Cypress Grove
Ms. Natural, Vermont Creamery Fresh Goat Cheese

**RECOMMENDED BRANDS
(REGIONAL):** Goat Lady Dairy,
Prodigal Farm

**AROMA:** Goat milk, or vaguely
lemony milk

**TEXTURE:** Creamy crumble,
moist morsel

**FLAVOR:** Bright, citrine,
mouthwatering

**IN SHORT:** Misunderstood

Perhaps more than any other, unaged goat cheese is one of the first styles a fledgling cheese maker (at least, one with goats) will pursue. The cheese can be made quickly and simply, and then sold immediately for cash flow. As a result, it's a style I urge you to look for at your local farmers' market or when you're traveling. You're likely to find wonderful makers and impeccably fresh cheese that you'll never see at the local supermarket or even the best cheese stores.

*Chèvre* translates as cheese made with goat milk, but the word has become synonymous with fresh, rindless goat cheese, most commonly sold in a log shape. It is the cheese that put goat cheese on the American eating map in the late 1970s, thanks to makers and chefs in Northern California, and remains the placeholder in people's minds for what goat cheese can be. Unfortunately, there's a lot of mediocre chèvre out there. In particular, this means a gritty, grainy, or watery texture, as opposed to the smooth, smearable *mouth clouds* (as described by Prodigal Farm) you want to find. As for flavor, chèvre is a tart, acidic cheese. But this should never mean sour or harsh—it should be pleasantly citrusy and anchored by creamy milk, like a great Key lime pie.

Fresh goat cheese isn't going to be a good melter—the cheese will soften under heat but won't become gooey or stretchy. Despite this, it's an impressively versatile addition to practically anything: eggs, flatbread, salad, or as a stuffing for meat. Its bright, mouthwatering flavor means a little goes a long way.

# Banon PDO

You cannot find real Banon in the States because its PDO guidelines require the use of unpasteurized milk and a typical aging period of fewer than thirty days. Nevertheless, I include it here for several reasons. When you are in Europe (particularly France, where it hails from one of four southeastern *départements*) and can buy the cheese legally, it is worth doing so. Unlike many fresh goat cheeses that coagulate slowly overnight, thanks to the power of acidification, Banon relies on rennet for a quick set, resulting in a dense, velvety paste. The cheese may be washed in eau-de-vie, which imparts a hot burn before the round is wrapped in chestnut leaves. As Banon ages over several weeks, the leaves impart a tannic, earthy quality—and the eau-de-vie a high fruity note. It's a delicate and complex combination. But be forewarned: despite the clear restrictions on U.S. importation of Banon, you may find an insipid hockey puck being sold under the same name. Made of pasteurized cow milk and wrapped in tough, sanitized green leaves, the cheese bears no resemblance to its stolen namesake. Avoid it, save your dollars, and hop a transatlantic flight to get the real deal.

**FRANCE | GOAT**
**UNPASTEURIZED**
**AROMA:** Tea leaves and cream
**TEXTURE:** Velvety and dense
**FLAVOR:** Cider by the autumn leaf pile
**IN SHORT:** Feisty

# O'Banon FROM CAPRIOLE GOAT CHEESES

A most brilliant example of an American riff on a European classic. Pioneering goat cheese maker Judy Schad, based just over the Kentucky line in Indiana, has been making this southern reinterpretation of Provençal Banon since 1988 (back when, as she points out, no one would buy a goat cheese that did not have a French name). The French original is a fresh puck of goat cheese, which may be soaked in eau-de-vie before being wrapped in chestnut leaves. Judy's O'Banon relies on Woodford Reserve bourbon for vanilla–oak intensity that complements the natural tannins of chestnut leaves. The result is a dense yet creamy round of rindless cheese imbued with nuances of tobacco and marzipan, minus the sweetness. Its name is a riff on French Banon, by way of Judy's buddy and former Indiana governor, the late Frank O'Bannon. I've been known to describe cheeses as masculine or feminine. If you doubt the applicability, taste this husky boy.

**UNITED STATES | GOAT**
**PASTEURIZED**
**AROMA:** Bourbon barrel
**TEXTURE:** Packed clay
**FLAVOR:** Mouthwatering yet tannic, a remarkable push-pull
**IN SHORT:** The Southern gentleman of goat cheese

# Feta (PDO)

GREECE | SHEEP/GOAT

PASTEURIZED

**RECOMMENDED BRANDS (PDO):** Dodoni, Mt. Vikos

**RECOMMENDED BRAND (NON-PDO):** Valbreso Feta (France/Sheep)

**AROMA:** Clean, deep sea

**TEXTURE:** Moist and crumbly, but creamy under tooth

**FLAVOR:** Tangy, lemony, milky-rich

**IN SHORT:** Dairy Pop Rocks

I am the first person to advocate for cheeses made in the United States, constantly explaining that American cheese does not mean bad cheese. Feta is one cheese where you won't hear my typical party line. While Greek feta is a PDO cheese, made of sheep milk blended with up to 30 percent goat milk, the name feta has been co-opted for any brined white cheese, often precrumbled in cups. There are some excellent feta-style cheeses made in the Balkans and France, but large-scale U.S. production is a sad situation indeed. Most of the time, American feta is salt-dusty cow milk cheese bearing no resemblance to the savory chunks of fatty, tangy feta commonly eaten throughout the day in Greece. The difference is remarkable; the original is so far superior to cheap imitators that no comparison is warranted. There are a number of smaller American farms making goat milk feta that can be wonderful in a lean, lemony way; but again, the fat and heft of sheep milk is integral to the delicate balance that makes this cheese great. Traditionally made feta is dry-salted before it is ripened in salt brine. Essentially, the cheese is pickled. The combination of sea-saltiness and gamy edge from the sheep milk make it the most intense fresh cheese I know. While it will keep for weeks submerged in its milky juice, once exposed to air it is nearly as perishable as Mozzarella. Replacing the brine with water won't do the trick, but you can easily make replacement brine at home with 1 cup of warm water and 3 tablespoons of kosher salt (just be sure to cool it before returning the cheese).

# MY PICKS: APPROACHABLE MOZZARELLA TYPES

Approachable fresh cheeses can be meals unto themselves, easily augmented by many of the vegetables or fruit that are likely hanging out in your fridge. Or, as we often do in my house, enjoy them as a solid snack or instantly prepared appetizer to nosh on while prepping dinner. Clean, light, and delicately sweet or briny is the name of the game, as in:

## Burrata (ideally, DiStefano or Lioni Latticini)

Upgrade your Mozzarella to burrata and you've made a special occasion out of Tuesday night. The bulging, cream-laced interior spills out so conveniently that you have no choice but to wipe it up with a slab of semolina bread, slice of tomato, or sliver of salumi, whichever you have handy (see page 49).

## Ricotta Salata (ideally, Mitica)

Okay, so technically it's not a cheese as it's made of whey, not milk. But who's judging when you can break a hunk into dry, slightly squeaky chunks and improve any night's salad? The whey gives a restrained, slightly cooked milky flavor, and the whole experience is like eating crackers made of dairy (see page 53).

## Halloumi (ideally, Mt. Vikos)

On the edge of intense due to its high salt content but ultimately guaranteed to be crowd-friendly. This cheese is just so awesome. You grill it and slice it; it's hot but not melted, briny but not heavy, and the ultimate appetizer alongside grabbable summer fruits and veggies. I don't mean salads. I mean bulging cherry tomatoes or slices of sticky peach. The most wondrous of finger foods (see page 53).

## MY PICKS: INTENSE MOZZARELLA TYPES

I appreciate the escalation in salinity that comes with more intense fresh cheeses. But even more so, the intense end of the flavor spectrum is a chance to experience the flavors of milk other than cow. Citrus and lemon give way to fatty, woolly roundness, in which you can taste the animal that brought you these fine cheeses:

### Fresh Goat Cheese, aka Chèvre (ideally, Vermont Creamery)

You can buy it in the standard log, but there's a second, better option: their creamy goat cheese is sold whipped for an airy, silken texture. Lemony, soft, and delicately tangy with no grit, sourness, or chalky aftertaste. This is what goat cheese can be (see page 56).

### Buffalo Mozzarella (ideally, Annabella Creamery)

Notice I don't say Mozzarella di Bufala Campana PDO because there are some fantastic options being made outside of Italy that deliver the ideal combination of higher fat and buffalo milk flavor: tangy and full, with notes of wet hay and pleasant gaminess. Avoid balls that are mushy or disintegrating, a sure sign the cheese is too old, and hold out for those like the fat of a baby's leg roll (see page 54).

### Sheep Milk Feta (ideally Mt. Vikos or Valbreso)

Usually Greek (and blended with goat milk), although possibly French or Balkan, real feta is never made of cow milk. It's moist and fatty, breaking apart into sizable chunks, not dusty bits. Its flavor is tangy, the aroma rich. If you find the brine pickling too salty, cut it with chunks of watermelon or tomato (see page 58).

## TASTING ONE
# A COMPARISON OF MILKS

Fresh cheese made from each of the three major milk types will give you a benchmark for understanding characteristic flavors and textures. As you move into aged cheese tastings, notice how these qualities anchor other styles.

**1. COW: Quark** (see page 41)**, mascarpone** (see page 44) **or fromage blanc** (see page 56) **are possible substitutes, but their recipes call for cream or milk skimming. I want you to start with pure, unadulterated, whole cow milk, made into cheese.**

**2. SHEEP: Driftless from Hidden Springs Creamery (or other fresh sheep cheese)** (see page 50)

**3. GOAT: Fresh Goat Cheese** (see page 56)

## TASTING TWO
# A MOZZARELLA VERTICAL

Beginning with real Mozzarella and moving into buffalo milk's more intense flavors, this vertical exposes you to the full range of what's possible beyond the block in the dairy case.

**1. Fresh (high-moisture) Mozzarella** (see page 43)

**2. Burrata** (see page 49)

**3. Mozzarella di Bufala Campana PDO or buffalo Mozzarella** (see page 54)

## TASTING THREE
# FRESH CHEESES TO BE COOKED

Tasted straight from the fridge, these cheeses may strike you as bland or plain. Breaded and fried, toasted, or grilled, you'll find yourself with discrete and delicious meals.

**1. Battered and Deep-Fried Cheese Curds** (see page 40)

**2. Toasted Bread Cheese** (see page 45)

**3. Grilled Halloumi** (see page 53)

# PAIRINGS WITH MOZZARELLA TYPES

## PAIRING OVERVIEW

SWEET MILK

TANGY MILK

GAMY MILK

BRINE

## BEAR IN MIND

These are the ingredient cheeses—instead of milk, butter, cream, or cream cheese.

Just as a swallow of milk cuts excessive spice, these cheeses absorb smoke, heat, and flavorings admirably.

Because of their dairy neutrality, Mozz types agree more readily with unusual food pairings.

## CLASSIC PAIRINGS

(Sweet milk) with acidic fruit: Smooth, elastic Mozzarella and succulent, juicy tomatoes (aka caprese salad)

(Tangy milk) with sweet vegetables: crumbly fresh goat with dense roasted beets (or squash)

(Gamy milk/brine) with sweet fruit: chunked feta with juicy, sugary watermelon

### 1. CRACKERS AND FLATBREADS WITH HERBS AND SPICES

Mozz types replace dips, spreads, or butter, so you can appreciate the crunch of your cracker. The relative neutrality of the cheeses means you don't have to worry about the crackers' flavor dominance.

**FLAVOR SPECTRUM: 1–10**

### 2. SMOKED OR SPICED NUTS

Crunchy flavor bombs whose intensity is cooled and cut by the moisture and essential milkiness of mozz types.

**FLAVOR SPECTRUM: 1–10**

### 3. COFFEE OR CHOCOLATE-COVERED COFFEE BEANS

If you take cream, that is. Sweet, milky cheeses play the same role and are barely removed from the cream cheese bagel you might eat alongside your cuppa.

**FLAVOR SPECTRUM: 1–2**

### 4. BUCKWHEAT HONEY

This black, molasses-like honey is astringent, intense, and malty. Ricotta was the first fresh cheese I enjoyed with it.

**FLAVOR SPECTRUM: 1–2**

### 5. SMOKED FISH

Take a note from lox and cream cheese, and this gateway's general affinity for smoky foods. Fish and cheese is generally discouraged, but I especially like tart, lemony notes with smoked mussels or salmon.

**FLAVOR SPECTRUM: 3–7**

### 6. 'NDUJA

This heavily spiced spreadable salami is insanely delicious and intense enough that it overwhelms most cheeses. Layer with savory Mozz types and you can have your meat paste and eat it too.

**FLAVOR SPECTRUM: 3–8**

### 7. CANDIED CITRUS PEEL

Chewy, fruity, tart, and best suited to wet, crumbly, acidic, or intensely briny Mozz types.

**FLAVOR SPECTRUM: 7–10**

ROBIOLA BOSINA

HUMBOLDT FOG

# Brie

CAMEMBERT

FROMAGE DE MEAUX

GOAT BRIE

LA TUR

BONNE BOUCHE

**SPECIALTY SHOP**

**Margie**
PAGE 76

**St. Nuage**
PAGE 82

**Moser Screamer**
PAGE 84

**Teleeka**
PAGE 88

**Bermuda Triangle**
PAGE 91

**Mt. Tam**
PAGE 82

**Kinderhook Creek**
PAGE 86

**Green Hill**
PAGE 78

**AVAILABILITY   SUPERMARKET** ➤➤

**Moses Sleeper**
PAGE 77

**Saint Angel**
PAGE 80

**Brillat-Savarin**
PAGE 83

**Goat Brie**
PAGE 84

**La Tur**
PAGE 91

**Triple Crème Brie**
PAGE 80

**Pierre Robert**
PAGE 84

**Robiola Bosina**
PAGE 85

**Le Delice de Bourgogne**
PAGE 83

**Bonne Bouche**
PAGE 86

**Fromager d'Affinois**
PAGE 78

**(Double Crème) Brie**
PAGE 76

**Saint André**
PAGE 80

**Humboldt Fog (Grande)**
PAGE 88

**Bûcheron/ Bûcherondin**
PAGE 91

**FLAVOR   APPROACHABLE** ➤➤

| ❶ | ❷ | ❸ | ❹ | ❺ |
|---|---|---|---|---|
| WHITE BUTTON MUSHROOM | CREAM | BUTTER | YEAST ROLLS | CRÈME FRAÎCHE |

**Nocetto di Capra**
PAGE 94

**Champlain Triple**
PAGE 97

**Adelle**
PAGE 99

**Kunik**
PAGE 94

**Goat Camembert**
PAGE 98

**Dancing Fern**
PAGE 101

**Weybridge**
PAGE 98

**Nancy's Hudson Valley Camembert**
PAGE 93

**Tunworth**
PAGE 102

**(wannabe) Camembert de Normandie PDO (aka Camembert with traditional aspirations)**
PAGE 104

**Cremont**
PAGE 93

**St. Albans**
PAGE 99

**L'Édel de Cléron**
PAGE 94

**Brebisrousse d'Argental**
PAGE 98

**(wannabe) Brie de Meaux PDO (aka Fromage de Meaux)**
PAGE 102

**Harbison**
PAGE 97

**Pont l'Évêque PDO**
PAGE 100

INTENSE

| **6** | **7** | **8** | **9** | **10** |
|---|---|---|---|---|
| WOODSY | PORCINI MUSHROOM | COOKED MUSHROOMS/ TRUFFLE | COOKED CRUCIFEROUS VEGETABLES | ALL THAT, PLUS BITTER GREENS |

# Every time I'm asked to bring cheese to a gathering, one of my selections is creamy, runny, or drippy and swathed in a downy, white skin.

Inevitably, folks circle 'round to watch the unwrapping of cheese, and I get the eager inquiry, "Is that a Brie?!" Which isn't surprising, since one of the first cheese associations to be cemented in people's minds is that buttery cheese with a snow-white rind must always be a Brie.

Actually, not necessarily.

First off, the name Brie can be given to any cheese. Historically, Brie was a northern French cow milk cheese with soft texture and edible white rind. These days, there are cheeses called Brie made from multiple milk types in myriad countries. Second, know that "Brie" can refer to a cheese that tastes bland and listless, or a cheese that's mildly buttery, or even an intensely pungent cheese, with flavor edging on bitter greens. Finally, to further complicate and confuse the issue, there are hundreds of cheeses that look like Brie but are made with a different recipe and called by a different name.

So what will the Brie Gateway introduce you to? The same qualities that would make you guess I'd brought Brie to your party. The Brie types are unified by their texture, which should be some version of butter, ranging from cold and flaky butter to room-temperature butter to whipped or even melting butter and, finally, to buttercream frosting. A range, to be sure, but buttery all the same. And the cheeses in this chapter all share an edible rind that can be the cheese's greatest asset or most devastating downfall. Traditionally this edible rind (known to Cheese Folk as a "bloomy rind") is a mottled alabaster hue, thanks to a mold called *Penicillium candidum* (or *camemberti*). The traditional white mold may be combined with or replaced by a brainy-looking yeast called *Geotrichum candidum*. Much of the cheese's aroma and character is determined by this rind, and the rind's flavor and texture is what makes one Brie type bad while another is good. The rind matters, and it's there to be eaten.

And yet, like so many people, I spent my first Brie-eating years carefully cutting away that skin-like edge of white. Brie was the fancy cheese in our house. Every two or so years my parents would have a party for which a wedge of plastic-wrapped Brie would appear alongside Stoned Wheat Thins and, if I was lucky, Boursin garlic and herb spread. What I knew about Brie was that I wanted to like it, the way I deeply loved and cherished the shrimp cocktail that also appeared on rare and lauded occasions. I knew Brie meant: Fancy! Special occasion! Holiday(?)! But I didn't like it. The juxtaposition of sticky smear and thick, chewy rind bothered me. Something medicinal about the rind permeated the whole cheese. It tasted the way its plastic wrapper smelled: at once bland and like chemicals.  In my eight-year-old heart, I wanted Brie to be as miraculous as that Boursin, which reminded me of thin, silky cream cheese, its flavor determined by its few simple ingredients.

The truth is, Brie can be miraculous. What I got as a kid wasn't. It was tough and firm, the rind bitter and thick. But that's not to suggest that good Brie types aren't readily available in the supermarket or that you have to go to Europe for a delectable bloomy rind. It's a matter of knowing what you like and knowing what to avoid. Many cheese snobs insist that the only Brie worth eating is the kind you can't get in the States. That only raw milk Brie de Meaux PDO is "real" and that all others are vapid imitations. Actually, Brie de Meaux is a 9 out of 10 in flavor intensity when it comes to Brie types. While I personally worship the stanky broccoli-soupiness at the strong end of Brie's flavor spectrum, not everyone does, or should. Many Brie types don't taste like cooked mushrooms and cauliflower, and they don't have to. Instead, they aspire to be whisperingly soft, luscious cheeses and are accordingly mild and decadent. It doesn't make them any less real or good, they just offer another dimension of flavor. What shouldn't fly in the Brie Gateway are sharp, chewy rinds that taste like aspirin, or cheeses that burn the eyes and throat with ammonia. These are my yardsticks for determining "bad." If it hurts my mouth or makes my eyes water, I don't want it. But "good" is a far more subjective thing. I still remember the day, a few months into my fledgling cheese career, when I brought a relatively common, "industrial" Brie type home to my boyfriend, along with a smattering of hyper-obscure, cheese geek finds. The one he swooned over was the one all the cheese geeks scoffed at. He kept going back for another swipe and exclaiming, "This is the best Brie I've ever had! It's so . . . creamy!" Never mind that it wasn't technically Brie. It looked the part, quilted like a goose-down pillow, all silky and spreadable, begging to be smushed across a cracker. It fulfilled every little kid's desire to eat the room temperature butter straight from its dish. (That cheese, BTW, was Fromager d'Affinois. see page 78). This chapter's approachable cheeses give you permission to eat the butter, straight up and unadulterated. The intense cheeses, meanwhile, may clear a small room when served at room temperature.

My point is, there's a whole world of Brie types out there. Best to clarify what you don't want to eat. From there, it's easier to find the flavors you will personally worship.

# Chapter Guide

I say Brie. And you think: White. Creamy. Buttery. First and foremost it's the soft, snowy rind that earmarks a cheese as Brie-like. That rind, in cheese techni-speak, is called a bloomy rind (or sometimes a soft-ripened, or even a surface-ripened, cheese). Brie type cheeses have a rind made of some combination of mold (*Penicillium candidum, Penicillium camemberti*) and/or yeast (*Geotrichum candidum*) that blooms like tiny flowers on the exterior of a ripening cheese. Over time, these patches of yellowish white fur are patted down to form a cohesive skin, or rind, on the cheese's surface. This live rind breaks down the fats and proteins of a cheese, resulting in an increasingly creamy to runny texture over time. This is why you may encounter that glistening layer just under the rind that I call the "creamline." The moister a cheese is to begin with, the faster this breakdown occurs.

## WHAT TO KNOW

**THE RIND MAKES A DIFFERENCE:** While traditional French Brie and similarly white-rinded cheeses are made using the mold *P. candidum* or *P. camemberti,* cheese makers are increasingly working with a yeast called *Geotrichum candidum* for their bloomy rinds. Why am I getting all cheese geeky on you? Because while both types of rind are edible (and, I'd argue, determine much of the cheese's flavor), the type of rind makes a difference in helping you find the cheese you'll prefer.

Remember with edible rinds that the flavor underneath the rind will always be milder than the rind itself, so if the flavor is going in a direction you don't care for you'll want to stop short of eating the rind.

➤ *GEOTRICHUM* **RINDS:**

• Make sweeter, mellower flavors

• Have flavors described as nutty and yeasty

• Look different: they are wrinkly and brain-like

• Often are yellower in color

• May have secondary mold growth—small blue or green spots that are naturally occurring and totally harmless

• Are less likely to get ammoniated over time

➤ *P. CANDIDUM / CAMEMBERTI* **(AKA CLASSIC BRIE) RINDS:**

• Are white, and may become mottled with brown over time

• Often make stronger, "sharper" flavors

• Have flavors best described as fungal/mushroomy or bitter greens

• Will become browner over time, with ammoniated smell and flavor

**DOUBLE AND TRIPLE CRÈME CHEESES:** You'll be more likely to find cheeses you like if you know how you feel about fat in your Brie types. This group is the most likely to be cream-enriched, which increases the natural fat level in the cheese, greatly influences texture, and impacts the cheese's flavor.

The terms *double crème* and *triple crème* (or triple cream) make numerous appearances in the world of Brie types, and refer to the fat content in a cheese's dry matter (the cheese minus all the water). No cheese is naturally 60 to 74 percent butterfat (the range defined by the French to qualify for double crème status), let alone the 75 percent plus that takes a triple crème from decadent cheese to a whisper shy of actual butter. Both types are cream-enriched to hit butter-bomb levels. Some makers tout this, others don't. And in fact, traditional Brie is neither double nor triple crème, instead weighing in around 45 percent butterfat. What's worth knowing is:

➤ Double or triple crème doesn't guarantee you inherently superior cheese. It does, certainly, guarantee you a mouth-coating paste that in careless hands gives the unfortunate impression of drinking margarine. There is such a thing as too buttery. And it doesn't feel good.

➼ These numerical standards are French, and cheese makers from other countries (most commonly the United States) may use the terms double or triple crème/cream simply to indicate that cream has been added.

➼ When a cheese is a double or triple crème Brie its flavor will be on the milder end of the flavor spectrum and its production is often more industrial or large-scale.

➼ Triple crèmes with unique brands and names (for example, Saint Andre or St. Nuage) have stronger flavors than triple crème Brie. The flavor boost starts with earthy and nutty qualities and builds to tart and mushroomy flavors.

➼ The best-made triple crèmes, whether or not they're triple crème Brie, should be like unsweetened buttercream frosting. And they should not be relegated to mere butter bombs—nutty, mushroomy, or tart flavors should be present, but just a whisper, like the vermouth in a proper martini.

## WHAT TO AVOID

➼ **COLOR:** A rind that has turned brown, sticky, red, or cracked (it need not be pristine white, but yellow or tan mottling is not the same as uniformly brown). Also, white, red, black, blue, or green spots on the cut surface of the cheese.

➼ **AROMA:** While Brie types, particularly at the intense end of the spectrum, may smell pungent ("fart in a bag" has been used more than a few times), they should never smell sharp or sour. Ammonia (like Windex or cat pee) is the surest sign that you've got off-quality cheese.

➼ **FLAVOR:** A cheese that tastes like aspirin or ammonia, or, I would add subjectively, tastes like nothing. Milk is not nothing, nor is lush, fatty cream. Those are mild, mellow hallmarks of dairy greatness. You don't have to love the most intense Brie type cheeses to appreciate good stuff, nor do you have to settle for bland, chemical-tasting cheese.

➼ **RIND:** Generally speaking, a triple crème cheese is going to be beaten fluff, like cheesecake, while other Brie types ripen to the texture of finger webbing (plump and soft with a little spring-back, like that bit of skin between your thumb and pointer finger). You want to avoid a rind that, when unwrapped and at room temperature, peels away from the interior paste. This is the cheese equivalent of being flipped the bird. Converserly, a rind that roots down into the cheese. The rind should be a uniform outer layer, and shouldn't form pockets or veins of white mold that eat into the yellow paste. Thick, chewy, or excessively papery rinds are a flaw, as is firm cheese. Yielding, sticky, cheese-cakey are all fine. But no stiffies. Finally, beware a liquid Brie type. Spoonable is okay but flowing cheese is generally a sign of overripeness.

## STORAGE AND SHELF LIFE

Because the Brie types are encased in a live rind that is actively breaking down the cheeses' fats and proteins, there is an objective life span: a cheese is young, ripe, perfectly ripe, overripe, and, finally, dead. You want to eat the cheese before it's over-ripe (certainly before it's dead) and ideally at peak ripeness.

The bloomy rind of Brie types is quickly smothered by plastic wrap, but paper wrap alone (unless it's specially designed cheese paper) will shorten shelf life, as the cheese will rapidly dry out. My preference is zip-top plastic bags, so you can squeeze all the air out and have individual storage units. You can also wrap first in parchment paper, followed by plastic wrap. A small Tupperware container can work similarly well, but the key is that the container be as close to the size of the cheese as possible to prevent its drying out.

Once cut, the Brie types are best consumed within seven days.

Small spots or patches of blue, green, or white mold may develop on the cut surface of the cheese; these can be easily scraped away or a paper-thin slice cut off to remove it, though they are a reliable warning sign that you're pushing the limit on storage life.

### IN A WORD: SOFT

#### LIGHT AND AIRY
AIRY  CREAMY  FLUFFY
MARSHMALLOWY  SILKY  SLIPPERY
TENDER  VELVETY  WHIPPED

#### SMOOTH AND/OR SPRINGY
BULGING  CHEWY  ELASTIC
FINGER-WEBBING  GELATINOUS
PLUMP  SLICEABLE  SMOOTH
SMUSHABLE  SPRINGY  STICKY
STRETCHY  SUPPLE  TENDER

#### HEAVY AND/OR WET
BEATEN BUTTER  CHALKY
CHEESECAKEY  CLAY  COLD BUTTER
FATTY  FUDGE  HEAVY  MOIST
PUDDING  SPONGY
TEMPERED BUTTER  YIELDING

#### LIQUESCENT
DRIPPY  LIQUID  MOLTEN  RUNNY
SCOOPABLE  SMEARABLE  TWO-TONE

#### FLAWS
GRAINY  HARD

# WHAT IS "BRIE," EXACTLY?

The original recipes for Brie are for the specific cheeses Brie de Meaux and Brie de Melun, both made east of Paris in the Île-de-France, with histories dating back to AD 774. The traditional size and shape of these cow milk Bries—large, flat circles with a diameter of fourteen to sixteen inches—coupled with their high moisture content (during cheese making the curd is barely cut, gently ladled, and allowed to drain with no additional pressing) made them highly perishable and minimally transportable. They were made near Paris, sold to Paris, and eaten in Paris. More than a thousand years later the north-western region of Normandy began producing a similar type of cheese—Camembert de Normandie—with small but critical cheese-making tweaks that yielded a more durable soft cheese neatly suited to span a longer distance to urban markets.

Unlike the cheeses Brie de Meaux PDO and Brie de Melun PDO, still produced in the Île-de-France today, "Brie":

➤➤ Need not meet specific production criteria.

➤➤ The milk type can be anything.

➤➤ It may be pasteurized or unpasteurized (though in the United States most Brie types are pasteurized as they're under sixty days, the legal requirement for raw milk cheeses).

➤➤ Runs the gamut in size from the original large, flat discs to small, four-inch rounds contained in wooden boxes.

# BRIE TYPES: FLAVOR & AROMA WHEEL

# (Double Crème) Brie

**FRANCE/UNITED STATES**

**COW**

**PASTEURIZED**

**RECOMMENDED BRANDS:**
Brie Couronne, Notre Dame,
Tour de Mars, Marin French
Cheese "Traditional Brie"

**AROMA:** Little to a whiff of
damp mushroom

**TEXTURE:** Sticky and
smushable

**FLAVOR:** Cream, white button
mushroom

**IN SHORT:** The Little Black
Dress of cheese

It's good to know that while the standard recipe for Brie produces a cheese that's 45 percent butterfat, neither cream-enriched nor 60 percent "double-crème," nearly all Brie on the market today has some cream added to it. Those that don't tend to be individually portioned, in rounds or sticks, and are usually hard, tasteless and generally wretched, with the confounding ability to morph overnight from not ripe to ammoniated. They are also disproportionately made in the United States. When in doubt, buying French is always the best. Most cheese shops consider double-crème Brie their "starter" Brie, though they're likely to offer many of the Brie types described in this gateway. The best-tasting versions are cut fresh from a traditional size six-pound wheel; their cream enrichment contributes richer flavor and texture while tempering the fungal notes of rind. You can expect a whiff of uncooked, white button mushroom but you'll be largely focused on the silky, mouth-coating texture and unapologetic dose of salt.

# Margie FROM SPROUT CREEK FARM

**UNITED STATES** | **COW**

**PASTEURIZED**

**AROMA:** Very little

**TEXTURE:** Sticky and smooth

**FLAVOR:** Salt and milk

**IN SHORT:** What industrial
Brie wants to be, but never is

A nonprofit farm and children's education center, Sprout Creek makes a broad range of primarily unpasteurized cow milk cheeses. While Margie is pasteurized, it shares their healthy dose of salt and, accordingly, their concentrated flavor boost. This approach is critical to the cheese's appeal, as it prevents an otherwise mild cheese from being bland. Encased in a plump, velvety rind, Margie's paste is smooth and sticky, as a good Brie should be. Buttery and delicate, it's an especially good option for tri-staters looking for a local food upgrade.

# Moses Sleeper
**FROM JASPER HILL FARM/THE CELLARS AT JASPER HILL**

Moses is named for the Revolutionary War scout who was buddies with the namesake of Jasper Hill Farm's first soft-ripened cheese (Constant Bliss). Unfortunately, both men lost their scalps during an ill-fated scouting mission, leaving us their legacy in the form of good cheese. Moses is an impeccable presentation of Classic Brie, albeit in a smaller wheel. The ridged bloomy rind has delicate sandy-colored striations, the interior is sticky and smooth, pocked with intermittent air holes. It stays impressively mild and mellow without relying on cream and butter flavors. Instead, expect muted white mushroom and the faint suggestion of buttered summer corn.

**UNITED STATES | COW PASTEURIZED**

**AROMA:** Mold and damp button mushrooms

**TEXTURE:** Finger webbing

**FLAVOR:** Muted, mellow, beginning of buttered corn

**IN SHORT:** The Basic Brie upgrade

## FAT IN CHEESE

Understanding how much fat you're eating when you enjoy a piece of cheese is complicated by the fact that a cheese's fat content is derived from the amount of fat in dry matter. Or, to put it another way, if I were to remove all the water from a piece of cheese, how much fat would be left in the solids that remained?

The reason fat is measured this way is because cheeses lose moisture over time. Water evaporates. If we were to measure fat in a piece of cheese that included water weight, the fat content would change as the cheese dried out.

This leads me to the point that bloomy rinds, including double and triple crème cheeses, are higher in moisture (they are softer, creamier, more spreadable) than aged cheeses such as Swiss or Parmesan. So while they have 60–75 percent butterfat in dry matter an ounce of double or triple crème is predominantly water, while an ounce of Parm is almost entirely solids. Ounce for ounce, there is less dry matter in soft, creamy cheeses, and so, ounce for ounce you are consuming less fat.

It's also worth bearing in mind that sheep milk, with nearly double the solids of cow or goat milk, will contribute a markedly creamier mouthfeel. It's rare to find a Brie-like cheese that's 100 percent sheep milk, but there are many blended milk varieties and that glug of sheep milk makes for universally richer cheese.

Eat on.

UNITED STATES | COW
PASTEURIZED
**AROMA:** Very little, milk
**TEXTURE:** Sticky to bulging
**FLAVOR:** Cream-thinned crème fraîche
**IN SHORT:** Crowd-pleasing

# Green Hill FROM SWEET GRASS DAIRY

Jeremy and Jessica Little followed the pioneering lead of Jessica's parents as grass-based dairy farmers in the American South to become the first artisan cheesemakers in Georgia. They make cheese that show cases the pristine quality of the family's electric yellow milk, higher in fat due to the use of Jersey cows, and buttercup-hued because of copious beta-carotene from the pastured forage. Years of refinement on Green Hill have led to a plump, eight-ounce round that is at once shorter and milder than a traditional French Camembert. The rind is marvelously thin, the interior sticky and nearly stretchy in texture. Over several weeks the paste breaks down into a runnier goo that manages to avoid any bitterness or acridity. Instead, it's a continuous smear of delicate butter, with just enough tartness to recall crème fraîche or sour cream. Green Hill is an easy-to-like cheese, surprisingly durable and well made, and the perfect American upgrade from an imported French double crème.

# Fromager d'Affinois

Could this be the Greek yogurt of cheese? Technically, perhaps. The cheese is made by Fromagerie Guilloteau, who pioneered the process of ultrafiltration. Meaning: the milk going into this cheese has had its solids filtered out from its water prior to cheese making. There is a bit more protein and calcium than in a cheese where the curds are drained during the make process. Why does that matter? The resulting texture is an almost otherworldly smearability, and that textural appeal extends to the gossamer-thin rind. So totally innocuous is its flavor that you'll be hard-pressed to tell the outer from inner. That's a good thing for everyone who's been turned off Brie types by a bitter, chewy skin. However, don't write this cheese off as a simple fat bomb. It's actually quite tart, more like cultured butter, though it does qualify as a double-creme with 60 percent butterfat. It is the ultimate newbie upgrade. Also look for little brother Pave d'Affinois, with all of the same benefits but a shorter shelf life due to its smaller size.

FRANCE | COW
PASTEURIZED
**AROMA:** Fresh milk, yogurt
**TEXTURE:** Silky
**FLAVOR:** Cultured butter
**IN SHORT:** The better Brie

## DO YOU EAT THE RIND?

If you are someone who does not eat the rind, you are in esteemed company. The first Holy Roman Emperor, Charlemagne (Charles the Great), refused the rind on a soft-ripened cheese when he first encountered such a thing in the nineteenth century. His biographer recounted that "taking up his knife he cut off the skin, which he though unsavoury, and fell on to the white of the cheese." I beg you to be open minded, like Charlemagne. When told he was "throwing away the very best part"

the Emperor "put a piece of the skin in his mouth, and slowly ate it and swallowed it like butter." His conclusion? "Send me every year to Aix two cart-loads of just such cheeses."*

The rinds on Brie type cheeses are meant to be eaten, and contribute vast complexities to the aroma and flavor of the cheese.

This being said, if you simply can't bear the rind, don't eat it. Perhaps you will have a Charlemagne at your table to pick up the loose ends.

*Eignhard and the Monk of St. Gall, *Early Lives of Charlemagne*, trans. A. J. Grant (London: Chatto and Windus, 1922), 79–80

## ORIGINS OF THE BLOOMY RIND

The most likely cultural and historical origins of the bloomy-rind style are linked to the households of French manors or peasant farms, where women would make small batches of small-format cheeses for household consumption. With only one or two cows, families pooled the milk of several days before making a single batch of cheese. Accordingly, the milk sat for hours, naturally and slowly developing acid as it soured before being warmed and coagulated. The resulting

fresh cheese was high in moisture and relatively high in acidity, making it hospitable to ambient gray and white molds of the household cellars where these cheeses would be aged. Without this particular combination of moisture, salt and acid (itself the direct result of northern French women's life rhythms), soft, creamy cheese with an edible white rind wouldn't have developed. If you like Brie types, thank a housewife.

# Triple Crème Brie

**FRANCE/UNITED STATES**

COW

**PASTEURIZED**

**RECOMMENDED BRANDS:** Belletoile (Henri Hutin), Marin French Cheese Company

**AROMA:** Little to a whiff of damp mushroom

**TEXTURE:** Sliceable butter

**FLAVOR:** Lemon curd

**IN SHORT:** Classic Brie, but fattier

Unlike the triple crème cheeses listed below, each of which is sold under its own name and has its own shape, triple crème Brie looks like the traditional large flat disc one associates with Brie. Its texture is also smoother, stickier, and more cohesive, while the triple crèmes below tend to resemble cheesecake or stiff pudding. If pure butter intensity is what you desire I'd steer you away from triple crème Brie: Hutin's offering is moist but still sliceable, while Marin French's has delicious but surprisingly tart, nearly lemony notes. Both are rich, but you wouldn't necessarily know all that extra cream was there. Worth noting is that despite Marin's competitive pricing and increasingly broad distribution, their cheeses are still entirely handmade. The milk is hand ladled into forms to preserve its fragile texture—something that's a rarity in the world of Brie.

# Saint Angel

**FRANCE | COW**

**PASTEURIZED**

**AROMA:** A whiff of mold

**TEXTURE:** Sticky butter

**FLAVOR:** Butter

**IN SHORT:** Pure comfort

Produced with the ultra-filtered milk Fromagerie Guilloteau is known for (see Fromager d'Affinois for more, page 78), but enriched with cream for 71 percent butterfat, Saint Angel enjoys official triple crème status. While the plump, quilted-looking rind is a soft shade of white, it is not grown from the traditional Brie mold *P. candidum*, but exclusively from *Geotrichum* yeast. Accordingly, it has the remarkable ability to never throw off fungal flavors or bitter notes. The strongest thing about it is the aroma while the entire eating experience is smooth and easy. Despite its richness the cheese finishes clean, so you're not left with a heavy dairy film along the roof of your mouth. I've used this in place of butter with great success (though mediocre cost-effectiveness).

# Saint André

**FRANCE | COW**

**PASTEURIZED**

**AROMA:** Glass of milk

**TEXTURE:** Butter crumble topping

**FLAVOR:** Sour cream topping, sans sugar

**IN SHORT:** The lightest feeling of the triple crèmes

Produced by Bonnegrande, this is the cheese that built the American market for a triple crème . It's still one of the best-known brands, originally made in a four-pound wheel and these days also available in a little paper box, personal snacking size. The bright white, fluffy *P. candidum* rind can be quite thick, and given enough weeks the larger wheels will develop a sizable creamline and some separation of the chewy exterior from the crumbly insides. Though these melt on contact with your tongue, the texture is remarkably flaky for a triple crème. This, coupled with the briny, edging-on-tart flavor, makes Saint André feel hardly cream-enriched at all.

SAINT ANDRÉ

UNITED STATES | COW
PASTEURIZED

**AROMA:** Very little, whiff of mold

**TEXTURE:** Two-tone

**FLAVOR:** Creamed corn

**IN SHORT:** The California cuisine of triple crèmes

# Mt. Tam FROM COWGIRL CREAMERY

The first aged cheese produced by the creamery (which got its start in 1994 in Point Reyes, California, and now also makes cheese in Petaluma), Mt. Tam is named for Mount Tamalpais, the landmark peak an hour north of San Francisco. Its rind is produced with *P. candidum*, making the flavor profile more likely to head mushroomy than yeasty and sweet. That said, the use of Straus Family Creamery organic milk anchors each cheese in the flavors of mild, grassy milk. During cheese making, whey is drained off the coagulated curds and replaced with warm water. This "washing" of the curd decreases acidity, making Mt. Tam one of the least tangy triple crèmes available. Add to this that demand for the cheese far outstrips supply, and it is often sold to the market quite young. The size of a double-decker slider, Mt. Tam is best when firm with a slight give. Inside, the paste looks like stiff mousse and dissolves on the tongue, like the greatest mouthful of creamed corn you've ever experienced. Unlike the French triple crèmes, Mt. Tam is never intensely salty. The Creamery also offers a rotating selection of seasonal cheeses that look like Mt. Tam with various action on the rind. Look for St. Pat (spring), Pierce Pt. (summer), Chimney Rock (fall), and Devil's Gulch (winter).

FRANCE | COW
PASTEURIZED

**AROMA:** Wildflowers or honey

**TEXTURE:** Proper gelato: airy and light

**FLAVOR:** Briny cream, like oyster velouté

**IN SHORT:** Cheese cloud

# St. Nuage

Aged by legendary French affineur Hervé Mons and sold primarily through Whole Foods, this *Geotrichum*-rinded triple crème is meltingly soft and tender. It manages to be gooey and fluffy at the same time. Careful tasters will notice great resemblance to mini Delice de Bourgogne (see page 83) and, I'd argue, they will experience the impact a talented ripener can make on a cheese. St. Nuage is buttery and intensely rich while benefiting from a discernible salinity that rounds out its flavor. The texture is airy and each bite is perfumed with the floral, almost honeyed, qualities a well-maintained *Geotrichum* rind can impact. You'll get why its name is "St. Cloud."

# Le Delice de Bourgogne

Burgundy throws its hat into the ring with this perennial favorite in the world of triple crèmes, made by Lincet. Perhaps because it's a larger format cheese (three plus pounds) it has much longer potential to improve over time before morphing into a mouthful of whipped fattiness with persistent acetone flavor. This is the best of what cheesecake can be, and when used to coat a simple water cracker, it becomes something wonderfully akin to a Ritz. The rind is concerningly thick and often separates from the interior. Though it's made of the temperamental mold *P. candidum* it avoids harsh, medicinal flavor, redeeming itself with mellow peanuttiness. A smaller format version is also produced which tends to be less salty, and more like a cooling cream river.

**FRANCE | COW**

**PASTEURIZED**

**AROMA:** Peanut butter, whiff of ammonia

**TEXTURE:** Whipped butter over beaten butter

**FLAVOR:** Salt, cream, peanuts

**IN SHORT:** Unsweetened Fluffernutter

# Brillat-Savarin

The cheese is named for Jean Anthelme Brillat-Savarin, who lived from 1755 to 1826 and, though officially a lawyer and politician, invented the concept of gastronomy. I think of him as the original Dr. Atkins, cautioning against excessive carbohydrates and celebrating the merits of a protein-rich diet. Who better, then, to be memorialized in the form of a triple crème cheese? Ten years ago you could find Brillat-Savarins from various makers, some of which were smaller in scale and producing handmade cheese. These versions were carefully aged, and the resulting cheese was denser and drier, with a paste that dissolved into wisps of delicious nothing on the tongue. These days what's out there is more industrial and thicker rinded but still hits the sweet spot I consider as making the perfect triple crème. It's salty, but not overwhelmingly so. There's a sour cream tang that admirably offsets incredibly rich mouthfeel. Over time its butter flavor can intensify to a nearly artificial degree, like movie theater popcorn, and the rind can become quite metallic. The younger the better here: it should be dense in texture, white in color. Like an M&M, let it melt in your mouth, not in your hand.

Also, be on the lookout for nouveau Brillat-Savarin which are produced not with the original, white *P. candidum* rind, but with a yellow, papery *Geotrichum* rind. These small-format cheeses are identical to Delice de Bourgogne.

**FRANCE | COW**

**PASTEURIZED**

**AROMA:** Very little

**TEXTURE:** Cut with a spoon

**FLAVOR:** Lightly cultured butter

**IN SHORT:** The best classic triple crème

## Pierre Robert

FRANCE | COW

PASTEURIZED

**AROMA:** Seasoned
cheese sauce

**TEXTURE:** Finger-swipeable

**FLAVOR:** Heavily salted butter
with a spicy edge

**IN SHORT:** High risk,
high reward

Produced in the Île-de-France, the original region of Brie production, Pierre Robert is made by Rouzaire, a fromagerie known for some of the better Brie de Meaux–type (see page 102) cheeses on the market. This triple crème is essentially an aged Brillat Savarin (see page 83). The three to four weeks spent in Rouzaire's aging caves leads to a concentration of salt, an increasingly dense-yet-whipped texture, and a greater likelihood of fungal or mushroomy flavors. As with many smaller format cheeses, the risk here is that the cheese sits at a store, languishing and forgotten, and then you take it home to find a thick, chewy, bitter rind and intense lick of salt. Seek white, fluffy cheeses and be rewarded with crème fraîche buttercream frosting.

## Moser Screamer

SWITZERLAND | COW

PASTEURIZED

**AROMA:** Brown butter

**TEXTURE:** Flourless cake,
or stiff mousse

**FLAVOR:** Mushroom and
salted crème fraîche

**IN SHORT:** Out-Frenching
the French

Sold in individual three-pound rounds packed in a charming wooden box, Moser Screamer is likely to immediately confuse you as it's repeatedly printed "triple cream, double cream." While it's 72 percent butterfat, and thus a triple cream cheese, the Swiss call any cheese over 60 percent butterfat a double cream. Accordingly, this cheese says both. You'll rest assured of its cream enrichment when you lay a pat on your tongue, where it will sit heavy and sticky before ever so slowly dissolving. Unlike classic French triple crèmes whose white molded rind can grow quite thick and bitter, Moser Screamer has only the barest skim of a rind and thus an even texture, rather than a gooey creamline atop firmer core. It's a remarkable cheese—undeniably rich and luxurious, but boasting flavors beyond salt and cream. In particular, it has a fungal depth like the finest swallow of porcini cream soup you can imagine.

## Goat Brie

FRANCE/UNITED STATES

GOAT

PASTEURIZED

**RECOMMENDED BRANDS:**
Chèvre d'Argental, Florette,
Joan of Arc, Soignon, Laura
Chenel's Chèvre Goat Brie

**AROMA:** Little to none,
tart dough

**TEXTURE:** Sticky to runny

**FLAVOR:** Sweet, cream,
hint of lemon

**IN SHORT:** The Sleeper Hit
(Yes, folks! It *is* goat milk!)

French Brie-like cheeses made of goat milk never hail from true Brie country (Île-de-France) but tend to be made in the Rhône-Alpes and Poitou-Charentes regions. I have no proof, but my theory is that the French seized on the opportunity to create a buttery, rich cheese made with goat milk for an American audience who still today, shies away from what it assumes will be piquant or animally. Goat Brie was a way to make the undesirable ready for primetime. You wind up with cheeses that are nearly as mild as their cow milk inspiration—the rinds are remarkably thin, the paste spun cream, and the flavors sweet and delicate with only the barest undercurrent of citrusy tang one might associate with goat milk. It's rare to encounter fungal, vegetal, or bitter flavors.

APPROACHABLE

# Robiola Bosina

ALSO SOLD AS ROBIOLA DUE LATTE AND ROBIOLA TWO MILK

The fresh and soft cheeses of Italy, by comparison with France and the Unites States, taste markedly less salted. As a result, their flavors tend to be more muted. Some would say subtle, others would say bland. What I notice is that acidity, or tartness, figures more prominently. In some Italian softies this twang is out of whack, but with Robiola Bosina it balances the plump, bursting paste. I love that the rind is always thin, never aspiriny, and adds minerality to an otherwise rich mouthful. It works in the way that roasted oysters with Parmesan garlic butter do—you'd think these a bad idea but they're compulsively edible. Robiola Bosina manages to look like it will spill across the plate but never becomes liquid. Its stickiness makes it more akin to true Brie than the cream-enriched cheeses that are stiff and cheesecakey.

**ITALY | COW/SHEEP**
**PASTEURIZED**
**AROMA:** Pastry dough
**TEXTURE:** Plump, springy to runny
**FLAVOR:** Butter, minerality
**IN SHORT:** New recipe, old soul

## Bonne Bouche FROM VERMONT CREAMERY

**UNITED STATES | GOAT**

**PASTEURIZED**

**AROMA:** Yeasty, wet hay

**TEXTURE:** Creamy to runny

**FLAVOR:** Milk, Meyer lemon, bread dough

**IN SHORT:** No rough edges, despite its goat origins

Choosing to include Bonne Bouche in a chapter of Brie-like cheeses felt bold and a little scary, since this diminutive, ashed round so closely resembles Selles-sur-Cher (see page 374), one of the classic goat cheeses of France's Loire Valley. Unlike its French inspiration, Bonne Bouche (which, BTW, means "good mouthful") has a rind produced exclusively with *Geotrichum candidum*.  That brainy, wrinkled skin (gray due to the inclusion of ash on the outside of the cheese) quickly breaks the interior cheese down to a drippy, spreadable smear within several weeks. I've had overripe Bonne Bouche that's been on the market for twelve or fourteen weeks, and by that point the flavors are piquant, with persistent animal notes. But that's atypical, and what's remarkable to me is how yeasty and nutty the cheese remains, even as it liquefies. The goat milk produces a flavor that will strike pure butter lovers as somewhat intense, but the cheese is utterly lacking the black walnut astringency of French cousins.

## Kinderhook Creek FROM OLD CHATHAM SHEEPHERDING COMPANY

**UNITED STATES | SHEEP**

**PASTEURIZED**

**AROMA:** A whiff of milk and white button mushroom

**TEXTURE:** Cream-over-chalk

**FLAVOR:** Tangy milk or untangy yogurt

**IN SHORT:** Delicate flavor, hefty texture

Tom and Nancy Clark are American cheese-making pioneers who put Columbia County, New York, on the map as home to a sheep dairy (this is still a relative scarcity, more than twenty years later). It's rare to find a pure sheep milk cheese with a bloomy rind, let alone one without traces of "sheepiness." That's the aromatic impression of a damp wool sweater, or a barn crowded with rained-on sheep. While some find this essence complex and unique, others find it distasteful. I love a whiff of it, but with Kinderhook Creek I welcome its absence. Instead, in both the larger format and its 3.5-ounce sidekick, you get a lemony spin on stiff, beaten butter. The rind on the little guy tends to be more tender, but larger wheels develop a thick, oozing creamline I enjoy. It's a brilliant introduction to the fatty heft of sheep milk, and one of the rare American-made options likely to be seen in supermarkets.

## Teleeka FROM TOMALES FARMSTEAD CREAMERY

UNITED STATES

GOAT/SHEEP/COW

PASTEURIZED

**AROMA:** Cultured dairy, like crème fraîche

**TEXTURE:** Cheesecakey

**FLAVOR:** Tangy nut milk

**IN SHORT:** Nuanced

The organic, farmstead creamery arm of Toluma Farms can be found a meandering twenty minutes west of Petaluma, California. There, 200 goats and 100 East Friesian sheep loll at the base of a steep hill from which, if you're lucky, you might catch a glimpse of the Pacific. The creamery's cheeses all take their names from the indigenous Miwok. In this case, *Teleeka* means "three" (referring to the milk types it utilizes). There is also *Kenne,* meaning "one" (milk type, goat; it also happens to be a comparable age and recipe to Teleeka) and Atika, meaning "two" (milk types, sheep and goat, though it differs completely in age, texture, and flavor from the others). Teleeka is my top pick, with its wetly packed texture so reminiscent of Piedmontese cheeses, like La Tur (see page 91).  The flavor is at once soft and crème fraîchey, though the acidity is fleeting, leaving you (especially with Teleeka) with the faint nuttiness of the blended milks. Salting is restrained, and as a result the cheese is both more delicate and more nuanced than its Italian counterparts.

## Humboldt Fog (Grande) FROM CYPRESS GROVE

UNITED STATES | GOAT

PASTEURIZED

**AROMA:** Yogurt, whiff of mold

**TEXTURE:** Crumbly cake

**FLAVOR:** Sour cream, citrus

**IN SHORT:** Bright

Many a cheese counter suggests that this cheese takes its name from the superior weed grown in Humboldt County, California. That's not actually the case, but its origins are trippy and wonderful enough that it could be. Cypress Grove founder Mary Keehn dreamt of Humboldt Fog on a 1980s plane ride home from France, imagining it in painstaking detail, from its tall, layer-cake shape to the interior line of blue-gray vegetable ash, included as an homage to the French mountain cheese Morbier (see page 135). Folks new to cheese think that the wavering line is blue mold, as in "Blue cheese," but it's not. It's merely a decorative, daily acknowledgment of the history of French cheese making that so moved one American woman. While Humboldt Fog's texture isn't sticky or silky like Brie, it looks like an *Alice in Wonderland* Brie that's been hit with a growth potion and made magically taller (there is also a mini version but I like it less because the rind quickly breaks down the flaky interior, destroying the sour cream crumble that makes this cheese special). Because Humboldt Fog is dusted in vegetable ash and inoculated with *P. candidum* to develop its edible white skin, it lacks the acidic or animal notes one might associate with fresh goat cheese. Its flavor is saltier, with buttermilk tang laced throughout the flaky cheesecake texture. Hovering over each bite is the brightness of lemon, shining through all that fog.

BÛCHERON/BÛCHERONDIN

# La Tur

La Tur looks like cheesecake, but it's mushier and creamier on the palate. Because you can eat it with a spoon, the creamline running so heavily it will drip onto the plate, my mom declared it the ice-cream cheese when I first served it up. The blend of milks gives a marvelous balance of sweet milkiness, tangy finish, and fatty heft to carry you through. As with many of the lesser-aged cheeses from Piedmont, there's a distinctively yeasty, fermented fruit edge to the flavor. By comparison, French double crème Brie tastes like a salt bomb, slick and heavy on the tongue. Despite its high moisture content, La Tur is quite durable and now widely available. For these reasons, it's my go-to exotic upgrade.

**ITALY | COW/GOAT/SHEEP**
**PASTEURIZED**
**AROMA:** Yogurt
**TEXTURE:** Wet cheesecake
**FLAVOR:** Salty, milky, tangy
**IN SHORT:** The ice-cream cheese

# Bermuda Triangle FROM CYPRESS GROVE

Similar in taste and texture to the flagship Humboldt Fog (see page 88), Bermuda Triangle's triangular-shaped loaf was changed in 2014 to be larger in diameter. The goal in doing so was to make more interior paste and less rind. This way the rind's breakdown of fat and protein would occur more slowly, the flavor-intense creamline that resulted would be smaller and more gradual, and the whole cheese could be neatly portioned into fat, moist triangles. As with Humboldt Fog, a modest quarter- to half-inch creamline is an indication of natural ripening. A cheese dominated by a fat inch of gray goo will be soapy, bitter, and can be written off as too old. Because of its increased size, Bermuda Triangle is flakier than Humboldt Fog and less salty, but its buttermilk and citrus notes are more pronounced, making the flavors ultimately more intense.

**UNITED STATES | GOAT**
**PASTEURIZED**
**AROMA:** Yogurt, whiff of mold
**TEXTURE:** Crumbly cake
**FLAVOR:** Sour cream, citrus
**IN SHORT:** Lemon-kissed

# Bûcheron/Bûcherondin

While "Bûcheron" was recently trademarked by Montchevrè, the name is commonly used to describe white, bloomy-rinded, two-pound log-shaped goat cheeses from France. Traditionally produced in Poitou, the cheese can develop some of the brainy wrinkling characteristic of Le Chevrot (see page 369), but its rind, and identity, are largely shaped by the white Brie mold P. candidum. Bûcheron is one of the first aged goat cheeses folks encounter that goes beyond the realm of a fresh log, usually because it's on the relatively affordable side. Plump, young, white Bûcheron has an interior on the chalky side of clay-like, with a perimeter of softened to oozing cream. Flavors intensify greatly just under the rind, so expect a spectrum of clean, bright, and tangy edging out to saltier and earthier. What you shouldn't experience is spicy or soapy.

**FRANCE | GOAT**
**PASTEURIZED**
**RECOMMENDED BRANDS:** Montchevrè, Sèvre, and Belle Laiterie
**AROMA:** Hopefully not much
**TEXTURE:** Liquidy cream with chalky clay center
**FLAVOR:** Bright lemon and good salt
**IN SHORT:** Mouthwatering

CREMONT

# Nancy's Hudson Valley Camembert FROM OLD CHATHAM SHEEPHERDING COMPANY

Here is proof that, with cheese at least, size matters. Nancy's is available in a small, individual square and a larger two-pound wheel that can be cut at store level (there's also a precut, prewrapped wedge that comes from a big wheel). Common wisdom would suggest that the larger wheel, freshly cut, would deliver superior eating. Surprisingly, that hasn't been my experience. The larger Camembert is considerably more acidic. The little square, meant to go it alone in the big world, tends to be balanced, rich, and crowd-friendly. Do beware, however, that a cheese wrapped in opaque paper is often left to languish for weeks on a store shelf. Give the cheese a squeeze before buying. You want to feel spring and slight resistance. A package of goo will be bitterly displeasing. Whether you're getting a square or a wedge, you can expect lavishly thick, rich paste, thanks to higher fat and protein from the sheep milk in the mix. It's noticeably lusher than a typical (cow milk) Brie. Accordingly, its flavors are grassy and mellow rather than intensely mushroomy or vegetal. Nancy's Camembert is the brainchild of American cheese pioneers Tom and Nancy Clark, who began production in Old Chatham, New York, back in 1993. Despite its East Coast heritage, its attitude is West Coast surfer. It's all good, man.

UNITED STATES

COW/SHEEP

PASTEURIZED

**AROMA:** Sour cream, damp grass

**TEXTURE:** Tempered butter

**FLAVOR:** Briny cream, peanuts

IN SHORT: The tongue Snuggie

# Cremont FROM VERMONT CREAMERY

The line between goat milk, cow milk, and cream in this cheese is as indistinguishable as Cremont's rind from its interior. They meld together into one succulent and puzzlingly complex flavor. The blending of milks (and introduction of cream) make this not only a double crème but a cheese with a split personality. The twang of goat milk (and a whisper of the animal notes often dubbed *goaty*) are fully present, but the smotheringly rich cloak of cream feels like a low moisture mouthful of cheesecake. Unlike a traditional white-rinded Brie, Cremont relies on the yellowy yeast *Geotrichum candidum*, responsible for its distinct nuttiness. A brilliant foray into the unknown for those who love decadent texture but are insistent on something more than a scoop of butter.

UNITED STATES

COW/GOAT

PASTEURIZED

**AROMA:** Buttermilk, wet hay

**TEXTURE:** Creamy, whipped, cheesecakey

**FLAVOR:** Cream, bread dough, nut

IN SHORT: Cheese cake

# Noccetto di Capra

ITALY | GOAT

PASTEURIZED

**AROMA:** Woodsy, with the barest whiff of ammonia

**TEXTURE:** Squishy with an airy, molten core

**FLAVOR:** Lightly goaty, with a backbone of nutskin and mushroom

**IN SHORT:** Woodland fairy

A bloomy-rinded goat cheese from Lombardy is a double "not in these parts" offering; the region is known for washed rind, Blue, and pressed cow milk cheeses. Using Bergamo's indigenous Orobica goats, maker Ca de Ambros has managed to produce a delicately gelatinous round of goat cheese with a flavor so delicate I'm reminded of baby powder. While thicker and sturdier than a Brie rind, Noccetto's exterior is tender and mild, encasing insides so soft as to seem whipped. What's brilliant about this one is the great contrast between its texture (pure butter) and its flavor (unapologetic but balanced salt, white mushroom, and a bright, piney tang from the goats). It looks like it will be boring, one-note, industrial. Nothing could be further from the truth.

# L'Édel de Cléron

FRANCE | COW

PASTEURIZED

**AROMA:** Damp hay, forest floor

**TEXTURE:** Slatherable

**FLAVOR:** Cooked button mushroom, spruce gum, and cream

**IN SHORT:** The Vacherin wannabe

Long before Harbison (see page 97) was made in the United States, the French recognized the sales potential of Vacherin Mont d'Or (see page 174). As that cheese was produced only seasonally, L'Édel de Cléron was invented as a year-round alternative. Made of pasteurized milk, its export to the United States was assured. A spillingly creamy pool bound in pine bark from the Jura Mountains (near its region of production in Franche-Comté), the appeal was equally dependable. Its complexity pales in comparison to Vacherin and Harbison, but it is spoonable and luscious, with the woodsy essence that makes bark-bound cheeses so magnificent. Should you be unable to find the others, go with Old Reliable, at any time of year.

# Kunik FROM NETTLE MEADOW FARM

UNITED STATES

GOAT/COW

PASTEURIZED

**AROMA:** Whiff of mold, butter

**TEXTURE:** Tender rind, whipped insides

**FLAVOR:** Boiled peanut

**IN SHORT:** The edamame of the Northeast

In the southeastern corner of the Adirondacks, a *P. candidum*-rinded goat cheese is elevated to plush triple crème status with the addition of Jersey cow cream. That mixing of milks creates a layering of flavor, and Kunik's base of goat milk contributes a delicate, tangy edge up front and a final finish that, at its best, is straight-up boiled peanut. The cream spreads the whole bite around better but never smothers with a muffler of fat. Kunik is regional in distribution, so look for it in Philly, New York, and Boston.

KUNIK

## MORE FROM PIEDMONT

La Tur and Robiola Bosina are the most commonly found cheeses from the Piedmont, Italy, producer Caseificio Dell'Alta Langa. La Tur has a particularly beguiling wet cupcake-like texture that manages to feel fresh and buttery simultaneously. Look for these other cheeses from the same maker if you dig La Tur but want an upgrade on flavor and rarity:

**BRUNET:** Think thick pancake, made of 100 percent goat milk for a tangy linger.

**CRAVANZINA:** More like a cross between La Tur and Robiola Bosina, but made from a blend of cow, goat, and sheep milk.

**ROCCHETTA:** Looks just like Brunet but is made from all three milks. Basically, this is La Tur's flattened brother and may also be sold under the brand Guffanti as Robiola Tre Latte.

## WHAT'S THE DIFFERENCE BETWEEN BRIE AND CAMEMBERT?

Traditionally, the differences are these:

➤ Brie is produced in France's Île-de-France outside Paris; Camembert hails from the northwestern region of Normandy.

➤ Brie is made in a large 14-inch flat disc; Camembert is a smaller 4-inch round packed and sold in a wooden box.

➤ Brie curd is barely cut; Camembert curd is always sliced vertically (and sometimes horizontally). This contributes to an expulsion of whey and a denser texture.

Camembert curd is ladled into perforated draining molds in multiple layers and is topped with a metal plate for overnight pressing. This also contributes to an expulsion of whey and a denser texture.

These days, the names Brie and Camembert can both indicate many different origins, flavor profiles, sizes, even milk types. So don't get too hung up on what it's called.

# Harbison

**FROM JASPER HILL FARM/THE CELLARS AT JASPER HILL**

Like all of Jasper Hill Farm's cheeses, Harbison is named for a local legend. Anne Harbison is known as the Grandmother of Greensboro, Vermont. She's an apt namesake for a cheese that swaddles you in its soft, lavish embrace, and welcomes even the most nervous guest to sit down and be pleased. Harbison is fantastically nuanced at the same time that it's imminently more approachable than its initial aromatic funk would suggest. It smells all stinky and broccoli-ish, but its flavor is soft, woodsy, addictive—the kind of cheese people wind up sticking their fingers into it without realizing what they're doing. Each round is bound in the cambium (inner) layer of spruce bark, harvested from trees on the farm's property, and this moist band imbues each bite with the aromatics of a Christmas tree. The damp, earthen smells give way to the taste of porcini mushrooms and warm cream, all laced with a sweet pine essence. That you can stick a spoon into the center and scoop the cheese out makes it all the more beguiling. Some Francophiles may find it looks like L'Édel de Cléron (see page 94); while similar in appearance, the eating experience is blissfully greater.

**UNITED STATES | COW**

**PASTEURIZED**

**AROMA:** Mushroom, garlic, cooked cruciferous veggies

**TEXTURE:** Scoopable to liquid

**FLAVOR:** Sweet, woodsy, hint of broccoli

**IN SHORT:** I dare you not to love it

# Champlain Triple

**FROM CHAMPLAIN VALLEY CREAMERY**

A relatively small producer, Champlain Valley Creamery makes cheese that is most commonly found in the New York market. Pocket-sized three-ounce drums of organic, cream-enriched milk, Champlain Triple is fluffier than the butter-like smear of most triple crèmes. What makes it interesting is an earthier flavor with animal aromas reminiscent of barns and leather, rather than the typical triple crème equation of lactic tang, briny balance, and bite of butter.

**UNITED STATES | COW**

**PASTEURIZED**

**AROMA:** Very little

**TEXTURE:** Cold, stiff butter

**FLAVOR:** Musky yet milky

**IN SHORT:** Earthy

# Brebisrousse d'Argental

FRANCE | SHEEP

PASTEURIZED

**AROMA:** Vegetal, wet wool

**TEXTURE:** The best of Velveeta cheese packets

**FLAVOR:** Butter, seawater, "wooliness"

**IN SHORT:** Sheep in wolf's clothing

This is a fake-out cheese! Conventional wisdom tells you if a cheese is orange on the exterior it has been washed with salt water and will have a barny aroma and meaty flavor (see the Taleggio Gateway, page 149). Then a cheese like this comes along. Its name, translated from French, means "red sheep." Its coloration, however, is due not to brine washing and bacterial cultivation, but to the addition of annatto, a plant-derived additive that gives orange Cheddar its hue. For lovers of buttery soft smearability, though, there's no faking out. Pure sheep milk delivers a thick fattiness unlike a cream-enriched double or triple crème. It's slick and sweet but briny, with a "sheepiness" that keeps it interesting. A good score for those who prefer their Brie types on the more extreme end of the flavor spectrum.

# Weybridge FROM SCHOLTEN FAMILY FARM/THE CELLARS AT JASPER HILL

UNITED STATES | COW

PASTEURIZED

**AROMA:** Crème fraîche, whiff o' manure

**TEXTURE:** Two-tone

**FLAVOR:** Lactic and animal, sour cream and leather

**IN SHORT:** Lingering

Made from the organic milk of Dutch Belted cows, those beautiful creatures whose midsection is banded in black fur, Weybridge has evolved as a collaboration between Scholten Family Farm and The Cellars at Jasper Hill, who manage its aging and distribution. Once upon a time this cheese was a small, thin disc that ripened to gooey liquescence. Now it resembles a tall hockey puck, blanketed in an impressively thin bloomy rind. Despite being pasteurized, Weybridge captures a lingering complexity both tart like sour cream, and rustic, with the intensity of a working dairy barn. The rind has the right edge of bitterness, like dandelion greens, the cheese a two-tone texture (sticky underrind/flaky center) that delivers an impressively layered tasting experience.

# Goat Camembert FROM IDYLL FARMS

UNITED STATES | GOAT

PASTEURIZED

**AROMA:** Goat breath

**TEXTURE:** Velvet-lined milky river

**FLAVOR:** Delicately fungal

**IN SHORT:** Remarkable

Owned by Mark and Amy Spitznagel, Idyll Farms bridges a mythic gap between the dales of Northport, Michigan; inner-city Detroit; and France's Loire. The couple is actively involved in the revitalization of Detroit, with a particular focus on urban farming. If you see goats on a city tour, they were likely dropped by the Spitznagels. Their unapologetically French-style goat cheeses come from a herd of 200 Alpine goats whose seasonal, pasture-based forage yields cheese from late March through December. While the production and distribution is extremely limited, these are some of the best soft-ripened goat cheeses in America. The moist, papery thin rind on Goat Camembert barely contains its burstingly drippy insides. The flavors are much yeastier and more fungal than I'd expect from goat milk, balanced by a gently acidic finish.

APPROACHABLE

# St. Albans

Cheese eaters in the know are likely to see this small ceramic crock of nearly liquescent goodness and mistake it for the French classic Saint Marcellin. In fact, that cheese is no longer exported to the United States and into the void has arrived this newcomer from Vermont Creamery. Just as a given style of cheese has a widely ranging texture and flavor spectrum, so, too, do certain cheeses vary so widely (with age) that you might as well be eating two or three different things. Young St. Albans is soft and dewy, moistly firm and relatively mild—milky with some nutty notes, thanks to the *Geotrichum* on the rind. Let a few weeks pass and you wind up with spoonable cheese pudding, earthy and stalwart, often boasting a few spots of (totally safe and edible) blue or green mold. Accelerate those pudding tendencies with a quick blast of heat in the toaster oven (pottery container and all) for instant fondue that can be drizzled atop a baguette or used to bathe leaves of endive and radicchio.

**UNITED STATES | COW**
**PASTEURIZED**
**AROMA:** Yeast and cow barn
**TEXTURE:** Plumply resistant to liquid
**FLAVOR:** Melted butter, cooked cauliflower
**IN SHORT:** Pudding cup

## Adelle FROM ANCIENT HERITAGE DAIRY

This cheese has changed so much in the years that I've known it. It's gotten thinner, with a drippy interior belying the sheep milk blended in. It reminds me of Saint Marcellin, in its riff on the mushroomy stink of good Meaux Bries—unapologetically barnyardy. For Adelle, the animal breath is of lanolin: damp sheep wool, persistent and slick with fat. It's a bold departure from the many cow milk choices out there, and meant for those willing to embrace the wet wool sweater of cheeses.

**UNITED STATES**
**COW/SHEEP**
**PASTEURIZED**
**AROMA:** Leather, wet wool
**TEXTURE:** Drippy
**FLAVOR:** Lactic, dandelion, lanolin
**IN SHORT:** Pronounced

## CHEESE ALLERGY?

Folks allergic to the antibiotic penicillin often ask if cheeses made with penicillium (*camemberti* and *candidum* in the case of Brie types, *P. roqueforti* and *P. glaucum* in the case of Blue types) will cause a reaction.

My answer is: I'm not a doctor! So talk to yours.

But: the antibiotic is made with a different strain of penicillium (*chrysogenum*) than the cheeses, and is made only with penicillin extract rather than with the whole mold.

For this reason, it is quite possible that someone allergic to the antibiotic can enjoy the cheeses with abandon. That said, some people are allergic to both and may experience similar reactions (hives, tingly mouth, anaphylaxis) to the cheese as to the medicine.

# Pont l'Évêque PDO

FRANCE | COW

(UN)PASTEURIZED

**AROMA:** Cooked cruciferous

**TEXTURE:** Stretchy, sticky, soft dough

**FLAVOR:** Roasted garlic and bitter greens

IN SHORT: The imposter

For years I sold Pont l'Évêque as a small, boxed square. Pudgy and plump, it had a rind like a Creamsicle—sherbet orange and edged with snowy white. These days, you're more likely to find large-format Pont l'Évêque. Sliced like a pie, the cheese has a quilted, yellowy rind and looks confusingly Brie-like. This ambiguity continues with each ensuing whiff and smear, the cheese heady with cooked broccoli intensity and Brie de Meaux (see page 102) aspirations. Recent changes to PDO guidelines suggest Pont of old was colored orange with annatto, and that this is no longer allowed. Additionally the cheese is no longer defined by the presence of classic washed-rind *brevibacterium linens*; in fact, as stated in the 2015 Amendment Application related to the cheese's PDO classification, "these cultures do not develop systematically, nor are they necessarily desirable." In the States, Pont l'Évêque is often categorized as a washed rind (see page 150), but its flavor has both feet planted firmly in the Brie de Meaux camp.

## WHO TOOK MY REBLOCHON?

The classic French cheese Reblochon (or Reblochon de Savoie) PDO hasn't graced American shores in almost ten years. Made exclusively from whole, raw cow milk that is gently pressed but never cooked, the cheese fails to meet FDA import criteria related to raw milk, aging minimums, and permissible water content. While *fermier* (farmhouse) Reblochon may develop orange bacteria and a ruddy, pinkish rind, its sticky, slippery interior and buttered-hay flavors put it more squarely in the Band of Brie than with the persistently pungent Taleggio types. Some retailers sell the cheese Fromage de Savoie under the Reblochon name: it's a lower-moisture, more industrial imitation; chewy and bland though hardly offensive. Ironically, it is a tiny farm in Tennessee that is putting out the closest cheese I've tasted to real Reblochon, so if you can find Sequatchie Cove Creamery's Dancing Fern (see page 101), treat yourself.

# Dancing Fern FROM SEQUATCHIE COVE CREAMERY

Padgett Arnold describes herself and husband Nathan not as cheese makers looking for a home, but people rooted to a place who wanted to become cheese makers. That's how they came to lead the cheese-making revolution in Tennessee. Dancing Fern looks like real Reblochon, a cheese no longer imported into the United States: shaped like a diminutive Frisbee, blanketed in a firm but velvety white rind bespeckled with gray molds. I tasted the cheese recently with a group of mixologists, and one announced immediately upon smelling the cheese that it was reminiscent of an aquarium, or maybe a pet store. I loved this because the smell reminds me faintly of a cow barn— there are lingering animal associations. In the mouth, though, it's all butter and pleasantly bitter vegetal notes; that flavor edge cuts through an otherwise slippery, fatty mouthfeel. I find it (and all of Sequatchie's cheeses) to be impressively restrained and brilliantly executed. This is simply one of the most complex and thoughtful cheeses being made in America.

**UNITED STATES | COW**

**UNPASTEURIZED**

**AROMA:** Pet store

**TEXTURE:** Stretchy yet slippery

**FLAVOR:** Buttered bitter greens

**IN SHORT:** American Reblochon

INTENSE

# (wannabe) Brie de Meaux PDO

**(AKA FROMAGE DE MEAUX)**

FRANCE | COW

PASTEURIZED

**RECOMMENDED BRANDS**
(from mildest to strongest):
Brie de Nangis (Rouzaire),
Le Châtelain Brie (Lactalis),
Fromage de Meaux (Rouzaire),
Brie Fermier Jouvence
(Ferme de Jouvence),
Brie Fermier (Ferme de la
Tremblaye)

**AROMA:** Cooked broccoli
and cauliflower, farty

**TEXTURE:** Sticky, slightly
stretchy, slippery

**FLAVOR:** Infinitely layered,
vegetal, truffly

**IN SHORT:** Ecstatic

ENGLAND | COW

PASTEURIZED

**AROMA:** Cooked cabbage

**TEXTURE:** Smooth, silken,
sticky

**FLAVOR:** Rich, truffle, cabbage

**IN SHORT:** Out-Frenches
the French

It's not just the illegality of Brie de Meaux and Camembert de Normandie (see page 106) that makes cheese geeks covet them (and worthy imitators). It's the intense flavor benchmark they anchor, especially for an American audience that may know Brie only as buttery and mild. The extreme culmination of what Brie can be is a place I'm pleased to visit as often as possible, but it does evoke very overcooked broccoli—simmered in well-salted water. These cheeses are garlicky, with rich, condensed flavor; exhaling after a small slice is like catching a whiff of damp hay. They taste savory, like the finished swallow of broccoli cheese soup, which is to say mainly fat and sweet cream. This is the character of Brie de Meaux. Do note that actual Brie de Meaux is, by French law, a raw milk cheese aged less than sixty days and is therefore not available in the States. Shops claiming to sell Brie de Meaux are not actually doing so. Luckily, there are a few producers who bother to make pasteurized cheeses that successfully approximate the raw-milk version.

If you can find Brie Fermier Jouvence, snatch it up. You will bow down before the offerings from the "farm of rejuvenation." This is the only farmstead Brie available in the States, made from the milk of 160 cows reared on the farm's land. The farm is owned by the head of a large French conglomerate who has opted to funnel his wealth into traditionally scaled cheese production that would otherwise be cost-prohibitive. This personal lark means we get to savor something remarkably close to authentic Brie de Meaux. Golden, garlicky, and remarkably savory.

# Tunworth

When I first tasted this cheese I was moved to tweet. I believe what I said was "Like a fart in a bag in the best possible way." This is a cheese that bucks all assumptions: You think the Brits make only hard cheese? Wrong. You think that a Camembert-looking cheese must come from France to be complex and wondrous? Nope. You imagine that a white rind equates merely to mild, rich, and creamy? Get a whiff of this. Produced in Hampshire by Stacey Hedges and Charlotte Spruce, and exported in partnership with British mongers and cheese-agers Neal's Yard Dairy, Tunworth is a brilliantly rich and buttery morsel with cabbage-y flavor that lingers as few bloomy rinds do.

APPROACHABLE

FROMAGE DE MEAUX

# (wannabe) Camembert de Normandie PDO

**FRANCE | COW**

**PASTEURIZED**

**RECOMMENDED BRANDS**
(from mildest to strongest):
Le Châtelain Camembert
(Lactalis), Hervé Mons
(Whole Foods exclusive),
Camembert Fermier
(Ferme de Jouvence)

**AROMA:** Wet hay, mushroom, and truffle

**TEXTURE:** Springy, heavy, and moist

**FLAVOR:** Broccoli rabe and porcini cream

**IN SHORT:** Proof that bitter can be sweet

These are exclusively French-made, small-format, eight-ounce rounds packed in charming wooden boxes. The pâté of Camembert is denser and springier than Brie, and because its rind is more proportional to the interior, ripening is slower, and creamy breakdown less dramatic. This said, Camembert's flavors tend to be danker and more concentrated, with a slight bitter-green edge that makes Camembert de Normandie and its worthy imitators, ultimately, the most intense Brie type of all. As with Brie de Meaux (see page 102), Camembert de Normandie's PDO regulations make it illegal for import into the United States, being a raw milk cheese aged for less than sixty days. Thankfully, there are a few French producers turning out remarkably excellent pasteurized Camembert.

What's essential to know when looking for Le Châtelain Camembert is that there are two versions: one wrapped in papery printed parchment (score!) and the other wrapped in shiny, plasticized white paper (bummer!). The latter has a whiff of promise but tends to fall short with bland flavor and a tough, chewy rind. The former can come tantalizingly close to the mercurial wonders of the raw real deal. The can't-miss version is, once again, Ferme de Jouvence's. This is the small, fat yardstick by which American cheese geeks measure Camembert. Properly ripened, the thin, downy rind will be mottled russet with slightly red edges. The interior paste is sticky and golden, with a perfume of damp hay, truffle, and garlicky bite on the finish.

# MY PICKS:
# APPROACHABLE BRIE TYPES

For these cheeses, "approachable" flavor hinges first and foremost on the rind. The most common complaint I hear is that a Brie type rind is thick, chewy, or bitter—none of that will do. Additionally, I'm looking for some version of pure butter. The flavors here aren't meant to be challenging—they're rich and easy, all bundled in a silken mouthful.

## Saint Angel

While Fromager d'Affinois (see page 78) might be snubbed by the geek squad, it's a revelation for people discovering the world of cheese. Then you add more cream to it and get Saint Angel. This is everyone's idea of Better Brie. (see page 82)

## St. Nuage

For anyone like me who assumes triple crèmes are one note, overly rich, and boring, here is a collaboration to change your mind. French cheese-ager Hervé Mons and one of the greatest triple crème makers in France prove earthen complexity and 75 percent butterfat can be merry friends. You'll probably have to go to Whole Foods to get it. (see page 82)

## Goat Brie (ideally, Florette or Chèvre d'Argental)

Play my favorite game, where you feed this cheese to your goat-hating friends and watch them wax poetic about how delicious the cheese is. Then, tell them it's made of goat milk. (see page 84)

## Robiola Bosina

The rind is always great; the sheep milk makes it fattier; it's Italian by way of France. It's consistently well done. And somehow, it seems to never be overripe, so you can buy with almost 100 percent confidence. (see page 85)

## MY PICKS: INTENSE BRIE TYPES

While intense Brie types hold fast to luscious, smearable, finger-lickin' texture, their flavors amp up considerably from butter and button mushroom. Truthfully, this leap is one of my favorites in cheese. I adore cooked broccoli, a hint of bitter greens, and a mouthful of cheese that reminds me of butter-sautéed porcini. That being said, not everyone embraces the pungency of these cheeses:

## Harbison from Jasper Hill Farm

Simply one of the greatest cheeses on the market—woodsy, scoopable, savory-yet-sweet, and easy. It's just a brilliant cheese. (see page 97)

## Tunworth

Play my second-favorite game, and find a very proud French friend and ask them to blind taste this against the Camembert de Normadie PDO you've snuck home from Paris in your luggage. Watch them stumble in confusion because Tunworth is equally cabbage-y, funky, and savory. (I've never actually played this game, but I would really enjoy it.) (see page 102)

## (wannabe) Brie de Meaux (ideally, Brie Fermier Jouvence from Ferme de Jouvence)

This wannabe is better than several actual Brie de Meaux PDOs I've enjoyed. A garlicky revelation of fungal-ness. (see page 102)

TASTING ONE
## THE CLASSICS

Moving from approachable to intense in flavor, this is the traditional flavor arc of what cow milk bloomy rinds can be.

**1. Double-crème Brie** (see page 76)

**2. A triple crème** (see page 80)

**3. A Meaux-ish Brie or Camembert** (see page 102)

TASTING TWO
## BEYOND THE COW

Experiment with the impact a bloomy rind makes on the flavors of goat and sheep milk. And see how they differ from the cow-milk classics.

**1. Goat Brie** (see page 84)

**2. Robiola Bosina** (see page 85)

**3. Cremont from Vermont Creamery** (see page 93)

TASTING THREE
## AN AMERICAN INTERPRETATION

These American cheeses appear Brie-like and, in some cases, are directly inspired by European recipes. Their flavors, however, are decidedly New World.

**1. Green Hill from Sweet Grass Dairy** (see page 78)

**2. Humboldt Fog from Cypress Grove** (see page 88)

**3. Dancing Fern from Sequatchie Cove Creamery** (see page 101)

## PAIRING OVERVIEW

BUTTER

CRÈME FRAÎCHE

MUSHROOM

CRUCIFEROUS VEGETABLES

## BEAR IN MIND

The rind will impact pairings: spicy or bitter flavors are amplified.

Although these cheeses are rich and buttery they have a fair amount of acidity/tartness.

Texture is a dominant quality. These cheeses coat the mouth. Look to cut that.

Because of their "dairy neutrality," approachable Brie types agree more readily with unusual food pairings.

The approachable end of the flavor spectrum has commonalities with Mozzarella types.

## CLASSIC PAIRINGS

(Butter/crème fraîche) with Sparkling Wine: Cream-enriched triple crèmes are cut by dry, effervescent Champagne

(Whole flavor spectrum) with Sliced Apple: Smearable, buttery, and potentially fungal cheese atop thin, crunchy, acidic fresh fruit

### 1. CRACKERS AND FLATBREADS WITH FRUITS AND NUTS

Brie-ish cheeses are meant for slathering and spreading on something thin and crispy; little nuggets of sweet and crunch cut the salt and butter.

FLAVOR SPECTRUM: 1–8

### 2. UNOAKED CHARDONNAY

Oaky Chardonnay, with its thick, buttery texture and woody, vanilla flavor, makes rich, buttery Brie types feel flabby on the tongue. Unoaked Chardonnay offers great acidity and round, yellow fruit flavors that complement tangy and earthy milk flavor. No tannin means no bitterness with that edible rind.

FLAVOR SPECTRUM: 1–8

### 3. COFFEE OR CHOCOLATE-COVERED COFFEE BEANS

If you take cream, that is. Sweet, milky cheeses play the same role and are barely removed from clotted cream or cream cheese that you might eat alongside your cuppa.

FLAVOR SPECTRUM: 1–3

### 4. COARSE OR BITTER CHOCOLATE

"Mexican chocolate" is sweet but gritty; high cacao chocolate is smooth but dark and bitter. Even sweeter dark chocolates have bitter, coffee, and roasted flavors, balancing the cream/butter/tang of approachable Brie types. Both types offer a hard, snappy contrast to lush spreadability.

FLAVOR SPECTRUM: 1–5

### 5. (DRIED) CHERRIES OR CRANBERRIES

Tart-sweet fruit with a juicy or chewy texture avoids the sticky sugar pitfall of condiments like honey, which become cloying layered with thick, rich Brie types.

FLAVOR SPECTRUM: 1–7

### 6. RAW CRUCIFEROUS VEGGIES AND BITTER GREENS

Raw broccoli and cauliflower or an arugula side salad offer crunch while complementing the vegetal character of intense Brie types. The shared bitterness recedes, pushing other flavors to the fore.

FLAVOR SPECTRUM: 8–10

CASTELROSSO

(YOUNG) GOUDA

QUESO TETILLA

TOMME DE SAVOIE

TOMA

NUVOLA DI PECORA

# Havarti

SPECIALTY SHOP

**Wagon Wheel**
PAGE 124

**Pata Cabra**
PAGE 128

**Ashbrook**
PAGE 138

**Nuvola di Pecora**
PAGE 128

**Toma**
PAGE 123

**Asiago PDO (Fresco)**
PAGE 124

**Queso Tetilla PDO**
PAGE 125

**Raclette (French)**
PAGE 140

**Butterkäse**
PAGE 120

**Colby**
PAGE 120

**Monterey Jack**
PAGE 120

**Havarti**
PAGE 121

**Fontina PDO**
PAGE 134

**(Young) Gouda**
PAGE 126

AVAILABILITY   SUPERMARKET ➤➤

**FLAVOR** APPROACHABLE ➤➤

**1** MILKY, BARELY TANGY

**2** MILKY, SLIGHTLY TANGY

**3** CULTURED BUTTER

**4** LACTIC, CRÈME FRAÎCHE

**5** BRINE

**Seascape**
PAGE 128

**Puits d'Astier**
PAGE 132

**Ogleshield**
PAGE 136

**Thomasville Tomme**
PAGE 141

**L'Amuse Brabander Goat Gouda**
PAGE 131

**Bethmale**
PAGE 138

**Ashbrook (Aged)**
PAGE 138

**Casatica di Bufala**
PAGE 141

**Tomme (de) Crayeuse**
PAGE 134

**Pata Cabra (Aged)**
PAGE 128

**Raclette (Swiss)**
PAGE 140

**Saint-Nectaire PDO**
PAGE 141

**Pawlet**
PAGE 136

**Tomme de Savoie PGI**
PAGE 142

**Fontina PDO**
PAGE 134

**Young Sheep Gouda**
PAGE 131

**Kinsman Ridge**
PAGE 132

**Morbier PDO**
PAGE 135

**Castelrosso**
PAGE 132

**Young Goat Gouda**
PAGE 131

INTENSE

| 6 | 7 | 8 | 9 | 10 |
|---|---|---|---|---|
| CARAMEL-SCENTED | COOKED MUSHROOM | CURED MEAT WITH TANG | LOAMY | ALL THAT, PLUS BITTER GREENS |

# In today's foodie culture, Havarti, red wax Gouda, and the like are written off as commodity cheeses—or at the very least as boring and pedestrian.

They often come in a block; they're rindless; they're semisoft; and you're most likely to see them as a sad little cube, impaled on a toothpick atop a supermarket catering tray.

But to me, Havarti is the gateway to everyday eating cheese. In our house, that means cheeses that are reliably tasty; not terribly expensive; and most important, hold the promise of lavish melting, softening into cheese rivers with only the slightest encouragement of toaster oven or microwave. Havarti (or red wax Gouda, or young Asiago, or Fontina, or Monterey Jack, all of which are included in the following pages) occupies a space of essential flavor comfort that is both sweetly milky and pleasantly tangy. These are what the world turned to before processed cheese products came along; they do the same thing, without added emulsifiers, whey, coloring, or other junk. They're also an approachable introduction to French tommes and Italian tomas, which, in their countries and regions of origin, are considered table cheeses intended for everyday eating and melting. The continental cousins have more earth and rusticity to them, but their purpose is the same: casual, multi-generational noshing.

There was a period of time in elementary school when I went grocery shopping with my father every Saturday. Our ritual was to eat at Wendy's before going to Stop & Shop. There we would divide the list and I would proudly troll the aisles with my own cart, responsible for all the shelf-stable goods that we needed. I loved those weekly trips, and in my memory they are anchored by three foods. To start: the Chocolate Frosty at lunch. To end: the pint of Ben & Jerry's New York Super Fudge Chunk that we would eat while unloading at home. But between, there were the stolen trips to the supermarket cheese counter. Tucked into a corner of the windowless store was a full-size cheese department, its walls lined with exotic foods like bulk coffee for grinding and Portuguese rolls shaped like dusty Nerf footballs. (This was the mid-1980s, mind you. Those were pretty fancy offerings.) On each of the counter's four sides was a plastic dome protecting samples of cheese and a small vial of help-yourself toothpicks. I would circle the counter, tasting each of the four samples, marveling that they were just sitting there, free, and that you could eat as many as you wanted. The specific cheese I recall is Havarti with dill. The little cubes were edible pillows, smushing down with each bite. They were a texturally superior version of mac and cheese, with the brine of a cautiously pickled cucumber. The weekends when Havarti with dill was out for sampling were great indeed.

When I started working in cheese, I wasn't surprised to learn that practically every European country has its version of Havarti (although usually without the dill). Traditionally, Havarti is made in Denmark. The Dutch have Gouda, usually encased in red wax. The Italians have Fontina in the northwest and Asiago in the northeast. When nineteenth-century immigrants from all of these countries arrived in the United States, they began making cheeses from home, and those basic cow milk recipes inspired two American originals—cheeses unique to the States. In Wisconsin it was Colby and in California it was Monterey Jack. They're both mild but eminently satisfying, and perfect starter cheeses to some of the lesser-known table cheeses of Spain, France, and the United Kingdom. What many (but not all of them) share is a cheese-making process called curd washing. After the curds have formed in the cheese-making vat, a portion of the acidic whey is removed and replaced with water. This bathes the curds, and the removal of acid enables a sweeter (rather than sharper) flavor profile. Even as curd washing falls by the wayside and the flavor spectrum of Havarti types intensifies into the French tommes, reminiscent of earth, wet soil, and hay, you can still expect to find these cheeses on the breakfast buffet at whatever little European B&B (or even hostel) you're crashing in.

What I love about this group of cheeses is the very concept of a table cheese. For cheese to be a part of every meal, one must believe that cheese is an everyday food. It's not a special occasion food or an elite food. Quite the opposite, in fact: cheese is humble and ordinary, it's regional and part of a local cuisine. Eating it is no big deal. Across much of the States, we share a vision of this possibility, but too often only for the junkiest of cheeses—the processed ones, the slices individually wrapped in plastic. I'd like to replace pasteurized prepared cheese product with the cheeses on the following pages, and encourage you to start enjoying cheese with eggs, or white bread, or a glass of whatever you drink when you get home from work. These are the cheeses for everyone.

# Chapter Guide

Many of the cheeses in this gateway, especially those at the approachable end of the flavor spectrum, are well-known and readily available. Because they are such common eating cheeses, the original recipes, unique to specific countries, are now replicated all over the cheese-making world. While in the case of Brie I point out that French-made is still generally better than non-French, that's not as true with the cheeses here. One of the most eye-opening trips I've taken in my cheese career wasn't to a remote mountain farm in Europe, but to several regional factories in Wisconsin that were making block cheeses I had previously overlooked as boring. What I discovered is that these can be mild, tangy, buttery, and deeply satisfying cheeses when well made—or gummy and utterly bland when made poorly. To be honest, the worst offenders I've found are the European-made versions of European cheeses from other countries. So I will always recommend a cheese made in its country of origin (Italian Fontina, say), and I may very well recommend a classic European table cheese made in the States (red wax Gouda from Wisconsin, say). But you will almost never catch me endorsing a European-made version of another European classic (like Swedish Fontina or German Havarti). These cheeses exist to compete on price alone, and they're just not as good.

## WHAT TO KNOW

**WASHED CURD CHEESE:** Not every cheese in this chapter is a washed curd, but Jack, Havarti, and Gouda all share this crucial cheese-making step, and all to varying degrees have a milky, sweet-tart flavor profile. I've been nerdily thrilled to find that many of the more exotic European cheeses included here are also washed curd, even though they look very different from a block or a waxed wheel.

**WASHING THE CURD IS PART OF THE CHEESE-MAKING PROCESS:** Acidic whey is drained off, usually by about a third, and water is added to the vat. The process is repeated so the curds bathe in a highly diluted whey solution, which contributes to a lower final acidity (and therefore a milder, sweeter flavor). It also prevents the curd constriction (harder curd bits) that comes with acid development and encourages a softer, airier mouthfeel even though the cheese is semisoft to semifirm in texture. It's not sticky or smearable like Brie, but it feels pillowy or squishy when you bite it.

**WASHING THE CURD IS DISTINCT FROM WASHING THE RIND OF A CHEESE:**
The latter happens after the cheese is formed and is an integral step in developing microflora that contribute pungent or stinky qualities to the cheese's aroma and flavor (Taleggio Gateway; see page 148).

## WHAT TO AVOID

➻ **COLOR:** A dark perimeter of discoloration under the rind is a sign that the cheese, although not spoiled, has been kept at too warm a temperature or is old. Additionally, avoid cheeses that have a perimeter of bright pink beneath the rind. Those cheeses, which are waxed or rindless, should not have any molds or color on them at all. None of these cheeses, rinded or not, should have specks of mold on the cut surface of the cheese.

➻ **AROMA:** Particularly at the intense end of the flavor spectrum beware strong ammonia smells, especially if they don't dissipate after unwrapping the cheese.

➻ **FLAVOR:** While the cheeses at the approachable end of the spectrum are mild, milky, and gently tangy, they should not be tasteless. At the intense end of the spectrum, the most common flavor flaw is bitterness. Vegetal bitterness, like arugula, is okay, but crushed aspirin is not.

➻ **RIND:** While most cheeses at the approachable end of the Havarti Gateway are rindless, those with a rind will often have weird-looking rinds! Thick, brown, smattered with yellow or rusty patches of yeast and smelling of earth. That's all normal. What you don't want to see are wet or smearing rinds. They should be nice and dry. As these rinds are more crust-like than they are skin-like, I don't generally recommend that you eat them. But feel free to try. They won't hurt you and you could discover something delicious.

## STORAGE AND SHELF LIFE

Although these cheeses are firm enough to hold their shape and be cut, they are often quite airy. Part of their appeal is their yielding spring, which is lost over time as the cheese dries out.

Paper wrap alone (unless it's specially designed cheese paper) will shorten shelf life because the cheese will rapidly dry out. My preference is zip-top plastic bags, so you can squeeze all the air out and have individual storage units. A small Tupperware container can work similarly well, but the key is that the container be as close to the size of the cheese as possible to prevent its drying out. Plastic wrap becomes a legitimate possibility here because these cheeses are more durable than any of the Brie types. My trick when wrapping in plastic is to always "face" the cheese before serving. Meaning: run a knife along the cut surface of a cheese to scrape off the paper-thin layer that's been in contact with the plastic. Taking the time to expose the fresh cheese underneath costs you very little and buys you instantly renewed and refreshed flavor.

Ideally, Havarti types should be eaten within two weeks of being cut, although they can last for three weeks with diminished flavor and complexity.

Small spots of blue or green mold may develop on the cut surface of the cheese. These can be easily scraped away or a paper-thin slice cut off to remove it, and the cheese beneath consumed, although they are a reliable warning sign that you're pushing the limit on storage life.

## HAVARTI TYPES: TEXTURES

### IN A WORD: PILLOWY

#### LIGHT AND AIRY
AIRY  CREAMY  FLUFFY
MARSHMALLOWY  OPEN  SILKY
SLIPPERY  TENDER  WHIPPED

#### SMOOTH AND/OR SPRINGY
BOUNCY  BULGING  CHEWY
DOUGHY  EVEN  FINGER-WEBBING
GELATINOUS  PLIABLE  PLUMP
PRESSED  SLICEABLE  SMOOTH
SMUSHABLE  SUPPLE  TENDER

#### HEAVY AND/OR WET
SPONGY  TEMPERED BUTTER
YIELDING

#### FLAWS
GLUEY  GUMMY  HARD  RUBBERY

# Colby

**UNITED STATES | COW**

**PASTEURIZED**

**RECOMMENDED BRAND:**
Widmer's Cheese Cellars

**AROMA:** Briefly cheesy

**TEXTURE:** Airy and moist, though firm

**FLAVOR:** Milky and mild

**IN SHORT:** The better mild Cheddar

If you've ever had Colby, you might have thought it was mild Cheddar. In fact, Colby is a Wisconsin original recipe, invented in 1885 by the Swiss immigrant Joseph Steinwand. The primary distinction between Colby and young (high-moisture) Cheddar is that Colby is a washed curd cheese. It's lower in acid, creamier in texture, and meant to be open and airy. In the mid-1990s, the U.S. Department of Agriculture changed Colby's grade standards so that holes weren't required, thus blurring the line between it and Cheddar. This is a bummer, because it's got an important place in Wisconsin, and American, cheese history. Joseph Widmer, the Wisconsin Master Cheesemaker who makes my preferred brand, laments this change because it's enabled mediocre Colby to flood the market and undermine what this American original is meant to be. Which is: moist and pillowy, peppered with holes the size of split peas. The flavor is totally mild, milky, and easy. But that paste is pure dairy succulence.

# Monterey Jack

**UNITED STATES | COW**

**PASTEURIZED**

**RECOMMENDED BRANDS:**
Cabot, Maple Leaf Cheese (flavored), Sierra Nevada, Vella Cheese Co. (Original High Moisture Monterey Jack)

**AROMA:** String cheese

**TEXTURE:** Semisoft and springy

**FLAVOR:** Mild, milky, barely tangy

**IN SHORT:** Nacho-rific

Jack cheese was invented in Monterey, California, making it, like Colby, an American original. The two share more than their American origins—both are stirred, washed curd cheeses. In this case, washing the curds in cool water keeps them firm and stops acid production early. By comparison with Havarti, Monterey Jack is firmer, springier, and less plush; but like its Danish brethren, the cheese is all about the flavor of milk. It's buttery, mild, and eminently meltable, although I find most Jack to be less seductive than Havarti, mainly because it lacks the incredibly lush texture. The most common way to take it up a notch is by adding hot pepper, to produce the world's greatest nacho topper: Pepper Jack. For this, I especially admire Cabot's lack of fear when it comes to heat.

# Butterkäse

The name means "butter cheese." Can we leave it at that? Like many German, Austrian, and Swiss recipes, Butterkäse found its way to Wisconsin with the immigrating influx of Swiss-German dairymen. One of my favorite producers, Edelweiss, notes that the cheese may be known as *dämenkäse*—or ladies' cheese—because it's delicately flavored,

## MONSTER CHEESE

Another American original (one that I'm less proud of than Colby or Monterey Jack) is Muenster. Or, as I called it as a kid, Monster Cheese. You might know it from your local supermarket deli counter: a block of floppy slicing cheese that's construction-cone orange on the outside. Muenster is typically made of cow milk, although I've seen goat versions.

It melts really drippily but is pretty bland. I believe everyone, even the kiddos, can appreciate a small flavor upgrade to Colby or Jack or Havarti. Don't confuse Muenster with the French stank-o cheese Munster (see page 166). If you buy Munster by accident, you will pay about six times more and get a salty cow patty of a rude awakening.

odorless, and complementary to many foods. I guess this was before the days of women sporting full-sleeve tattoos and slinging cheese for a living. Aged only two to four weeks, Butterkäse is cream-enriched for reliably rich texture, round mellowness, and minimal aroma. It's insanely plump and melts on command like a well-trained dog. Given its mild, delicate flavor, you can pair it with nearly any vegetable or carb and guarantee that it won't overwhelm.

**GERMANY/UNITED STATES**
COW
PASTEURIZED
**RECOMMENDED BRANDS:**
Edelweiss Creamery,
Roth Cheese
**AROMA:** None to speak of
**TEXTURE:** Bubbie's arm
**FLAVOR:** Butter (duh)
**IN SHORT:** Like buttah

# Havarti

Pockmarked with irregular holes, a slab of good Havarti is akin to the irresistible pillow of a fat baby's thigh. It's so unbelievably plush and sexy in its squishiness that I struggle to understand why people write it off as a nothing-special cheese. It also melts like molten lava, thick rivers of ooze spreading mercilessly across any potatoes, tortilla chips, or slab of bread you put in its way. Havarti is totally approachable in an essentially cheese-y way; it's familiar, but aspiring to something a little more flavorful. It's mouthwatering. Originally made in Denmark, Havarti was a creamed cheese, meaning cream-enriched to 60 percent butterfat levels. It's also a washed curd cheese, with an accordingly sweet, low acid flavor. Of the milder Havarti cousins like Jack (see page 120) and young Gouda (see page 126) I prefer Havarti for its open, moist texture and perfect balance of milky freshness and pleasant tang.

**DENMARK/UNITED STATES**
COW
PASTEURIZED
**RECOMMENDED BRANDS:**
Castello, Roth Cheese
**AROMA:** Mac-and-cheese powder
**TEXTURE:** Baby's thigh
**FLAVOR:** Approachable, deeply buttery, familiar without being boring
**IN SHORT:** The always-have-around cheese

HAVARTI

# WHAT'S A TOMME?

The world of French cheese is replete with tommes—Tomme de Savoie (see page 142), Tomme Crayeuse (see page 134), Tomme fraîche, and on and on. The Italians have toma. Even the Americans have been inspired, as in Point Reyes Farmstead Cheese Company's Toma (below), or Twig Farm's Goat Tomme (see page 193). So what is a tomme?

What I can tell you is that, to the best of my understanding and findings, tomme's an *-ish*. Smallish. Roundish. Semisoftish. It's traditionally a cheese whose name describes its most basic qualities—a cheese from Savoie, a chalky cheese, a fresh cheese. One universal characteristic of the European tommes is a natural rind, meaning a crusty exterior that isn't made of wax or cloth, nor washed or inoculated. It's a rind that's grown, not made, and built of layers of ambient mold and yeast that sprout on the cheese's exterior over several months' aging.

More subjectively, tommes are rustic cheeses. A cheese friend describes it like this: "Grass. If it didn't taste like grass, it wouldn't be a tomme." More broadly, the tommes remind me of the outdoors: turned soil; mown hay; damp, rocky caves; the best of warm-breathed, stabled horses. I find the tommes maintain the plush texture and essential, milky tang of Havarti (see page 121), but the presence of that knobby, brown, gray, dappled rind introduces a whole new layer of earthiness (and usually flavor intensity) to the eating equation.

## Toma FROM POINT REYES FARMSTEAD CHEESE COMPANY

While *toma* is regarded as the Italian equivalent to the French *tomme* (a smallish, roundish cheese with a natural rind), the Giacomini family originally envisioned their cheese as a handmade Havarti (see page 121). They didn't want precious or fancy cheese, but everyday good eating for folks who didn't care for their signature Blue cheese (and folks who did). They adopted the name "Toma" in homage to their Italian heritage, and because they feared that referencing Havarti would lead consumers to dismiss the cheese as throwaway. Table cheeses are quite common in Italy—regionally produced; semifirm to firm in texture; and served at breakfast, lunch, or dinner interchangeably. Like Gouda (see page 126) and Havarti, Toma's curds are washed in warm water, replacing lactose; delivering a sweeter flavor profile, and with a few months' age, the beguiling aroma of warm butter. Wheels like this remind me that cheese need not be overwrought and high concept. Cheese can be good, everyday food, beckoning you to have another bite. As a friend notes, "It needs to have enough flavor cold to taste like something." This cheese does.

**UNITED STATES | COW**

**PASTEURIZED**

**AROMA:** Warm butter

**TEXTURE:** Like milk fudge that gets stuck in your molars

**FLAVOR:** Sweet and buttery, with a cultured milk tang

**IN SHORT:** The everyday upgrade

# Asiago PDO (Fresco)

**ITALY** | **COW**

**PASTEURIZED**

**RECOMMENDED BRAND:** Mitica

**AROMA:** Kraft singles

**TEXTURE:** Sticky, airy, chilled dough

**FLAVOR:** Fresh and sweet

**IN SHORT:** The panini go-to

The Italians make aging distinctions for the cheese protected under the Asiago name, but it's all called Asiago. Officially, there's pressed or ripened (*mezzano*: four to six months; *vecchio*: over ten months; and *stravecchio*: over fifteen months), but in the States the cheese is sold as young Asiago (Fresco) aged for thirty days and aged Asiago (*vecchio*, *d'allevo*, or *stravecchio*) that's anywhere from two- to fifteen-plus months old and bears an increasingly great resemblance to Parmigiano-Reggiano (see page 320). Young Asiago earns my respect for being a valuable cooking cheese at a generally affordable price point. Firm yet sticky, the flavor manages to be milky sweet with an underlying twang that prevents it from melting into mindless glop. When I created a recipe for the ultimate breakfast sandwich, I used Asiago fresco because its tartness offset the butter, bacon, and egg, which can otherwise overload a little English muffin. It's a cheese that must be purchased from an Italian producer, as American brands tend to wind up in the indecisive middle age of aged Asiago and lose the fresh, tangy backbone that keeps the cheese balanced.

# Wagon Wheel FROM COWGIRL CREAMERY

**UNITED STATES** | **COW**

**PASTEURIZED**

**AROMA:** Cooking cream

**FLAVOR:** Brown butter balanced with tart

**TEXTURE:** Supple and luxurious

**IN SHORT:** The *buerre noisette* of cheese

Known for their Brie-ish, small-format, mold- and bacteria-ripened cheeses, Cowgirl made their foray into large-format aged cheese with the hefty Wagon Wheel. A rosy rind is evidence of brine washing, but the cheese is all about everyday approachability rather than impressive levels of stinkdom. You can look forward to a glossy, supple interior that melts luxuriously. As with all Cowgirl cheeses, the milk is exclusively organic, from local northern Cali dairy Straus Family Creamery. I'm convinced the milk is a major contributor to the rich flavors of cream and brown butter that keep this everyday cheese worth eating daily.

## GIVE THE BREAST A REST

The breast-shaped Tetilla is by far the most common semisoft cow milk cheese of Galicia, Spain. But keep your eyes peeled for its two brethren: Arzua Ulloa PDO and Gallego. Both are buttercup yellow rounds with plump, bulging insides. While Tetilla may have a thick, coarse, waxy rind and stiff interior, these two never fail to disappoint on the meltingly tender side of things. They share Tetilla's tangy, buttery flavor, but their texture is much more seductive.

# Queso Tetilla PDO

Galicia's famous [cheese] nipple is referenced in correspondence dating back to 1753, although its production likely predates this. Juan Bermudez de Novoa, chaplain of San Xoan de Torés, announced sending "two bacons, leg cow, half a dozen cheeses; three dozen and a half of nipples" to his master, the Marquis of Camarasa. I've been told the robot-boob shape of the cheese started when curd was drained in the bras of female cheese makers, but I'm pretty sure that's a tall tale. The most popular cheese in northwestern Galicia, Tetilla benefits from the area's temperate, wet climate, which grows stellar pasture for cows. PDO regulations specify that only the Friesian, Pardo Alpine, and Galician Rubia breeds may be milked for the cheese. At the end of the day, you wind up with the ultimate kid's cheese: a smooth, thin, straw-yellow crust containing gently bulging insides with mildly acidic, briny, fresh milk flavor. Not surprisingly, it makes crazy good cheese toasties.

SPAIN | COW
PASTEURIZED
**RECOMMENDED BRAND:** Celga
**AROMA:** Mild, acidic milk
**TEXTURE:** Creamy and smooth
**FLAVOR:** Tangy butter
**IN SHORT:** The after-school snack

# (Young) Gouda

NETHERLANDS/
UNITED STATES

COW

PASTEURIZED

**RECOMMENDED BRANDS:**
Beemster Mild, Beemster
Vlaskaas, Maple Leaf Cheese

**AROMA:** Yogurt and butter

**TEXTURE:** Moist, smooth, limp

**FLAVOR:** Lactic, unexpectedly
cultured

**IN SHORT:** Zip-a-dee (doo-dah)

Somewhere in the midst of tasting hundreds of cheeses to write this book, I made a bunch of hard-core cheese people sit down and taste good old Gouda. I mean Young Gouda. Red Wax Gouda. Gouda with no aspirations to be aged or caramelly or Parm-like, but content to be smooth and springy, with a milky tang. It quickly led to a spirited discussion about whether young Gouda was a lay-low cheese or a lame-o cheese. I've decided it's lay-low. The average Dutch person eats forty-plus pounds of cheese a year, and this is a primary reason why. Young Gouda isn't sexily complex, with layers of unfolding flavor. But good Gouda is surprisingly cultured (as in buttermilk). It has a wonderfully supple texture that sits heavy on the tongue, rather than a waxy or gluey paste you have to gnash your way through. It melts seamlessly and offers more tang than the Jack so commonly called for in nacho recipes. Serious cheese people might find it pedestrian, but balanced flavor and creamy texture make for worthwhile eating.

# WHAT'S GOUDA DOING IN THE HAVARTI GATEWAY?

When it comes to their flavor and texture, young Gouda and aged Gouda might as well be two different cheeses. Younger (less than a year) Gouda is semifirm, springy, and smooth, with sweet/tart, edging-into-vanilla flavor. Aged Gouda, meanwhile, bridges from firm to hard and crystalline, with noticeable crunch. Its flavors are intense and redolent of toast, roasted nuts, and bourbon.

For these reasons, you'll find Goudas aged up to a year in the Havarti Gateway and those with twelve-plus months of age in the Parmesan Gateway. You'll also find the newly popular Parm/Gouda hybrid cheeses like Parrano in the Parmesan Gateway (though, technically, they are aged for less than a year).

➻ The Havarti Gateway includes younger versions of the Netherlands' most famous cheese, Gouda, made of various milks.

➻ Gouda is a washed curd cheese.

➻ Gouda is named for the town of Gouda in the South Holland province of the Netherlands.

➻ Like Cheddar, the name Gouda doesn't guarantee much: Gouda can be made anywhere, and while traditionally made of cow milk, it may also be made from sheep or goat milk.

➻ The Dutch, in a nod to tradition, typically call the sheep and goat milk cheeses Gouda-style rather than Gouda.

➻ Gouda Holland is a name under application for a Protected Designation of Origin (PDO). To be called Gouda Holland, a cheese has to be:

- Produced and ripened in the Netherlands

- Full-fat

- Flat and cylindrical or block/loaf

- 48 percent to 52 percent fat in dry matter

- Maximum 42.5 percent moisture (twelve days after production)

- Naturally ripened (not in foil, aged above 50°F / 10°C)

- Produced with animal rennet

SPAIN | GOAT

PASTEURIZED

**AROMA:** Mildewy outside, doughy inside

**TEXTURE:** Crumbly yet creamy, almost processed

**FLAVOR:** Salt, crème fraîche, lemon

**IN SHORT:** Crisp and clean

ITALY | SHEEP

PASTEURIZED

**AROMA:** Muted, fresh mushroom

**TEXTURE:** Pocket-warmed toffee

**FLAVOR:** Polenta cream

**IN SHORT:** Snackable but impressive

UNITED STATES

GOAT AND COW

PASTEURIZED

**AROMA:** Caramel whiff

**TEXTURE:** Semisoft to firm, smooth and creamy

**FLAVOR:** Raw hazelnut

**IN SHORT:** Hard to find, easy to like

# Pata Cabra

Here is Julian Cidraque's "leg of the goat," produced from his herd of a hundred in the Spanish region of Aragon. Unusually for Spain, Pata Cabra is a washed curd cheese. Although it's often photographed with a yellow or brackish rind, it can just as easily be found with a thin, powdery bloomed rind, all gray and brown lichen. Every cheese changes with age, but young Pata Cabra is a truly different experience from aged. What remains consistent over time is the insanely smooth, creamy interior, so slick it feels almost processed. Less-aged cheeses taste refreshing and crisp, inasmuch as a cheese can be, with moderately intense citrus and crème fraîche flavors. With age, Pata Cabra becomes markedly drier and saltier, its flavor so reminiscent of olives and mushrooms that I see why some want to put it in the Taleggio Gateway (see page 148). For me, its soul is more like a luscious version of Gouda (see page 126).

# Nuvola di Pecora

I love Italians. They do things like name a cheese "cloud of sheep" after making a silken slab that closely approximates what an ovine cumulus nimbus might taste like. Looking like a square of Taleggio (see page 159), but cloaked in a soft grayish-white rind, this supple darling from Emilia Romagna is aged for a mere month to retain its heavy, moist paste. It's crowd-pleasing and easy, yet the rind has the earthen complexity of a wet-cement creamery floor. It's enough to keep everyone interested, and while the rind is chewy I rather enjoy the biscuity flavors it lends to the cheese. Alone, the interior is a thick pudding-like silken polenta but with a nearly floral, milky finish. The tang prevents boredom.

# Seascape FROM CENTRAL COAST CREAMERY

Paso Robles' Central Coast Creamery calls Seascape a "Cheddar-style cheese." I find it more akin to a young goat Gouda with its semisoft paste and smooth, creamy mouthfeel. I like these guys, though their distribution is primarily on the West Coast, because they focus on aged styles of cheese and are purchasing their milk from California farms. Their cheese generally hits the market at $15 to $17 per pound, which makes it among the most affordable aged goat cheeses I know. This is a no-brainer crowd cheese. It is likely to please everyone with its complex tang and sweet, rounded finish. Also look for their caramel-scented goat Gouda, one of the only American-made goat Goudas I know of.

APPROACHABLE

# 2-2-2 GRILLED CHEESE SANDWICH

Never again shall you suffer through a greasy grilled-cheese sandwich made with Cheddar. The secret is that the perfect grilled-cheese cheeses come from the approachable end of Havarti types' flavor spectrum. Expect a flowing river of milky, sweet, tangy cheese that can be improved only with bacon (if you eat pork) and tomatoes (in season).

**2 SLICES WHITE BREAD**
(don't try to health it up with multigrain)

**2 TABLESPOONS BUTTER**

**2 OUNCES HAVARTI, MONTEREY JACK, OR RED WAX GOUDA**
(wax removed); cheese cut into thin rectangles

**OPTIONAL:**
**2 SLICES GOOD BACON, COOKED**
(Nueske's, say)

**2 THIN SLICES TOMATO**
(May through September only, depending on your locale)

1. Butter one side of each slice of bread with ½ tablespoon butter.

2. Layer cheese on one unbuttered side.

3. Add bacon and tomato, if desired. If so, ideally layer cheese, then bacon/tomato, then cheese. Top with remaining slice of bread, butter side up.

4. Melt 1 tablespoon butter in cast-iron frying pan over medium heat.

5. Place sandwich in pan. Cover with a saucepan lid.

6. Cook for 2 minutes. Don't move it around.

7. Flip sandwich over. Cover with a saucepan lid.

8. Cook for 2 minutes. Don't move it around.

9. Remove, cut in half, devour.

# Young Goat Gouda

Because Gouda is traditionally made of cow milk, you may notice that Dutch makers label their sheep and goat offerings Gouda-style goat cheese, whereas American retailers just call it goat Gouda. Regardless of the name, you can expect a dense, smooth, firm cheese that looks like very white-pasted Gouda. Because these wheels are typically aged three to eight months, they are older than many goat cheeses, resulting in a mellower, sweeter flavor. Compared to a red-wax–covered cow milk Gouda, goat Gouda begins to taste downright candied. I like these cheeses as a teaser for people who hate the lemony, curdy quality of unaged chèvre. Velvety smooth, this goat cheese smells like warm caramel and scalded milk.

**NETHERLANDS** | **GOAT**

**PASTEURIZED**

**RECOMMENDED BRAND:** Arina

**AROMA:** Caramel

**TEXTURE:** Dense and smooth

**FLAVOR:** Starbucks Caramel Flan Latte

**IN SHORT:** The safest cheese risk out there

# Young Sheep Gouda

Ewephoria is the readily available brand, and the matured version is aged for four months. It's mellow and rich, with the beginnings of the candied sweetness that makes one-year versions of sheep Gouda swoon-worthy. But if you can, get Terschelling. It's made in extremely limited quantity from the organic milk of sheep grazing the salt grass of Terschelling Island. Over ten months' aging, Terschelling develops the rounded fattiness that makes aged sheep cheese special. It's got nutty, caramel flavors, but what makes it really complex is the whiff of beefiness in that dense, smooth paste. It's not just cheese candy. Given Terschelling's scarcity, you might hold out for some of the longer-aged sheep Gouda brands detailed in the Parmesan Gateway (see page 296).

**NETHERLANDS** | **SHEEP**

**PASTEURIZED**

**RECOMMENDED BRANDS:** Ewephoria Matured, L'Amuse Terschelling

**AROMA:** Herbaceous and sweet

**TEXTURE:** Fatty and smooth

**FLAVOR:** Coconut

**IN SHORT:** Like eating summer's first whiff of suntan lotion

# L'Amuse Brabander Goat Gouda

Technically a young goat Gouda aged six to nine months, Brabander is so exceptional that it warrants consideration as its own cheese. You pay for the privilege, but I'd rather indulge occasionally and eat something truly spectacular. In the Brabandt region of southern Holland, where sandy soil doesn't support the lush pasture needed to graze cows, goats can flourish on marginal land. Betty Koster oversees the maturation of L'Amuse at one of several facilities that prioritizes warmer ripening conditions for more intense flavor development. Start by eating this cheese with your fingertips. It's like white velvet, never crumbly and never greasy. Betty delivers a cheese made the way Americans are assumed to want it: sweet and pineappley. Brabander smells like butter pecan ice cream and tastes like crème brûlée. It's long and big and lingering and exceptionally delicious.

**NETHERLANDS** | **GOAT**

**PASTEURIZED**

**AROMA:** Juicy Fruit gum and butter pecan ice cream

**TEXTURE:** Cheese velvet

**FLAVOR:** Crème brûlée

**IN SHORT:** Tropical

# Puits d'Astier

FRANCE | SHEEP
UNPASTEURIZED

**AROMA:** Clean and sheep milky

**TEXTURE:** Thick

**FLAVOR:** Bright, lemony pop

**IN SHORT:** A study in contrasts

From French affineur Rodolphe le Meunier comes this insane giant doughnut of a cheese, with a firm gray rind that's typically covered in a powdery coat of pale yellow mold. Like many of the intense-tasting French tommes, its appearance is all earth and soil rusticity. The rind smells like dirt, or the inside of a vaguely damp cave; you wouldn't be surprised to stumble upon the cheese wedged among the rocks on a lonely hillside hike. But from there, Puits d'Astier veers from tradition. For one, it's made of sheep milk, not the typical Auvergnese cow. Then there's the taste. Neither lanolin/sheepy nor moist and hazelnutty, it's surprisingly acidic, which contrasts beautifully with the fat, round texture of the sheep milk. There are whiffs of grass, of ground, of mold, but at the end of the day it's like eating a bite of lemon cream.

# Castelrosso

ITALY | COW
PASTEURIZED

**AROMA:** Lobster butter—sweet, melted, with a whiff of lemon

**TEXTURE:** Lacy and fragile, flaky and fine

**FLAVOR:** Mushroom butter

**IN SHORT:** One of the great unsung cheeses

The traditional cheese of northwestern Italy's Piedmont is Castelmagno, a hulking drum of semiskimmed cow and/or sheep and goat milk with a nearly sandy texture and a sour, earthy flavor. It often develops blue veining and has been produced since at least 1277. By comparison, Castelrosso seems positively modern-day, although it's hardly new-fangled. The Rosso family has been making it since 1894, and although it looks like a shorter Castelmagno, it's always cow milk, always pasteurized, and never Blue. Castelrosso is a chronically underappreciated cheese and, I believe, tastes consistently better than Castelmagno despite its pasteurization. The first bite teases with a promise of tartness, but the taste is butter-sautéed mushrooms splashed with cream. It feels rich and deep, but manages to be light and delicate. Couple this with its lacy, almost flaking texture and the contrast is shockingly incongruous.

# Kinsman Ridge   FROM LANDAFF CREAMERY/THE CELLARS AT JASPER HILL

UNITED STATES | COW
UNPASTEURIZED

**AROMA:** Mac and cheese, with a rind like wet cement

**TEXTURE:** Plump and plush, peppered with oblong holes

**FLAVOR:** Celery gratin

**IN SHORT:** A taste of France via New England

From the farm that makes the Caerphilly-like Landaff (see pages 236 and 237) comes this gloriously moist, plump take on a French tomme. For some reason that I utterly fail to understand, tommes aren't especially favored in the States. As a result, good Saint-Nectaire (see page 141) and the like are difficult to find. Enter Kinsman Ridge. Its muted, wet-chalk aroma suggests a mild and potentially forgettable flavor. Don't fall for that trick. The paste is rich and savory, capturing what it must feel like to be a ruminant ripping broad mouthfuls of lush grass from damp, loamy soil. It's a cheese of the earth, perfectly salted and never bitter, and always anchored with a deep butteriness.

APPROACHABLE

CASTELROSSO

# Tomme (de) Crayeuse

FRANCE | COW

(UN)PASTEURIZED

**AROMA:** Mushroom, milk

**TEXTURE:** Nearly gelatinous but with a chalky center

**FLAVOR:** Heavily buttered pasta with shaved truffle

**IN SHORT:** Proof that eating dirt can be delicious

Said quickly, the name sounds like "Tom Cruise," and I know more than a few mongers who colloquially call this the Top Gun cheese. I'm no great fan of Tom's but am a rabid proselytizer of this relatively new tomme from Savoie. Invented in 1997 by Max Schmidhauser, Tomme Crayeuse is now handled by several affineurs and exporters with varying degrees of success. Although its name translates as "chalky tomme," it's only in France that you'll find a fresh and flaky texture. What makes it so glorious in the States is the ripening that happens during transit: the powdery, velvety gray rind breaks down a solid half inch of paste into gelatinous, mushroomy ooze. The inside core remains chalky—bright and tart in contrast to the drooping edges. Despite its technicolor mold patches, the rind can be quite tasty if, like me, you're into earthy flavors. It reminds me of the first time I bought celery from a farmers' market instead of the supermarket. It was intensely green and pleasantly bitter, the aroma of soil still clinging to the leaves. A Tomme Crayeuse with no chalk is an old cheese likely to be ammoniated and overwhelmingly salty, and I would argue that one with only chalk is pleasantly tangy if somewhat boring. You want the two-tone, so ask to see the cheese cut open. When you find it, you will be rewarded with a bite of moist earth of eastern France.

# Fontina PDO

ITALY | COW

(UN)PASTEURIZED

**AROMA:** Rehydrated porcini mushroom

**TEXTURE:** Dense and dangerously close to gummy

**FLAVOR:** Fruit-forward and spicy on the finish

**IN SHORT:** Mushroom cream sauce without the mushrooms or cream

Poor Fontina. It's one of those maligned cheeses whose name has been used and abused so much it's hard to predict what kind of cheese you're going to get. Traditional name-protected Fontina must come from Italy's Valle d'Aosta and is made from whole cow milk and aged for a minimum of three months. It's typically marketed in the States as Fontina Val d'Aosta and has a toothsome, buttery texture and huskier flavor with truffle undertones. You can tell the real deal by its Consorzio Producttori Fontina stamp. And then there are the ripoffs sold under names like Fontal, Fontinella, and Fontella, which may be produced in Italy or the United States or other European countries. These are younger, pasteurized cheeses designed to be milder in flavor and softer in texture. I put those at about a 3 on the intensity spectrum— semifirm and buttery, but with less tang than young Asiago. Real Fontina is fruity and mushroomy, and intense enough that fonduta— what some call the Italian version of fondue—combines the melted cheese with cream, milk, and eggs before pouring it over bread (and blanketing it with shaved white truffle, if you're lucky).

# Morbier PDO

Morbier is one of the first cheeses to really enchant, because it comes with a line of romance straight through its middle. Traditionally, Morbier was made with excess milk or curd from Comté (see page 278) production. A smaller wheel, it ripened more rapidly and could be consumed in a few rather than many months. Produced over two days, the first layer of curd was covered with ash to protect the surface from insects; the following morning, a second layer of curd was added and the two were pressed together. One could taste, it was said, the difference in richness between morning and evening milk. These days, it's still produced in the departments of Doubs, Jura, Ain, and Saône-et-Loire, using only the milk of Montbéliard or Simmental cows. It's still demarcated by a horizontal black furrow of charcoal or vegetable ash that must be applied by hand. But it's no longer a side project of communal dairy farmers, and the cheese is cranked out on a daily production schedule and intended for international sale. Expect a supple, glossy interior with scattered openings the size of a currant. Like Havarti (see page 121), the curds may be washed in warm water during cheese making. Wheels are ripened for a minimum of forty-five days, always on wood planks, although the hefty ten-pound rounds require four-plus months to develop flavor intensity that goes beyond light, creamy, fruity notes. With age, roasted, spicy, and vegetal flavors make the whole bite considerably more interesting, although, to be frank, I rarely find that in cheeses arriving to the States. In 2014, there was an import alert related to the ash used to decorate each wheel; despite its moisture content of 58 percent (relatively springy and dry), the future of this raw-milk classic remains unclear.

NOTE: In 2014, the U.S. Food and Drug Administration began challenging the importation of Morbier because of bacterial counts associated with raw milk and the cheese's signature line of ash. The Morbier-like, pasteurized Secret de Scey was quickly introduced. It pales in imitation.

FRANCE | COW
UNPASTEURIZED

**AROMA:** Peanuts and damp rocks

**TEXTURE:** Supple, glossy, creamy

**FLAVOR:** From vanilla and cream to peanut and cooked vegetable

**IN SHORT:** Familiar but radically different

## Pawlet FROM CONSIDER BARDWELL FARM

UNITED STATES | COW

UNPASTEURIZED

**AROMA:** The strongest thing about it. Some wet dog

**TEXTURE:** Almost floppy, pleasantly limp

**FLAVOR:** Complex salty tang

**IN SHORT:** The melter for cheese geeks

Technically a washed-rind cheese, Pawlet boasts a tacky, mottled orange exterior that might have you thinking it's gonna be stinky. And in truth it's relatively aromatic. But it tastes like the washed curds, and I'm reminded of what I want the Italian import Fontina (see page 134) to be. That is: as I've eaten it in Piedmont, vaguely truffly, with a yogurt tang that balances the richness. Pawlet may look like Consider Bardwell's other orange cheese, Dorset (see page 158), but taste-wise it's another thing entirely. Imagine Havarti (see page 121) with duskier intonations: mushroom and nut, bolstered with fruity acidity and salt.

# Ogleshield

ENGLAND | COW

UNPASTEURIZED

**AROMA:** Straight-up nut butter

**TEXTURE:** Pleasantly plump, a little slippery, easy to bite

**FLAVOR:** Roasted peanuts; beef jerky but less salty

**IN SHORT:** Peanut butter and bacon

Jamie Montgomery, the revered maker behind Somerset's Montgomery's Cheddar (see page 251), is one of two men responsible for this creamy, pliant cheese. While technically a brine-washed (washed rind) cheese, Ogleshield has evolved over the past fifteen years. It began its life as a recipe cross between Monty's Cheddar and a French tomme. Made from high-fat Jersey cow milk, the cheese was buttery, vaguely nutty, and pleasant, but nothing to write home about. When Neal's Yard Dairy (see page 233) cheese maturer William Oglethorpe began brine washing the wheels, moisture was locked in; a softer, more melting texture established; and the flavors deepened into roasted peanut and rich white wine. Still, there is a savory anchor that makes this the ultimate British noshing cheese.

PAWLET

# Bethmale

FRANCE | COW OR GOAT

(UN)PASTEURIZED

**AROMA:** Hay and clean goats

**TEXTURE:** Lovely and limp

**FLAVOR:** A little bit Juicy Fruit, sans sugar

**IN SHORT:** Goat breath solidified

The cow version is often sold as *vache*, the goat as *chèvre*. They share a larger wheel size; a thick natural rind; and a plump, airy interior smattered with irregular holes. Then there are numerous Bethmale variants, often sold as Pyrenees tommes, made from cow or goat milk, potentially a blend, and even with sheep milk added. Point being: the name Bethmale is broad and can deliver a wide range of eating experiences. I've had over-aged versions of Bethmale that look fine (the injustice! There was no visual tip-off) but smell of mothballs and taste bitter and vegetal. And I've had cow milk versions that were innocuous to the point of being bland. Not bad cheese, but why-bother cheese. It's the goat wheels that I find beguiling. They are firm enough to be sliceable, but succulent and plump. And they walk a fine line between high, fruity acidity (serious tang that you wouldn't expect from the pillowy texture) and the soft, fresh hay quality that I instantly associate with goatiness, in all the best ways.

# Ashbrook FROM SPRING BROOK FARM

UNITED STATES | COW

UNPASTEURIZED

**AROMA:** Vaguely boggy but not terribly stinky

**TEXTURE:** Air-puffed down pillow

**FLAVOR:** Layered and big; at the crossroads of fruity, savory, and sweet

**IN SHORT:** Better than Morbier

In 2014, the seminal French cheese Morbier (see page 135) began vanishing from American cheese counters. Even before this, most of what I was tasting was middling at best. The cheese was fine, but never mind-blowing. Enter the triumphant Ashbrook. While it was created to diversify the farm's cheese portfolio, it turned out to be so much better than the Morbier arriving on our shores. The texture is truly special—smooth and glossy but puffed with air when you bite into it. Like a cheese pillow, it compresses under pressure. Maker Jeremy Stephenson describes the flavor as "brighter and cleaner than Morbier, without the funk or earthy notes." I find that well-aged wheels capture the umami complexity of a superior washed rind: layered and big, so that your tongue tingles and your mouth waters on the perfect, tenuous edge of fruity burst, cured pork, and caramelized onion. This being said, younger wheels are considerably milder, and while they lack the mind-blowing complexity that I know this cheese is capable of, they are clean and sweet, with a delicate yellow fruitiness.

ASHBROOK

# Raclette

FRANCE/SWITZERLAND

COW

UNPASTEURIZED

**RECOMMENDED BRANDS:**
Raclette du Valais AOP
and Risler Raclette

**AROMA:** Stinky, bodily,
far-off gas station

**TEXTURE:** Pillowy, holes the
size of pencil erasers

**FLAVOR:** Olive and
cooked onion

**IN SHORT:** The cheese
for scraping

I can't think of a time I've encountered someone wanting to buy Raclette for eating. People seek it out for melting, specifically in the dish from which the cheese takes its name ("to scrape"). To make raclette, the exposed surface of a partial wheel—or small rectangular slabs of the cheese—are melted in a special machine. It's not unusual to run through half a pound of cheese per person, and because of this, people too often purchase on price alone. French Raclette is universally cheaper than Swiss; it's younger, its production is more industrial, and it melts like a dream. That it doesn't taste like much gets lost in the spasms of delight triggered by molten rivers of cheese. Because Americans tend to make raclette once a year at most, I encourage you to find a really good one, with depth and bodily reek. Otherwise, you might as well melt up some Havarti (see page 111). These two superior Swiss Raclettes balance on a flavor seesaw of briny olive and caramelized onion. You can expect the unusual aromatics of good Riesling: petrol, or newly opened rubber raft. If you go with French Raclette, expect a 5 in flavor intensity, with a mildly pungent smell and a tentatively meaty/salty meal.

## MELTING RACLETTE

There may be no greater comfort food than melted cheese, except for melted cheese with a good dose of starch. Accordingly, raclette has been enjoyed since the thirteenth century. Originating in the Swiss Alps, the name derives from the verb *racler* (to scrape). If there is any shortcoming to this simple, utterly satisfying meal, it's the requirement of special equipment: you need a raclette machine, which allows you to melt small rectangular pats of cheese, or preferably quarter- (or even half-) wheels, which makes for great gooey fun with a crowd. The exposed face of cheese bubbles and blisters and is then scraped in a great, undulating cascade over a plate of potatoes (I prefer boiled), pickles (cornichons and onions), and air-dried beef (buendnerfleisch or bresaola). I add more vegetables than is traditional, both for fiber and conscience-easing, and find I'm no less happy if I skip the meat entirely.

The cheese of choice here is Raclette du Valais AOP or Risler Raclette.

**FOR 8 PEOPLE**
Get the quarter-wheel raclette machine and a quarter-wheel of Raclette
16 potatoes, boiled in well-salted water
2 jars cornichons
2 jars pickled pearl onions
Parboiled broccoli and cauliflower

# Thomasville Tomme FROM SWEET GRASS DAIRY

Talk to Jeremy Little, co-owner at Sweet Grass Dairy, and he'll tell you about moving to Georgia and becoming a cheese maker. He watched as the locals zipped through the grocery store throwing food in their carts and then spent an hour at the video store carefully picking out a movie. That was the food attitude he first confronted; luckily, it's going the way of the video store. A key to establishing a foothold with his local market, new to fancy cheese, was embracing tradition. Playing with the tomme traditions of Italy and France, Jeremy created a Southern table cheese. As a monger friend explained, "You're helping someone pick cheese. You recommend a soft and/or stinky, then a Cheddar and/or Alpine, and then what? This is your third cheese. It's the eating cheese." Named for the farm's hometown, the cheese manages to be moist but dense, with a flavor I can describe only as sharp. It's beyond tart, acidic in a way that might seem Cheddar-like, but with a sticky, buttery chew totally unlike Cheddar. The folks at Sweet Grass suggest using it to make pimento cheese. Southern France, by way of the South.

**UNITED STATES | COW**
**UNPASTEURIZED**

**AROMA:** Clean, stony, minimal

**TEXTURE:** Gluey in a good way

**FLAVOR:** High, bitter greens, anchored in buttery chew

**IN SHORT:** Southern table cheese

## Casatica di Bufala

From Bergamo's Quattro Portoni, Casatica looks like a white mold-ripened bread loaf, ridged and indented from the straw mats on which it has aged. That innocuous rind suggests a cheese that will be mild, safe, and a little boring. In fact, Casatica's flavor edges on bitter greens, with a tangy persistence. This is especially unexpected because of the high-fat, high-protein richness of buffalo milk. The first moment of each bite promises to be puffed and fatty, a satisfying if short-lived mouthful of milk dough. Then comes the spike of flavor: a cheese pillow with attitude.

**ITALY | BUFFALO**
**PASTEURIZED**

**AROMA:** Fermenting milk, fruity

**TEXTURE:** Moist pillow

**FLAVOR:** Bitter greens

**IN SHORT:** Wolf in sheep's clothing

## Saint-Nectaire PDO

Full confession: I love Saint-Nectaire passionately. When tasting it with an esteemed cheese friend, he said, "I've always had a problem with this cheese." I got all miffed because I'm such a fan. When pressed, he explained, "It's one of those cheeses that's three different cheeses, depending on how it's made. I feel like I can see potential between the lines, but it's hidden under shitty imported versions, under terrible care by distributors and retailers. It sits in the warehouse and gets mistreated and keeps on not selling." Heartbreakingly, he's right. When I visited the Monts-Dore region of Auvergne, where Saint-Nectaire has been made

**FRANCE | COW**
**(UN)PASTEURIZED**

**AROMA:** Damp rye, earthen nooks

**TEXTURE:** Dough

**FLAVOR:** Celery, raw hazelnut, brine

**IN SHORT:** Bovine

on high-altitude farms by farmers' wives since the seventeenth century, I experienced what this cheese can be. It was a soft, creamy dough that I rolled between my fingers. It had a brown mottled crust, flecked with gray, yellow, and rusty red flowers of mold. There was a refined aroma of straw, earth, and undergrowth—all mildly damp—and a frank, lactic, nutty taste. Ideally and traditionally, it was made with raw milk. What it should not be is bland, semisoft, and blush-rinded, nor should it be brackish brown and hard to the touch, all bitterness and dirt. I won't lie. It's hard to find in its proper incarnation. But, oh, for anyone who has hiked in open meadows, ridden horses with abandon, or whiled away an afternoon in a hayloft. . .if you find a good piece of Saint-Nectaire, you'll be back to that happy place in no time.

# Tomme de Savoie PGI

Recently, I tasted Tomme de Savoie with a French friend whose family has been in the cheese-aging business for generations. I asked her what Tomme de Savoie should taste like and she sighed, "My dad, on his truck, has ten different Tomme de Savoies. And they all sell really well." She's from Savoie, naturally, where the local cheese is aged to varying degrees of intensity such that there's Breakfast Tomme and Children's Tomme and After-Dinner-with-a-Drink Tomme. In the United States, I find it to be a maligned and misunderstood cheese. It's either industrially produced, gummy, and utterly bland ("It's boring!" consumers say, and they're right), or it has a classic flavor profile that's alien to many Americans because it is truly reminiscent of dirt. Good Tomme de Savoie looks and smells like soil turned into lush green grass. The rind is thick and knobbly, sandy brown, and ideally cloaking the deep yellow paste that's a sign of grass-fed milk. It's moist and loamy but retains the acidic tang of milder Havarti types. Its flavor hints at bitter greens without being imbalanced. We just don't have a lot of foods that are supposed to taste like that. Proper texture makes or breaks this cheese—the good stuff is airy and squishy, its texture peppered with irregular openings.

FRANCE | COW

UNPASTEURIZED

**AROMA:** Moist hay, open barns, and valley grass after the rain

**TEXTURE:** Sticky, semisoft, a little open

**FLAVOR:** Tangy and edgy

**IN SHORT:** The ultimate rustic cheese

# MY PICKS: APPROACHABLE HAVARTI TYPES

The seduction of these cheeses is their plush, springy, airy texture, the possibility of which, melted, becomes an undulating river with enough tang to ensure some backbone. While mild, none of these are so boring that you wouldn't be happy to keep a hunk in the fridge for quick noshing.

## Butterkäse (ideally Edelweiss Creamery or Roth Cheese)

Havarti (see page 121) will do if you can't find this consummate floppy cheese, but the cream-enriched plushness is worth seeking. It's so rich that it feels softened straight out of the fridge. Make a tray of nachos with this and a good glug of hot sauce and blow some minds next Football Sunday. (see page 120)

## Nuvola di Pecora

An exotic Italian cheese unlikely to be found in any but the best specialty cheese shops, made of sheep milk, and yet . . . somehow like eating flowery polenta. In other words, creamy and easy. (see page 128)

## Young Goat Gouda (ideally, Arina)

This is often the first aged goat cheese that folks can get their teeth on. It's dense and buttery like red wax Gouda, but the goat milk contributes caramel flavor that's so sweet as to be edging on candied. (see page 131)

# MY PICKS: INTENSE HAVARTI TYPES

While the American version of everyday eating cheese may be mild, buttery, and kid-friendly, many European versions are decidedly saltier and earthier (although equally kid-friendly, I assure you). Their texture is conveniently sliceable, but flavors are amped up with mushroom and peanut notes, overlaid with decidedly rustic aromatics:

## Tomme Crayeuse

One of my all-time favorite cheeses, with mushroom smear under the rind and a chalky, lactic center. It's increasingly difficult to find—the closest comparable I've found for the vegetable butter I love is Kinsman Ridge from Landaff Creamery/The Cellars at Jasper Hill. (see pages 132 and 134)

## Ashbrook from Spring Brook Farm

It may fake you out, appearing to be Morbier (see page 135), but this Vermont newcomer delivers the flavor complexity imports have virtually lost: fruity and savory, anchored with the clean sweetness of milk. (see page 138)

## Saint-Nectaire

Another favorite from France, although you must find an artisanal or fermier version with the brown mottled rind, not the uniform pinkish exterior that signifies a Saint-Nectaire tasting like nothing. The real deal is like a horseback ride across a cool, foggy meadow. (see page 141)

TASTING ONE
## APPROACHABLE TABLE CHEESES, BY COUNTRY

While these cheeses share a plump, moist texture and mildly tangy, butter-driven flavor, each country has their own spin on easy eating.

**1. United States: Colby or Monterey Jack** (see page 120)

**2. Denmark: Havarti** (see page 121)

**3. Spain: Tetilla** (see page 125)

TASTING TWO
## YOUNG GOUDA, BY MILK

Here are young Gouda recipes interpreted through the three basic milk types. I'd argue that they make sheep and goat milk more approachable and prove that cow milk Gouda can be delicious rather than gummy and bland.

**1. (Young) Gouda** (see page 126)

**2. Young Goat Gouda** (see page 131)

**3. Young Sheep Gouda** (see page 131)

TASTING THREE
## INTENSE TABLE CHEESES, BY COUNTRY

These share a core identity of buttery spring and pleasant tang, but the difference brine washed or natural rinds makes is profound.

**1. England: Ogleshield** (see page 136)

**2. Switzerland: Raclette** (see page 140)

**3. France: Tomme de Savoie** (see page 142)

# PAIRINGS WITH HAVARTI TYPES

## PAIRING OVERVIEW

TANGY MILK

TART MILK

CARAMEL

SUPER EARTH

## BEAR IN MIND

Although the texture of these cheeses is semisoft/semi-firm (i.e., sliceable), they are extremely buttery and palate-coating.

Until the intense end of the flavor spectrum, these are easy, cheesy cheeses—milky and relatively neutral.

The intense end of the flavor spectrum has commonalities with approachable Taleggio types and intense Cheddar types.

## CLASSIC PAIRINGS

(Tangy/tart milk) with strong herbs and spices: Havarti (or Gouda) seasoned with dill or caraway, Monterey Jack with pepper. The cheese becomes a textural vehicle for other flavors.

### 1. CRACKERS AND FLATBREADS

Semisoft with buttery tang, the Havarti types and their straightforward, cheesy flavors are extremely versatile atop crunchy crackers and flatbreads, flavored or plain.

**FLAVOR SPECTRUM:** 1–10

### 2. CRUNCHY, ACIDIC FRUIT, OR GOOD DRIED FRUIT CRISPS (SUCH AS SIMPLE & CRISP)

Apple; nonmushy pear; plump, tight-skinned Concord grapes; or unsweetened dried apple and pear crisps. The operative words here are crunchy, crisp, and unsweetened. The fruit cleanses and refreshes, allowing the cheese to be satiating, snackable. This is snack or lunch for me.

**FLAVOR SPECTRUM:** 1–10

### 3. ROASTED TOMATOES OR TOMATO JAM

Cooking tomatoes concentrates their sweetness and their acidity. Alongside tart-milk Havarti types, the acidity in both recedes, leaving the ultimate tomato and cheese sandwich, well beyond tomato season.

**FLAVOR SPECTRUM:** 1–5

### 4. OAKED CHARDONNAY

Creamy and full-bodied, oak-aged Chardonnay is saved from flabbiness by the tart, tangy notes at the approachable end of Havarti types' flavor. The pairing is crowd-friendly cheese and Wine 101: easy, eatable, and drinkable, if not especially thought-provoking.

**FLAVOR SPECTRUM:** 1–6

### 5. LIGHTER TANNIN RED WINES, LIKE PINOT NOIR, GRENACHE, AND SYRAH

From light to dark fruit, with good acidity but lacking mouth-puckering tannin that can draw out the bitterness of intense Havarti types. You'll get a PB & J-type effect, minus the sugar.

**FLAVOR SPECTRUM:** 7–10

GRAYSON

EPOISSES

LIMBURGER

# Taleggio

TALEGGIO

NICKAJACK

RED HAWK

WINNIMERE

**AVAILABILITY** **SUPERMARKET** ➤

**FLAVOR** APPROACHABLE ➤

| **1** | **2** | **3** | **4** | **5** |
|---|---|---|---|---|
| SALTED BUTTER | PIZZA DOUGH | STONE FRUIT | VEGETAL | UNSWEETENED CHOCOLATE |

INTENSE

| 6 | 7 | 8 | 9 | 10 |
|---|---|---|---|---|
| PROSCIUTTO | BACON | *SAUCCISON SEC* | BOUILLON, ONION SOUP | ALL THAT, PLUS THE BODY |

# The number-one question I am asked at dinner parties is "What's your favorite cheese?"

I usually hem and haw about how I like all cheeses before I get to the truth: What I really love are the soft, stinky cheeses.

The cheeses of this chapter are the ones I mean.

I thought a lot about the Taleggio types while tasting for this book because there is a technical classification that cheese people use to sum up the soft stinkers. Technically, they are known as washed-rind cheeses. This means that once the cheese is formed into a wheel (or square, or whatever shape it's going to be) the rind is washed in a brine solution, often with alcohol (beer, wine, or spirits) added to the brine. This causes two things to happen: 1) the rind turns some shade of orange; and 2) the cheese stinks, usually in ways reminiscent of the sweaty human body. But I've chosen not to place every washed-rind cheese in this book in the Taleggio Gateway, and here's why:

Back in 2002, when I was struggling to master the world of cheese from my post behind the Murray's counter, the soft, stinky cheeses were the least familiar style. Customers would stand there looking sadly at the 200-plus offerings under glass and say, "Well. I like Brie. But I want something. . .stronger." At which point I would confidently reach for Taleggio. These days, Taleggio is hardly novel. It can be found on panini at Panera Bread and in Food Network recipes aplenty. Lots of people ask for it by name. In fifteen years, Taleggio has become its own gateway to some very specific texture and flavor assumptions.

Although there are washed-rind cheeses in the Havarti and Swiss Gateways, they are firm in texture. They lack the gorgeous, sticky smear that makes Taleggio types so luscious on their own, no melting required. Then there's flavor. The Taleggio types are stronger than other soft cheeses, and by this I mean more pungent. Heavier, richer, saltier, more lingering. Persistent. But these cheeses *aren't* sharp or acidic. Bitterness is not an acceptable dimension of flavor as it is with intense Brie types, which can be reminiscent of broccoli rabe or arugula. Here, the cheese (no matter how smelly it may be) is about an absence of bitterness. Its flavor is also about other foods, most notably fruit and cured meat. On the approachable end of the flavor spectrum, it's stone fruit such as apricots; midrange, there's a lot of mellow porky notes happening (bacon and salami); by the intense end, it's fermentation, both fruit and animal. These cheeses get bodily. Finally, there's salt. Salt is an important component of the flavor, left by the brine washing that the cheese's exterior receives.

Now, about the rind of the Taleggio types. Early in my life of cheese, I discovered a French classic called Epoisses. I don't have a single favorite cheese, but if I was forced to choose one, Epoisses would get serious consideration. Back then it was my newest, greatest find. I told my mom all about it, rhapsodic with descriptions of its porky flavor and scoopable texture, like some kind of heavenly meat pudding. Sometime after this she called me, sounding mildly distressed. She had gone to her local cheese shop to find that cheese I had told her was so good. Now she was sitting at the dining room table with a small round in front of her, wondering how she was supposed to pick off what looked like neon-orange Vaseline coating That Very Expensive Cheese I Told Her About.

Egad. She wasn't supposed to pick it off. That was the rind. She was supposed to dip in and eat the whole thing. All the flavor was in the rind! That's what made it great! And then I imagined the scene through her eyes. I saw a sticky, wet, orange quilt reeking of some fairly unpleasant things, draped across the opening of an otherwise charming wooden box. No wonder she was flummoxed. It violated every basic tenet of what our food is supposed to look and smell like. Of course she would think the whole thing was spoiled.

But that is part of what comes with these cheeses. Even at the approachable end of the flavor spectrum, handling these cheeses will leave you with smelly fingers. We're taught that bad-smelling things are bad. Here, bad smelling things are good. That's the magic of a bacterial cocktail that develops with a particular combination of moisture, salt, and lowered acidity. Our mouths can detect sweet, salty, sour, and bitter; each inspires a certain response in the taster. Sweet and salty make you want to keep eating, while sour and bitter offer contrast that shocks. Umami is an elusive fifth taste—a compulsive savor imparted by the amino acid glutamate. It's what MSG relies on to make food addictive. Your brain tells you to keep eating—just one more bite. The Taleggio types deliver a particular combo of sweet-salty flavor; soft, fatty texture; and amino acid power punch that make them a veritable tsunami of umami. Once you pop, you can't stop.

# Chapter Guide

These are the creamy to semisoft washed-rind cheeses, the best known of which is Taleggio. It's what I pushed on the cheese counter back in 2002 when customers told me that they liked Brie but wanted something stronger. Taleggio was the gateway to Stinkdom, back when stinky cheese was a relatively new phenomenon to the American cheese-eating world.

## WHAT TO KNOW

**THE RIND MAKES A DIFFERENCE:** Unlike the rinds of Brie types, which are made of molds or yeast, these rinds are comprised of bacteria. Like Brie types, the rind is made by the cheese maker, cultivated through repeated washings in brine, and it relies on particular levels of salt, moisture, and acidity to flourish. Washed rinds:

➻ Are some shade of orange from pale blush to neon safety vest.

➻ Smell bad, and will make you smell bad when you touch them. Think sweaty socks/dirty diapers/sticky armpits.

➻ Are edible and impart a lot of the cheese's flavor, though they may have a gritty texture from residual salt that has dried on the exterior.

➻ Taste stronger than the cheese itself, so if the flavor is going in a direction you don't care for, stop short of the rind.

## WHAT TO AVOID

➻ **COLOR:** A rind that has turned brown or cracked, or has spots of mold on its cut surface.

➻ **AROMA:** A cheese that smells putrid, like rotting garbage. (This is different from normal bad smells of this style, which are reminiscent of the body and its functions. Let's leave it at that.) Also, avoid an ammonia whiff.

➻ **FLAVOR:** The most common defect is an ammonia burn. Also beware of cheeses with a pronounced bitter or bile-like taste that catches you in the back of the throat. This, as opposed to the brothy, beefy, savory, or sweaty qualities that are normal and desirable for this type.

➻ **RIND:** A rind that is dry and flaking off, or a rind that is hard. Even a thick, firm washed rind should be pliant and a bit sticky.

## STORAGE AND SHELF LIFE

Because the Taleggio types are encased in a live rind that is actively breaking down the cheeses' fats and proteins, there is a true life-span when a cheese is young; ripe; perfectly ripe; overripe; and, finally, dead. You want to eat the cheese before it's overripe (certainly before it's dead), and ideally at peak ripeness.

For the most part, these cheeses start out moist and plump and become dry and petrified over time. There are a few exceptions, such as my blessed Epoisses, which start firm and chalky and become increasingly scoopable to liquid over time. Hard is not a good sign for these cheeses.

The washed rind of Taleggio types is quickly smothered by plastic wrap, but paper wrap alone (unless it's specially designed cheese paper) will shorten shelf life because the cheese will rapidly dry out. My preference is zip-top plastic bags, so you can squeeze all the air out and have individual storage units. You can also wrap first in parchment paper, followed by plastic wrap. A small Tupperware container can work similarly well, but the key is that the container be as close to the size of the cheese as possible to prevent its drying out.

Once cut, the Taleggio types are best consumed within seven to ten days.

Small spots or patches of blue, green, or white mold may develop on the cut surface of the cheese. These can be easily scraped away or a paper-thin slice cut off to remove it, and the cheese beneath consumed, although they are a reliable warning sign that you're pushing the limit on storage life.

# TALEGGIO TYPES: TEXTURE SPECTRUM

## IN A WORD: TENDER

### LIGHT AND AIRY
CREAMY  CURDY  MARSHMALLOWY
OPEN  SLIPPERY

### SMOOTH AND/OR SPRINGY
BOUNCY  BULGING  DOUGHY
ELASTIC  EVEN  FINGER-WEBBING
GELATINOUS  PLIABLE  PLUMP
SLICEABLE  SMOOTH  SMUSHABLE
SPRINGY  STICKY  STRETCHY
SUPPLE  TENDER

### HEAVY AND/OR WET
MOIST  PUDDING  SPONGY
TEMPERED BUTTER  YIELDING

### LIQUESCENT
DRIPPY  LIQUID  MOLTEN  RUNNY
SCOOPABLE  SMEARABLE  TWO-TONE

### FLAWS
GUMMY  HARD  MUSHY  RUBBERY

# TALEGGIO TYPES: FLAVOR & AROMA WHEEL

**UNITED STATES** | COW

**UNPASTEURIZED**

**AROMA:** Unsweetened cocoa

**TEXTURE:** Satisfyingly buttery

**FLAVOR:** Tangless, grassy, butter

**IN SHORT:** Havarti lovers' foray into pungency

**IRELAND** | COW

**PASTEURIZED**

**AROMA:** Olives

**TEXTURE:** Toothsome, bite-down

**FLAVOR:** Smooth, tangy, butter

**IN SHORT:** Spring picnic cheese

# Dorset FROM CONSIDER BARDWELL FARM

The recipe and aging profile for Dorset have changed considerably since the farm began making this cheese nearly ten years ago. It's now typically sold right at sixty days, meaning the cheese is mellow when it hits the market, even on the West Coast. It's accordingly milder in flavor because it's moist and airy in texture. My favorite wheels have a bulging, creamy muffin top just beneath the rind. Made with the high-fat milk of Jersey cows from one of two farms from where Consider Bardwell exclusively sources, "salted butter" captures Dorset in a nutshell. Unlike Taleggio (see page 159) there's no yeasty quality. Instead, you get the pleasure of dense, grassy butter. The first tenuous signs of stinkdom come only from the undulating sherbety rind, although a dank, unsweetened chocolate flavor develops in older cheeses. Most of the time, though, it's a gentle entry into barely pungent, more like eating cheese and white bread sandwiches without the white bread.

# Gubbeen

Produced by the Ferguson family in West County Cork on land they have farmed for multiple generations, Gubbeen is one of the triumvirate of washed rind cow milk cheeses that put Ireland back on the artisanal cheese-making map. While this cheese looks like Taleggio and the stinky cheeses, eating it reminds me of the occasional sample of Havarti (see page 121) that I got as a kid in the supermarket cheese shop. Gubbeen's rind is a triple layer of yeast, the classic washed-rind bacteria *Brevibacterium linens*, and a final bathing of white wine–infused brine. The top of each wheel is often blanketed in edible white mold. The result is a complex aroma—at once mushroomy and boggy—and a bouncy, pressed paste that tastes more of tang and butter than anything funky or off-putting.

# Taleggio PDO

The day after I accepted my first job in cheese, I celebrated by purchasing three exotics to taste. It's a testament to the fact that this was in March 2002, as Taleggio was one of those three. These days, Taleggio is often regarded as a has-been that everyone has eaten. But back then, it was, according to my tasting notes, "total funk smell—barnyard—meaty—mellower taste; soft, not runny; dewy gooey and yum." Since then, I've tasted enough washed rinds to downgrade my comments about funk and barnyard, but the rest of it holds true. Taleggio is the cheese that led me to the term "gateway cheese." It was the way I first introduced customers to stinky cheese, and could easily do so because Taleggio is only the barest bit stinky. It's more like briny dough—comforting and only a bit challenging. Taleggio has been made for over 1,000 years in the Valsassina region of Lombardy, once with the milk of cows on their annual migration down from mountain pastures, but no longer. Don't fear cheese that has patches of grayish mold on the exterior, but do insist on a plump, moist wedge with no cracks.

**ITALY | COW**

**PASTEURIZED**

**RECOMMENDED BRANDS:** Ca De Ambros, Ciresa, Pondini Imports Organic Taleggio

**AROMA:** Yogurt, mold, dough

**TEXTURE:** Squishy, sticky, smooth

**FLAVOR:** Sea-salt-sprinkled pizza crust

**IN SHORT:** The Pillsbury Doughboy of cheeses

# Nababbo

ITALY | GOAT

PASTEURIZED

**AROMA:** Bread dough, no hint of goat

**TEXTURE:** Floppy (almost processed) smooth and slippery

**FLAVOR:** Yeast, stone fruit, chalky finish

**IN SHORT:** The nonstinky stinky cheese

Like its better-known and more traditional Lombardian brother Taleggio (see page 159), Nababbo is a marvelous gateway to the World of Stink, primarily because it's not that stinky. I actually consider it to be a double gateway, because it's a chance to eat a goat cheese without any of the citric acidity most goat-haters wish to avoid. Instead, there's the friendly, doughy taste of pungency's beginning, and the barest whisper of tanginess. Nababbo is all about salt and yeast with a little linger of fruity acid. On the finish, you get the soft minerality of many aged goat cheeses—it's a quality that reminds me of baby powder. Nababbo is a new innovation, taking traditional cow milk Taleggio and turning it into a goat milk block.

# Abbaye de Tamié

FRANCE | COW

UNPASTEURIZED

**AROMA:** Subtly barny

**TEXTURE:** Glossy, pancake-pocked, still springy

**FLAVOR:** Hay-ey milk with a delicate fruitiness

**IN SHORT:** Quintessentially French

As the import landscape into the States has become narrower, with greater restrictions established by the U.S. Food and Drug Administration, classic cheeses from the European canon have begun to vanish. Among these is the Savoie standard Reblochon (see page 100), and the lesser known but far more glorious Abbaye de Citeaux, both banished for their moisture content, combined with their exclusively unpasteurized status. Before being banned, the Reblochon Americans got was usually industrial, chewy, and blandly mild—more like salty Brie. Citeaux, meanwhile, captured the rusticity of *fermier* Reblochon. Abbaye de Tamié is what's now available. It does several things well, beginning with its texture, which is glossy and somewhere between slippery and sticky, punctuated by little openings like bubbles in cooking pancake batter. It's a cheese that's about milk and hay, with subtle fruitiness. The rind, while chewy, is peanutty and delicious unless the cheese is nearing its life's end, in which case it's bitter. In either case, it tends toward the color of pumpkin pie filling, overlaid with a white skim of *P. candidum* mold. It's a good cheese, with a savory anchor and complexity that many cheese makers struggle to capture. Even so, it will leave raw-milk Francophiles longing for the classics of yore.

# Quadrello di Bufala

Of the twenty-five cheeses that Lombardian producer Quattro Portoni makes, this is the best. I think of it as a buffalo milk Taleggio (see page 159), which immediately counters any dismissal one might make that Taleggio is pedestrian, predictable, or boring. Here, you get Taleggio's mellow approachability, but the megafat of buffalo milk contributes amazing, mouth-filling texture. It's like eating a savory marshmallow. Expect the opposite of sharpness, followed by brine and stone fruit under the rind. Unlike in some of the farm's other cheeses (Casatica, see page 141), there's no acidity or bitterness. Each time I'm asked to pick a washed rind that will impress people with its obscurity but delight everyone with its flavor, this is my go-to.

**ITALY** | **BUFFALO**

**PASTEURIZED**

**AROMA:** Yeast dough

**TEXTURE:** Fat made airy, but moistly so

**FLAVOR:** Sea spray, with fleeting apricot on the finish

**IN SHORT:** Savory marshmallow

# Grès des Vosges

FRANCE | COW

PASTEURIZED

**AROMA:** Promisingly stinky

**TEXTURE:** Smooth and sticky

**FLAVOR:** Yeasty, lactic, with some mushroom and garlic notes

**IN SHORT:** The new kid from Alsace

I recall this Alsatian cousin of real French Munster (see page 166) hitting American shores around 2003. It was about the same time that importing unpasteurized Munster, with its age profile of less than 60 days, became truly impossible. Everyone was forced to buy pasteurized Munster, most commonly made by Fromagerie Haxaire, which is often gummy, its rind bitter. Enter this alternative. The handheld, oval round is decorated with a dried fern, and while Grès des Vosges (translation: sandstone from the Vosges) becomes velvety and supple after three to four weeks, its flavor remains in the realm of easy-yeasty. It's a sweet little cheese, and good proof that mild need not mean tasteless. It won't, however, deliver the take-no-prisoners intensity of raw-milk Munster PDO. If that's what you crave, you've got to go to Europe. There are versions of Grès des Vosges washed in the cherry brandy kirsch, which imparts a bit of burn and high fruitiness to the finish.

## Isabella FROM ANCIENT HERITAGE DAIRY

When I first tasted Isabella, its thin, mold-dusted top rind had been sliced off, and the round was offered to me like a dairy bread bowl. Dipping a spoon in, I discovered the savory cannoli filling of my fantasies. The interior looks doughy, but when it hits your tongue you realize it's unbelievably plush. That richness can be credited to both the addition of cream and the use of 15 percent to 40 percent sheep milk, depending on the time of year. Despite the mixing of milks, there are no sheep wool flavors to be found, as with other blended milk cheeses from this Oregon farm. Instead, it's waves of stone fruit: apricot and green olive most profoundly. Unlike the characteristic meaty or stinky profile of brine-washed cheeses, Isabella is racy, delicate, and generously fruity.

UNITED STATES

COW AND SHEEP

UNPASTEURIZED

**AROMA:** Berries and cream

**TEXTURE:** Scoopable custard

**FLAVOR:** Apricots and green olives

**IN SHORT:** Diaphanous

## Nicasio Square FROM NICASIO VALLEY CHEESE COMPANY

Lovers of Taleggio, take my hand and come on a journey into greater complexity and flavor evolution. While the Big T can at times feel slippery and somewhat processed in texture, Nicasio Square is wonderfully plump and marshmallowy. It's got the addictive, super-comforting flavor of yeasty dough but the complexity contributed by the barest hint of stone fruit's acidity. I regularly taste apricot on the finish of this cheese. Huskier large-format San Geronimo was unfortunately pitched to me as "reminiscent of cigar ash" (note: don't sell cheese this way). In fact, both cheeses have the aroma of fresh tobacco, and upon melting (which they

APPROACHABLE

do, brilliantly) offer up strong savory notes of cooked milk and bacon. This Nicasio, California, farmstead operation has roots dating to 1919, when Swiss ancestors established the Lafranchi dairy; the addition of cheese making is merely the next step for this third-generation ranch, with its commitment to sustainable agriculture and pasture-based dairying.

UNITED STATES | COW
PASTEURIZED

**AROMA:** A pinch of tobacco from a newly opened pouch

**TEXTURE:** Marshmallow

**FLAVOR:** Apricot strudel, salted not sweetened

**IN SHORT:** Meaty mousse

# Red Hawk FROM COWGIRL CREAMERY

Cowgirl Creamery is the first maker I know of to brine wash a triple crème. Red Hawk's demand has always outstripped its supply, and mongers from coast to coast are resigned to rarely seeing a fully ripened puck. Nearly always, it boasts some layer of chalky interior. While this makes most Red Hawk markedly milder than the cheese's full potential, with layers of texture come layers of flavor. A good creamline gives you the wonder of whipped butter—rich despite its light, airy mouthfeel. Left on the plate to warm sufficiently, the cheese's exterior pulls apart from the clinging insides in peaks of goo. At the center is a nearly crumbling core. While the cheese is surprisingly odorless for its type, the rind tastes vegetal and pleasantly tart, the insides like movie theater popcorn atop salted sour cream. Each time I taste Red Hawk, I like it far more than I remember. Its summer corn flavor and multilayered texture distinguish it from the crowd.

UNITED STATES | COW
PASTEURIZED

**AROMA:** Surprisingly little

**TEXTURE:** Whipped butter atop butter atop cold butter (outside in)

**FLAVOR:** Buttered corn with a spinach edge

**IN SHORT:** The disruptor

UNITED STATES | COW

PASTEURIZED

**AROMA:** Hoppy

**TEXTURE:** Sticky

**FLAVOR:** Cooked collards, well buttered and salted

**IN SHORT:** New tricks from an old dog

# Schloss FROM MARIN FRENCH CHEESE COMPANY

The oldest continually operating creamery in the United States has been making cheese since 1865 and making Schloss (that's "castle," in German) since 1901. The recipe for the creamery's signature washed rind has been modified in recent years. Marin French found the cheese got truly great at about seventy days, toward the end of its lifespan. The hard decision: sell it young and not terribly interesting, or hold it back to greatness and short shelf life. The answer was: neither. Instead, they added more cream for faster ripening. It's now 5.5 percent cream—unusual and much improved. Despite its high butterfat content, the texture is smearable and sticky, never runny as one might assume. And it's markedly more assertive and complex than it used to be. While the rind has an edgy flavor of hops and baker's chocolate, the dairy's unapologetic use of salt offsets the risk that the cheese's slippery, buttery insides might come off as bitter.

# Livarot PDO

What I recall of Livarot (still sometimes known as "the Colonel" for the dried vegetable fiber strips that encircle the wheel, not unlike the stripes on an Army Colonel's uniform) is the 500-gram piece we used to import from affineur Hervé Mons around 2003. It was a *fermier* (farmhouse) cheese, unpasteurized, with each bite floating on a cloud of earthen complexity. These days, you'll find far more industrial rounds in four sizes ranging from petit (250 grams) to grand (up to 1,500 grams), made across the whole of Normandy, and by 2017 exclusively from the milk of the Normande cow, though it will be pasteurized for U.S. export. Every size is still bound with three to five strips of fiber, and while the feed and aging regulations of the cheese are strictly dictated, much of what's available has lost its complexity thanks to pasteurization. That being said, good Livarot is restrained in a way I associate uniquely with the French. It's not a loud, salty, overly stinky cheese; it veers more toward corn, onion, and leafy green flavors, with a hay-like bouquet. PDO regulations allow the cheese's washing liquid to contain annatto, a plant-derived coloring that imparts orange hue; thus, some Livarot are a pale, orange sherbet color while others are raucous, nearly lipstick red. Don't expect an appreciable difference in flavor. Where possible, here or abroad, seek this cheese in raw milk form. The differences will astound you.

FRANCE | COW

PASTEURIZED

**AROMA:** Vegetal

**TEXTURE:** Camembert-like, glossy, occasional small openings, breakdown under rind but no actual creamline

**FLAVOR:** Succotash, with a whiff of petrol

**IN SHORT:** Restrained in the way the French do it best

## THE HYBRID RIND

One day, I tasted nine washed-rind cheeses and realized all of them had some amount of white mold speckling or even blanketing a rind I expected to be orange. More and more commonly, washed rinds have some combination of the brine-induced bacteria *B. linens* and the fluffy white Brie-mold *P. candidum*. As a result, the whole category is a lot tamer than it used to be. Cheeses with a significant amount of *candidum* tend toward vegetal or fungal flavors and away from the insistent, stinky, animal and bodily aroma/flavor profile associated with washed rinds. Of the nine I tasted, only one was solidly orange. It was correspondingly more complex and layered in all the classic ways. If you want unadulterated funk, look for a safety cone–orange rind.

# Nickajack FROM SEQUATCHIE COVE CREAMERY

Nathan Arnold (backed by his wife Padgett) has emerged as one of the best cheese makers in the States. But if you didn't know that, you might buy this cheese for its name alone. It's an homage to Nickajack Cave, site of endangered gray bats and Johnny Cash's attempted-suicide-turned-spiritual-enlightenment. But that's just the fun trivia. The truth is, like all of this Tennessee maker's cheese, Nickajack is quietly and brilliantly complex. It's somewhere between a tomme, with toothsome texture and earthy finish (see page 123) and the meaty savor of French washed rinds. The rind's washing with hard cider contributes subtle fruitiness and the tannic pucker of black tea, but the flavor hit is akin to the lingering, concentrated tingle of oil-cured black olives. The higher fat content of Jersey/Holstein cow milk serves only to prolong that slow burn.

**UNITED STATES | COW**

**UNPASTEURIZED**

**AROMA:** Vaguely Cheddary

**TEXTURE:** Semisoft and springy

**FLAVOR:** Black olives

**IN SHORT:** Ring of fire

# Durrus

Invented in 1979 by Jeffa Gill, Durrus started a local washed-rind revolution. Perhaps because Durrus, unlike Ardrahan (see page 167) and Gubbeen (see page 158), is unpasteurized, I've always found it to taste the most complex, intense, and layered of the County Cork Three. This being said, it also seems to undergo the most extreme change from the cheese you will encounter for purchase in the United Kingdom. On the other side of the Atlantic, it's much sweeter and milder. Here, though, even suspicious-looking wheels—those that have darkened to a nearly russet hue and throw off a serious cow pie smell—have a light, nearly slippery texture and flavors reminiscent of unsweetened hot chocolate. They're all cocoa and cooked milk at first, with a husky olive/corncob finish.

**IRELAND | COW**

**UNPASTEURIZED**

**AROMA:** Straight-up cow patty

**TEXTURE:** Pudding skin and the layer just underneath

**FLAVOR:** Unsweetened cocoa, followed by chicory

**IN SHORT:** The reviver of Irish artisan cheese

UNITED STATES | COW

PASTEURIZED

RECOMMENDED BRAND:
Widmer's Cheese Cellars

AROMA: Wet dog

TEXTURE: Spongy smush

FLAVOR: Unsweetened chocolate, brown bread

IN SHORT: Limburger for
the timid

FRANCE | COW

(UN)PASTEURIZED

AROMA: Baby diapers

TEXTURE: Plump,
smooth, glossy

FLAVOR: Salty, yeasty,
and vegetal

IN SHORT: Worth waiting
for the real thing

# Brick

While an entire loaf of Brick resembles a block of deli-slicing cheese, the yellow-orange lichen of a rind tells you there's more afoot. A whole bunch of history, for one. The original recipe was created by a Swiss-born cheese maker in 1877, and took its name not from the cheese's rectangular shape but from the fact that it was originally pressed under bricks. Brick was meant to be the firmer, milder interpretation of Limburger (see page 175). Joe Widmer of Widmer's Cheese Cellars makes this cheese better than anyone, still using his grandfather's bricks to press moisture from the curds. The cheese is hand-flipped three times before it's floated in brine. After that come rubdowns with whey-based paste to cultivate the trademark washed rind. As a bigger hunk of cheese, Brick needs more time to properly ripen: at least two months, although Joe likes it at four or five. By then you get the inimitable combo of moist, airy smear and perfectly salted brown bread flavor. Plus, you can say you're eating a bit of American (Wisconsin) cheese history.

# Munster or Munster-Géromé PDO

Petit Munster, or Géromé, merely describes a smaller version of Munster cheese, meeting the same production criteria as the Frisbee-size rounds most often seen in the States. Lest lovers of the mild, floppy American deli-cheese Muenster (see page 121) get confused, this is NOT the cheese you seek. The classic washed rind of eastern France's Vosges in Alsace and Lorraine, real Munster stinks. Its origins date back to the sixth century when Irish monks, followed by Italian Benedictine monks, established themselves around the market town of Munster (so named from the Latin *monasterium*). When I sold cheese to restaurants in the early aughts, the cheese cart at Manhattan four-star temple Jean-Georges was presided over by JG's brother Philippe. He used to tell me how his Alsatian mother would send rounds of Munster to New York, and he would leave them on the radiator, properly ripening to rank, oozing glory. Predictably, the downstairs neighbor called the landlord, thinking something had died in the heating system. The pasteurized Munster we get here is inoffensive if gummy, but lacking the vegetal, manure pungency that this cheese offers at its best. For that you'll need to go to Europe and get it unadulterated and unpasteurized.

APPROACHABLE

# Ardrahan

While Ardrahan used to be an exclusive export of Neal's Yard Dairy, it is now sold by Ornua (formerly the Irish Dairy Board), making it far more available to U.S. retailers and thus the most commonly seen of the County Cork Three: Ardrahan, Durrus (see page 165), and Gubbeen (see page 158). Unlike its two cousins, it's also the export that most closely resembles the cheese you would encounter in the United Kingdom. Durrus and Gubbeen, meanwhile, are so much more intense in the States than at home that you might think them different cheeses. Ardrahan was first made by Eugene and Mary Burns in 1983. Mary has continued to make the cheese since Eugene's death in 2000. Many cheese people talk about Cork as an ideal environment for washed rind cheese—the land shrouded in salty fog from the sea and the cheeses naturally bathed in briny air. It's Mary Burns who first made this connection in association with her cheese. Ardrahan is washed only in brine, fortified with nothing more. While the smell is poopily pungent, the flavor stays in the realm of savory and smoky, with a core of lactic tang. I find it to be more consistent than Durrus, if less likely to reach that cheese's potentially soaring heights of complexity.

**IRELAND | COW**
**PASTEURIZED**
**AROMA:** Peat bog
**TEXTURE:** Curdy and sticky
**FLAVOR:** Savory, edging on smoky
**IN SHORT:** Old reliable

# Robiola Vecchia Valsassina

This is essentially a quarter Taleggio that is cut and allowed to ripen with rind on all sides; many cheese stores sell this as aged Robiola. Each eight-ounce square is the cheese equivalent of a personal pan pizza. Its smaller size contributes to faster ripening, creamier textural breakdown, and more intense mushroom and truffle flavors layered atop the comforting yeasty note that Taleggio is loved for. I think of this as a really special flatbread, sans bread.

**ITALY | COW**
**PASTEURIZED**
**RECOMMENDED BRAND:** Ciresa
**AROMA:** Yeast, dough, mold
**TEXTURE:** Springy, sticky, slick
**FLAVOR:** Prosciutto-draped pizza
**IN SHORT:** The Taleggio upgrade

# Oma FROM VON TRAPP FARMSTEAD/THE CELLARS AT JASPER HILL

UNITED STATES | COW

UNPASTEURIZED

**AROMA:** Earthy

**TEXTURE:** Tender and plush

**FLAVOR:** Approachable barnyard

**IN SHORT:** Supremely balanced

In Vermont's Mad River Valley, the pillowy washed-rind cheese Oma is named in honor of Oma (German for "grandmother") Erica von Trapp. She started the family farm more than fifty years ago, and her grandson Sebastian now makes this cheese (among others) from the farm's organic, high-fat Jersey cow milk. A relatively stocky wheel, Oma has a quilted orange rind overlaid with white flora that mellows the barnyard and delivers a complex, savory, and eminently balanced mouthful of cheese. With textures ranging from springy to puddingy (but never runny), Oma is peppered with irregular openings, its flavor buttery and sweet, occasionally garlicky.

# Rosso di Lago

ITALY | COW AND SHEEP

PASTEURIZED

**AROMA:** Spring cow field

**TEXTURE:** Sticky stretch

**FLAVOR:** Salt-buttered garlic scapes

**IN SHORT:** Finger-lickin' good

The Piedmont producer La Casera is responsible for many of the more interesting robiolas exported to the U.S. *Robiola* refers to small, usually mixed milk and often fresher (younger) cheeses traditional to northwestern Italy. While many of La Casera's robiolas remain rindless due to leaf or cabbage wrappings, Rosso di Lago is neon orange, thanks to a combo of brine washing and annatto coloring. Salt permeates a paste at once sticky and stretchy, and that initial manure-y funk translates into garlicky, porky flavor. I embrace total smearability and generously layer Rosso di Lago between thin slices of raisin fennel bread, with a draping of Prosciutto di Parma for good measure.

# Brescianella Stagionata

ITALY | COW

PASTEURIZED

**RECOMMENDED BRANDS:** La Casera, Luigi Guffanti

**AROMA:** Doughy, porky

**TEXTURE:** Melting, slippery

**FLAVOR:** Delicately meaty, as in prosciutto

**IN SHORT:** The lardo pizza of cheese

Although relatively industrial in production, Brescianella feels like a special discovery. I chalk this up to the fact that, although it's made in Lombardy and looks, smells, and tastes a lot like Taleggio (see page 159), it's much rarer in the States—and its thinner, smaller size means it ripens more quickly and intensely. That's not to say it's overwhelmingly stinky—it's not. Each thin, flattened square is, at its best, sweet and doughy, with a salty finish. Lil' Frankie's in New York's East Village makes a pizza with nothing on it except salt and lardo (softened shavings of pork lard). That's Brescianella in a nutshell.

# Hooligan FROM CATO CORNER FARM

Of Cato's more than twenty farmstead cheeses from Colchester, Connecticut, Hooligan remains my favorite. I've loved it since 2002, when I first discovered it at New York City's Union Square Greenmarket and tried to convince the old-school counter guys at Murray's that we should sell it (everyone told me it was way too expensive and inconsistent, and that I was nuts). Recently I was reminded of what makes this cheese astounding. The two-tone texture, gelatinous underrind, and moist chalk at the center is so slippery and whipped that it feels indecent. Hooligan's rind is more yellow than orange, reminiscent of Portuguese cheeses that have a high, sharp aroma that's a bit fruity, like heavily brined green olives. Despite all these layers, it's the straightforward seduction of salty, lobster-buttered corn flavor that gets me every time. Vegetal, briny, and rich, this is a cheese I could eat all day long.

**UNITED STATES | COW**

**UNPASTEURIZED**

**AROMA:** Baby diapers

**TEXTURE:** Slippery at the rind, chalky at the center

**FLAVOR:** Vegetal and buttery, baker's chocolate on the rind

**IN SHORT:** Voluptuous

# Försterkäse

There are two Försterkäses floating around the United States. One is made in the St. Gallen dairy Käserei Stofel, whose cheese maker Thomas purchased the name Försterkäse when its inventor retired. The other is made of unpasteurized milk by Willi Schmid, who apprenticed with the cheese's inventor. Thomas's cheese is made in an elevated vat so the curds don't need to be pumped out but can run down with gravity, preserving their moisture-laden texture. When Försterkäse first appeared in the States, sometime around 2004, it was so runny as to barely be contained by the spruce bark lashed around the exterior. These days, it's a more succulent, semisoft paste; and although the rind is unapologetically orange, its character and flavors are more about cream and Christmas trees. Worth noting, this is the cheese that inspired the seasonal American treasure Winnimere from Jasper Hill Farm (see page 171).

**SWITZERLAND | COW**

**UNPASTEURIZED**

**RECOMMENDED BRAND:**
Käserei Stofel

**AROMA:** Christmas and eggnog

**TEXTURE:** Pockmarked, squishy

**FLAVOR:** Cream and spruce

**IN SHORT:** Holiday magic

# Rush Creek Reserve FROM UPLANDS CHEESE COMPANY

Inspired by Vacherin Mont d'Or (see page 172), the famed seasonal cheese of France that is produced only in winter months from the fat- and protein-rich milk of hay-fed cows, Rush Creek Reserve captures the impressive complexity of what a hybrid-rinded cheese can be. The cows milked for Vacherin Mont d'Or travel to grassy pasture in summer and spend winter months in lower valleys, sustained on dried hay that fuels richer milk. Similarly, Uplands' cows (a herd carefully crossbred

APPROACHABLE

from nine breeds selected for their ability to thrive on pasture) spend Wisconsin spring and summer on grass, when their milk is used to produce Pleasant Ridge Reserve (see page 284). From early September to early November, the animals' diet shifts and this spoonable, bark-bound round is produced. The cheese begins its life with the same brine washings as Pleasant Ridge Reserve and, aged in shared caves, develops a slick and pungent washed rind thanks to ambient yeasts and *B. linens*. This washing ceases for the last stage of ripening, at which point a blanketing of white *P. candidum* takes over, producing a peach-colored mottled rind with an undercurrent of brothy, meaty flavor offset by the sappy, pine astringency of Christmas trees.

UNITED STATES | COW
UNPASTEURIZED

**AROMA:** Savory cream and Christmas

**TEXTURE:** Custard

**FLAVOR:** Brothy, sweet, woodsy

**IN SHORT:** The eat-alone-in-a-closet-so-you-don't-have-to-share cheese

# Winnimere FROM JASPER HILL FARM

With a complexity as deep as the northeastern Vermont lake it's named for, Winnimere's skin is prone to patches of Brie-ish white fluff that overtake the orange stickiness. Inspired by seasonal Jura Mountain cheeses like Vacherin Mont d'Or (see page 172), and, specifically by Swiss Försterkäse (see page 170), Winnie is made only in winter, when the farm's Ayrshire cows eat a higher fat and protein diet of dried hay. The cheese finishes aging at a texture somewhere between panna cotta and trickling river. To contain this, wheels are bound in a strip of spruce cambium, the tree's flexible inner bark layer, which permeates the cheese's flavor with a high, piney note. This astringency is happily balanced by a salty, sweaty finish. Winnie tastes like cured pork but is so spillingly creamy as to deliver an incongruous flavor/texture mash-up.

UNITED STATES | COW
UNPASTEURIZED

**AROMA:** Wet pine tree

**TEXTURE:** Scoopable to liquid

**FLAVOR:** Bacon cooked by sapling campfire

**IN SHORT:** Lappable

# Langres PDO

The crinkle rind of a Langres looks blaringly neon next to many washed rinds: darker and redder, with elegant ridges and nearly dry edges. While the cheese is brine-washed, it is additionally colored with plant-derived annatto. Cupcake-sized, with a long lactic-acid coagulation and three weeks of aging, Langres is unusually dense and dry, almost crumbly at the center, with bright, sour cream notes and a spicy finish. That complexity is enhanced in unpasteurized versions readily found in Europe. No porky, yeasty stuff here. The flavor is lean and elegant, a quality further complemented by its traditional service, for which the concave top is filled with Champagne. A waterfall of steely effervescence soaks into the cheese (facilitated by a few small cuts), bringing a dimension of dry yellow fruit to the party. The whole thing is refined, which is how they do in the departments of Champagne-Ardenne.

FRANCE | COW
PASTEURIZED

**AROMA:** Briny mushroom

**TEXTURE:** Dry clay

**FLAVOR:** Lactic, spicy

**IN SHORT:** Sharp-tongued society lady

# Epoisses PDO

FRANCE | COW

PASTEURIZED

**RECOMMENDED BRANDS:**
Fromagerie Berthaut, Gaugry

**AROMA:** Farty

**TEXTURE:** Silken and spoonable

**FLAVOR:** *Saucisson sec*

**IN SHORT:** Bark worse than its bite

It is said (although I've never found it proven) that it's illegal to carry Epoisses on the Parisian Métro, so profound is its stink. It is amazing how a small cheese can so quickly fill a room with the reek of dirty diapers and then taste salty, boozy, and utterly delicious. Dating back to the sixteenth-century Cistercian monks of Burgundy, Epoisses was resurrected in the mid-twentieth century by the farmer Berthaut, whose brand is now most commonly associated with the cheese. Produced in parts of the Côte d'Or, Yonne, and Haute-Marne departments, Epoisses spoonable cheese is pale orange to brick-red in color, and made exclusively from the milk of local breeds Brune, Montbéliarde, or Simmental Française. In the States, you'll find only pasteurized versions, but do seek out raw-milk versions in Europe. They're all the better for lack of tampering. Washed in brine and the local spirit Marc de Bourgogne, Epoisses is nestled in a wood box, covered with what looks like a sunny orange quilt. You can control the ripeness at which you purchase Epoisses because the cheese is sold in individual rounds. A cheese to be eaten a week from purchase should be evenly orange, relatively smooth, and almost springy to the touch. A cheese to be eaten immediately will have a thick, glistening, undulating rind and yielding texture under pressure. Avoid cheeses that are dark russet to brown because they're past their prime. After you break through the yielding skin of a ripe Epoisses, your reward is a spoonful of pale beige, scoopable paste that carries a meaty savor, followed by the pleasant, residual burn of alcohol.

# (so-called) Vacherin Mont d'Or

FRANCE/SWITZERLAND
COW

(UN)PASTEURIZED

**AROMA:** Hay and Christmas

**TEXTURE:** Soft-boiled egg

**FLAVOR:** Sweet cream and resin

**IN SHORT:** The scoop-for-a-group cheese

Vacherin is the Holy Grail of cheese. Its production is seasonal, and getting your hands on some over the Christmas holidays once represented the greatest sport of food-obsessed urbanites. Today, there are several Vacherin-ish cheeses coming out of Switzerland that emulate the true PDO cheese, which is categorically unavailable in the United States. The PDO cheese is Vacherin du Haut-Doubs or Mont d'Or, made exclusively in the Haut Doubs region of France along the Swiss border. It is made from unpasteurized milk between August 15 and March 15, and available only for sale between September 10 and May 10. The scoopable, lightly pressed wheels are bound in spruce and packaged in a charming wooden box. Vacherin developed as a late-season counterpart to summer Alpine cheeses. Those large wheels, made

APPROACHABLE

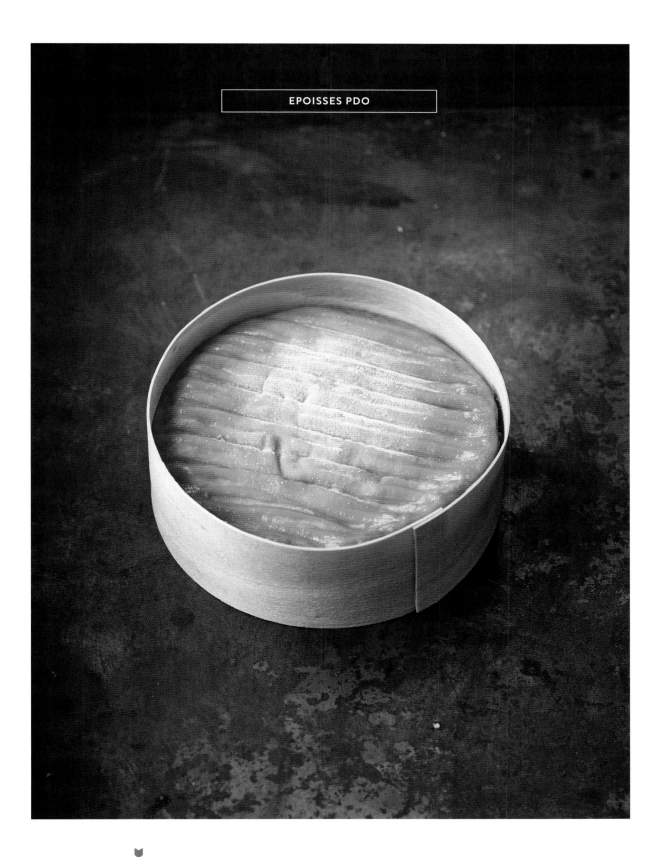

during the summer when cows grazed on mountain grasses, were returned to the valleys once fall set in. There, the cows were kept indoors, eating hay and making smaller amounts of fattier milk. That rich rocket fuel is spun into this silken, spoonable delicacy of a cheese. Vacherin's moisture content is high enough that the bark and box are necessary to contain it, and while it can resemble a rusty, wrinkled washed rind, its flavors are much subtler: sweet cream, with the restrained brine of a proper oyster and a whiff of pine forest.

## MORE CHEESE-IN-A-BOX

Epoisses is the most common French washed-rind-cheese-in-a-box you're likely to encounter. If you like the savory/scoopable/alcohol-laced experience, look for these other (albeit harder to find) Burgundian cheeses:

**L'AMI DU CHAMBERTIN:** Smaller and taller than Epoisses, but similarly washed in Marc de Bourgogne, l'Ami tends to be dense and cakey in texture, with a moist, clay-like interior. The bit under the rind breaks down into tempered butter, while the fermented fruit burn of the Marc is much more prominent than in Epoisses.

**SOUMAINTRAIN:** Pending PDO registration, Soumaintrain is currently a PGI cheese. It's basically a big Epoisses, and the top tends to bulge over the wood box like a glorious muffin top. Bigger size, longer aging, and generally greater intensity are the names of the game. The Marc de Bourgogne–washed rind becomes tacky and caramel-colored, the interior supple but one degree firmer than runny. The flavors are beefy and savory with addictive umami edibility.

**TROU DU CRU:** If Soumaintrain is Epoisses' big brother, then Trou du Cru is its little brother. Invented by the producer Berthaut (the Epoisses brand most likely to be found in the States) in the early 1980s, Trou du Cru are like golf balls of stinkdom. Because of their petite size (two ounces each), they are too often dried out or slimy and ammoniated. A good one has a tacky orange rind and supple, squishy interior. Thanks to a high rind-to-paste ratio, the flavor intensity is extreme, with all the meaty, Marc-y, salty character of Epoisses but crammed into a bite-size cheese.

# Limburger

So famed is the stench of Limburger that old folks stop me to reminisce about cheese mischief they used to get up to (my favorite was a story about some college pranksters who stuck Limburger in the engine of their fraternity brother's car before a long drive so the cheese slowly melted over the course of 300 miles, its stench permeating the vehicle's heating system). These days, Limburger is much less of a cultural touchstone for stinky cheese than it used to be, and people who know it have often eaten it in sandwich form with slivered onions and brown bread while visiting Wisconsin. In the 1920s, Green County produced eight to ten million pounds annually. Now, there's a single plant, overseen by Master Cheesemaker Myron Olson. Young Limburger (say, two months) is more like feta than anything else, but by five months you can expect supple texture and livery intensity. Ironically, I find German-made Limburgers milder in flavor (if not aroma) than Myron's. They tend toward mushroom and grassy flavors—more about the milk than the exterior smear.

**GERMANY/UNITED STATES**

COW

**PASTEURIZED**

**RECOMMENDED BRANDS:** Chalet Cheese Company (U.S.), Käserei Champignon (Germany), Käserei Zurwies (Germany)

**AROMA:** Bad. And really strong

**TEXTURE:** From crumbling to supple, depending on age

**FLAVOR:** Dark chocolate, liver, salt

**IN SHORT:** Offal. Some would say awful

# Grayson FROM MEADOW CREEK DAIRY

Just looking at this cheese, you can see it's been washed. The rind is safety-cone orange and thick with nearly visible layers of brine and damp, pasty smear. Inside, it looks like undercooked cake, evenly spotted with small, round air pockets. Made seasonally at Helen and Rick Feete's grass-based dairy in Galax, Virginia, Grayson is an unapologetically stinky cheese. It has the bodily qualities, the crotchy, footy essences that you're not supposed to talk about, but that stinky cheese lovers worship. But this is no loud, bad-smelling novelty cheese. It's got the deep complexity of long-simmered French onion soup, where the onions' sulfuric sting slowly caramelized into bronzed sweetness, only to be married with the meaty savor of proper beef stock. Grayson captures each of these layers without tasting like any one specifically.

**UNITED STATES | COW**

**UNPASTEURIZED**

**AROMA:** Rubber raft (wine folks call that petrol)

**TEXTURE:** Undercooked cake, heavy and slippery on the tongue

**FLAVOR:** Big! Kalamata olives, beef broth, caramelized onion, a whiff of petrol

**IN SHORT:** Bodily

# ORIGINS OF THE WASHED RIND

As opposed to the cultural and historical origins of the bloomy rind style, the washed-rind cheeses likely took hold as an all-male, all-business venture in monasteries during the early Middle Ages. Larger volumes of milk from monastery herds could be transformed into cheese on a daily basis, providing a protein- and fat-rich alternative to meat (especially important for Franciscan orders) and, later, a reliable income stream for the monastery. Unlike peasant women, who made cheese in between the running of the households, monastic cheese makers had a rigid schedule of worship, around which morning and afternoon milking and cheese making could occur.

The result? Fresh milk quickly coagulated meant low-acid, higher moisture cheese most hospitable to colonization by yeasts and orange-pigmented coryneform bacteria.[*] The smearing of this bacteria with hands moistened in salt brine (or the beer and wine which was also produced by monasteries) led to a uniform washed rind of pungent orange bacteria. If you like stinky cheese, thank a monk.

[*] Paul Kindstedt, *Cheese and Culture: A History of Cheese and Its Place in Western Civilization*, White River Junction, Vermont: Chelsea Green Publishing, 2012, page 130.

## MY PICKS: APPROACHABLE TALEGGIO TYPES

Approachable washed rinds take your hand and whisper, "It's safe with me. Step away from the world of purely buttery cheeses and experience what a bit of salt, an embracement of yeast, and the embodiment of savory can be." Your fingers may smell a bit, but it's okay. You can wash them.

### Taleggio PDO (ideally, Ciresa)

Before I ever worked in the cheese biz, I used to splurge at a Brooklyn gourmet store and write notes on the cheeses I bought there. In my first group of entries is Taleggio "total funk smell—barnyard—meaty—mellower taste; soft, not runny; eewy gooey and yum." I was sold even in 2001. (see page 159)

### Quadrello di Bufala

Because you only ever hear about buffalo milk being made into Mozzarella (if you're even hearing that!), here's proof that it has amazing applications beyond fresh cheese. Imagine barely baked pizza dough topped with Mozzarella di Bufala and an apricot for dessert. (see page 161)

### Nicasio Square from Nicasio Valley Cheese Co.

Truth be told, I don't often see this cheese outside of California. But imagine: a perfect, savory cheese marshmallow. Now go West. (see page 162)

## MY PICKS: INTENSE TALEGGIO TYPES

When I'm eating the intense washed rinds, I innately appreciate that this style evolved, in part, as a meat substitute for Franciscan monks (see page 176). If I close my eyes, I am reminded of the great firsts of my cured meat-eating life: *jamón serrano ibérico de bellota, sauccison sec,* even the Genoa salami studded with green peppercorns that we got on occasion when I was a kid. These cheeses are pungent and layered, and when I was a cheese newbie they were my revelation that food could smell really bad and taste really amazing.

### Försterkäse (ideally, Käserei Stofel)

On the approachable end of intense, with wet wood aromatics that are as much about evergreen snowball forts as they are about beefy, salty cheese. (see page 170)

### Epoisses PDO (ideally, Berthaut)

You never forget your first great love, and even as decades pass it's impossible not to romanticize about how special it was (and maybe still is). Epoisses is that cheese for me: savory pudding with a fermented, alcoholic edge. I occasionally eat the whole 12 ounces by myself and feel only fleetingly regretful about doing so. (see page 172)

### Grayson from Meadow Creek Dairy

Over the years, the European washed rinds exported to the United States have gotten increasingly tuned down in animal intensity. Here, then, is the American answer to how stinky cheese should be: big, bodily, and beefy but anchored in a caramelized sweetness like slow-cooked onions and the flour-dusted fat cap of a good roast beef. (see page 175)

TASTING ONE
## LOMBARDY'S TAKE ON WASHED RIND

The region of Italy from which Taleggio hails is fertile ground for experimental washed rinds, using unexpected milks. Tasted in tandem, the influence of fruity goat milk or fatty buffalo milk on an approachable stinker are astounding.

**1. Taleggio PDO** (see page 159)

**2. Nababbo** (see page 160)

**3. Quadrello di Bufala** (see page 161)

TASTING TWO
## AMERICAN INTERPRETATIONS ACROSS THE FLAVOR SPECTRUM

Although the washed rind style is traditionally associated with France, there are more and better washed rinds coming from American producers than anywhere in the world, and they come in all degrees of intensity.

**1. Dorset from Consider Bardwell Farm** (see page 158)

**2. Oma from Von Trapp Farmstead/ The Cellars at Jasper Hill** (see page 168)

**3. Grayson from Meadow Creek Dairy** (see page 175)

TASTING THREE
## BARK-BOUND HOLIDAY HITS

Some of the finest and best known washed rinds are released seasonally, just in time for the holidays/New Year. Several American classics have been directly inspired by European counterparts.

**1. Försterkäse** (see page 170)

**2. Rush Creek Reserve from Uplands Cheese** (see page 170)

**3. Winnimere from Jasper Hill Farm/ The Cellars at Jasper Hill** (see page 171)

**4. (so-called) Vacherin Mont d'Or** (see page 172)

## PAIRING OVERVIEW

YEAST

STONE FRUIT

CURED MEAT

BEEFY

## CLASSIC PAIRINGS

(Yeast/stone fruit) with sweet and grainy (add flatbread for crunch): Taleggio and fig jam panini

(Cured meat/beefy) with pungent, acidic, and astringent: Limburger with raw onion on dark bread

### 1. CRACKERS AND FLATBREADS WITH OLIVE OIL AND/OR FENNEL

The salty, meaty qualities of Taleggio types are tamed by buttery olive oil and balanced by aromatic anise and fennel. Creamy texture begs for a crunchy pairing.

**FLAVOR SPECTRUM:** 1–10

### 2. FRESH, CRUNCHY VEG

If the washed rinds are the meats of the cheese world, their salt, funk, and fat can be balanced by watery crunch. Slices of raw veg such as fennel and celery are among my favorites. I avoid sweeter veggies like carrots and red peppers because I want to taste the cheese and get the benefit of a palate cleanser.

**FLAVOR SPECTRUM:** 1–10

### 3. AROMATIC AND ACIDIC WHITE WINES, LIKE RIESLING AND GEWÜRZTRAMINER

Wines that smell like flowers, honey, or apricots can be so beguiling that you think they're sweet, even when there's no residual sugar in the glass. And those bottles that are produced to be off-dry (a little bit sweet) still have serious acidity which keeps them bright. Drinking a glass of Riesling with a washed rind gives you the balancing benefits of a fennel slice, a dried apricot, and a pickle all in one swallow. Plus (in my humble opinion) it's a lot more fun.

**FLAVOR SPECTRUM:** 1–10

### 4. DRIED APRICOTS

Playing to the softer, stone fruit tendencies at the approachable end of the flavor spectrum, dried apricots draw out those musky, succulent notes while offering the textural counterpart of chew. A favorite appetizer of mine is a Devils on Horseback variant: slice a dried apricot in half, smear it with a mellow Taleggio type, and toothpick the parcel closed. You can wrap it in a slice of sweet cured pork like prosciutto or speck if you wish (I find bacon is too porky and overwhelming). Throw in the toaster oven at 400°F for five minutes until the meat is crisped and the cheese is runny.

**FLAVOR SPECTRUM:** 1–7

## 5. PICKLED FRUITS AND VEGGIES

Pickled things are ideal with washed rind cheeses. Crunch balances buttery paste, whereas acidity cuts meaty savor and salt. These days, there are countless options in a jar, as well as super-quick pickles that you can make at home in less than twenty minutes. Pickled fruits such as raisins, figs, cherries, or apricots (Boat Street Pickles is my favorite brand) are softer and sweeter, whereas pickled vegetables ranging from red onion to okra to the ubiquitous cuke often introduce smoke or heat and do better at the extreme end of the washed-rind flavor spectrum.

**FLAVOR SPECTRUM (PICKLED FRUITS):** 1–5

**FLAVOR SPECTRUM (PICKLED VEGGIES):** 6–10

## 6. ROOT VEGGIE CHIPS

The spoonable, scoopable washed rinds in a box such as Försterkäse (see page 170), Rush Creek Reserve (see page 170), Epoisses (see page 172), so-called Vacherin Mont d'Or (see page 172) and Winnimere (see page 171) can play the role of orgiastic dip. A small, crispy disc is the perfect vehicle to enjoy them, but one that respects earthy flavor and plays down salt and acid. The cheeses are balm for the soul and you don't want to cut that, you want to savor it. Root vegetables like beets and carrots have a natural sweetness that doesn't become cloying. In dehydrated form, they're delicately crunchy.

**FLAVOR SPECTRUM:** 6–10
COUPLED WITH SPOONABLE, SCOOPABLE TEXTURE

## 7. SHAVED WHITE TRUFFLE

I realize that the likelihood of getting your hands on a seasonal, winter white truffle from northern Italy to shave at home is very, very small. But if you plan to propose marriage or ensure the immediate and successful closing of a massive business deal, you may well go out and find one. Then insist that all parties sit reverent and silent and smell a box of truffle-blanketed cheese before everyone partakes with their own tiny spoon. Possibly this will happen once in your life, and I hope it's when you're relatively young, so you can talk about it for the next fifty to sixty years.

**FLAVOR SPECTRUM:** 6–10
COUPLED WITH SPOONABLE, SCOOPABLE TEXTURE

## BEAR IN MIND

Salt! These are all brine-washed cheeses, and as a result are saltier (and potentially finely gritty if you eat the rind).

As such: consider the rind. Like Brie types, the rind will have more concentrated flavor than the interior paste, more salt and more stink/funk.

As a group, these are less acidic cheeses than Brie types.

I think of these as the meats of cheese. Cooked and cured meat flavors are a common thread. What would you pair with those?

Sweetness balances salt and funk.

Acid cuts meaty savor.

The approachable end of the flavor spectrum has commonalities with intense Havarti types.

The intense end of the flavor spectrum has commonalities with intense Swiss types.

OSSAU IRATY

MANCHEGO

MADELEINE

CABRA AL VINO

MANCHESTER

# Manchego

FIORE SARDO

PECORINO ROMANO

MALVAROSA

PECORINO GINEPRO

GARROTXA

SPECIALTY SHOP

**Goat Tomme and Square Cheese**
PAGE 193

**Grazalema**
PAGE 196

**Madeleine**
PAGE 198

**Lord of the Hundreds**
PAGE 200

**Paški Sir**
PAGE 200

**Ticklemore**
PAGE 192

**Oriol de Montbrú**
PAGE 196

**Berkswell**
PAGE 198

AVAILABILITY SUPERMARKET ➤➤

**Manchester**
PAGE 194

**Queso de Murcia (Curado) PDO**
PAGE 197

**Gabietou**
PAGE 198

**Garrotxa**
PAGE 193

**Pecorino Toscano PDO (Fresco)**
PAGE 196

**Pecorino Toscano PDO (Stagionato)**
PAGE 197

**Ossau-Iraty-Brebis Pyrénées PDO**
PAGE 201

**Queso de Murcia al Vino PDO**
PAGE 194

**FLAVOR** APPROACHABLE ➤➤

**1**
SOFTLY FLORAL, HERBACEOUS

**2**
TART-N-TANGY

**3**
MAC-N-CHEESE POWDER

**4**
GREEN OLIVE

**5**
MELLOW MEAT

INTENSE

| 6 | 7 | 8 | 9 | 10 |
|---|---|---|---|---|
| CARAMEL INTO BUTTERSCOTCH | FIVE-PART FLAVOR (FRUIT/ACID/FAT/SALT/BUTTER) | FERMENTED FRUIT | SMOKE-N-GAME | ALL THAT, PLUS SALT |

## Although Italian Americans have been cooking with Pecorino for years, and Greeks invented authentic feta, it's Spanish Manchego that

gets credit for putting sheep cheese on the map. It's remarkable how completely Manchego has assumed its dominance of the sheep cheese niche when, fifteen years ago, it was still an exotic offering on New York's best cheese counters. I started selling it in 2002; offering a young and an aged version got many conversations going. A mere five years later, Manchego was old hat in New York and San Francisco and showing up regularly in cooking magazines as a universally available ingredient. As my work took me away from the coasts, however, I rediscovered the thrill of introducing people to sheep milk cheese. While Manchego's name had a vaguely familiar ring to customers, or its common mispronunciation (Man-chang-go) did, their newfound excitement reminded me of the old days. If I got fancy and served them a little triangle of cheese smeared with Manchego's common bedfellow *membrillo* (aka quince paste), they got gleeful in the supermarket aisles. Quite simply, when I fed someone Manchego, they liked it.

Manchego is the gateway to aged sheep and goat cheeses, or, as I fondly think of them, the cheeses that you're least likely to have heard of but most likely to enjoy. Aged sheep cheeses have an essentially cheesy flavor to them, reminiscent of boxed mac-and-cheese sauce, but with the  sweetness of macadamia nuts. The fat content of sheep milk is approximately double that of cow or goat milk. Because of this, aged sheep-milk cheeses that are firm or even hard in texture still have a smooth, dense mouthfeel. You can feel the fat. And it feels good. Sheep-milk cheeses, while relatively unknown, aren't burdened by the same negative associations as goat milk cheeses, which are simply assumed to be goat cheese (as in white, crumbly logs that are tangy and mouthwatery—what haters would call sour). That aged goat cheeses don't exhibit any of these characteristics is no matter. Many folks hear "goat" and they head for the hills. This is really unfortunate because the countries that excel at making aged sheep cheeses—notably Spain, France, Italy, and, increasingly,

England—also make a huge range of aged goat cheeses that are similarly likable. Unlike the familiar, meltable cheeses that the Havarti Gateway ushers in, Manchego introduces a world of firm but pliable cheeses full of smooth, subtle, mellow complexity; herbaceous, nutty, and caramel flavors abound. It's only at the most intense end of their flavor spectrum that Manchego types could possibly alienate. If anything, the criticism I most often hear about these cheeses is that they're not strong enough. Thoughtful tasting, deft pairing, and good company can silence that criticism. These aren't loud cheeses, but they aren't bland either.

Sometime in my late twenties, before that five-year mark when Manchego morphed into a New York has-been, I had a summer party in the backyard of my brownstone rental. I was dating a guy with whom I built a relationship around food; he worked in one of the city's best restaurants, ran its cheese program, and knew ceaseless amounts about wine. He entered my life as a customer and introduced me to a new way of cooking and eating, one that he discovered during the year he lived in Spain. When the downstairs apartment was vacated a few weeks before my birthday and the landlady offered me use of the yard, he suggested that we cook for a group. "Cook," that is, in the loosest sense of the word. "Assemble" would be more accurate. Inspired by the Madrid tapas bars he'd haunted as a grad student, we put cheeses together with all kinds of condiments and spreads, cured meats, figs from the backyard tree, and copious amounts of wine. It was to be a never-ending cocktail party, but more thoughtfully arranged. Two of our platters held thin triangles of cheese: Manchego smeared with quince paste and the Catalan goat cheese, Garrotxa, dolloped with fig jam. It's a genius arrangement: guests need no utensils and cheese plays the role usually reserved for crackers. The only thing to be concerned with is what to do with the thin strip of inedible rind. (In our case, the answer was, "throw it on the ground.") Guests were ecstatic about our tapas well before the booze-haze set in. The food was satiating but simple, the fruit pastes sweet-tart atop pleasantly salty, mellow cheeses. The whole thing felt new and exotic, but the flavors were easy and oddly familiar. To this day, I describe quince paste as being like a better version of the canned cranberry jelly that you serve at Thanksgiving. That cranberry jelly is good! Why eat it only once a year? Dragging the butter-dredged turkey skin through a medallion of cranberry is a mere sliver removed from the pleasure of eating Manchego and quince paste. No wonder everyone likes it.

It's true that aged sheep and goat milk cheeses can be intense. Typically, this means more acid (mouthwatering), more piquancy (peppery), and ultimately more animal flavors. In particular, some sheep milk cheeses can taste quite gamy, like the fat-capped rare meat of a lamb chop just next to the bone. Cheese folk call this flavor lanolin, referring to the oil in sheep wool. Recently, a sheep farmer indignantly told me that lanolin has no aroma or flavor, but wet wool does and intense sheep milk cheeses are decidedly reminiscent of it. Salt will concentrate these flavors, producing cheeses often described as rustic. But for the most part, aged sheep and goat cheeses have a softness to their flavor: aromas of dry grass rather than freshly mown grass; nut skin rather than roasted nuts; brined green olives as opposed to oil-cured black. And beneath it all, there is a round sweetness at first suggestive of caramel and then deepening into butterscotch. Most important, remember that these cheeses tend to be subtle. This may be a turnoff for the sharp-cheese seekers of the world, or a reason to move past them because they're just okay. But for many, the subtlety makes this family of cheeses compulsively edible and a compelling reason to throw away the cracker, once and for all.

# Chapter Guide

While Manchego has put sheep milk cheese on the American map in the last 15 years, it's only one of dozens of aged sheep- and goat-milk cheeses that share a mellow approachability. Despite the relative exoticism of many Manchego types, these are easy-to-like cheeses that buck expectations of what goat cheese (sour, sharp, tangy) and sheep cheese (dirty, meaty, weird) supposedly taste like.

## WHAT TO KNOW

➼ **FAT:** Sheep milk has roughly twice the fat and protein of cow or goat milk. Resultingly, aged sheep cheeses become sweaty at room temperature. As the cheese warms up, butterfat leaches out of the paste, beading up on the cut surface of the cheese. There's nothing wrong with this, but be mindful not to leave the cheese out for hours at a time. Additionally, it's more likely to dry out when allowed to warm, sweat, be refrigerated, be taken out, warm, and sweat again. As the cheese loses fat, it more readily absorbs flavors from its surrounding environment.

➻ **AROMA:** Aged sheep milk cheeses, especially those from the French Pyrenees, often have a strong fishy smell on the rind. Let the cheese air out for half an hour and don't be put off.

➻ **RIND:** While eating the rind won't hurt you, I don't endorse eating hard, dry, sharp-edged rinds. Aged cheeses have been sitting somewhere for many months, and the rind is the barrier between the interior and air during that entire time. Hard, dry rinds are typically chewy and taste like a cheese's aging environment. All this being said, it's fun to experiment. You'll sometimes stumble upon a hard rind that's delicious. I find the rind of Berkswell (see page 198), for example, to taste like biscuits.

## WHAT TO AVOID

➻ **COLOR:** A dark perimeter of discoloration under the rind is a sign that the cheese, although not spoiled, has been kept at too warm a temperature or is old. Particularly avoid any cheese with a perimeter of bright pink. This is nature's warning sign and can indicate unintentional bacteria beneath the rind. Also, the exposed, cut face of these cheeses should not have specks of blue or green mold. This is an indication the cheese has been sitting, precut in plastic, for too long. The mold won't hurt you and may be scraped off, but the cheese is likely to taste like plastic wrap.

➻ **FLAVOR:** While the rinds of some of these cheeses smell like fish, the cheese should never taste like fish. The most common flavor flaw of aged sheep and goat cheeses, especially at the more intense end of the flavor spectrum, is bitterness. A bitter edge to the flavor, as in arugula, is acceptable, but a lingering, medicinal bitterness is not.

➻ **RIND:** Many of these cheeses, including Manchego, are encased in wax. Don't eat the wax. Avoid cheeses with smushy, damp, or pasty rinds.

## STORAGE AND SHELF LIFE

Lower moisture, aged cheeses are hardy but they're not impermeable. Paper wrap alone (unless it's specially designed cheese paper) will shorten shelf life because the cheese will rapidly dry out. My preference is zip-top plastic bags, so you can squeeze all the air out and have individual storage units. Plastic wrap becomes a legitimate possibility here because low-moisture cheeses are more durable than any of the Brie types. My trick when wrapping in plastic is to always "face" the cheese before serving. Meaning: run a knife along the cut surface of a cheese to scrape off the paper-thin layer that's been in contact with the plastic. Taking the time to expose the fresh cheese underneath costs you very little and buys you instantly renewed and refreshed flavor.

Ideally, cheeses in the Manchego Gateway should be eaten within two weeks of being cut, although they can last for three to four weeks with diminished flavor and complexity.

Small spots of blue or green mold may develop on the cut surface of the cheese. These can be easily scraped away or a paper-thin slice cut off to remove it, and the cheese beneath consumed, although they are a reliable warning sign that you're pushing the limit on storage life.

## MANCHEGO TYPES: TEXTURES

### IN A WORD: FIRM

### SMOOTH AND/OR SPRINGY
CHEWY  COMPACT  PRESSED  SLICEABLE  SMOOTH

### DENSE AND/OR CRUMBLY
CHUNKY  CRUMBLY  DENSE  DRY  FLAKY  OILY-YET-DRY  UNCTUOUS

### FLAWS
GREASY  MEALY  WAXY

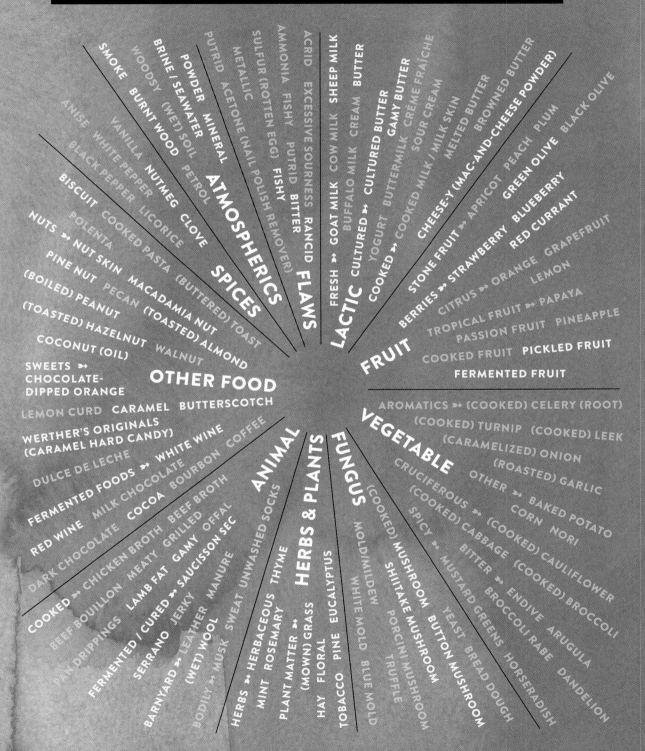

# MANCHEGO TYPES: FLAVOR & AROMA WHEEL

# Ticklemore

ENGLAND | GOAT

PASTEURIZED

**AROMA:** Powdery, delicate

**TEXTURE:** Moist crumble

**FLAVOR:** Floral, herbaceous (chervil), and minerally

**IN SHORT:** Ladylike

As is the case with many of the best farmhouse cheeses in Britain, Ticklemore's continued existence may be credited to the collaboration and transparency within the cheese community. Robin Congden is the inventor of this exquisite cheese. After several years of assistance from Debbie Mumford, maker at Devon's Sharpham Creamery, Robin suggested she take over production of Ticklemore full time so he could focus on his goat and sheep milk blue cheeses. Buying goat milk from the same supplier Robin worked with for more than a decade, Debbie gets the continued benefit of goats on the browse, allowed free rein to munch at pastures and their preferred scraggly brush—in this case, hedgerows. The wheels of cheese bear the impressions of the plastic molds in which the curd is formed and drained, two halves that meet in a thick seam at the equator, creating its distinctive flying saucer shape. Ticklemore has spectacularly delicate and nuanced flavor— moistly floral, with a cool, herbaceous finish. Aged goat cheeses often have a soft minerality that reminds me of baby powder; Ticklemore is the first cheese that really drove this association home.

## JUST BROWSING

Goats are natural browsers. While cows graze on grass, goats prefer to browse through leafy and scrubby vegetation. They'll happily strip the leaves off branches and make short work of scrappy bushes and undergrowth. In many parts of the cheese-making world, it was traditional to keep both goats and cows. The goats performed the job of Weedwackers, clearing paths so cows could more easily reach lush, seasonal pasture. This doesn't mean that goats won't also chow down on grass. I know more than a few farmers who keep goats around just to maintain their lawns.

# Goat Tomme and
# Square Cheese FROM TWIG FARM

Michael Lee and Emily Sunderman's goats browse in the scruffy woods that surround their West Cornwall, Vermont, house. While their cheeses are seasonal and extremely limited in production, they are so special as to warrant mention for those in the Northeast, particularly Boston, New York, and Vermont. Both Goat Tomme and Square Cheese are aged a minimum of sixty days (more like eighty, actually), but the Tomme can go longer and sometimes bridges the winter months when no cheese is being produced. Because they are taking great pains to make great milk, the farm's cheeses are not pasteurized, so the changing nuances of bark and brush come through in each bite. While Goat Tomme is made with a blend of theirs and a neighboring farm's milk, Square Cheese is 100 percent Twig goats. Both offer a moister, more succulent version of Garrotxa, with deep, lingering pine-nuttiness and a rind that, despite its delicate fuzz, tastes wonderfully vegetal.

**UNITED STATES | GOAT**
**UNPASTEURIZED**
**AROMA:** Shady woods
**TEXTURE:** Firm but creamy
**FLAVOR:** Pine nut milk
**IN SHORT:** Bosky

# Garrotxa

It's a blessing and a curse when the first encounter you have with a cheese is with the very best version that is made. On the one hand, you're instantly and completely seduced. On the other hand, there's nowhere to go but down. That was my experience with Toni Chueca's Garrotxa, called "La Bauma." The Cheucas once had goats, but they sold their herd to a neighbor and now buy the milk back so they can focus solely on cheese making. This focus has paid off in a remarkable cheese, its rind thick and fuzzy, the color of moleskin and the texture of kitten fur. All Garrotxa is dense and aged, the expected lemony tang of goat milk softened into flavors of nut skin and toasted hazelnuts. La Bauma has the added wonders of deep aromatics, like scrub brush growing in the foothills of the Pyrenees, and damp wood. Garrotxa is not yet a protected cheese, but I'm told this process is underway. It should always hail from Catalonia and is always made of pasteurized milk. I often talk about aged goat cheeses' ability to change the opinions of those who dislike fresh goat cheese. Garrotxa is the prime, and now readily available, example.

**SPAIN | GOAT**
**PASTEURIZED**
**RECOMMENDED BRANDS:**
La Bauma (Murray's Cheese exclusive), Sant Gil
**AROMA:** Dry summer grass and slight mustiness
**TEXTURE:** Moist chew that softens in the mouth
**FLAVOR:** Hazelnut skin, pine nuts
**IN SHORT:** The converter

## Manchester FROM CONSIDER BARDWELL FARM

UNITED STATES | GOAT

UNPASTEURIZED

**AROMA:** Almost metallic but earthy, sharp dirt

**TEXTURE:** Moistly granular

**FLAVOR:** Saline, mineral, soft earth

**IN SHORT:** Like eating the air around goats

The virtue of unpasteurized milk is that you truly taste a place. There is no filter between you and the feed, air, water, soil, and animal whose milk made the cheese you're eating. I find this especially true of Consider Bardwell's goat cheeses, perhaps because I have visited the farm and can easily embrace the sensation of eating the place. Their seasonal Manchester, produced with the farm's first milk of March, and continuing until the goats dry off in early December, is ideal at four to five months of age. By then, the salt has coalesced, pulling together green goat-milky notes with the earthy anchor of open-air cave aging. Female goats are remarkably clean animals. They smell of hay and grass, of warm breath and fresh milk. These gentle qualities shine on in the cheese. It's enough to make you hop in the car and take a drive to Vermont.

## Queso de Murcia al Vino PDO

SPAIN | GOAT

PASTEURIZED

**RECOMMENDED BRAND:** The Drunken Goat

**AROMA:** Somewhere between grape juice and red wine

**TEXTURE:** Pliant

**FLAVOR:** Smooth, sweet, winey

**IN SHORT:** Fruity

I'd be lying if I said this was one of my favorite cheeses. I don't tend to go for flavored cheeses in the first place, and wine-washed choices often have a disturbingly grapey quality. Still, I appreciate Queso de Murcia al Vino's ability to coax cheese newbies over to the goat side—more specifically, the most common brand found on the American market, the charming Drunken Goat. It's got a great name, and people pay attention. Its story goes that a cheese maker and his friends were sitting around drinking and knocked a wheel of cheese into a barrel of red wine. After bobbing around for several days, the cheese was fished out, tasted, and determined to be even more delicious. These days, barely firm wheels of goat cheese, boasting a smushable, pliant texture, are made friendlier and fruitier with a washing in one of the red wine appellations of Murcia (Jumilla, Yecla, and Bullas), which imparts a violet hue to the rind. Most important, the cheese retains the soft, hay-ey flavor of goat milk, rather than succumbing to an overwhelming wine hose-down.

QUESO DE MURCIA AL VINO PDO

# Pecorino Toscano PDO (Fresco)

ITALY | SHEEP

(UN)PASTEURIZED

**AROMA:** Mild, tangy milk

**TEXTURE:** Firm, yet creamy and moist

**FLAVOR:** Briny tang

**IN SHORT:** Fresh

Commonly sold as young Pecorino Toscano, as opposed to the aged or officially stagionato versions, this rindless, white, moist Pecorino exemplifies the walnutty and tangy simplicity of what briefly aged Pecorino can be. Pecorino Toscano qualifies for DOP/PDO status with a history dating back to Etruscan times, when sheep farming provided a viable use for otherwise marginal land. Today, Pecorino Toscano can be made anywhere in Tuscany, as well as parts of Umbria and Lazio. Matured for a minimum of twenty days, most of what's exported is two to three months, although Cryovac packaging maintains its fresh briny smack. In Italy, the first Pecorinos of spring are enjoyed with delicate fava or broad beans. My most memorable encounters have been at breakfast in Tuscany, dragging the cheese through brackish chestnut honey in lieu of cream and sugar with a small, intense Italian caffè.

# Grazalema

SPAIN | SHEEP/GOAT

PASTEURIZED

**AROMA:** Buttery citrus

**TEXTURE:** Firm yet creamy

**FLAVOR:** Chocolate-dipped orange peel

**IN SHORT:** Lush

Here's a cheese I have Spanish cheese expert Enric Canut to thank for an introduction. El Poyoyo (the "Grandaddy"—although Poyoyo is also an indigenous breed of goat) hails from a cooperative on an Andalusian nature preserve that formed in 1997. When Enric first unveiled this Manchego-size wheel, encased in a hatch-marked wax rind, I thought, "Boring." It looked young, the paste pliable, the yellowy hue like chicken fat. But oh, how unboring it was. The blend of milks (85 percent goat to 15 percent sheep) captures the fatty heft of sheep milk; the goat adds a tang and lightness that in overly aged wheels becomes piquant and fermented—fruity, like unsweetened grape soda. Ideal wheels are firm but creamier and moister than Manchego (see page 202), the aroma full and buttery, and the flavor herbaceous and citrusy and never acidic. It's expensive but rare and special. It begs to be thinly shaved, each translucent piece left to dissolve on the tongue.

# Oriol de Montbrú

When I first saw a solid, elegant round of Oriol de Montbrú, I thought it was a miniaturized Garrotxa (see page 193). It had the same gray kitten-fur rind, the same firm-but-yielding texture. And to say it was inspired, or at least influenced, by Garrotxa wouldn't be far off. But this is some serious transnational collaboration happening. Produced by Oriol Antunez, who has been making goat cheese on his parents' farm

APPROACHABLE

outside of Barcelona since 1996, this recipe was developed in response to the arrival of 1,500 water buffalo, moved from Lombardy, Italy, when their owner ran out of space. As it happens, this man is the neighbor of famed Italian cheese maker Quattro Portoni (see page xx), making some of the finest and most innovative buffalo milk cheeses available. So Oriol de Montbrú reinterprets a classic Catalan cheese recipe through the lens of heavy, fatty, and rich buffalo milk. The densely moist chew is impressive; a smaller wheel size means that the earthy, pleasantly bitter rind can be tasted throughout.

SPAIN | BUFFALO

PASTEURIZED

**AROMA:** Damp mustiness

**TEXTURE:** Impeccably dense and fatty

**FLAVOR:** Mellow gamy tang

**IN SHORT:** The cross-country collaborator

## Queso de Murcia (Curado) PDO

For decades, the milk of local Murcia-Granada goats has been made into this firm, compact cheese, and aged for a minimum of four but often closer to six months. Its appeal beyond the regional market of Murcia was limited, leading to the development of Queso de Murcia al Vino in 1986 (see page 194). I wonder, though, if Queso de Murcia's time is finally arriving. Larger wheels and longer aging deliver an aged goat cheese more Pecorino-ish in texture, with full, buttery flavor. It's an ideal appetizer cheese, made for pairing with spreadables like fig or tomato jam that use the cheese in lieu of a cracker or toast. It's mellow and lactic—both easy eating and good eating.

SPAIN | GOAT

PASTEURIZED

**RECOMMENDED BRAND:** Naked Goat

**AROMA:** Buttery

**TEXTURE:** Compact

**FLAVOR:** Mellow and lactic, cheesy

**IN SHORT:** The nosher

## Pecorino Toscano PDO (Stagionato)

Pecorino Toscano stagionato must be aged for a minimum of four months. Unlike Fresco (see page 196), the curd is cut into much smaller, corn-kernel-size bits during cheese making and may be briefly heated to further expel moisture. The cheese is then pressed and brined to ensure a drier paste suited for longer aging. The firm, compact interior develops a lovely straw color over time, its rustic brown rind a shell that encases the cheese's insistent fragrance. Here, then, is the consummate all-purpose cheese. It's meant to be put down in a chunk, picked at communally, and enjoyed alongside whatever olives, salumi, or fruit are around. It's hard enough to grate or shave over veggies from blanched broccoli to roasted Brussels sprouts but is always restrained enough to be eaten straight up. It has an essentially cheesy flavor, like the good parts of boxed mac and cheese. It avoids the predicament a cheese friend describes of mediocre cheese: "I totally nothing'd it. Like pretzels, where I eat a whole bag and don't even realize." Great all-purpose cheese will keep you coming back mindfully, even sneakily.

ITALY | SHEEP

(UN)PASTEURIZED

**RECOMMENDED BRAND:** Mitica

**AROMA:** Full and fragrant

**TEXTURE:** Dense, firm, and occasionally waxy

**FLAVOR:** Rustically cheesy

**IN SHORT:** The all-purpose cheese

## Madeleine FROM SPROUT CREEK FARM

Inspired by Pecorino recipes, with a moistly firm and flaky texture, Madeleine is noticeably more delicate than other aged cheese produced by Sprout Creek, but markedly more intense than most aged goat cheeses from other countries. I chalk this up to cheese maker Colin McGrath's judicious use of salt. Many aged goats walk the dangerously boring line of bland and underseasoned; here, the seasonal milk's natural floral notes are pushed to the fore by the briny presence of salt, and the natural sweetness of goat milk, aged, is emphasized. The cheese is a study in contrasts, managing to be approachable but interesting enough for the guy who wants some special cheese.

## Gabietou

A riff on the traditional wheels of the Pyrenees, Gabietou is made of a two-thirds/one-third split between cow and sheep milk. The cheese was invented by Gabriel Bachelet in 2001, making it a positive newborn in the region where Ossau-Iraty (see page 201) has been made the same way for 5,000-plus years. Bachelet sells Gabietou to the two cheese agers (affineurs) Hervé Mons and Jean d'Alos, who each have their own treatment for maturation before selling it at roughly five months. When I first discovered Gabietou, it was revelatory: less pressing and less aging than its 100-percent sheep counterparts made for a moistly plump, pillowy texture. Brine washing imparted additional salt and a meaty funk otherwise unseen in these parts. The danger with Gabietou is that it's sold too young, when the texture can feel almost processed, the flavor muted. As a cheese friend says, "At this price, you shouldn't have to stop and think about what it tastes like." That is the difference between bland and subtle. Too-young Manchego types are tasteless; additional aging enables those subtle, fleeting flavors to unfold before you.

## Berkswell

The Fletchers' farmhouse has been known as Ram Hall since the sixteenth century, although Berkswell's production began in the early 1990s. Tasting Berkswell was the first time I "got" cheese seasonality. The idea that a cheese changes depending on when it's made, what the animals are eating, the humidity, the temperature, and the singularity of a place is a beautiful and romantic notion. I had cynically concluded that it was often employed as an excuse to cover up inconsistencies

---

**UNITED STATES** | **GOAT**

**UNPASTEURIZED**

**AROMA:** Wet rocks

**TEXTURE:** Flaky but smearable, chewy

**FLAVOR:** Good salt, floral, sweet on the finish

**IN SHORT:** The interesting everyday cheese

**FRANCE** | **COW/SHEEP**

**UNPASTEURIZED**

**RECOMMENDED BRAND:** Hervé Mons (primarily found at Whole Foods)

**AROMA:** Damp hay and curing pork

**TEXTURE:** Pillowy soft

**FLAVOR:** Green olive and *saucisson sec*

**IN SHORT:** Sensuous

APPROACHABLE

## SEND ITALY TO YOUR DOOR

Most cheese stores are supplied by the same handful of importers and distributors. Some import themselves, meaning they find cheeses in Europe and buy them direct. This is logistically complex, slow, and often expensive (if you're only buying for one store, volumes are low, and fixed costs are high). If you want to taste Italy without leaving the United States, there is no better retailer than New York City's DiPalo. They have never failed to confound me with half a dozen Italian cheeses I've never heard of, many of which are unpasteurized and small production. Still located in Little Italy, DiPalo has recently expanded its e-commerce business and ships cheese across the country. Still, there's no substitute for walking in the joint so you can talk and taste your way to a new discovery.

## THE MOST MISUSED WORD IN CHEESE

My fascination with cheese, and food generally, is fueled by the panoply of words that can be used to describe it. One that pops up a lot these days is "unctuous." It's typically used to describe a rich, runny, buttery cheese like a custardy-ripe Camembert.

In fact, the word means oily, and there's no better category for its use than sheep milk cheeses. At room temperature, they readily sweat butterfat, often beading up like a guy in an interrogation room. Even straight from the fridge (which is never the temperature at which I recommend eating cheese, but sometimes you've just gotta), their texture is often firm but just a shade from greasy. Unctuous they are, but don't expect a spreadable or slathery cheese in the mix.

and problems with cheese. And, in truth, it can be that excuse. But with Berkswell, I could taste the evolution, undeniable, right in front of me. Early season (spring) wheels are biscuity and delicate, laced with the undeniable fruitiness of wild strawberries (themselves nearly impossible to find, pure and more intense than the mammoth supermarket varieties most of us are used to). Later season (fall) wheels are preferred by the French export market, according to my friend and Neal's Yard co-owner Jason Hinds. They are husky and gamy, their lambiness amplified by unapologetic but appropriate salting. This spectrum of possibility exemplifies the wonder of farmhouse cheese.

**ENGLAND | SHEEP**

**UNPASTEURIZED**

**AROMA:** A whiff of fish

**TEXTURE:** Dense yet powdery

**FLAVOR:** Strawberry shortcake (spring wheels) or lamb chops (fall wheels)

**IN SHORT:** Triscuity

# Paški Sir

CROATIA | SHEEP
PASTEURIZED

**AROMA:** Saline and musky

**TEXTURE:** Dense but
incredibly moist

**FLAVOR:** Sage-rubbed lamb,
yet sweet

**IN SHORT:** A true taste
of place

Made on Pag Island in the Adriatic, off the coast of Croatia, this cheese is a testament to the resourcefulness of sheep and the amazing food that can be coaxed from a marginal landscape. The island's environment is remarkably harsh, with very little vegetation. Those grasses that do survive are buffeted by salt-water spray. The best fields for grazing, while studded with thousands of rocks, boast great quantities of sage, which impart a musky complexity to the sheep milk and its resulting cheese. The Paska Ovca sheep is the indigenous breed, smaller than average, and producing extremely limited quantities of milk (which is still harvested by hand!). A single wheel of cheese requires ten to twelve sheep, and the wheel is then aged for one year. Accordingly, it's not cheap. But it's worth it. It looks like just another Pecorino but manages to balance a flavor seesaw between toffee and game.

# Lord of the Hundreds

ENGLAND | SHEEP
UNPASTEURIZED

**AROMA:** Grass, cooked
mushroom

**TEXTURE:** Supple but grainy

**FLAVOR:** Sautéed shiitakes,
hint of caramel

**IN SHORT:** Elegant

In East Sussex, Cliff and Julie Dyball left careers in finance and insurance in 2002 to start making cheese. They named this unusual, blocky square after the Saxon tax collectors who worked on behalf of local lords, each one of whom oversaw a region of 100 shires. On the farm's property stands a marker where people would gather to pay their dues to the Lord of the Hundreds. In many European countries, medieval taxes were paid not in money but in food (often cheese), although I'm not sure that's the case here. It's a spectacular cheese, golden yellow, amber beneath the rind and slightly grainy from a minimum of six to eight months of age. It walks a remarkably fine line between savory and sweet. Rather than a gamy or lamb quality, there is the deep savor of butter-roasted mushrooms and underneath that, a suggestion of brown-butter caramel. It's been described as an English Manchego (see page 202), but I think it's more interesting than that.

# Ossau-Iraty-Brebis Pyrénées PDO

Lesser known than Manchego (see page 202) and Pecorino, but easily sexier and more approachable than either, are the aged sheep cheeses of the French Pyrenees. Firm, smooth, and supple, these cheeses strike a balance between fatty chew, impressions of grass and hay (without actually tasting like grass and hay), and a sweet nuttiness like aromatic clouds surrounding the carts of New York City nut vendors. The most aged and complex of them have a floral intensity that goes well beyond common if likable caramel tendencies. Some might call these cheeses boring. I'd argue that they're subtle and lingering, but quietly so. A word of warning, however: they often smell (bizarrely and intensely) of old fried fish. This aroma should dissipate with half an hour's exposure to air and should never impact flavor.

**FRANCE | SHEEP**

**(UN)PASTEURIZED**

**RECOMMENDED BRANDS:** Abbaye de Belloc, Agour, Onetik

**AROMA:** Hay, nut skin, sometimes fishy

**TEXTURE:** Moist break, firm yet sumptuous

**FLAVOR:** Toast, caramel, and green olive

**IN SHORT:** Red wine's best friend

# Queso Manchego PDO

SPAIN | SHEEP

(UN)PASTEURIZED

**RECOMMENDED BRAND:**
El Trigal

**AROMA:** Werther's Originals, peanuts

**TEXTURE:** Oily, chunky, dry

**FLAVOR:** Werther's Originals with the possibility of gaminess

**IN SHORT:** Crowd-pleasing

Although Manchego production is regulated, the guidelines are broad enough that a cheeses's final flavor and texture span a huge range. All Manchego must be produced from the milk of the Manchega sheep (those wheels labeled *artesano* or *artisanal* will always be made of unpasteurized milk) and within designated parts of the provinces of Albacete, Ciudad Real, Cuenca, and Toledo. Additionally, all wheels have a braided basket-weave imprint around the outside, meant to evoke the imprint of traditional esparto grass molds. But that's where the commonalities end. Wheels can be aged from sixty days to fourteen or more months; rinds may be treated with wax or other protective substances; milk can be raw or pasteurized; production can be automated or handmade. The upshot is this: Manchego is rarely offensive. It's also rarely mind-blowing. It's usually quite approachable and snackable; and with increased age comes increased piquancy, spice, and granularity. I've found a growing consistency of flavor across producers: a sweet, candied undertone that I believe has boosted Manchego's popularity enormously.

# The Best Queso Manchego PDO

SPAIN | SHEEP

UNPASTEURIZED

**BRANDS:** 1605 (Essex St. Cheese) and Manchego Curado (Pondini Imports)

**AROMA:** Orange blossom, mint, candied nuts

**TEXTURE:** Compact and fatty, never waxy or greasy

**FLAVOR:** Scrambled egg, chocolate-dipped citrus

**IN SHORT:** Game-changing

There are two Manchegos that deserve their own mention, so different are they from the rest of what's available. While Manchego production has come to be dominated by larger scale producers working with pasteurized milk, these are both made from unpasteurized, single-herd milk sources. I think of them as embodying the two extremes of what refined Manchego flavor can be. Pondini's certified organic Manchego is clean and fruity with discernible citrus notes. It's delicate and prone to a minty herbaceousness just beneath the rind. On the Sierra de la Solana farm, José Luis Martin produces the natural, unwaxed 1605 Manchego. The moist, compact paste smells like damp sheep and hay but tastes of the deeply comforting combination of scrambled eggs and serrano ham. Its finish is spicy, but akin to nutmeg and allspice rather than the harsh, fermented fruity spice that more industrial-aged Manchegos deliver. Just as Manchego can be many cheeses, these two offerings differ from each other. Together, however, they capture the wondrous spectrum of what exceptional, handcrafted, and authentic cheese can be.

# Malvarosa

SPAIN | SHEEP
PASTEURIZED
**AROMA:** Sweet milk and hay
**TEXTURE:** Sliceable but springy
**FLAVOR:** Butterscotch
**IN SHORT:** Candied

Tasting Malvarosa was the first time I made an immediate connection between aged sheep milk cheese and the concentrated yellow syrup of a cellophane-wrapped butterscotch candy. Not brown sugar and butter, but those crinkly lozenges that someone's grandma might have given you as a kid. To this day, such a butterscotch finish takes me by surprise because the cheese begins with a pleasant, full, buttery persona that appears to be completely straightforward. Then that sunny sweetness pops up at the end. Malvarosa is a singular cheese, made in Valencia from the milk of native Guirra sheep and aged in a knotted hammock of cheesecloth, which impresses the cheese with folds and ridges where the cloth has lain. Despite its unique production, it sets a standard for the easy likeability of many similar recipes. Do watch out for rock-hard Malvarosa, often smattered in green-gray mold. Such a wheel is too old and won't give you the moist, yielding texture that you deserve. Plus, it's likely to taste more like wax than anything else.

APPROACHABLE

# GranQueso FROM ROTH CHEESE

I've been calling this an American cow-milk Manchego (see page 202) for years. Partially it's the waxy, basket-weave rind and the dense, granular texture. But more so its sweetness. The six-plus-month original is all coconut and Werther's Originals. The fifteen-plus-month reserve looks fearfully waxy and dry, but under tooth is the equivalent of Girl Scout Samoas: coconut, cocoa, and buttery crunch studded with protein clusters so dense they're not crystalline as much as food unto themselves. By comparison, the original seems almost boring. The rusty rind is rubbed in a proprietary spice blend including cinnamon and paprika, which may well contribute to the aromatics. I guess this is the cheese equivalent of a juicy red wine—something wine folks might call pedestrian. Laypeople, on the other hand, rave at its deliciousness and gulp it down. Eat on!

# Verano and Invierno FROM VERMONT SHEPHERD

People who've worked in cheese for several decades will remember when Major Farm in Westminster West, Vermont, started making a cheese called Vermont Shepherd. That was in the early 1990s, and in one fell swoop the Majors proved that Americans could make great cheese from sheep milk. In so doing, they cemented Vermont's sustaining reputation as a leader in the resurrection of craft American cheese. Their cheese was a direct homage to France's Ossau-Iraty (see page 201), and it was superb. Today, David Major and Yesenia Ielpi continue to work David's family farm, now simply called Vermont Shepherd. The flagship cheese, made seasonally when the sheep are on summer pasture, is aged in a small cave mounded beneath the hillside. *Verano* (summer) is distinguished from the off-season mixed-milk cheese *Invierno* (winter). It's rare to find Verano outside of the Northeast; often it's gone from shelves by New Year's. Production is small, and its limited availability is testament to its enduring greatness. As many of the French Pyrenees sheep cheeses become increasingly candied in flavor, I especially appreciate well-aged (six-plus months) Verano. It's got a complex balance of lanolin; fruity acid; salt; and a delicious whiff of damp earth just beneath the rough, sandy rind. The mixed-milk Invierno tends to be milder and more buttery, with mushroomy mellowness. Look for a wheel shaped like a flying saucer, where the seams of two plastic colanders used to drain the cheese curd have met around the perimeter. Each wheel is stamped with the batch number and a small, woolly sheep.

**UNITED STATES** | COW

**PASTEURIZED**

**AROMA:** Butterscotch candy

**TEXTURE:** Crayons

**FLAVOR:** Coconut butter cookies

**IN SHORT:** The Samoa of cheese

**UNITED STATES**

SHEEP AND SHEEP/COW

**UNPASTEURIZED**

**AROMA:** The aging cave (Having been there, I can confirm it's more about grass, sheep milk, and exposed earth than dank rock.)

**TEXTURE:** Firm, dense, and incredibly smooth

**FLAVOR:** Too many layers to capture—sweet, rich, gamy, acidic, balanced

**IN SHORT:** The new American classic

# Good Shepherd Sheep Cheese (Pyrenees-style) FROM GOOD SHEPHERD FARM

**UNITED STATES | SHEEP**

**UNPASTEURIZED**

**AROMA:** Mac 'n' cheese

**TEXTURE:** Cold butter pastry

**FLAVOR:** Intense, complex, layers, fruit, brine

**IN SHORT:** Once you pop, you can't stop

At the edge of the Appalachian mountains, in Kentucky's first sheep dairy, you can find a brilliant example of what makes the best aged sheep cheeses compulsive. You keep eating them even as you ask yourself why you're eating them. The answer: you can't stop. There is some potato chip/Frito-like collision of fat, salt, and acidity that feels elemental and compels you to one more bite. Let's start with the texture. It's firm, but very buttery, punctuated by crunchy bits. These aren't fine and granular but are buried in the smooth, dense expanse like a nugget. The presence of salt makes other flavors pop more brightly without the cheese ever tasting salty. There is the essence of something red and juicy, like small spring strawberries, buried under butter pastry. The Dotsons make cheese seasonally from the milk of entirely pastured East Friesian sheep. While this is laudable, it's the taste of their cheese that makes it exceptional.

# Boont Corners FROM PENNYROYAL FARMSTEAD CHEESE

**UNITED STATES**

**SHEEP/GOAT**

**UNPASTEURIZED**

**AROMA:** Grassy

**TEXTURE:** Dense and smooth to crumbly, but always buttery with fat

**FLAVOR:** Ranging from mild tang to complex caramel to subtly smoked game

**IN SHORT:** Truly a different cheese each time you taste it

Mendocino, California's Pennyroyal Farm is a mind-blowing model of agricultural synergy and seasonal cheese making. Land costs in this part of the world are largely prohibitive for cheese makers. Pennyroyal manages as a partner vineyard/creamery hybrid. The prices that can be claimed for wine essentially subsidize a painstaking farmstead cheese operation of sheep and goats, with production lasting from March until December. Their signature Boont Corners is made from a blend of sheep and goat milk. Because these animals produce milk seasonally, the cheese begins with a higher percentage of sheep in March and evolves into a 100 percent goat-milk cheese by season's end in December. Additionally, the age profile changes from a minimum of two months to a maximum of six-plus. As a result, one cheese (Boont Corners) is really hundreds of different cheeses, each comprised of its own milk blend and age profile. The vintage (four to six months) that I've tasted was like a complex goat Gouda (see page 131), caramelly and dense, while the reserve (180-plus days) had become firmer and nuttier, with more pronounced acidity. At any age and blend, this cheese is anchored by a seductive and lingering sweetness that makes it approachable enough for the masses but fascinating for the connoisseurs.

# Queso Zamorano PDO

The prevalence and importance of sheep dairying and cheese making in the region of Castile and León is well documented as far back as the eleventh century. From this tradition comes the aged sheep cheese Zamorano, made exclusively with the milk of indigenous sheep breeds Churra and Castellana. If you get a chance to see the label on the wheel of cheese, look for the identifier craftsman, which signifies raw milk and animal rennet (i.e., the most traditional recipe). The cheese must be produced in the province of Zamora and aged for a minimum of 100 days, although it takes six months to really get good. It's said that you get better wine from vines that have to struggle in inhospitable soil for water and nutrients. Zamora presents a comparable situation for cheese: a harsh climate with minimal forage means that sheep must extract maximum nutrition from limited feed. This influences the flavor and quality of Zamorano, and differentiates it from other Spanish sheep cheeses. I look forward to warm, buttery flavor up front, with a toasted nut and spice finish on well-aged wheels.

**SPAIN | SHEEP**

**(UN)PASTEURIZED**

**RECOMMENDED BRAND:** Marques del Castillo

**AROMA:** Sheep milk

**TEXTURE:** Granular but smooth with fat

**FLAVOR:** Spicy, balanced by buttery fat

**IN SHORT:** As the locals say, warm and friendly

# Pastorale FROM SARTORI

Wisconsin maker Sartori has a number of limited-edition cheeses that are produced seasonally and available only until the batch runs out. Pastorale was their first foray into cheese made with sheep milk. The rind is electric orange, rubbed with paprika for a sweet and smoky finish. Unlike most of their Parmesan type cheeses, I find Pastorale to be surprisingly rustic—less candied than BellaVitano (see page 310) and boasting a subtle smokiness more like a hot dog cooked on a campfire than the actual smoke itself. While most of Sartori's cheeses have a wet-yet-crumbly texture, Pastorale is smoother and denser owing to the high-fat sheep milk. After forty-five minutes at room temperature, it goes greasy like a good Manchego (see page 202).

**UNITED STATES**

**SHEEP AND COW**

**PASTEURIZED**

**AROMA:** Whiff of smoke

**TEXTURE:** Firm but grainy

**FLAVOR:** Muted smoke

**IN SHORT:** Idiazabal by way of Italy by way of Wisconsin

# Queso Ibores PDO

SPAIN | GOAT
UNPASTEURIZED

AROMA: Acidic, buttery

TEXTURE: At the crossroads of crumbly and elastic

FLAVOR: Piquant, goat milky

IN SHORT: Spicy goat

In western Spain, adjacent to the Portuguese border, lies the harsh province of Extremadura (even its name captures the extremity). Blistering hot, dry summers make it a challenging land for ruminants, although indigenous breeds of goats and sheep have adapted to the tough grazing. Ibores relies on the milk of three local breeds, primarily the Serrana because the other two are nearly extinct. In a reversal of the typical seasonal milking cycle of goats, Ibores goats begin milking in autumn and are dried off (finished milking) by spring. They spend their summers on mountain slopes instead of in the punishing, arid valleys. The best Ibores delivers subtle piquancy and clean edging-on-caramel goat milk.

# Pecorino delle Balze Volterrane PDO

ITALY | SHEEP
(UN)PASTEURIZED

AROMA: Red currant and sheep oil

TEXTURE: Firm and fatty, the slightest bit mealy

FLAVOR: Fruit acid and nut butter, where the whole exceeds the sum of its parts

IN SHORT: One of the Pecorinos you go hunting for

Young, rindless Pecorino (see page 196) is tart and tangy, but many wheels have an unfortunate sour-milk imbalance. Then you encounter the rare aged Pecorino that has a high, red fruit acidity anchored by round, savory flavors: toasted nuts; a bit of lamb; tight, plump Castelvetrano olives. Pecorinos like this have a complexity rarely encountered outside of Italy. It's a flavor layering in which big, obvious qualities, like salt or caramel, are absent, leaving you to return again and again for another small bite that might finally reveal what it is that you're tasting, and why it is so revelatory.

# Pecorino Ginepro

ITALY | SHEEP
PASTEURIZED

RECOMMENDED BRAND: Mitica

AROMA: Sheep yogurt

TEXTURE: Moistly crumbly, mealy in the mouth

FLAVOR: Tart, almond

IN SHORT: Super lactic

This Roman Pecorino is so shockingly white that you might think it was made from goat milk. Its name and its rind come from repeated bathings in balsamic vinegar steeped with juniper. The resulting layers are so dark that they appear black and often flake off like paint chips when you handle the cheese. The romantics would say that this careful treatment imbues the moist, crumbling paste with essences of woody balsamic or resinous juniper. In truth, I find it's more of a window dressing: the cheese is about well-made, medium-aged Italian sheep milk. Next to French sheep cheeses, it's remarkably lean and lactic, with the pronounced potency of almond extract. Eating this cheese proves the purpose of fruit mostarda: chunky and sweet, with the singing high spice of mustard seed or powder, it tames the cheese's acidity and focuses your attention on the smooth, fatty finish.

PECORINO GINEPRO

# Queso Idiazabal PDO

SPAIN | SHEEP

UNPASTEURIZED

**AROMA:** First night of fall, a few blocks from a smoking chimney

**TEXTURE:** Firm, can be mealy

**FLAVOR:** Tang and fruitwood smoke

**IN SHORT:** Autumnal

A tip from a cheesemonger friend: this nearly unpronounceable Basque cheese is loosely spoken as "idiots having a ball" (id-ee-ah-tha-ball). Take it from someone who judged almost fifty Idiazabals in one day: there is a range of possibility with this cheese. I've found that the least industrially produced wheels are smaller in size. Those that resemble Manchego (see page 202) tend to be the blandest and least interesting (more like a 3 on the flavor intensity scale), but by no means bad. While you're highly unlikely to find the unsmoked version in the United States, don't expect that you're relegated to eating something that tastes like a smoked sausage. Artisanal Idiazabal offers smoke as only one component of flavor; there's a fruity acidity, followed by the meatiness of rare lamb and then the lingering whiff of smoke. (Traditionally, the cheese was hung by the fire to cure, so it picked up some smokiness but wasn't directly smoked.) It's the difference between smelling a suggestion of smoke and having someone squeeze the bottle of liquid smoke onto your tongue.

# Queso Roncal PDO

SPAIN | SHEEP

UNPASTEURIZED

**RECOMMENDED BRAND:** Puente del Esca

**AROMA:** Woolen

**TEXTURE:** Pressed and granular

**FLAVOR:** Lamb-chop fat cap

**IN SHORT:** Manchego's country cousin

The first Spanish cheese to receive PDO status (in 1981), Roncal is now made by only five producers. Milk must come from the Latxa sheep, a breed native to Navarra and Basque Country. Fluffy and long-haired, Latxa are used primarily for milking and graze in the wild, rolling hills of Navarra. Production and aging of the cheese must occur in one of seven municipalities in the Valle de Roncal. Unlike the better known Manchego (see page 202), Roncal has a rough, bark-like rind and shies away from sweet or caramel flavors. Cheese folk often describe it as spicy Manchego. Its character is more rustic, with piquant fruity notes. As the table cheese of its area, Roncal is meant for snacking alongside ubiquitous bottles of red wine and cider.

# Tomme du Haut Barry

FRANCE | SHEEP

PASTEURIZED

**AROMA:** At the intersection of yeasty and fruity

**TEXTURE:** Chewy

**FLAVOR:** Fermentation, like pickled fruit

**IN SHORT:** The bresaola of cheese

Although it's made in the cradle of Ossau-Iraty (see page 201) Land—Aveyron in the Midi-Pyrénées—there's nothing recognizable about this cheese. To begin with, it looks like a stone cannon ball. The paste is dense and smooth, chewy, but not quite as fatty-limp as Ossau-Iraty. You can feel the cheese the moment it hits your tongue, like a swig of kombucha, full of fermented fruit. It's floral and reminds me of cured beef. There's a complexity and intensity to this one far beyond the normal range of pleasant, easy sheep-cheese eating.

APPROACHABLE

# Fiore Sardo PDO

Different from the PDO cheese Pecorino Sardo, Fiore Sardo may be smoked as part of its ripening process. This cheese is made across Sardinia, and its legitimacy for name protection comes from the historically critical role of sheep farming on the island (often the sole source of income for farmers on otherwise marginal lands). Its name (*fiore* means "flower") refers to the flowering plants that were traditionally used to coagulate the curd of the cheese. These days, makers use either lamb or kid (goat) rennet; I've found these rather than calf rennet produce a cheese more rustic and animally in flavor. Many brands of Fiore Sardo are semifirm; vaguely smoked; and generally insipid, if inoffensive. True Fiore Sardo is crackly and flaky—Pondini's is aged four to six months—the wheels tacky with lard and reeking powerfully of acidic smoldering wood. The curd remains uncooked during cheese making and the cheese avoids sweet or caramel flavors entirely. Instead, a powerful, sheepy rusticity is overlain with damp, dark smokiness from the bark of local cork trees. It's a cheese for cold, wet weather: hearty, fortifying, and glorious.

**ITALY | SHEEP**

**(UN)PASTEURIZED**

**RECOMMENDED BRAND:** Pondini Imports

**AROMA:** Wet, smoldering fire pit

**TEXTURE:** Hard and chunky

**FLAVOR:** Piquant, gamy, smoky

**IN SHORT:** Big

# Gran Cacio Etrusco

ITALY | SHEEP
PASTEURIZED

**AROMA:** Musty cellar

**TEXTURE:** Firm with tiny, jagged pockmarks

**FLAVOR:** Salty, nutmeg spice

**IN SHORT:** The companion cheese

A great pleasure of visiting cheese makers is witnessing how they eat their cheese and remembering that having a piece on a cracker isn't necessarily The Way. Gran Cacio is made by a Pecorino Romano (below) producer, still based in Lazio. With milk hand-selected from four to five dairy farmers, this smaller format wheel is hand-salted with Sicilian sea salt and allowed to age for six months, during which time a thin, knobbly brown rind develops. On the tongue, Gran Cacio is salt, like an accidental swallow of ocean. Then there is an insistent burn, but somehow less fiery than Pecorino Romano. Many people would say it's too salty. But like Pecorino Romano, it's not made to be eaten alone. That cheese is made for cooking with, this one as a companion finger food. It makes you crave a bite of something wet, sweet, and juicy. A perfect slice of cantaloupe. A dribbly fall pear. Maybe even—sacrilege!—the sweet-tart succulence of satsuma. I like cheeses that make me think differently about cheese, as this one does.

# Pecorino Romano PDO

ITALY | SHEEP
PASTEURIZED

**RECOMMENDED BRAND:** Fulvi

**AROMA:** Sheepy

**TEXTURE:** Firm and moistly flaky

**FLAVOR:** So intensely salty, but more . . .

**IN SHORT:** The cheese for seasoning

Pecorino Romano is so called because, until the 1950s, it was made exclusively in the countryside of Rome. Then, the Sardinian president of Italy expanded its approved production area to include Sardinia. The cheese can be produced between October and July, and there is now a single producer left in the approved four provinces of Lazio (Rome). Pecorino Romano is generally regarded as a cooking cheese, and mistakenly, as interchangeable with Parmigiano-Reggiano (see page 320). In fact, the cheese is far more intense and saltier than Parm-Reg, and while it's most often grated it need not only be. Fulvi is the last Roman maker of a traditionally Roman cheese. It's aged for ten to twelve months, although the PDO guidelines mandate only six months. The Sicilian and Soprevisana breeds of sheep in Lazio yield less, but richer, milk. As a result, the cheese is firm, moist, and flaky rather than hard, dry, and crumbly. It's like Maldon sea salt as opposed to Morton's. Speaking of salt, Fulvi still hand salts its wheels, allowing dry salt to migrate into the cheese during aging, rather than brining the cheese and sealing its exterior with a crust. All this said, Pecorino Romano is salty. Its flavor is so assertive that your tongue feels instantly hairy. My prescription is to eat this cheese with other foods. When I was a kid, at the beach, I used to wash my plum or peach in the surf before I ate it. It coated each bite with the luminescent brine of the ocean. That's what Pecorino Romano does for fava beans, or pesto, or amatriciana. Straight up, your lips are likely to burn, but paired properly it is a wash of milky sea.

APPROACHABLE

## MY PICKS: APPROACHABLE MANCHEGO TYPES

I'm looking for firm yet buttery texture. Crowd-pleasing flavor that's subtle, not boring. Hints of sweetness that don't bash the palate like cheap candy. And perhaps most of all, cheeses that defy expectations of what sheep or goat milk taste like.

### Ticklemore

It's English, and goat milk, and flying saucer–shaped. The texture is two-tone, and the cheese manages to capture floral and herbaceous notes. It's like eating spring air made solid. (see page 192)

### Gabietou

For those who've known and loved an Ossau-Iraty (see page 201), here is a fleshier, silkier cousin at once savory and delicate. In my tasting notes it reads, "This cheese strokes your tongue."

### Good Shepherd Sheep Cheese from Good Shepherd Farm

I'd never heard of this cheese, although I know and love Verano, the first American interpretation of Ossau-Iraty (see page 201). It was so layered and complex that I couldn't stop until I chewed up the little strip of rind. One of the best cheeses I ate in 2015. (see page 206)

### Manchego (ideally, 1605 from Essex Street Cheese and/or Organic Manchego from Pondini Imports)

For everyone who thinks they know what Manchego is about, you don't until you eat one of these. Supremely balanced, radically different from one another, new tricks from an old dog. (see page 202)

## MY PICKS: INTENSE MANCHEGO TYPES

Intense Manchego types start sweet and candied, whereas those butterscotch or caramel flavors are layered and persistent. From there, the flavors arc into the piquant and gamy—rustic, lamb choppy, spicy, and ultimately unapologetically and seriously salty.

### GranQueso (Reserve) from Roth Cellars

The cheese equivalent of the Girl Scouts' famed Samoas, sans sugar: coconut, butter cookie, and chocolate. (see page 205)

### Fiore Sardo PDO (ideally, Pondini Imports)

In a sea of boring Fiore Sardos, this one embodies the rusticity of a land so wild and Spartan that only sheep could thrive there. Blanketed in piquant cork wood smoke, heady with gamy milk fat. (see page 211)

### Pecorino Romano PDO (ideally, Fulvi)

For everyone who treats this cheese like mere salt, take note. I remember the day I showered it atop a bowl of canned cannellini beans and fed it to my ten-month-old daughter. It became a simple yet elevated meal. She ate the whole thing. (see page 212)

### TASTING ONE
## MANCHEGOS

See for yourself how one name encompasses myriad cheeses. Young Manchego should be buttery and easy; aged offers more caramel or spicy notes. My two favorite Manchegos promise a superior level of complexity.

**1. Young Manchego (aged less than six months)** (see page 202)

**2. Aged Manchego (aged more than six months)** (see page 202)

**3. The Best Manchego** (see page 202)

### TASTING TWO
## THE INFLUENCE OF THE PYRENEES

France's region for aged sheep cheese has inspired makers to innovate and reinterpret the classic recipe.

**1. Gabietou** (see page 198)

**2. Ossau-Iraty PDO** (see page 201)

**3. Verano from Vermont Shepherd** (see page 205) **or Good Shepherd Sheep Cheese** (see page 206)

### TASTING THREE
## THE FLAVOR ARC OF AGED SHEEP

From fresh and tangy to subtly savory to fermented and fruity, sheep milk can be many things. What remains constant is a full, rich fattiness that sits heavy on the tongue.

**1. Pecorino Toscano PDO (Fresco)** (see page 197)

**2. Lord of the Hundreds** (see page 200)

**3. Tomme du Haut Barry** (see page 210)

### TASTING FOUR
## GOAT CHEESE, BEYOND THE LOG

I say it again and again: goat milk is maligned and misunderstood by folks who have had only poorly made fresh goat cheese. Aged goat cheese offers a new world of herbaceous, grassy, and nutty flavors.

**1. Garrotxa** (see page 193)

**2. Queso de Murcia al Vino PDO** (see page 194)

**3. Madeleine from Sprout Creek Farm** (see page 198)

# PAIRINGS WITH MANCHEGO TYPES

## PAIRING OVERVIEW

**SOFTLY HERBACEOUS**

**MAC-AND-CHEESE POWDER**

**BUTTERSCOTCH**

**SALTY/SMOKY/GAMY**

## BEAR IN MIND

Fatty sheep can stand up to a lot (of acid, tannin, bitterness).

Mouth-coating richness that feels heavy with straight-up sweet or buttery pairings.

Because of their firm texture, these cheeses are a good vehicle for soft, smearable things. The cheese becomes the cracker.

## CLASSIC PAIRINGS

(Whole flavor spectrum) with acidic/tannic wine: aged sheep milk cheeses with Merlot, Nebbiolo, Tempranillo, Sangiovese

(Mac-and-cheese powder/butterscotch) with tart, fruity, smear: Manchego and quince paste

(Salty/smoky/gamy) with smooth, sweet starch: Pecorino Toscano (Fresco) and fava beans

(Salty/smoky/gamy) with high-acid effervescence: Idiazabal and Basque white wine Txakoli(na)

### 1. RAW NUTS

Almonds, hazelnuts, pistachios, and walnuts are my picks over sweet, fatty cashews, pecans, macadamias, or peanuts. Each offers crunch and notes of astringency, tartness, or bitterness that balance fatty-rich cheese, while complementing the soft, nut skin essence of many Manchego types.

**FLAVOR SPECTRUM:** 1–10

### 2. SMEARABLE FRUIT PASTES/SPREADS

I avoid smearable condiments with creamy, buttery cheeses because I don't want a mouthful of goo. The Manchego types are the first of the firm cheeses that can act as cracker or bread slice, and a favorite (incredibly easy) appetizer of mine is one of these cheeses smeared with fruit paste. What's key? Acidity! And, toward the more intense end of the flavor spectrum, the possibility of spice. Honey or strawberry jam on these cheeses feels like a sticky, drippy mess. A tart or spicy fruit spread cuts fat and salt while complementing nutty, earthy, and gamy flavors.

**FLAVOR SPECTRUM (TART FRUIT):** 1–7
**FLAVOR SPECTRUM (SPICY FRUIT):** 3–10

### 3. BROWN ALE

There is a place on the flavor spectrum of Manchego types where the cheeses have a lanolin or sheep flavor anchored by smooth, fatty paste and an essential caramel quality. In this place, the chocolaty, grassy flavors of brown ale become symphonic. A critical and important component: the ale has scrubbing bubbles that slice through sheep fat so you can eat and drink more.

**FLAVOR SPECTRUM:** 3–7

BARELY BUZZED

MONTGOMERY'S CHEDDAR

TOUSSAINT

# Cheddar

BARBER'S CHEDDAR

CORRA LINN

CHESHIRE

HOOK'S
CHEDDAR

**SPECIALTY SHOP**

**Toussaint**
PAGE 234

**Wensleydale**
PAGE 230

**Cheshire**
PAGE 234

**Caerphilly**
PAGE 236

**Lancashire**
PAGE 236

**Red Leicester**
PAGE 230

**Double Gloucester**
PAGE 233

**Landaff**
PAGE 237

**AVAILABILITY  SUPERMARKET ➤➤**

**Mild Cheddar**
PAGE 231

**FLAVOR  APPROACHABLE ➤➤**

| **1** | **2** | **3** | **4** | **5** |
|---|---|---|---|---|
| BLAND | MILD (NOT BLAND) | GRASSY MILK | BUTTERMILK | SOUR CREAM |

**INTENSE**

| **6** | **7** | **8** | **9** | **10** |
|---|---|---|---|---|
| MEET *HELVETICUS* | MALTY | ACID BALANCED BY CARAMEL | OF THE EARTH, GAMY | ALL THAT, PLUS SOUR |

# I say "Cheddar" and you think mild. Medium. Sharp. How can you not? Cheddar is the first cheese that most of us understand to exist along a

flavor spectrum. For cheese geeks, Cheddar draws immediate associations with the specific cheese-making process of Cheddaring, during which curd is allowed to form thick layers that are cut and stacked atop one another to press out moisture (and enable acidity to develop).

Whether you prefer your Cheddar white or yellow gives away your hometown faster than a nasally drawl or pronouncing car like "cah." Even the British classify their Cheddar comparatively, although their equivalent to sharp is known, far more politely, as mature Cheddar (which to this day makes me think of a cheese that will refrain from calling me names). Cheddar is still the most common reference point for firm cheese. People tell me, "Well, I mean, obviously, I like Cheddar." Or, "I want something really strong. Not like Cheddar strong but, you know, strong." Cheddar is the closest thing that Americans have to a national cheese, and with good reason. We've been making it, or some variant of it, since settling the colonies in the seventeenth century.

But when I say Cheddar, I'm thinking beyond the block. Mild, medium, and sharp are benchmarks of flavor intensity, to be sure; but as I learned when I met English-style or clothbound Cheddar early in my mongering gig, the old familiar cheese could be anything but. It could be enormous and cylindrical, its texture dry and feathery rather than the moist crumble I grew up on. The biggest shock was Cheddar's potential flavor range. Suddenly I met cheeses that were dank and earthy, or high and bright like lemon, or with horseradish's spicy prickle. Some Cheddars bordered on candied with butterscotch or caramel innuendo. And then there were all these English cheeses that weren't Cheddar but were Cheddar-like: each bite broke apart into distinct chunks under tooth—and the tastes were lactic, tangy, and savory. I learned those were called the Territorials, named for distinct regions of England such as Cheshire, Gloucester, Lancashire, and Leicester, each one a precursor to the only cheese that has become known to, I would wager, everyone. The most profound revelation to be found by stepping through the Cheddar Gateway is that mild, approachable cheeses of this type need not be rubbery, bland, or so-called mild any more than intense and strong Cheddar types need be overly acidic, mouthwatering, or so-called extra sharp.

The possibility of these nuances was so foreign to me that I assumed that all good Cheddar was British (and, by association, that all American Cheddar was, if not bad, then predictably uniform and uninspiring). The week before I transitioned from full-time cubicle-goer to full-time cheesemonger, my office threw me a going-away party. I agreed to bring the cheese and included a dense, buttery, lemony white Cheddar. There was nothing smooth or gummy about it. Each tiny crumble veritably exploded on the tongue. It dissolved creamily, in infinite layers of milk, then brine, then citrus. I guess you could call it sharp, but it was so much more than a burning feeling. Needless to say, everyone loved it. When the one Brit in the office asked what the cheese was and where it was from, I realized I wasn't sure. So, I committed the number-one Cardinal Sin of Mongering and lied. I knew the name was Grafton Cheddar; as for the provenance I had no clue. There was nothing Cracker Barrel–ish about it and so I guessed. "England," I claimed (hoping I sounded authoritative). "Really?" he asked. "Are you sure?" Of course that made me defensive (I mean, after all, I had been working on a cheese counter at night after work. Surely I knew the difference between American and English Cheddar) and I assured everyone that yes, we were eating an English Cheddar. Couldn't everyone tell? I mean, it was so much better than the Cheddar we all grew up with. The Americans nodded solemnly.

Indeed. Of course, I was completely wrong. Grafton 2 Year was a Vermont Cheddar, and simply better than the ones I ate as a kid. It was the first block Cheddar I encountered that was mind-blowing, just as Montgomery's Cheddar (see page 251) was the first clothbound version that revealed to me the world of Cheddar beyond the block.

Cheddar, more than any other cheese type, can be divided into two camps: the thinking person's Cheddar and the eating person's Cheddar. I don't mean that you're not a thinker if you want to eat, any more than someone who wants to ponder isn't going to end up taking that piece of cheese down, eventually. But there is a lot (billions of pounds) of Cheddar that's wholly unremarkable. It's not bad, it's just not interesting. It offers the comfort of fat, protein, and salt, perhaps with a little zip at the end if you're into that sort of thing. And that's just fine.

I'm concerned here with the evolving flavors of Cheddar types. Some of the most extraordinary and easy-to-adore cheeses I've met in the past few years have been block Cheddars that are made with an adjunct culture that delivers a wild and addictive new flavor to the world of cheese. You keep going back for a small bite, a little crumble, a piece of your friend's piece, thinking, "What is that?" Or not thinking at all, just sensing that you want more.

There is a resurrection of British farmhouse cheese happening, and many of the original Cheddar types that were nearly destroyed by industrialization in postwar Britain are returning. Their complexity and grace, their handcraftedness, are especially humbling to anyone who has tasted the stuff that rolls off factory lines. And there are the outliers, which as history shows are really the originators of the Cheddar type. These are cheeses (French!) that taste of ancient volcanic soil, of a dying art and lifestyle.

With this enormous range, a particular pet peeve of mine is the common inclusion of Cheddar in recipes calling for melted cheese. The truth is, most Cheddars aren't great melting cheeses. Unless they're very young (mild), they don't melt smoothly but separate greasily, immediately congealing moments away from heat. But Cheddar *is* a consummate eating cheese. The Brits have an entire meal based on this premise: a ploughman's lunch is simply a hunk of cheese, a piece of bread, and a pickle for much-needed acidity (and juice!). My most common lazy-weeknight family dinner is a sizable hunk of Cheddar (usually clothbound), a second cheese that's usually spreadable, bread, and a salad (maybe pickles too). Cheddar is so familiar that we tend to ignore its possibilities. In my house, it's the meat substitute, the weekend lunch you eat standing at the kitchen counter, the post-gym snack. If you think you know Cheddar, I'm here to tell you the fun is only just beginning.

# Chapter Guide

Cheddar, not unlike Brie, has become a placeholder word to refer to a general flavor and texture type. There is no Brie de Meaux (see page 102) equivalent in the world of Cheddar—no single Cheddar whose origin, ingredients, make process, or aging are so singular as to lock down a protected name. There is a PDO for West Country Farmhouse Cheddar, but this encompasses five separate producers of five differently named English Cheddars.

The U. S. Department of Agriculture has a standard for American-made Cheddar dating back to 1956, and producers today must adhere to it. Cheddar is a cheese "made by the Cheddaring process or *another procedure* which produces a finished cheese having the same physical and chemical properties as the cheese produced by the Cheddaring process" (*my emphasis*).

## WHAT TO KNOW

**SO WHAT'S CHEDDARING CHEESE?** When I started teaching cheese classes, I neatly explained Cheddar as being a cheese that is Cheddared. Cheddaring is a potential step in the cheese-making process: Whey is drained from curd, which is allowed to knit into a mat at the bottom of the cheese vat. This mat is then cut into strips or blocks that are stacked atop one another, unstacked, and restacked in an effort to press out whey (moisture) and encourage the development of acidity. As the U.S. Department of Agriculture explains, however, if one can achieve the same textural and chemical properties without Cheddaring, the resulting cheese can still be called Cheddar. The Cheddaring process is slow and labor-intensive; using it rather than some combination of heating, pressing, and bacterial culture blends is an unlikely choice for a larger, more industrialized producer. Cheddaring requires time and hands. Although you can make impressive cheese without Cheddaring, I regard those cheeses which are Cheddared as truer and more authentic. At the end of the day, however, Cheddaring doesn't guarantee a tastier cheese.

**WHAT MAKES A CHEESE A CHEDDAR TYPE (IF IT'S NOT CHEDDARED)?** To start with, the U.S. Department of Agriculture has cheese-making parameters that define Cheddar. The cheese must be "made from cow's milk with or without the addition of coloring matter and with common salt, contains not more than 39 percent of moisture, and in the water-free substance, contains not less than 50 percent of milkfat." But for the purposes of Cheddar as a gateway cheese, there is something more experiential. There's a particular mouthfeel to Cheddar types, a texture that is moist yet firm and that breaks into chunks as you bite down. It's not granular. It's not elastic. You can feel that before your cheese was a cohesive piece, it was comprised of curd chunks that were pressed together. This texture is shared between cheeses of France, England, and the United States whether or not they are Cheddared. Cheddar types need not be restricted to cow milk, although this is both traditional and predominant.

## WHAT'S THE DIFFERENCE BETWEEN BLOCK AND CLOTHBOUND?

Block Cheddars, as the term suggests, are cheeses produced in a larger block format (in some factory settings, up to several thousand pounds). This block is then cut up into smaller blocks for aging and distribution.

➻ Block Cheddar is more likely to be aiming for a typical American identity of mild, medium, or sharp (though not always).

➻ Block Cheddar is more likely to cost less because it can be aged in plastic in big refrigerators and doesn't require the same kind of labor-intensive care as clothbound Cheddar.

➻ Clothbound Cheddar has flavors that are less about sharpness (acid) and more about complexity: earthy, caramel, brothy, or fruity flavors prevail.

➻ Clothbound Cheddar is made in a wheel typically ranging from twenty to sixty pounds. This wheel is wrapped in muslin or similar fabric and sealed with a semipermeable fat layer, usually lard.

➻ As a result, clothbound Cheddar loses more moisture as it ages, resulting in a drier, flakier texture than block Cheddar.

➻ Because clothbound cheeses have a breathable outer layer, and because the cheese is contracting as it loses moisture, it's not uncommon to see cracks around the perimeter of the cheese that have blue mold in them. This is totally harmless and doesn't have an appreciable impact on flavor.

➻ Clothbound Cheddar will cost more money. Its aging (typically nine to eighteen months long) requires flipping, brushing, and hands-on maintenance that's quite intensive.

➻ Making cheese in a large block that can be sealed in plastic and aged in refrigeration is a choice driven by increased efficiencies. When you are presented with two similarly named cheeses (Cheddar, or Double Gloucester, see page 233; or Lancashire, see page 236), one made in a block and the other in a wheel (clothbound or not)—the wheel cheese will always cost more. You are rewarded with a cheese whose flavor and complexity are infinitely greater, more nuanced, and more alive.

➻ Some Cheddar types (block and wheel) are developing a new flavor identity (sweeter, nuttier, hedging toward tropical fruity), thanks to the introduction of adjunct cultures not traditional to Cheddar making (see page 232).

➻ While eating the rind won't hurt you, I don't endorse eating hard, dry, sharp-edged rinds. Aged cheeses have been sitting somewhere for many months, and the rind is the barrier between the interior and air during that entire time. Hard, dry rinds are typically chewy and taste like a cheese's aging environment.

## WHAT TO AVOID

➻ **COLOR:** Darker yellow or tan color just beneath a cloth rind is typical. This shouldn't be more than a quarter-inch thick, nor should it permeate the center of the cheese. While clothbound cheeses may develop cracks and harmless blue veining, the exposed, cut face of these cheeses should not have specks of blue or green mold. This is an indication the cheese has been sitting, precut in plastic, for too long. The mold won't hurt you and may be scraped off, but the cheese is likely to taste like plastic wrap. To avoid this predicament, especially in a supermarket context, I opt for cheeses wrapped in a waxy parchment-looking paper by the producer. These are vacuum-sealed and are least likely to have off-flavors. Or I opt for cheeses that are freshly cut in front of me.

➻ **FLAVOR:** The earthy, root cellar aromas of clothbound Cheddar types permeate the paste just beneath the rind; this is part of their character. But sharp flavors lacking balance from other components of the cheese (salt, fat, and milky qualities) are undesirable. Cheddar types should never taste like bile.

➻ **RIND:** Clothbound Cheddar types are wrapped in cloth. Remove it before eating. Most makers who wrap in cloth also brush this cloth with melted lard. If you want to avoid contact with pork, seek alternatives to clothbound. That might be block or natural-rinded Cheddar types.

## STORAGE AND SHELF LIFE

The original Cheddar type was made in France to be sold across medieval Europe via land and sea transport. In other words, these are hardy cheeses. That said, they're not impermeable. Paper wrap alone (unless it's specially designed cheese paper) will shorten shelf life because the cheese will rapidly dry out. My preference is zip-top plastic bags, so you can squeeze all the air out and have individual storage units. Plastic wrap becomes a legitimate possibility here because low-moisture cheeses are more durable than any of the Brie types. My trick when wrapping in plastic is to always "face" the cheese before serving. Meaning: run a knife along the cut surface of a cheese to scrape off the paper-thin layer that's been in contact with the plastic. Taking the time to expose the fresh cheese underneath costs you very little and buys you instantly renewed and refreshed flavor.

Ideally, cheeses in the Cheddar Gateway should be eaten within two weeks of being cut, although they can last for three to four weeks with diminished flavor and complexity. Clothbound cheeses fade more quickly than block versions.

Small spots of blue or green mold may develop on the cut surface of the cheese. These can be easily scraped away or a paper-thin slice cut off to remove it, and the cheese beneath consumed, although they are a reliable warning sign that you're pushing the limit on storage life.

## CHEDDAR TYPES: TEXTURES

**IN A WORD: CHUNKY**

**SMOOTH AND/OR SPRINGY**
CHEWY  COMPACT  PRESSED
SLICEABLE

**DENSE AND/OR CRUMBLY**
CHUNKY  CRUMBLY  CRUNCHY
DENSE  DRY  FLAKY

**FLAWS**
GLUEY  GRAINY  GREASY  WAXY

# CHEDDAR TYPES: FLAVOR & AROMA WHEEL

**ATMOSPHERICS**

SMOKE · WOODSY · BRINE / SEAWATER · POWDER · PUTRID · ACETONE (NAIL POLISH REMOVER) · METALLIC · SULFUR (ROTTEN EGG) · AMMONIA · ACRID

BURNT WOOD (WET) SOIL · PETROL · MINERAL · FISHY · PUTRID · FISHY · BITTER · RANCID

**SPICES**

ANISE · WHITE PEPPER · VANILLA · NUTMEG · CLOVE · BLACK PEPPER · LICORICE

**FLAWS**

EXCESSIVE SOURNESS

**LACTIC**

FRESH ➤ GOAT MILK · COW MILK · SHEEP MILK · BUTTER · BUFFALO MILK · CREAM · CULTURED ➤ CULTURED BUTTER · GAMY BUTTER · CRÈME FRAÎCHE · YOGURT · BUTTERMILK · SOUR CREAM · COOKED ➤ COOKED MILK / MILK SKIN · MELTED BUTTER · BROWNED BUTTER · CHEESE-Y (MAC-AND-CHEESE POWDER)

**OTHER FOOD**

NUTS ➤ NUT SKIN · POLENTA · BISCUIT · COOKED PASTA · (BUTTERED) TOAST · PINE NUT · PECAN · MACADAMIA NUT · (TOASTED) ALMOND · (BOILED) PEANUT · (TOASTED) HAZELNUT · WALNUT · COCONUT (OIL)

SWEETS ➤ CHOCOLATE-DIPPED ORANGE · LEMON CURD · CARAMEL · BUTTERSCOTCH · WERTHER'S ORIGINALS (CARAMEL HARD CANDY) · DULCE DE LECHE · FERMENTED FOODS ➤ WHITE WINE · RED WINE · MILK CHOCOLATE · COCOA · BOURBON · COFFEE · DARK CHOCOLATE · CHICKEN BROTH · BEEF BROTH

**FRUIT**

STONE FRUIT ➤ APRICOT · PEACH · PLUM · BERRIES ➤ STRAWBERRY · BLUEBERRY · RED CURRANT · GREEN OLIVE · BLACK OLIVE · CITRUS ➤ ORANGE · GRAPEFRUIT · LEMON · TROPICAL FRUIT ➤ PAPAYA · PASSION FRUIT · PINEAPPLE · COOKED FRUIT · PICKLED FRUIT · FERMENTED FRUIT

**VEGETABLE**

AROMATICS ➤ (COOKED) CELERY (ROOT) · (COOKED) TURNIP · (COOKED) LEEK · (CARAMELIZED) ONION · (ROASTED) GARLIC · OTHER ➤ BAKED POTATO · CORN · NORI · CRUCIFEROUS ➤ (COOKED) CABBAGE · (COOKED) CAULIFLOWER · (COOKED) BROCCOLI · SPICY ➤ MUSTARD GREENS · BITTER ➤ ENDIVE · ARUGULA · BROCCOLI RABE · HORSERADISH · DANDELION

**ANIMAL**

COOKED ➤ CHICKEN BROTH · BEEF BOUILLON · BEEF BROTH · MEATY · GRILLED · OFFAL · PAN DRIPPINGS · LAMB FAT · GAMY · SAUCISSON SEC · FERMENTED | CURED ➤ SERRANO · JERKY · LEATHER · MANURE · BARNYARD · (WET) WOOL · MUSK · SWEAT · UNWASHED SOCKS · BODILY ➤

**HERBS & PLANTS**

HERBS ➤ MINT · ROSEMARY · THYME · HERBACEOUS · PLANT MATTER ➤ (MOWN) GRASS · HAY · FLORAL · PINE · EUCALYPTUS · TOBACCO

**FUNGUS**

MOLD/MILDEW ➤ (COOKED) MOLD/MILDEW · WHITE MOLD · BLUE MOLD · MUSHROOM ➤ SHIITAKE MUSHROOM · PORCINI MUSHROOM · TRUFFLE · BUTTON MUSHROOM · YEAST · BREAD DOUGH

# Red Leicester

ENGLAND | COW
(UN)PASTEURIZED

**RECOMMENDED BRANDS:**
Long Clawson Aged, Sparkenhoe (exported by Neal's Yard Dairy, unpasteurized only), Devonshire Red (the name Quicke's gives its version of Red Leicester)

**AROMA:** Very little—moist wood from the cloth binding

**TEXTURE:** Chewy and moist

**FLAVOR:** Rich, simple, milky

**IN SHORT:** The texture cheese

Red Leicester looks fake, like someone who has spent too long in a tanning booth or a waxen wedge of acorn squash. In the 1700s, red dye was used to distinguish the cheese from Cheshire (see page 234) and Cheddar, and the lurid orange hue has remained its hallmark. That, and a remarkably mellow, savory flavor. Some might call it boring or bland, but well-made Red Leicester is in fact a Perfectly. Balanced. Cheese. It has a lovely, long, moist bite—not as chunky or flaky as other Cheddar types—and easy taste. David and Jo Clarke make Sparkenhoe, which I regard to be the best. It's certainly the most authentic: clothbound, and made from the raw milk of the farm's 150 Holstein-Friesian cows. It's the only raw milk, farmhouse Leicester cheese made in Leicestershire.

# Wensleydale

ENGLAND | COW
PASTEURIZED

**RECOMMENDED BRANDS:**
Hawes (made by Wensleydale Creamery, exported by Neal's Yard Dairy), Wensleydale Creamery, Singleton's

**AROMA:** Cold milk

**TEXTURE:** Smooth and creamy

**FLAVOR:** Milky

**IN SHORT:** Cold salted butter

Most likely to appear tarted up with all kinds of hideous fruits and candies (cranberry, orange, chocolate, you name it), good old-fashioned Wensleydale is a straightforward territorial traditionally hailing from Yorkshire. When threatened with the closure of the local Hawes Creamery (and loss of its purchasing power from nearby dairy farms), employees and locals purchased the plant to keep production going. That creamery is now called Wensleydale Creamery, and it produces a traditional wheel for Neal's Yard Dairy, marketed under the name Hawes. This is a clothbound version, larger and cylindrical, made with animal rennet, and produced under slightly different make and aging conditions than their smaller, vacuum-sealed wheels. Other Wensleydales are now made outside the traditional region, most notably in Lancashire. The reason I recommend the brands I do is because they deliver a cheese that is dense and creamy, with a soft, buttery flavor. Much of what's found is called hard acid Wensleydale, and its flavor can be so acidic, its texture so dry and crumbly, that you'd practically beg for a sprinkling of chocolate chips to even the cheese out.

# MILD, MEDIUM, AND SHARP: SUPERMARKET UPGRADES

For those folks yearning for deeper, more complex flavor than can be found in the supermarket dairy aisle, but still watching their weekly budget, here are some of my favorite, readily available, better Cheddar types.

**MILD CHEDDAR:** A 1 on the flavor spectrum, mild Cheddars are firm, springy, and even a little squeaky. I find them bland, but if you like them, let's call them very mild. Treat yourself to an occasional English territorial listed at the beginning of this gateway and consider experimenting with upgrades. For example, one of my favorites is sold as:

**TILLAMOOK MEDIUM CHEDDAR:** They say medium, but I'd call it mild. That said, it's a good mild Cheddar, not a bland one. A whisper of tang, creamy and round, and dominant on the West Coast.

**MEDIUM CHEDDAR:** A 5 on the flavor spectrum, medium Cheddars are firm and chunky with creamier texture in the mouth and pleasantly tangy, buttermilk flavor. Some may embrace a sweeter, brown butter profile. My favorites:

**COLLIER'S CHEDDAR:** A Welsh Cheddar that does not bill itself as mild, medium, or sharp but as powerful. It's got a soft smush and pleasant sweetness that is complex enough to please but safe for those who don't want sharpness.

**DEER CREEK "THE FAWN" FROM THE ARTISAN CHEESE EXCHANGE (MADE BY HENNINGS):** This relative newcomer from Wisconsin isn't actually a block of Cheddar, but a wheel. Made to be milder, mellower, and sweeter, it's full and complex in flavor. But don't expect tanginess.

**DUBLINER:** I'm happy to confess that I buy this cheese every single week at my grocery store. It supposedly combines qualities of an aged Cheddar with the sweetness of Swiss and the piquancy of Parm. My family finds it endlessly eatable but flavorful, and it melts.

**GRAFTON CHEDDAR, 2 YEAR AGED:** Raw milk, signature age profile with creamy mouthfeel and restrained tartness.

**SHARP/ EXTRA SHARP CHEDDAR:** An 8 on the flavor spectrum, with high, tart flavor and persistent tongue prickle. These qualities are only to be outdone in intensity by extreme caramel or earth notes. My favorites:

**DEER CREEK VAT 17 FROM THE ARTISAN CHEESE EXCHANGE (MADE BY HENNINGS):** The goal for this cheese was not traditional sharp flavor but a combination of the best Cheddar attributes from around the world. It's deep, smooth, and layered, edging on caramel, with a persistence that should please those looking for intense Cheddar.

**CABOT EXTRA SHARP:** ten to twelve months of age, clean and consistent flavor with upfront acidity.

**CABOT FARMHOUSE RESERVE:** Roughly 18-month Vermont Cheddar with clean background and strong acid and sulfite notes.

# A BRIEF HISTORY OF CHEDDAR

Cheddar, the firm cow milk cheese originating in Somerset, England, is the culmination and perfection of cheese-making technology that most likely began in medieval France. At France's bellybutton, in the Massif Central, were Roman-built roads which, beginning in the first century AD, were used to transport salt north from the Mediterranean coast. Along these roads, the cheeses Cantal (see page 252) and Salers (see page 254) evolved: moist yet crumbly cylinders that were firm and durable enough to be transported back to the sea for export. Rather than cooking the curds and whey to extract water, as with Swiss or Alpine cheeses, makers pressed and broke the curd, crumbling it into bits that were heavily salted to draw out excess moisture.

Importantly, this difference in salt also has a profound impact on flavor—lower salt Alpine styles are known for their sweet flavor profile. The considerably higher salt content of Cheddar type cheeses, along with the unique cheese-making steps used to create this type, deliver a cheese that is more acidic. Or, in laymen's terms, one that tastes sharper.

The original French recipes are more likely to be called tangy, or pleasantly sour, while the English versions lean toward lemony, citrusy, and sour cream notes. But across country lines they share a general flavor and texture profile radically different from the other big cheeses of Europe. Because of Cantal's durability, it was exported across Europe by the end of the Middle Ages. Undoubtedly, its recipe was also carried by Romans inhabiting England's western regions. Its technique was adopted by cheese makers around the Roman town of Chester and was referred to as Cheshire (see page 234), the name of the county in which it was made. One could argue that we have the Romans to thank for the original Cheddar!

# WHAT ARE ENGLISH TERRITORIALS?

The territorials are traditional British cheeses named for their territory or county of origin. These would include Cheshire (see page 234), Wensleydale (see page 230), Lancashire (see page 236), and Gloucester, to name a few that are most similar to one another. Their make processes differ from Cheddar in two notable ways: the curd is neither scalded nor Cheddared. These two steps produce a cheese with denser, smoother paste and lower acidity. Accordingly, I find the territorials tend toward flakier, crumblier texture and flavors that are more lactic: cultured butter, buttermilk, and sour cream are typical.

APPROACHABLE

# Double Gloucester

Unless mild Cheddar types are skillfully crafted, they're just boring to eat. Fat, protein, sustenance, sure, but mindless eating. This is why I'd urge you to seek out the only unpasteurized Double Gloucester available. Although its firm, pale orange interior looks similar to Cheshire (see page 234), Double Gloucester undergoes a longer, slower acidification process. As a result, it's denser and smoother, the flavor mellower. It reminds me of golden brown toast that's heavily buttered. The area of Cheshire where the cheese is made has mineral and salt deposits that are said to impact green grass, and thus the milk of cows who eat it. I'm of the belief that additional feed, including silage (fermented fodder), overwrites the delicacies of the fresh grass, but the impact of higher fat and protein from this diet is undeniable. It's part of what makes the cheese so rich despite its simplicity. Double Gloucester is colored orange with annatto (and has been, traditionally, since the cheese's inception in the sixteenth century) and made exclusively of whole milk (Single Gloucester would indicate partially skimmed milk). If you can't find Appleby's, Double Devonshire is an exceptional pasteurized version of Double Gloucester; other brands taste like mild, orange Cheddar.

ENGLAND | COW

(UN)PASTEURIZED

**RECOMMENDED BRANDS:** Appleby's (exported by Neal's Yard Dairy, unpasteurized only), Double Devonshire (the name Quicke's gives its version of Double Gloucester)

**AROMA:** Minimal

**TEXTURE:** Dense and moist

**FLAVOR:** Mellow and buttery

IN SHORT: Easy like Sunday morning

## WHAT IS NEAL'S YARD DAIRY?

Neal's Yard Dairy is both a place and brand, but more than either it's an ethos about traditional British and Irish cheese. Beginning with owner Randolph Hodgson, who in the 1980s began visiting and cultivating the few remaining farm cheeses in the U.K., and continuing today with the buying, aging, and sales teams who run the retail and wholesale operations, Neal's Yard Dairy has always prioritized knowledge and selection of its cheeses. Its core cheeses, like the West Country Cheddars, are tasted and selected batch by batch every four weeks, before finishing their maturation at the Arches in Bermondsey, London. In the past thirty years the team at Neal's Yard Dairy has been responsible for the resurrection of dying cheeses (such as Kirkham's Lancashire, see page 236) and the invention of traditionally minded new ones (Stichelton, see page 350). Their mission is to know each batch of cheese that passes through their hands, and to be able to articulate the miraculous variations that make farmhouse cheese so neat and special in the first place.

# Cheshire

ENGLAND | COW

(UN)PASTEURIZED

**RECOMMENDED BRAND:**
Appleby's (exported by Neal's
Yard Dairy, unpasteurized
milk only)

**AROMA:** Not much, cheesy

**TEXTURE:** Looks very dry and
crumbly but moist in the mouth

**FLAVOR:** Yellow butterscotch
candy followed by a hint of earth

IN SHORT: For eating with a
pint at the pub

"Here, son. Try this. This is real Cheshire." So said Mr. Edward Appleby when he met Neal's Yard Dairy owner Randolph Hodgson back in the mid-1980s. Then, as now, the Applebys were the last remaining producers of traditional, unpasteurized, clothbound Cheshire. Cheshire production has come to be dominated by factories making a pasteurized and rather acidic cheese quite different from what nineteenth-century manors once made. The Applebys' cheese (directed by cheese maker Garry Gray) is both crumbly and moist, the flavor impacted by the salt and mineral deposits at the edge of the Cheshire plain where the family's Friesian-Holstein cows graze. It's a challenging cheese to sell, particularly to an American audience. Many wonder about the value of such a straightforward and mellow-tasting cheese that costs quite a lot of money. To be sure, it's a very good eating cheese, savory and hearty, with a sour cream twang that lightens the whole thing up. But the real value is that in buying and eating it, you're preventing a piece of English food tradition from going extinct.

UNITED STATES | COW

UNPASTEURIZED

**AROMA:** Damp stone and
Southern biscuits

**TEXTURE:** Feathery but crumbly in the mouth

**FLAVOR:** Sea salt-buttered
biscuits

IN SHORT: American territorial

# Toussaint FROM SPROUT CREEK FARM

Neither a block Cheddar nor a clothbound Cheddar nor technically a Cheddar at all, Toussaint—from Poughkeepsie, New York—reminds me of the English territorials. Produced in a solid ten-pound, natural-rinded wheel, the cheese at its best is like a biscuit thickly smeared with salted butter. The texture is unusual—dense and flaky, with a crumbly chew. It's slightly milled by hand, which I credit with its territorial-like-but-not-quite-territorial texture. As in many Sprout Creek cheeses, there's an unapologetic use of salt, which slows down the acid-heavy cultures used to make the cheese. In this case, salt is critical, pushing subtle, earthy, and—near the rind—red fruit flavors to the fore. I've also eaten Toussaint that is wildly sharp, the acid hitting you first and most intensely. I much prefer the softer flavor profile, achieved by carefully managing the curd-salting during the make process. While the English territorials are more focused on lactic and milky notes, I think of Toussaint as their American counterpart. You eat it and think it must be Cheddar, even though it looks and feels a little different.

CHESHIRE

# Caerphilly

ENGLAND | COW

(UN)PASTEURIZED

**RECOMMENDED BRANDS:**
Duckett's and Gorwydd
(exported by Neal's Yard Dairy,
unpasteurized milk only)

**AROMA:** Butter and celery,
earth at the rind

**TEXTURE:** Moister than
Cheddar or other territorials,
mealy in the mouth

**FLAVOR:** Buttery crumble,
lactic, the barest beginnings
of acidic bite

**IN SHORT:** The mild
Cheddar upgrade

Eating real Caerphilly was one of my first lessons in the profound difference between traditional cheese and commodified cheese. I'd had Caerphilly before. It was a white, crumbly block, a bit tangy. Pleasant enough, although utterly forgettable. Eating it made me wonder how the British maintained so many distinct yet fundamentally comparable cow milk cheeses. Then I tasted Gorwydd, then the only unpasteurized milk, traditional Caerphilly on the American market. Now there is Duckett's as well. These cheeses are two-textured, with a white, springy interior that's citric in flavor. My favorite bite is just under the brown rind, which is covered with white mold like some kind of rock lichen. Here, the paste is creamier and more yielding, the flavor saltier, more mushroomy. Chris Duckett of Somerset preserved the Caerphilly tradition (itself originating in southern Wales in the town of Caerphilly) and taught Todd Trethowan, who went on to make Gorwydd. In his old age, Chris moved production to Westcombe Dairy, where he continued cheese making and research until his death in 2009. Now, Tom Calver at Westcombe oversees the milky crumbled deliciousness of Duckett's, and Todd produces Gorwydd on the family farm in mid-Wales.

# Lancashire

ENGLAND | COW

(UN)PASTEURIZED

**RECOMMENDED BRAND:**
Kirkham's (exported by
Neal's Yard Dairy, unpasteurized
milk only)

**AROMA:** Tart, milky

**TEXTURE:** Buttery crumble or
dreamy creamies, take your pick

**FLAVOR:** Savory yogurt,
sour cream

**IN SHORT:** Streusel sans sugar

One of the first cheese descriptors to lodge itself in my brain was the seductive phrase "buttery crumble." It made me think of the streusel topping on a peach pie: butter and flour mashed together, albeit without the addition of sugar. Buttery crumble isn't just romantic wording, it's how the Lancashire, England, locals describe the ideal texture of their regional cheese. It should be moist yet crumbly, and creamy under tooth. I'd heard "buttery crumble" long before I experienced the lemony tang of proper, unpasteurized Lancashire cheese, which is like a slab of sour cream cake. Made today by Graham Kirkham, following his mother's recipe (that's Mrs. Kirkham, to a lot of old-school cheese people), the curd takes three days to prepare. Imagine a time when milk was allowed to sour naturally, a bit gathered each morning until enough milk was collected to produce a larger wheel of cheese. So it goes here. Very slow acidification, with primarily natural bacteria (rather than starter added by the maker), produces a brilliantly complex flavor. It's full of yogurt and cultured butter notes, essentially lactic but also ripe. Kirkham's is the only unpasteurized Lancashire left, and also the only maker not to coat its wheels in wax. If buttery crumble is what the locals call it, I'll add to this Graham's own characterization: the "dreamy creamies."

APPROACHABLE

# Landaff

FROM LANDAFF CREAMERY/THE CELLARS AT JASPER HILL

Good cheese is saving American dairy farms, but sometimes it takes a village. The Erbs' second-generation New Hampshire farm was, by the mid-aughts, struggling to support itself as milk prices plummeted. Doug Erb was able to study cheese making at the now-defunct Vermont Institute for Artisan Cheese, as well as at the side of Chris Duckett (maker of Duckett's Caerphilly, see page 236). Add to this that Landaff was the first farm outside of Vermont to turn the aging of its nascent cheese over to the Cellars at Jasper Hill in Greensboro, Vermont. This overseas/over state-line collaboration has brought us an American twist on a Welsh classic. Both smaller and drier than Duckett's or Gorwydd Caerphilly , Landaff manages to walk a line between rustic and rarefied. There's exceptional variation from winter to summer when the cows move on to grass, so if you prefer creamier brown butter notes, buy between January and July. For drier, denser cheese with golden yellow hue and buttermilk notes, buy between August and December.

**UNITED STATES | COW**

**UNPASTEURIZED**

**AROMA:** Rock cavern, grassy lawn

**TEXTURE:** Firm and crumbling

**FLAVOR:** Brown butter and bright buttermilk

**IN SHORT:** Harmonious

**UNITED STATES | COW**

**PASTEURIZED**

**AROMA:** Rich

**TEXTURE:** Buttery and dense

**FLAVOR:** Butter-bathed citrus

**IN SHORT:** Irish-inspired

# Promontory FROM BEEHIVE CHEESE COMPANY

Brothers-in-law Pat Ford and Tim Welsh of Beehive Cheese Company left their successful corporate jobs to make cheese. As Pat says, "When we got started, Timmy wanted to do something crazy." Unfortunately, their local market (central Utah) was decidedly uncrazy. To succeed, they needed to begin with a cheese that was recognizable. Luckily, Utah State, one of the country's top five agricultural schools for dairy milk research, had been working on a recipe they were calling "Old Juniper" and were happy to share it with Beehive Cheese for adaptation. Now called "Promontory," the cheese is Cheddared and serves as the base recipe for all of Beehive's other cheeses. It's also among a group of American cheeses to complicate the definition of Cheddar. It may meet the U.S. Department of Agriculture's guidelines on moisture and fat, but it includes an adjunct culture that contributes uniquely lush and tropical fruit flavors over time. Pat doesn't call his cheese a Cheddar because he (rightly) figures that people are inclined to buy Cheddar by price. The incredibly smooth, sweet, fruitiness of Promontory is all about defying that expectation.

Beehive makes flavored variations of Promontory at specific times of the year, depending on the fat content of the milk. These include Barely Buzzed (higher fat winter milk, rubbed in a proprietary espresso blend and French superior lavender); TeaHive (rubbed in bergamot tea); and SeaHive (lower fat summer/fall milk, rubbed in local honey and Redmond Real Salt, which is harvested from an ancient sea bed near Redmond, Utah).

**UNITED STATES | COW**

**PASTEURIZED**

**AROMA:** Like what you expect sharp Cheddar to smell like

**TEXTURE:** Moist crumble

**FLAVOR:** Butter-saturated diner toast

**IN SHORT:** Euphoric

# Prairie Breeze FROM MILTON CREAMERY

Rufus Musser starts our conversation by reminding me, "I'm a Pennsylvania Dutch boy." From there, it's a thirty-plus-years' journey to his Milton, Iowa, creamery, now making Rufus's spin on block Cheddar. Born and raised a Mennonite in the greater Lancaster area, Rufus and his wife moved West in search of cheap ground and a project different from his father's vegetable farm that was keeping him away from his family each summer. They began milking cows, and when a plan for a cheese factory in a nearby Amish community fizzled, Rufus saw his opportunity to make and market cheese, using milk from his Amish neighbors. After a rocky beginning, he tweaked a Cheddar recipe to make something new. When I asked Rufus if the tweak was introducing the adjunct culture *Lactobacillus helveticus*, he said briskly, "You won't get answers to all your questions today." I've long suspected this in Rufus's proprietary blend because Prairie Breeze is intensely flavorful, smooth and deep, with a buttery roundness that induces fits of ecstasy. The cheese is Cheddared, but other parameters such as acidity and moisture are on the perimeter for actual Cheddar. So Rufus calls it a Cheddar type. Aged at least nine months, "We do it the hard way and feel like it's a true artisan cheese."

## MEET *HELVETICUS*

About ten years ago, I noticed something shifting in the world of Cheddar. Previously, consumers had two possible flavor directions: either mild, medium, or sharp Cheddar (generally, from big name brands, made in big blocks, with lower price tags) or the newly (re)discovered English or clothbound Cheddars, often twice the price, meant for the connoisseur, and tasting amazing but not like the American concept of Cheddar.

Then, suddenly, there was a new option. Often, the cheese wasn't called a Cheddar, but it was described as a hybrid, or like a Cheddar and Swiss put together. What this meant was a cheese that looked like Cheddar and felt like Cheddar, but tasted sweeter. Smoother. Nuttier. It was practically addictive. It contained the adjunct culture *Lactobacillus helveticus*.

Makers add bacterial cultures to milk for two reasons: the first is to acidify the milk, converting sugar (lactose) into (lactic) acid.

Adjunct cultures do their work later, shaping a cheese's flavor profile over time, within proper temperature, acidity, and salt ranges. Many makers won't discuss their culture blends—they're proprietary and part of the secret sauce that makes each cheese unique. But as Pat Ford of Beehive Cheese Company (an open fan of the *L. helveticus* influence on his flagship Promontory recipe) explains it, "Ten years ago a technical judge would consider sweetness [in Cheddar] a flaw, but an aesthetic judge might give extra points." These days, he enters Promontory in Cheddar categories of cheese competitions because it's Cheddared. Cheese awards may question whether it's a true Cheddar, but as Pat reminds me, "People just like it."

Cheddar types containing *Helveticus* have a deep, lush sweetness, somewhere between heavily buttered white toast and cheese candy.

# (Raw Milk) Flagship

### FROM BEECHER'S HANDMADE CHEESE

**UNITED STATES** | COW

**(UN)PASTEURIZED**

**AROMA:** Cheese candy

**TEXTURE:** Moist smush

**FLAVOR:** Browned butter

**IN SHORT:** Ubiquitously likeable

In 2003, Beecher's Handmade Cheese founder Kurt Beecher Dammeier set out to change the way America eats by making cheese in front of as many people as possible in his Pike Place Market storefront in Seattle. But that cheese couldn't be too weird or too stinky if it was going to usher the masses into the world of artisan cheese. The model was Washington State University's Cougar Gold, made since World War II and, famously, sold in a can. Flagship is the first Cheddar type I recall tasting and thinking, "This is . . . different. Addictively delicious." Flagship is Cheddared, and the adjunct cultures that are a major dictator of its flavor do their work around ten to twelve months. Accordingly, the cheese is always aged for at least that long. The flavor of Flagship is browned butter. There's other lusciousness going on, notably pineapple flavors, but the defining quality is frothy, savory, sweetly nutty cooked butter. Those adjunct cultures also impact the texture of the cheese, and because Kurt is a chef, he was specifically interested in making a cheese that would melt well, which Flagship does far better than most block Cheddars. His mac and cheese is known as the world's best, and Flagship is a key component. The exact same recipe that makes Flagship is used in very limited runs of the unpasteurized Raw Milk Flagship, and is the baseline for Flagship Reserve (see page 246), although that cheese is made in a cylindrical form and clothbound. The final piece of cheese is significantly different and worth a side-by-side tasting.

## WHAT ARE THOSE WHITE THINGS ON MY CHEDDAR?

Aged cheeses of all sorts, whether they're Cheddar types, Swiss types, or Parmesan types, will begin to exhibit white patches in the paste at around nine to twelve months of age. These look like salt or sugar crystals and may expand to dime-sized rounds that are crunchy or gritty under tooth. These are amino acid clusters, typically tyrosine, and are considered a hallmark of great aged cheese. They don't impact flavor, but their texture is part of what makes the eating so great.

In Cheddar, especially younger cheeses, you're more likely to see white specks on the surface of the cheese. These tend to be calcium lactate crystals, and while they're considered to be a technical defect in Cheddar, they don't have an appreciable impact on the quality of the cheese.

What you don't want to see is white fur or white mold, which is likely a sign of cross-contamination from knives that were previously cutting a Brie type.

# Barber's 1833 Vintage Reserve Cheddar

When I visited Barber's, in the thick of English Cheddar Country (that would be Somerset), I was forced to reconsider my prejudices against block Cheddar. I'd previously assumed it was all machine-made mediocrity, but there I was, wandering along the rolling hills of Maryland Farm, which has been in the Barber family for six generations (since 1833). Most impressively, the farm has established a laboratory dedicated to the preservation of natural mixed-starter cultures historically used for Cheddar making. Barber's actually cultivates and maintains starters used by the most famous West County Cheddar producers, and theirs is the only block Cheddar to benefit from a collection of starters dating back to the nineteenth century. The complex balance of sweet and savory flavors is consistently impressive, as is the intensely creamy smear of the paste. Aged for a minimum of twenty-four months and made using milk from the farm's own herd of 2,000 cows, Barber's stands at the crossroads of Cheddar history and Cheddar possibility. It's outstanding, and due to its production scale, readily available.

**ENGLAND | COW**
**PASTEURIZED**
**AROMA:** Fruity milk
**TEXTURE:** Creamy with occasional crunch
**FLAVOR:** Savory, salty, a little beefy
**IN SHORT:** High-octane

# Lincolnshire Poacher

If I was to offer you a sliver of Lincolnshire Poacher, you'd ask, "What Cheddar is that?" I've always thought of it as just another English Cheddar, until I sat down recently and tasted it alongside Montgomery's (see page 251) and Isle of Mull (see page 253). I marveled at the nuanced differences. Makers Simon and Tim Jones of Lincolnshire learned from a Welsh maker whose own cheese was a Cheddar/Alpine (Swiss) cross. As a result, the sweeter, rounder flavors of Alpine mountain cheese echo through a wheel that otherwise subscribes to West Country Cheddar traditions (unpasteurized milk from the farm's herd and traditional animal rennet). What did I find putting Poacher next to clothbound Cheddars? A burnished rind and smoother, more densely knitted texture. A full, sweet aroma that was buttery and earthy with whiffs of warm hay. And flavor that goes far beyond what the aroma promises: melted butter and nuts but with a serious beefy quality. At other times it's been nearly pineappley.

**ENGLAND | COW**
**UNPASTEURIZED**
**AROMA:** Buttered hay
**TEXTURE:** Smooth, dense, and creamy
**FLAVOR:** The cheese equivalent of marrowbone
**IN SHORT:** Expectation defier

# Georgia Gold Clothbound Cheddar FROM NATURE'S HARMONY FARM

UNITED STATES | COW

UNPASTEURIZED

**AROMA:** Lemony earth

**TEXTURE:** Dense and flecked with crunchies

**FLAVOR:** Hold out for the pineapple-malty

**IN SHORT:** Inspired

There was no clothbound Cheddar made in the American South, which was reason enough for Nature's Harmony to pursue its own version. That, and the fact that the farm crafts its portfolio of cheeses based on traditional European artisan methods adapted to grass-fed cows in Elberton, Georgia. Of the bunch, Georgia Gold is my favorite, and the most recent piece I tasted only reinforced that. At fourteen months of age, it was edging on crunchy, with a savory, malty flavor. The farm typically sells it younger when it's a bit softer and fruitier. The bulk of what's available is six months, when the paste is smooth and densely creamy, the flavors just starting to pop with citric and pineapple notes. The feedback they've heard is that there are so many mature, brothy clothbounds out there that customers like the variety offered by their younger cheese. Sure, it may be the spice of life, but I'll take my Georgia Gold mature, thanks.

# Corra Linn

SCOTLAND | SHEEP

UNPASTEURIZED

**AROMA:** Wet sweater in an earthy cave

**TEXTURE:** Clothbound Cheddar but fattier

**FLAVOR:** Toasted nuts, and the woolliness of sheep

**IN SHORT:** Consummate autumn cheese

The Lacaune breed of sheep is known for the southern French cheese made from its milk, of which Roquefort (see page 356) is the most popular. I find it mildly shocking, then, that these animals have been so successfully adapted to the humid cold of Lanarkshire, Scotland, where Selina and Andrew Cairns milk their herd from late January until early August and make a drum of cheese which is aged for roughly six months. At quick glance, it looks like another clothbound Cheddar, but the use of sheep rather than cow milk translates into a softer—dare I say woollier—eating experience. You taste the sheep milk, round with fat, with a hint of wet sweater. It's approachable and not at all sharp, reminiscent of darkly toasted nuts. There's merely a tentative wave toward the intense wet-cave earthiness that characterizes traditional English Cheddars.

CORRA LINN

# Hook's Cheddar

**UNITED STATES | COW**

**PASTEURIZED**

**AROMA:** Mac-and-cheese powder

**TEXTURE:** Moist flakes

**FLAVOR:** High, lean, tart

**IN SHORT:** Extra-sharp Cheddar done right

Hook's Cheese Company, run by high school sweethearts Tony and Julie Hook, makes over thirty kinds of cheese, but it's the Cheddars and the Blues they're best known for (although Julie became the first, and is still the only, woman to win the World Cheese Championship with her Colby in 1982). The Mineral Point, Wisconsin, facility to which they expanded in 1987 provided ample aging space so they could begin holding Cheddars back for as long as fifteen and even twenty years. Working with the same group of local dairy farmers for nearly forty years, Hook's has mastered consistency and quality. While their baby Cheddars (sold as mild and medium, and aged one to four months and five to ten months, respectively) are perfectly pleasant, it's at around two years that things get interesting. Their one- to three-year Cheddars would be called sharp or maybe even extra sharp, but they successfully avoid the bilious flavors many long-aged Cheddars exhibit. That's the thing about sharpness. You want tart and edgy, but not an acidic burn deep in the back of your throat. By ten years, Hook's Cheddar is quite rare and considerably denser and creamier than the two-year version. It starts out with a deep sweetness, the paste studded with crystallization like the cookie topping on a Carvel ice cream cake. The finish is pronounced, edging onto bitter. It's a neat trick, but I'll take the two- to three-year for day-to-day exceptional eating.

## WHY IS CHEDDAR AMERICA'S CHEESE?

The migration of Cheddar types continued from England westward across the Atlantic to the American colonies. The settlers of the Massachusetts Bay Colony came from the dairying region of East Anglia, which was the original supplier of cheese and butter to the London market. As the demand for butter increased and East Anglian makers stripped increasing amounts of butterfat from their milk, their cheese became of poorer and poorer quality. Severe flooding and cattle disease in the 1640s further eroded production, and soon the cheeses of Cheshire and Somerset were sought out for London consumers.

Despite East Anglia's fall from cheese grace, its residents took their knowledge of, and interest in, dairying and cheese making across the ocean to their brave new world. The colonists kept careful tabs on advancements in English cheese making and adopted these for their own recipes. It was not until the mid-nineteenth century that other immigrating populations (German, Italian, and Scandinavian), arriving with cheese-making traditions of their own, began to influence the production of cheese in America. Today, more than three billion pounds of Cheddar are produced in the United States.

APPROACHABLE

HOOK'S CHEDDAR

# Flagship Reserve
**FROM BEECHER'S HANDMADE CHEESE**

UNITED STATES | COW

PASTEURIZED

**AROMA:** Toasted nuts and something damp

**TEXTURE:** Dense and waxy

**FLAVOR:** Brown butter and celery root

IN SHORT: Cheddar 201

Flagship Reserve begins its life as Flagship (see page 240), although the curds are molded into cylindrical forms that are clothbound and open-air aged. The moisture loss is extreme: 11 percent of its weight in twelve to eighteen months of aging. With this drop comes an intensification of both salt and acidity—and a cheese that veers back to the common characterization of aged Cheddar as sharp and clothbound Cheddar as earthy. Underneath this insistent edge, incredibly appealing brown-butter notes remain. For eaters who write off Flagship as being too easy, the Reserve has a drier chew and more complex flavor development. It's still ubiquitously likeable, but I think of it as the thinking person's Flagship.

## THE ORIGINS OF CLOTH BINDING

Cheese folk often distinguish between block Cheddar (traditional American) and clothbound Cheddar (traditional English). Block tends to be moister and more likely to fall on the mild/medium/sharp spectrum, whereas clothbound is drier, with flavors that are more about earthiness, nuttiness, and complexity.

It's entirely possible, however, that the practice of cloth binding a Cheddar actually began in eighteenth-century America. While the English developed closely watched Cheddar-making techniques, including heating the curd, crumbling or milling it, and salting the curd bits in the vat, the more extreme American climate demanded surface protection for cheeses that would otherwise lose moisture and suffer from accelerated decay. By wrapping their cheeses in protective bandages and coating those bandages with melted butter, Americans were able to minimize loss and maximize quality. Bandaging had been used in northern England, most notably for Stilton, but Americans embraced the technology and improved upon it over time, settling on melted lard as a more cost-effective outer coating. The technique of a lard-brushed binding is still used for clothbound Cheddars today. It's conceivable that American colonists were the first packagers of Cheddar.

APPROACHABLE

# Cabot Clothbound Cheddar

**FROM CABOT COOPERATIVE CREAMERY/THE CELLARS AT JASPER HILL**

In 2003, farmer-owned cooperative Cabot, beloved in the Northeast for various block Cheddars, approached fledgling Vermont cheese maker Jasper Hill Farm about aging a new recipe. The cheese was meant to be clothbound and cellar aged, and that experiment turned into a collaboration for the ages. Using the milk of a single farmer, George Kempton, Cabot makes thirty-pound drums that are immediately transported to the Cellars. There, each wheel is brushed in lard, and an additional layer of cloth is added before ten to fifteen months of aging ensues. This was the first clothbound Cheddar that really distinguished an American from a traditional English flavor profile, with discernible caramel sweetness layered atop savory notes. The roundness is well integrated, and I often find the first bite like a brown-buttered baked potato, followed by sour-cream tang and dairy sweetness.

**UNITED STATES | COW**
**PASTEURIZED**

**AROMA:** Pleasantly musty, like a root cellar

**TEXTURE:** Smooth, downy snowflakes

**FLAVOR:** Caramel, nuts, and sour cream tang

**IN SHORT:** The poster child for American clothbound

# Flory's Truckle  FROM MILTON CREAMERY

While Milton Creamery's Prairie Breeze (see page 238) results from a partnership with area Amish dairies, Flory's Truckle begins with the Flory family of Jamesport, Missouri. As Rufus Musser tells it, the Florys wanted to make cheese, not sell it. The challenge was finding the right recipe, milk, and environment. A Gouda style wasn't doing it, but this clothbound Cheddar type did. Truckle refers to the small, cylindrical shape typical of English Christmas Cheddar; its cloth wrap and aging period of twelve-plus months produce a drier, flakier paste than Prairie Breeze, with earthy cave aromas, particularly near the rind.

**UNITED STATES | COW**
**PASTEURIZED**

**AROMA:** Earthy cave

**TEXTURE:** Dry, layered

**FLAVOR:** Vegetal, grassy

**IN SHORT:** Austere

# Bandaged Cheddar  FROM BLEU MONT DAIRY

Willi Lehner is Wisconsin's Mad Scientist of Cheese, using other people's (organic and pastured) milk and production facilities to craft his portfolio of recipes. The cheeses are then aged in a private cellar behind his house. Willi's Bandaged Cheddar is inspired by British recipes but, aged for one to two years. That length of time is unusual because clothbound Cheddars typically dry out, their flavors fading into an imbalanced bite that's all wet dirt and acid. Willi's cheese, however, boasts a sharpness that is complex and layered, with toast and woodsy whiffs atop a foundation of crystalline crunch. Both the crusty binding and edge just beneath are distinctly cave-like, with a damp, mildewy persistence that keeps the cheese from being just brown-butter sweet.

**UNITED STATES | COW**
**PASTEURIZED**

**AROMA:** Damp subterranean cave, wasabi

**TEXTURE:** Dense and pasty with lots of crunchies

**FLAVOR:** Rich, woodsy, mouthwatering

**IN SHORT:** Experimental

CABOT CLOTHBOUND CHEDDAR

# Hafod

WALES | COW

PASTEURIZED

**AROMA:** Wet tilled soil, minerally

**TEXTURE:** Moist chew, smears on the roof of your mouth

**FLAVOR:** High-acid and super grassy at center, at the rind savory and nuttier

**IN SHORT:** Of the earth

In 2007, atop a wet hill on the longest-standing registered organic farm in Wales, an experiment began. What might an English Cheddar of 100 years ago have looked like? Tasted like? How could the milk of Ayrshire cows, with their lower yield but higher solids (and smaller fat globules) be best expressed? Sam and Rachel Holden began this experiment after learning cheese making from Simon Jones, maker of Lincolnshire Poacher (see page 241), who had himself learned cheese making from the late Dougal Campbell, a neighbor of Sam's father. By channeling Dougal, they began a Swiss-influenced Cheddar hybrid, but found the colder, wetter climate of Wales and the Ayrshire milk ill-suited to Simon's recipe. Enter Neal's Yard Dairy's Randolph Hodgson and his growing fascination with a true Cheddar of the nineteenth century. How to make such a thing? First and foremost, slow down. Let your starter build over two hours. Cut your curd blocks for Cheddaring and let them sit on the make table while you retrieve your kids from school. Integrate the recipe into life rather than the other way around. The resulting cheese, Hafod (Hav-odd), bears none of the fruity or butterscotchy impressions of its original Poacher inspiration. It's moister, all earth, the paste close-knit and buttery. A new-old cheese, it continues to evolve as the Holdens and Neal's Yard Dairy play around with its ideal age profile.

# Quicke's Cheddar

ENGLAND | COW

PASTEURIZED

**AROMA:** Citrus and grass

**TEXTURE:** Toothsome

**FLAVOR:** Lemony

**IN SHORT:** Lean and clean

Recently, when I asked some cheese friends to tell me which was their favorite Cheddar, one voted for Quicke's, among other reasons, because it's "a family farm since Columbus sailed the ocean blue." In this case, Mary Quicke's family has been working the land of Home Farm since it was bestowed on them by Henry VIII during the 1530s. It wasn't until the 1970s that the estate added a creamery and began cheese production under the name Quicke's Traditional Ltd. Its line includes a variety of Cheddars, from the newly minted Quicke's Buttery at three to four months up to the two-plus years Quicke's Vintage. Quicke's Mature is what's most likely to be found in the States, sold simply as Quicke's Cheddar. I rely on Quicke's, a traditional, clothbound wheel, to deliver a lighter, leaner flavor profile than other English clothbound Cheddars. Most notably, it has a lemony edge and horseradish astringency that tastes almost green. I wonder if the farm's emphasis on grass-based feed drives this. It's extremely clean, and while many of its neighbors are savory, brothy and even meaty, Quicke's has always tasted more delicate, and more akin to my childhood perceptions of sharp Cheddar.

# Montgomery's Cheddar

If ever there was a cheese that defends flavor variation from wheel to wheel, this Cheddar is it. While James (Jamie) Montgomery defined, with his Somerset neighbors, the conditions necessary to produce Artisan Somerset Cheddar, the chance to taste dozens of wheels from his aging cellar showed me the staggering range of what a cheese can be. Forget a type, I'm talking about a vast variety in one cheese, made by one maker (Steve Bridges crafts every mammoth sixty-pounder that comes off the manor). Famously, Montgomery's uses a different starter blend for each day of the week, meaning no two days of production are identical. Every wheel in the United States is hand selected by Neal's Yard Dairy for its unique flavor profile. The rigorous adherence to traditional Somerset Cheddar production, plus the nearly infinite variability of flavor that evolves more than one year later, has made this the most celebrated and beloved clothbound Cheddar in the world. A distinguishing characteristic is a drier paste than its Somerset kin; an old-fashioned mill creates a uniquely brittle curd, which, combined with clothbound aging, develops into a fissured flake by the time it hits the market. At its best, Monty's is like meat crackling, where fat and protein develop a caramelized edge of dark sweetness. As I get older, I'm finding my clothbound Cheddar preferences lean in the sweeter, more caramelized direction. I think this is scoffed at as the cheese equivalent of preferring a Napa Cab to a Bordeaux, but I don't really care. I like a caramel edge to offset the caveyness of clothbound Cheddar.

ENGLAND | COW

UNPASTEURIZED

**AROMA:** Caves, wood shelves, mown grass

**TEXTURE:** Flaky nubbins

**FLAVOR:** From meaty and savory to sweet and fruity

**IN SHORT:** Mercurial, with a chance for mind-blowing

# Cantal PDO

FRANCE | COW
(UN)PASTEURIZED
**AROMA:** Cultured butter
**TEXTURE:** Feathery
**FLAVOR:** Gamy sour cream
IN SHORT: The shocker

Although Cantal is a name-protected cheese, its production may be of unpasteurized milk (and relatively traditional) or of pasteurized milk, cranked out in great quantity by lowland factories. This means you have to inquire what's on offer, as *fermier* denotes "farmhouse" or unpasteurized milk, and *laitier* refers to pasteurized versions. There's also Cantalet, which is a briefly aged, small-format Cantal that tends to be much tamer in flavor. Cantal is a weird cheese, which is what I like about it. It looks like clothbound Cheddar (although without the cloth), but it doesn't feel or taste at all like Cheddar. Texturally, it's moister and more feathery, but it's the flavor that demands acknowledgment. While not as intense as its brother Salers (see page 254) or its neighbor Laguiole (see page 253), Cantal has a seriously rustic edge. Its base flavor is all cultured butter, but layered over that is a slightly sour, gamy edge that lingers persistently. It's a cheese that tastes of leather, horses, and dirt. At least, the unpasteurized milk versions do. Most pasteurized Cantal is perfectly pleasant and mildly acidic, but more akin to Cheshire (see page 234) or Caerphilly (see page 236).

## ARTISAN SOMERSET CHEDDAR

Since Cheddar is such a broad type and is not guaranteed by any name protection standards, three of England's greatest traditional Cheddar makers (James Montgomery of Montgomery's Cheddar, see page 251; George Keen of Keen's Cheddar; and Richard Calver of Westcombe Cheddar) got together to define what it means to be Artisan Somerset Cheddar. Their aim was to distinguish their cheeses from generic Cheddar and to clarify the distinctions from the West Country Farmhouse Cheddar Cheese PDO, which may include pasteurized and flavored cheeses. Artisan Somerset Cheddar:

1. Is made only in Somerset, England.

2. Is made with the unpasteurized cow milk of the farm's own herd.

3. Is made with milk that is acidified using traditional pint starters: cultures taken from naturally occurring bacteria in unpasteurized Somerset milk, rather than powdered starters that are purchased.

4. Curd is coagulated using animal rennet.

5. Must be cylindrical in form and clothbound; it is aged for a minimum of one year.

# Laguiole PDO

Produced across the central French départements of Aveyron, Cantal, and Lozère, Laguiole may only be produced from the milk of French Simmental and Aubrac cows. The curds are broken and pressed twice. During the initial press, curds are flipped over at least five times. The second press includes the formation of cylindrical wheels, which are salted before being pressed again. As a result, the texture is chunky and Cheddar-like, although the cheese is never technically Cheddared. Despite the fact that cheese has been produced in this region since the fourteenth century, the area's unique geography and climate make Laguiole what it is. High-altitude flora contribute to uniquely floral milk, while the harsh climate has necessitated the cold, damp, cellar ripening that teases out Laguiole's earthen, sour, and mushroomy flavors. Whereas the most intense English clothbound Cheddars are reminiscent of freshly turned wet dirt, the French Cheddar types are more restrained: older, colder, and stonier.

**FRANCE | COW**

**UNPASTEURIZED**

**AROMA:** Cold stone

**TEXTURE:** Moist and chunky

**FLAVOR:** Sour yet perfumed

**IN SHORT:** The redheaded stepchild (of English Cheddar)

# Isle of Mull Cheddar

My impression of Scotland, until I visited, was *Braveheart*. Rocky and green but manageable, even in a kilt. Once there, I found it to be bleakly beautiful. Wild, glossed in eerie light, like a land of ghosts. *Braveheart* was the Scottish highlands. Far to the west, off the jagged, fractured coastline, is the Isle of Mull. Population: 3,000. From this craggy rock comes a Cheddar unlike any cheese you will ever encounter. It tastes like it's made it the middle of nowhere. Edgy. Spiky. A salad of bitter and mustard greens. Mull is a Cheddar for someone who likes it sharp, even though the cheese isn't actually acidic. It's intense, and that should please the sharp-lovers. Given the unforgiving climate and extremely short growing season, Chris and Jeff Reade's 100 cows are fed a diet light on grass (hence the relatively white paste of the cheese) and heavy on spent grain husks from the local whisky distillery in Tobermory. For Harry Potter fans, imagine Madame Maxime's enchanted, whisky-drinking horses. Fiery, fruity, and fermented notes poke out in turn. The finish lasts more than thirty seconds. Somehow, you have found a tenuous rope hold to this remote and desolate bit of land and sky and sea.

**SCOTLAND | COW**

**UNPASTEURIZED**

**AROMA:** Horseradish

**FLAVOR:** Bitter greens, fermented fruit

**TEXTURE:** Practically soft, for a Cheddar

**IN SHORT:** Untamable

# Salers PDO

FRANCE | COW

UNPASTEURIZED

**AROMA:** Sour milk and damp, stony air

**TEXTURE:** Moist and Cheddary

**FLAVOR:** Floral yet sour, acidic yet earthy

**IN SHORT:** Ancient

I have encountered just a few cheeses that make me feel like I am touching history. And in the tradition of the Slow Food movement, if you want to save history you have to eat it. Demand keeps food alive. Salers is incredibly rare, made during summer months on the formerly volcanic plateau of Auvergne's Massif Central. The red-haired Salers cows are milked by hand in a field, using a portable milking unit, and are so finicky that they won't let their milk down if their baby calves are not tethered to them. The cheese is produced seven days a week in a small stone hut called a buron, with milk acidifying overnight in open troughs and then contributing its air-ripened flora to the next day's vat. There are fewer and fewer people who want to do this work, although the resulting cheese sings of the stark, unspoiled green hills, at once floral and gamy, long, lingering, sour, milky, and complex. It's a cheese that's not likely to exist in another fifty years, so get it while you can.

## FROM THE MOUTHS OF MAKERS

Cheese sits at the intersection of art and science, with, at its best, a bit of mysticism tipped in. When asked about their work, here's what Cheddar-type makers have to say:

When asked how long his cheese is aged: "Listen to the cheese. It will tell you what it wants to be."—Rufus Musser, Milton Creamery (see page 238)

"I prefer to let customers tell me what it [Promontory] is rather than putting myself in a box; there's an expectation of what Cheddar is."—Pat Ford, Beehive Cheese Co. (see page 239)

"My goal was to make a cheese that was clearly premium but ubiquitously likable."—Kurt Beecher Dammeier, Beecher's Handmade Cheese (see page 240)

Of clothbound Cheddar: "You get layers of flavor. You may not like those flavors but you will always have more layers, more complexity."—Mary Quicke, Quicke's Traditional Ltd. (see page 258)

## MY PICKS: APPROACHABLE CHEDDAR TYPES

Mild Cheddar types encompass both block (rindless) choices and clothbound wheels that hover in a familiar but often undefinable flavor family of rich, mellow dairy. Their texture is often a big draw for me: mashing into the roof of the mouth in densely moist smears, like a spoonful of clotted or sour cream.

### Red Leicester (ideally, Sparkenhoe or Devonshire Red)

For those committed to their mild block Cheddar, brighten things up with this electric orange alternative that manages to be moist (never gummy) and savory (never bland). (see page 230)

### Toussaint from Sprout Creek Farm

Unlike many of the English territorials, this American isn't afraid of judicious salt. As a result, the flavor is more about red fruit, the aroma subtle and earthy rather than the usual tangy milkiness. (see page 234)

### Lancashire (ideally, Kirkham's)

Like a slab of unsweetened sour cream cake, moist-yet-crumbly, buttery yet tangy. A cheese whose maker can only describe it as the "dreamy creamies," and whose neighbors call it the "buttery crumble," demands consideration. (see page 236)

# MY PICKS: INTENSE CHEDDAR TYPES

Intense Cheddar types start with cheeses delivering concentrated browned-butter and tropical-fruit notes. Lovers of approachable flavor are likely to enjoy this kind of intensity as it's more of the candied sort. For dirty earth intensity, I look to traditional English clothbound Cheddar: brothier, farmier, and generally more erratic (and, arguably, more interesting). These, for me, are the true embodiment of intense Cheddar types.

## Prairie Breeze from Milton Creamery

Rufus Musser won't confirm what cultures make his recipe unique, but everyone who eats this cheese freaks out and wants more. Think buttered Pullman toast, with the satisfying balance of moist crumble and occasional crunchy bit. (see page 238)

## Lincolnshire Poacher

Mild need not mean boring, and Poacher straddles the fence of the increasingly intense, sweeter, edging-on-Swiss flavors that evolve across the Cheddar types. Smoother than typical Cheddar's crumble, with beautiful buttered hay aromas. (see page 241)

## Montgomery's Cheddar

The English clothbound Cheddar that induces awe and has inspired a generation of American cheese people, myself included. Its variability is what makes it truly artisanal; its ability to taste like caramelized beef fat is what makes it my top pick. (see page 251)

## TASTING ONE
# AMERICAN BLOCK CHEDDAR

Don't knock the block. It's not all forgettable, interchangeable cheese confined to being mild or sharp. Great and complex Cheddar comes in block form.

**1. Medium Cheddar (from Mild, Medium, and Sharp: Supermarket Upgrades** (see page 231)

**2. Prairie Breeze from Milton Creamery** (see page 238)

**3. Hook's Cheddar** (see page 244)

## TASTING TWO
# ENGLAND, MAKING MORE THAN CHEDDAR

To an American palate, if it's firm and cow milk and English, then it's Cheddar. Tasting the territorials (see page 232) and newer English recipes together is an incomparable way to discover all the flavors that make these cheeses distinct unto themselves.

**1. Red Leicester** (see page 230)

**2. Appleby's Cheshire** (see page 234)

**3. Hafod** (see page 250)

## TASTING THREE
# NEW WORLD VERSUS OLD WORLD

As with wine, there are flavor trends in American cheese that differ from the traditional profiles of Old World comparables. Side by side, these become evident.

**1. Caerphilly** (see page 236) **and Landaff from Landaff Creamery** (see page 237)

**2. Flagship from Beecher's Handmade Cheese** (see page 246) **and Barber's 1833 Vintage Reserve Cheddar** (see page 241)

**3. Cabot Clothbound Cheddar** (see page 247) **and Quicke's** (see page 250) **or Montgomery's Cheddar** (see page 251)

## PAIRING OVERVIEW

LACTIC

BUTTERMILK

*HELVETICUS* (ADJUNCT CULTURE THAT MAKES CANDIED AND BUTTERED TOAST FLAVORS)

DIRTY EARTH

## BEAR IN MIND

Acid is a universal component of Cheddar types' flavor.

Fruit and sugar balance acid and dirty/earthy flavor.

Acid and bitterness tasted alongside acidic cheese can make these qualities recede, pushing secondary flavors forward.

Although Cheddar types are firm (and can play the role of cracker), they are also dense and moist. This makes them well suited to refreshing crunch/palate cleansing.

## CLASSIC PAIRINGS

(Whole flavor spectrum) with chutney

(Lactic/buttermilk) melted with mustard, Worcestershire sauce, and porter/stout: Welsh rarebit

(Dirty earth) with pickles: ploughman's lunch

### 1. SMEARABLE FRUIT PASTES/SPREADS

I avoid smearable condiments with creamy, buttery cheeses because I want to avoid a mouthful of goo. Firm cheeses can act as cracker or bread slice, and a favorite (incredibly easy) appetizer of mine is one of these cheeses smeared with fruit paste. What's key? Acidity! Honey or strawberry jam on these cheeses feels like a sticky, drippy mess. A tart fruit spread cuts fat and salt while complementing nutty, earthy, and gamy flavors.

Lighter fruit pastes such as pear, apricot, and pomegranate: **FLAVOR SPECTRUM 1–5**

More intense/tart fruit pastes such as plum, cherry, fig, and quince: **FLAVOR SPECTRUM 6–10**

### 2. SWEETER PICKLES

Take a cue from the classics, Cheddar and chutney and ploughman's lunch, which traditionally relied on sweeter pickles. Sweeter pickled pairings give you sugar and acidity, balancing earthy flavor and cutting Cheddar's moist, dense paste. Pickled fruits, such as raisins, figs, cherries, or apricots (Boat Street Pickles is my favorite brand); chutney (The Virginia Chutney Co.); or sweeter pickled vegetables, such as bread and butter pickles or pickled beets, are all winners.

**FLAVOR SPECTRUM: 1–10**

### 3. (HARD) CIDER

Only in the States do we call it "hard." What I mean is dry, alcoholic cider of the funky, earthy, and tannic sorts that the United Kingdom, France, and, increasingly, the United States specialize in. Here you can drink your apples, with the added benefits of acidity and effervescence to scrub the palate clean.

**FLAVOR SPECTRUM: 1–10**

RUPERT

COMTÉ

GRANDCRU

# Swiss

EMMENTALER

GRUYÈRE

TÊTE DE MOINE

TARENTA

HEUBLEUMEN

**SPECIALTY SHOP**

**Andeerer Schmuggler**
PAGE 276

**Heubleumen**
PAGE 275

**Beaufort PDO**
PAGE 277

**Abondance PDO**
PAGE 279

**Tarentaise (4-8 months)**
PAGE 288

**Tête de Moine AOP**
PAGE 280

**(Gruyère de) Comté PDO**
PAGE 278

**GrandCru (Original/Reserve)**
PAGE 276

**Appenzeller**
PAGE 279

**SUPERMARKET** ➻

**Baby Swiss**
PAGE 272

**Emmentaler**
PAGE 275

**Jarlsberg**
PAGE 272

**AVAILABILITY**

**FLAVOR** APPROACHABLE ➻

**1** COOKED MILK

**2** TOAST AND MELLOW TOASTED NUTS (ALMONDS)

**3** INTENSE TOASTED NUTS (FILBERTS)

**4** COFFEE

**5** WHITE PEPPER

**Rupert**
PAGE 288

**L'Etivaz AOP**
PAGE 284

**Rupert
(Reserve)**
PAGE 288

**Adelegger**
PAGE 289

**Holey Cow**
PAGE 280

**Viamala**
PAGE 282

**Tarentaise
(9 month+)**
PAGE 288

**GrandCru
(Surchoix)**
PAGE 276

**Alpha Tolman**
PAGE 281

**Pleasant
Ridge Reserve**
PAGE 284

**Der Scharfe
Maxx**
PAGE 286

**Challerhocker**
PAGE 290

**Le Gruyère AOP**
PAGE 282

INTENSE

| 6 | 7 | 8 | 9 | 10 |
|---|---|---|---|---|
| CURED MEAT | JERKY, SMOKE | CARAMEL, DULCE DE LECHE | PINEAPPLE PRICKLE | ALL THAT, PLUS CARAMELIZED ONION |

# Cheese people aren't supposed to hate any cheeses. It would be like hating one of your children. But Swissy cheeses have given me the

heebie jeebies from the time I was little. If you're anything like me, you grew up understanding Swiss cheese to be a plasticized block sliced at the deli counter alongside a glistening pink lobe of boiled ham. It was usually cut pretty thick, so each piece was slightly stiff. The reason I really hated Swiss cheese was because of its sweet, oddly nutty flavor, like milk boiled too long in a pot. At the same time, it was reminiscent of old socks. Swiss cheese was the one with the big holes, and I came to think of its particular flavor as sweet feet. Blessedly, this could be muted by a heavy slathering of Hellmann's and mustard on my ham sandwich, but whenever I had the option, I avoided anything purporting to be Swiss cheese.

It never occurred to me that Swiss cheese might be an unfair and incomplete catchall term, just as it never occurred to me that the floppy Kraft Singles standing in for American cheese were really selling our country short. A more accurate phrase for Swiss types is Alpine cheese, but only hard-core cheese folk and informed retailers are likely to use this descriptor. Traditionally, Alpine cheeses were large wheels made of unpasteurized cow milk, designed to preserve that milk for many months or even years. Historically, these cheeses were produced seasonally, when animals went to graze in the high-altitude pastures of surrounding mountains. What the Swiss Gateway ushers you into is a group of cheeses that are dense, firm, and ageable, but still moist (never dry or hard). They melt in glorious cheese rivers and are characteristically sweet (not too salty, not sharp or acidic). Each bite is full of cooked milk and toasted nut flavors.

When I started working in cheese, I was still dodging Swiss, but confronted with a dozen cheeses from Switzerland I had never heard of, I began to realize that there might be more on offer than sweet feet. The inspiration for common American deli Swiss is the cheese Emmentaler. It's still not my favorite cheese, but man, what a difference the real thing makes, in all its hulking, 180-pound, carefully aged, rinded glory. It's complex and layered, each piece practically perfumed with mountain grasses and flowers. Then, there were other cheeses from Switzerland. And the mountainous regions of France and Austria, even Italy. It wasn't long before I saw fledgling American cheese makers making cheeses inspired by Swiss types. Some of the first really stellar American artisan cheeses paid homage not to the block with holes but to the mountain cheeses of the Alps and Jura.

The ever-expanding choices on the cheese counter opened my eyes to the possibilities of Swiss, but it was New York City's restaurants that finally and completely seduced me as a wide-eyed twentysomething. I was drawn again and again to rustic, simple dishes that I'd never had but that reminded me of my childhood table. There was the after-hours menu at Balthazar, led by Onion Soup Gratinée. Little did I realize that the brown pottery crock of glistening mahogany broth, topped with a veritable boat of properly stale baguette, was generously capped with melted, bubbling Gruyère—a cheese that Switzerland has been making exactly the same way for the past 900 years. Picking crusty drippings of cheese off the bowl's sides warmed me with inimitable satisfaction.

Le Gamin, with its bowls (not cups) of café au lait, offered the sophisticated Croque Monsieur (or egg-enriched Croque Madame): essentially the greatest hangover food ever invented. Buttered bread with melted Emmentaler and ham sandwiched between, drowned in golden, bubbling béchamel. Inside all those layers, I'd never have known the cheese once had telltale holes, so distracted was I by its lingering, roasted nuttiness.

At the cheese restaurant Artisanal, I ate dozen-cheese fondue from a hammered copper cauldron simmering with an opaque, glistening cheese soup and accompanied by generous side plates of bread, crunchy apple slices, and nubbins of salami. Each swipe had a lingering, high fruitiness that I attributed to white wine, which somehow made eating an entire pot of melted cheese seem obvious, light, and balanced. It was so silken, so easy—the food equivalent to a cashmere turtleneck. Sated and stupefied, I barely registered the belated horror of learning that the fondue was comprised of 12 different Swiss cheeses, blended varyingly on any given night for layers of lactic, fruity, animal, and spicy flavor.

I loved them all. It dawned on me then that *this* was Swiss cheese. Cheeses that had been made to work this whispering, beguiling magic, and had been doing so in the classic recipes of Europe for centuries. From there, it was a small step to learning that eating a piece straight off a wheel brought nearly the same satisfaction. I had been duped, it turned out. Those childhood delis weren't selling Swiss cheese. They were selling bad cheese. Say good-bye to sweet feet and plasticky holes. Alpine cheeses are not only varied and magnificent, they are uniquely programmed to satisfy some carnal part of both mind and body: warm, melty, gooey, salt-sweet, moist, chewable, and tasting powerfully of the thin-aired, flower-dotted land from whence they come.

# Chapter Guide

Swiss is the catchall that refers to the firm, aged, cooked pressed cow milk cheeses of France's Jura, west into Switzerland, and farther west still atop the Alpine spine of Austria, Switzerland, and northern Italy. These days, Swiss types (or, more accurately, Alpine) cheeses can be found farther afield, most notably across the United States, from Vermont to Virginia, Wisconsin to California.

## WHAT TO KNOW

**WHAT DOES COOKED PRESSED MEAN?** For years, I've debated the merits of technical cheese classification. What's helpful about the technicalities is that specific choices in the cheese-making process result in specific flavors or textures when you eat the finished cheese. Here, what's relevant is that Alpine cheeses are made with a short acidification process and a long, slow period of heating, stirring, and cutting of the curd. The curd is then drained, pressed, and brined, for at least several hours and often as long as a day.

**WHAT WILL SWISS TYPES BE?** Because of the cooking/pressing process you can expect certain commonalities of texture, age, flavor, and more. Expect cheeses that are:

➡ Firm in texture but still elastic—never dry, rock-hard, or granular.

➡ Aged. Invented to preserve summer milk so it could be eaten in winter, they are designed for 5 to 24 months of aging.

➡ Larger in size (typically 15 to 80 pounds, although sometimes as big as 220).

➡ Sweet in flavor (meaning, not sharp, acidic, or overly salted). They are nutty, with a backbone of cooked milk and brown-butter notes.

➤ Brilliantly gooey when melted: not greasy, not prone to separation; just slick, stretchy, and runny.

➤ Potentially brine washed during aging, with an exterior anywhere from tan to dark sandy brown to tacky, damp, and orange.

**WHAT ARE SWISS TYPES NOT?**

➤ Necessarily from Switzerland. Swiss cheese is an American invention. In Switzerland, all cheeses have unique names and histories, and the majority of Swiss cheese in the United States is made somewhere other than Switzerland (often, the American Midwest).

➤ Necessarily made from cow milk. Most are, and the traditional mountain cheeses of Switzerland and France are, but this style can be made of other milk types.

➤ Necessarily a specific flavor. Each Swiss type has its own nuance; its own tweaks in the make process; its own origins of milk, of feed, of soil. Even wheels produced within a dozen miles of one another exhibit unique qualities.

**WHY ARE ALPINE CHEESES COOKED PRESSED CHEESES?** The historical origins of Alpine cheeses are among the most satisfyingly practical in the entire world of food. They come from poorer agricultural regions with a limited growing season, limited growing land, and a great dependence on cows (animals that require a lot of grass or hay to survive). With the melting of winter snows, cows were led into the alps (that's lowercase *a*, referring to the higher plains of whatever mountains were close by) for summer grazing. Typically this began not before May and ended by October. The reason for this seasonal migration was to clear lower grazing land for crop growing, in particular hay growing for those same cows that would need to eat during the following winter. While on the alp, the cows were milked and cheese had to be made efficiently and economically. This meant a few things:

➤ If it was to be a reliable food source, the cheese had to be durable enough to spend the summer aging in mountain huts and then durable enough to last through the winter.

➤ In order to make long-lasting cheese, water had to be removed from curd.

➤ Salt was both rare and heavy, so cheese making couldn't rely on huge amounts of salt to dehydrate the curd.

➤ Fires could be kindled and curd cooked to naturally expel moisture. This technique was first explored by cheese makers in the mountains of Switzerland.

➤ Larger wheels meant longer storage potential and fewer pieces of cheese to transport at season's end.

The author Paul Kindstedt writes movingly and brilliantly about the cultural origins of Alpine (and other) cheeses in his books *American Farmstead Cheese* and *Cheese and Culture*.

## WHAT TO AVOID

In the world of cheese, the big, brawny, aged cheeses are regarded as durable. And, compared with the limp Brie types and the flaky freshies, they are. They were invented to be. That does not, however, make them indestructible. I once had a customer call and complain that her Gruyère was bad after two months sitting on her counter. The Parmesan in the can, she pointed out, didn't get moldy when she did that. This is not cheese in a can.

➤ **COLOR:** When you see a sizable (half inch) perimeter of browning under the rind, you're looking at an old and dried-out cheese. Not spoiled, but not as good as it should be. The exposed, cut face of these cheeses should not have specks of blue or green mold. This is an indication that cheese has been sitting, precut in plastic, for too long. The mold won't hurt you and may be scraped off, but the cheese is likely to taste like plastic wrap. To avoid this predicament, especially in a supermarket context, I opt for cheeses wrapped in a waxy parchment-looking paper by the producer. These are vacuum-sealed and are least likely to have off-flavors. Or I opt for cheeses that are freshly cut in front of me.

➤ **FLAVOR:** Peppery flavors or tongue-burning sensations are not desirable in this style. Conversely, absolutely tasteless cheese is not acceptable. The flavor of more subtle and delicate Alpine cheeses, such as Comté (see page 278), dissipates into nothingness when wrapped in plastic and left to sit for several weeks. Whenever possible, get a taste from a larger chunk, and a custom-cut piece.

➤ **RIND:** Avoid cheeses with a mushy rind or ones that smell strongly of ammonia.

## STORAGE AND SHELF LIFE

Alpine cheeses were the original vehicles for preserving milk through long, cold, mountainous winters. Within the world of cheese, they have a relatively long shelf life. That said, they're not impermeable. Paper wrap alone (unless it's specially designed cheese paper) will shorten shelf life because the cheese will rapidly dry out. My preference is plastic zip-top plastic bags so you can squeeze all the air out and have individual storage units. Plastic wrap becomes a legitimate possibility here because low-moisture cheeses are more durable than any of the Brie types. My trick when wrapping in plastic is to always "face" the cheese before serving. Meaning: run a knife along the cut surface of a cheese to scrape off the paper-thin layer that's been in contact with the plastic. Taking the time to expose the fresh cheese underneath costs you very little and buys you instantly renewed and refreshed flavor.

Ideally, cheeses in the Swiss Gateway should be eaten within two weeks of being cut, although they can last for three to four weeks with diminished flavor and complexity.

Small spots of blue or green mold may develop on the cut surface of the cheese. These can be easily scraped away and the cheese beneath consumed, although they are a reliable warning sign that you're pushing the limit on storage life.

# SWISS TYPES: TEXTURES

## IN A WORD: PLIABLE

### SMOOTH AND/OR SPRINGY
CHEWY  COMPACT  ELASTIC  EVEN
PLIABLE  PRESSED  SLICEABLE
SMOOTH  SMUSHABLE  SUPPLE
TENDER

### DENSE AND/OR CRUMBLY
CRYSTALLINE  DENSE  FIRM

### FLAWS
GUMMY  MEALY  RUBBERY  WAXY

# SWISS TYPES: FLAVOR & AROMA WHEEL

# Baby Swiss

**UNITED STATES/
NETHERLANDS**

COW

(UN)PASTEURIZED

**RECOMMENDED BRANDS:**
Guggisberg Grass-Fed, Melkbus
58, Swiss Valley Farms

**AROMA:** Mild, sweet

**TEXTURE:** Springy but creamy

**FLAVOR:** Sweet, milk, Swissy

IN SHORT: Approachable

As the name implies, Baby Swiss is a not-especially technical description for a smaller, younger wheel of Swiss (aka Emmentaler, see page 275)-style cheese. Various producers take credit for inventing the cheese in the American Midwest during the 1950s and 1960s, supposedly because the American palate couldn't handle full-on Emmentaler recipes being made by Swiss immigrant makers. Less age means less time for the *Propionic shermanii* bacteria to do their work, resulting in smaller holes and a less pronounced sweet/nutty flavor wallop. Someone who doesn't love Emmentaler (see page 275) may prefer Baby Swiss because, essentially, it's milder. The better producers can be counted on for a moist and pliable but exceptionally creamy paste with a soft, yogurty flavor. For an eminently satisfying Cuban sandwich, you can't beat it. Some producers are doing a great job with milk sourcing (grass-fed, local, rBGH [genetically engineered hormone]-free, etc.), and these guys get a gold star from me.

# Jarlsberg

**NORWAY | COW**

**PASTEURIZED**

**AROMA:** Subdued, classic Swiss

**TEXTURE:** Pliable, slightly
gummy

**FLAVOR:** Buttered nuts

IN SHORT: Ubiquitous

Ironically, Jarlsberg is the cheese that gave generic Swiss its first (and still today, most powerful) brand name. Ironic because the cheese is actually produced in Norway and named for one of the counties where Swiss cheese-making techniques first took hold in the nineteenth century. The farmer-owned cooperative that makes Jarlsberg (pronounced Yarls-berg) is Norway's largest producer of dairy products, and their part-skim cheese is made to be as consistent and versatile as possible: block or wheel, low fat or regular, pliant and mild, sweet, and nutty. And of course smattered with holes. I think it's a pretty boring cheese, and the Lite (reduced fat version) is quite gummy. But it's an important reference point from which to begin upgrading. If you like it, you'll love the other approachable cheeses in this gateway.

BABY SWISS

EMMENTALER

APPROACHABLE

# Emmentaler

Here then is the cheese that inspired the name Swiss. Originally produced in the Emme valley in the Canton of Bern, Swiss Emmentaler is an AOP cheese, meaning its production is regulated within Switzerland. Emmentaler, Emmenthaler, or Swiss are hole-pocked cow milk cheeses striving for a similarly sweet and nutty flavor, and they may be produced anywhere. Swiss Emmentaler AOP must be made of raw, silage-free milk, and even the youngest wheels are aged for four months in humid cellars. During this time, a unique fermentation occurs within the cheese thanks to the work of propionic bacteria. The cheese's supple, elastic paste bulges and bends under pressure from the gas, causing the signature holes—or, as they are also creepily known as, "eyes." Do be prepared for the fact that freshly cut, cave-aged Emmentaler will leak butterfat from the holes. Crying eyes are a sign of quality, not spoilage. Each wheel can be traced back to its dairy of origin. A single producer in the United States, Edelweiss Creamery, makes traditional Emmentaler-sized wheels ripened from seventeen to twenty-four months, delivering a superior nutty flavor and less of the sweet Swiss-feety flavor that I don't personally care for.

**SWITZERLAND/ UNITED STATES**

COW

**UNPASTEURIZED**

**RECOMMENDED BRANDS:** Emmi, Edelweiss, Gourmino

**AROMA:** Sweet feet

**TEXTURE:** Firm yet pliable

**FLAVOR:** Moist nuttiness

IN SHORT: The Classic

# Heubleumen

An Appenzellerish-sized wheel, Heubleumen is one of thirty-plus cheeses invented by Thomas Stadelman. He's the gut man on the Swiss cheese scene. As he told me, he has visions of new cheeses and is constantly experimenting with traditional base recipes that he modifies following his intuition and dreams. Heubleumen begins as a recipe typical of the region, rubbed after three months of aging with dry hay flowers. When I asked if you're meant to eat the rind, he said, "No. The rind is the package. You don't eat the wrapper with the chocolate." But oh, what a wrapper, redolent of a dusty hayloft and contented animals. I fantasize about melting slabs atop buttered bread and enjoying grilled cheese and hay soup in one bite.

**SWITZERLAND | COW**

**UNPASTEURIZED**

**AROMA:** Hay dust

**TEXTURE:** Firm, a bit gummy

**FLAVOR:** Piece of hay, cowboy style

IN SHORT: Equine

SWITZERLAND | COW

UNPASTEURIZED

**AROMA:** Dry earth

**TEXTURE:** Lip-smacking

**FLAVOR:** Buttered almonds

IN SHORT: Surprising

# Andeerer Schmuggler

There are cheeses worth finding and tasting because to do so is to taste something magical. Fleeting, inconsistent perhaps, but coming from a place and a person that feels otherworldly. Such are the cheeses of Floh (Flea) Martin at Sennerei Andeer. A proponent of organic farming, a champion of cows with horns, and a revolutionary in the Canton of Grabunden, Floh is the creative vision behind a series of cheeses made by his wife Maria. Each follows a similar base recipe, but the final cheese varies greatly due to milk skimming, aging times, and seasonal milk supply. Schmuggler takes its name from Floh's time as a smuggler, when he would illegally ferry 100 wheels of cheese a year into Germany. Although the milk is partially skimmed, by nine months it has a shockingly dense and fatty-seeming texture. Each year at my childhood Thanksgivings, my mother would bake cookie sheets of almonds tossed in two sticks of butter. Eating Floh's cheese was an experience in time travel, back to those holidays and the sweet, slippery, satiating crunch of butter-toasted nuts.

UNITED STATES | COW

PASTEURIZED

**AROMA:** Minimal, toasty

**TEXTURE:** Firm and pliable, chewy

**FLAVOR:** Friendly, milky, nutty

IN SHORT: The house cheese

# GrandCru FROM ROTH CHEESE

Cousins Fermo Jaeckle and Felix Roth opened Wisconsin creamery Roth Käse USA Ltd. (now Roth Cellars) in 1991. They have family roots in Swiss cheese export and production dating back to 1863, so it's no surprise that a traditional Alpine-style cheese would be one of their first (and still signature) recipes. Relying on imported copper vats typically used for cheese making in Switzerland and eastern France, Roth's GrandCru reaches the market in a smaller wheel, thus requiring less aging time. Like Gruyère (see page 282), the wheels are smeared with brine before cellar aging of four months (Original) to more than nine months (*Surchoix*, which means "top quality"). The younger profiles, Original and Reserve (six to nine months), are solid eating and cooking cheeses. They melt beautifully, with consistently reliable flavors of cooked milk and lightly toasted hazelnuts. In my house, they are fridge cheeses, which should be considered a compliment. We keep them around for everyday noshing. The Surchoix offers a markedly deeper level of intensity, but unlike its Swiss inspirations it tends toward the smooth and butterscotchy rather than the beefy. Expect a softer, more pliable texture that can veer toward gummy.

# Beaufort PDO

In the high mountain valleys of Savoie and in parts of the Haute Savoie lie the massifs of the Alps. Here, Beaufort is produced from the milk of Tarentaise and Abondance cows that migrate from the valley floors to high Alpine pastures with the melting of winter snows. Although Beaufort is made like Comté (see page 278) or Gruyère (see page 282), it is distinguished by its high butterfat content and cold-cellar ripening. The cheese must be aged for a minimum of five months, and it gets spectacularly interesting at ten to sixteen months. The wheels of eighty-plus pounds are hooped in a concave wooden mold. The rind of the cheese forms a convenient track for ropes that were once used to strap wheels to the backs of animals for the return trip down the mountain sides. Beaufort été denotes a cheese made from June to October, including wheels made from high-altitude Alpine milk. Beaufort chalet d'alpage is reserved for wheels made from June to October twice a day in Alpine chalets at an altitude of greater than 1,500 meters. The cheeses must be made using traditional methods, and the milk is produced from a single herd. I don't find that Beaufort gets the same beefy, saline intensity of many Gruyère wheels arriving on U.S. shores. Instead, well-aged—and especially chalet d'alpage—wheels are a concentration of floral, fatty complexity. Subtle, but long-lingering and full-on *Sound of Music*. The creamy cling means a moist, succulent mouthfeel that bolsters flavors of toasted filberts and abundant, fresh hay.

**FRANCE | COW**

**UNPASTEURIZED**

**AROMA:** Marigolds and barely dried hay

**TEXTURE:** Dense but incredibly moist and fatty

**FLAVOR:** Toasted hazelnut and warm cream

**IN SHORT:** Von Trapp–errific

## WHERE DOES SWISS GET ITS HOLES FROM?

The fruity, nutty flavor and moist, foot-like aroma of Emmentaler (a combination I shudderingly think of as sweet feet) exist because the cheese is low in acid (sweet) and contains a bacteria called *Propionic shermanii*. This particular combo is also the key to the holes in Swiss. *P. shermanii* are anaerobic, meaning they thrive in the interior of low-acid cheese, particularly at warmer temperatures. By thrive I mean multiply, and in so doing creating a secondary fermentation that releases gas (carbon dioxide). The uniquely elastic texture of Emmentaler (and other Alpine cheeses) enables the cheese to bulge and expand around these interior gas bubbles, creating holes rather than cracks or explosions. Most Alpine cheeses have occasional holes the size of olive pits. Emmentaler is unique in its gaping eyes, which can be as large as peach pits.

# (Gruyère de) Comté PDO

**FRANCE | COW**

**UNPASTEURIZED**

**RECOMMENDED BRANDS:**
Alpage (made when cows are eating summer grass, mandated for all Comté in summer), Essex Street Comté (selected by Essex Street Cheese, aged at the Fort St. Antoine), Fort St. Antoine, Marcel Petite (the affineur at Fort St. Antoine, so essentially the same thing)

**AROMA:** Warm croissants

**TEXTURE:** So moist, firm yet barely knitted together

**FLAVOR:** Truly an extraordinary range, from sweet and gentle to coffee and cacao

**IN SHORT:** Varied and fascinating

Comté has much in common with Gruyère (see page 282). Produced in the Jura Massif region of eastern France, Comté is both an AOC and AOP regulated cheese resulting from a careful partnership between 3,000 family farms, roughly 170 *fruitieres* (village dairies) and a few select affineurs. The breeds of cow whose exclusively raw milk may be used are limited to Montbéliarde and French Simmental. A strict grass diet is enforced, and silage feed is not allowed. Unlike Gruyère, Comté milk is partially skimmed before heating in copper vats, but the final cheeses are graded like Gruyère. Top scorers get a green band, lower scorers a brown band, and the lowest don't receive the Comté name. Although some wheels are sold at 120 days, others age as long as 18 months and sometimes more. I attribute the greatest challenge facing Comté to this massive potential age range. It is essentially five cheeses in one. Younger wheels are mild to the point of timidity, and even well-aged wheels might be described (as one cheese friend puts it) as a Saturday afternoon cheese. You could eat it all damn day. It's subtle, complex, unbelievably moist. The flavor is smoother and less salty than Gruyère, with more stone fruit than beefy tendencies. Often, Comté's subtlety is lost on those expecting big, sharp, or butt-kicking flavor. It's none of those things, and that's what makes it so ephemerally delicious. Unfortunately it also dies quickly in plastic wrap, contributing to a perception of the cheese as bland, so have it cut in front of you whenever possible.

## ONE CHEESE, A THOUSAND SMELLS

The Comté Aroma Wheel was one of the first graphics that hammered home for me how complex a single cheese can be. It also inspired the flavor/aroma wheels that appear throughout this book.

CIGC/Comté Cheese Association

# Appenzeller

I give the Appenzeller Guild marketing credit for branding the cheese the "spiciest in Switzerland." I don't really agree with the description, but more on that in a minute. Appenzeller, although not an AOP cheese, is strictly regulated by the Guild. Silver-labeled Classic must be aged for a minimum of three months, gold-labeled Surchoix for four, and black-foiled Extra at least six. Production occurs, as it has for 700 years, in the Cantons of Appenzell Innerrhodden, Appenzell Ausserrhodden, and parts of St. Gallen and Thurgau. The monks of the Abbey of St. Gallen received land taxes in the form of cheese. Today, fifty-eight producers make the cheese from partially skimmed milk delivered twice each day to the village dairy. After production, wheels are sent to central aging facilities, where they are washed in the extra-secret herbal brine. My impression of Appenzeller as not particularly spicy is due to the fact that the vast majority of the cheese on the U.S. market is the Classic, youngest age profile. Add to this the explosion of singular and unique cheeses now being made in Switzerland, many of which boast intense, oniony, and beefy notes. By comparison, Appenzeller tastes rather tame. That being said, Appenzeller Extra has a black pepper tingle that would land it at 7 to 8 on the Swiss type intensity scale.

SWITZERLAND | COW
UNPASTEURIZED

**AROMA:** Cooked milk

**TEXTURE:** Dense, smooth, and firm

**FLAVOR:** Nutty, scalded milk, edging into spicy with age

IN SHORT: Robust

# Abondance PDO

Named for the village of Abondance in the French Alps of Haut-Savoie, Abondance is the twelfth-century child of Gruyère (see page 282) and Comté (see page 278). Like its parents, the cheese is made of unpasteurized cow milk, strictly regulated by AOC guidelines. The animals graze in Alpine pastures during warmer months, and the cheese's production is a careful balance between farmer (milk maker), fruitiere (cheese maker), and affineur (ager). It is made in a copper vat using animal rennet and then is cut, stirred, pressed, and aged on wood boards. From Mama Comté, it gets restricted cow breeds; in this case, Tarentaise, Montbeliarde, and Abondance. From Papa Gruyère, it gets a reliance on whole milk rather than skimmed, and like the most traditional Gruyère (Alpage), the cheese is made by gathering curd in a linen cloth secured around the neck of the cheese maker. It's littler than its better-known kin—wheels are typically fifteen to twenty-five pounds with a minimum aging time of 100 days. The concave sides recall French Beaufort (see page 277), and it's a size, shape, and flavor profile that have inspired several notable American producers, including Thistle Hill, Spring Brook Farm (see page 288), and Uplands Cheese Company (see page 284).

FRANCE | COW
UNPASTEURIZED

**AROMA:** Gently cooked milk, floral

**TEXTURE:** Supple

**FLAVOR:** Warm spice, red fruit

IN SHORT: Good potpourri

SWITZERLAND | COW
UNPASTEURIZED

**AROMA:** Plummy

**TEXTURE:** Meltingly tender

**FLAVOR:** Full and fruity

**IN SHORT:** Gently spicy

UNITED STATES | COW
PASTEURIZED

**AROMA:** Moist foot

**TEXTURE:** Plump and plush

**FLAVOR:** Brine, jerky

**IN SHORT:** Nobody puts baby
(Swiss) in a corner

# Tête de Moine AOP

The "head of the monk" exists for one reason alone: to be served with a nifty circular blade (*girolle*), which skims the outside of the cheese, shaving off paper-thin rosettes. Technically you can eat it by the chunk, but if you're going to do that, there are better Alpine cheeses to choose. What makes this one good is slipping a silky, barely there shaving on your tongue and letting it melt away into a fruity, slow burn finish. Beginning in 1192, Tête was paid out as taxes from the Abbey of Bellelay; these days it's produced by eight village dairies in the Swiss Jura. The small drums are aged seventy-five days (Classic) while being washed in a brine solution that develops the sticky, orange rind. The paste is remarkably soft and pliable compared with other mountain cheeses. Even the reserve cheeses of four-plus months are delicate and melting. It is said that the girolle shaving exposes the cheese to air, allowing its white pepper spice to unfold, like letting an aged wine breathe.

# Holey Cow FROM CENTRAL COAST CREAMERY

I'll admit it. When I encounter a cheese purporting to be in the style of another cheese (Baby Swiss, see page 272) that is itself a dumbed-down version of a third cheese (Emmentaler, see page 275), and that cheese's name is a questionable pun, I am immediately biased against it. Holey Cow hails from a California creamery that produces a wide variety of styles from all three of the major milk types. It is also a compelling example of why you should push past your food assumptions and try new things, even things you expect will be bad. Holey Cow certainly has the firm-yet-squashy mouthfeel of well-made younger Swiss, but its flavor is far more complex, edging into the pleasantly foot-y. It's not orange or stinky; actually, it's rindless, so you wouldn't expect to find the depth characteristic of larger, longer-aged Alpine cheeses. But there it is. American West Coast cheese folk will likely be familiar because it's celebrated across California for an approachability that doesn't sacrifice interest or complexity.

# Alpha Tolman FROM JASPER HILL FARM

One of the many great joys of Jasper Hill's cheeses is the genealogy of their names. Alpha Tolman was not only a philanthropist, building the local library in Greensboro, Vermont, but a dairy farmer as well. In his honor comes the farm's first readily available Alpine-style cheese. Relative to its European counterparts, Alpha is a little guy, more akin to Appenzeller (see page 279) or Abondance (see page 279) than hulking Gruyère (see page 282), Comté (see page 278), or Beaufort (see page 277) wheels. As such, it more quickly reveals the impact of aging. Typically sold at eight to eleven months, Alpha has by then developed meatier, caramelized onion flavor. Younger wheels are more delicate, all melted butter and red fruit. It's supple enough for a Raclette redux and full enough to be your fondue go-to.

**UNITED STATES | COW**
**UNPASTEURIZED**
**AROMA:** Meat and wood
**TEXTURE:** Dense, pliant
**FLAVOR:** From melted butter to French onion soup
**IN SHORT:** Manly

SWITZERLAND | COW

UNPASTEURIZED

**RECOMMENDED BRANDS:**
1655, Emmi Kaltbach, Gourmino, Mifroma (The consistently
best brand is 1655, where wheels
come from one of three dairies
with monthly average cheese
grading scores of 19 out of 20
over 5 years. All wheels are aged
a minimum of 12 months.)

**AROMA:** Unsweetened Nutella

**TEXTURE:** Dense chew

**FLAVOR:** Hazelnut skins,
cooked milk

**IN SHORT:** The king of
Alpine cheese

# Le Gruyère AOP

After spending the better part of a week visiting Gruyère producers, the three affineurs responsible for 99 percent of the cheese exported to the Unted States, and milk makers, my key observation is that the Gruyère in Switzerland is appreciably different from most of what's available in the States. The difference is mainly textural: the paste is dense but creamy in the mouth with no breaking and minimal crystallization. In the States, I've come to expect and celebrate Gruyère that's laced with little crunchy bits. Across the Atlantic, the flavors are also more fruity and lactic, with less savory, roasted, or beefy qualities. Gruyère tastes cleaner and sweeter in Switzerland. My favorite cheese of my last trip was a thirteen-month aged plug from the private store of Laiterie de Billens' maker Bernard Oberson. It sang with tropical fruitiness—papaya and pineapple—of the sort I've rarely encountered on counters at home. I chalk these differences up to poor storage and age. A lot of the Gruyère that makes it to American mouths has been sitting in cold, dry containers, and warehouses. It loses moisture, salt concentrates, and increasingly meaty flavors push to the fore. I like the beef bouillon intensity many Gruyères have, but going to the source revealed the possibility of a different typical standard for this magnificent cheese. For lovers of the rustic, Gruyère d'alpage is a rarity worth seeking as most wheels boast smoky, toasty undertones thanks to open fire cooking during cheese making.

# Viamala

Once known as Nufenen, the name of the village and dairy that produces this cheese, Viamala is tangible, edible proof of a new generation of Swiss cheese making. Individuals are moving away from the anonymous production of a regional type and creating a singular cheese sold under a unique name. The regional specialty is Bundner Bergkase; Viamala took that base recipe and aged it out to nine months. Brilliantly, the dairy has an underground pipe that allows cows to be milked through summer on higher altitude plateaus, and transports that milk down the mountain and into the cheesehouse. Although the dairy is quite modern, the cheese tastes of history. Even when it is as young as three months a whiff is smoky; by nine months it has lost the astringency of smoke but captured a eucalyptus edge. The creamy, dense flesh breaks cleanly. To eat the cheese is to pause, as I did, on a cold fogged-out mountainside, the eerie echo of cowbells rolling through the damp.

SWITZERLAND | COW

UNPASTEURIZED

**AROMA:** Corncob smoke

**TEXTURE:** Creamy and dense

**FLAVOR:** Eucalyptus
tongue tingle

**IN SHORT:** Fortifying

# WHAT DOES IT TAKE TO BE GRUYÈRE?

Gruyère has been made in western Switzerland since 1115, and remarkably little of its production and aging has changed in the ensuing 900 years. Much of this continuity is due to the strict production requirements that protect not only the Gruyère name but its historic cheese-making traditions.

• Cheese may be produced only in the five Swiss Cantons of Vaud, Neuchâtel, Jura, Bern (borders Emmentaler), and Friboug (where the town of Gruyère is located).

• Milk must be delivered twice each day, seven days a week, 365 days a year (no overnight storage).

• Milk may never be pasteurized.

• Milk is exclusively grass- and hay-fed. No silage is permitted.

• There are 170 village dairies (buying milk from local farms) and 53 Alpine dairies (milking at 1,000 to 1,800 meters from mid-May to mid-October and making only one to two cheeses daily).

• Alpine Gruyère curd is gathered by hand in a giant cloth, and many producers still heat the vat over an open fire.

• Gruyère is always made in a copper vat, and each vat can make only one batch of cheese each day.

• The evening milk acidifies overnight. In the morning, fresh milk is added; and then a whey-based starter culture is added; and the curd is coagulated with animal rennet.

• Village dairies hold their cheese for three months before it is transported to the aging cellar; Alpine dairies hold them for only one week due to space constraints.

• At four months, the cheese is graded and taxed, and permitted to be called Le Gruyère AOP only if it scores an 18 or higher on a quality scale of 1 to 20.

• The aging cellar matures the cheese for a minimum of five months before it may be sold as Le Gruyère AOP.

• The cheese hits market under various names:

➤➤ Le Gruyère AOP: six to nine months

➤➤ Le Gruyère AOP Réserve: at least ten months

➤➤ Le Gruyère AOP Bio: Produced using milk from farms certified by Bio-Suisse (organic)

➤➤ Le Gruyère d'alpage AOP: Produced from mid-May to autumn from mountain-pastured milk, pressed in a linen cloth, and made in smaller wheels (approximately fifty-five pounds)

# L'Etivaz AOP

SWITZERLAND | COW

UNPASTEURIZED

**AROMA:** Memories of woodsmoke

**TEXTURE:** Fine, smooth, firm but creamy

**FLAVOR:** Smoked Brazil nuts

IN SHORT: Concentrated

L'Etivaz is the cheese you get when a small group of cheese makers determines that Gruyère's AOP restrictions are too lenient and sets off to make a true mountain cheese, as one might have had 150 years ago. You could argue that this cheese would be Gruyère d'alpage. But if you were one of eighty-seven chalets in the Canton of Vaud, this cheese would be invented with an eye to history and named for the nearby town of Etivaz. Name protection would soon follow, making the cheese the first AOP in Switzerland. Production mimics Gruyère with the following modifications: cheese can only be made from May 10 to October 10; vat heating must occur over open flame; curds are gathered from the vat with a cloth; wheels can range from 10 to 38 kilograms (22 to 84 pounds); the cheeses are aged for a year or more. The two major flavor contributors to L'Etivaz are the Alpine grasses and herbs that cows are restricted to during the summer months, and the pungent spruce smoke swirling over open copper vats during cheese making. As the cooperative charmingly describes it, "After a long aging, the aromas of this birth resurface as childhood memories." The fine, firm, ivory-yellow paste has a flavor at once frank and aromatic: dusky hazelnut is typical, as are suggestions of smoke more than actual smoky taste. The fleetingly savory, herbaceous flavors fade quickly once the cheese is cut.

# Pleasant Ridge Reserve  FROM UPLANDS CHEESE COMPANY

UNITED STATES | COW

UNPASTEURIZED

**AROMA:** Cooked fruit, toast

**TEXTURE:** Tender. "You ought not to have to use your teeth," says Andy.

**FLAVOR:** Red fruit and papaya up front, followed by chicken stock

IN SHORT: Infinitely layered

This is the cheese that first demonstrated Americans' ability to make an Alpine style that rivaled Europe's greatest. First-generation founders Mike Gingrich and Dan Patenaude sold the business to second generation cheese maker Andy Hatch and farmer Scott Merika, who continue their commitment to seasonal, exclusively grass-based cheese making. Pleasant Ridge Reserve is the full name of the cheese, released as early as nine months; Extra Aged denotes wheels fifteen months and up, which are only five to ten percent of the total production. Summer is the best time to buy Pleasant Ridge, when stock is twelve to thirteen months old and the cheese is fudgy enough to smash between your tongue and the roof of your mouth. At that age, its complexity is in full force, anchored by distinct savory notes. As Andy says, "You want to taste that it came from an animal. There's so much sweet cheese out there." So he avoids making a cheese that's one-note caramel or butterscotch, delivering instead massive layers of flavor that continue unfolding long after you swallow. There's red fruit, followed by tropical, and the rich anchor of slow-simmered chicken stock. It's no wonder this cheese has won Best Cheese in America a record three times.

APPROACHABLE

# Der Scharfe Maxx

SWITZERLAND | COW

UNPASTEURIZED

**AROMA:** Remarkably stinky, oniony, and cooked cheesy

**TEXTURE:** Perfect toffee

**FLAVOR:** Caramelized onion soup and sometimes dulce de leche

IN SHORT: The mind-blower

Near Lake Constance, in the Canton of Thurgau, Daniel Studer oversees cheese making on the same grounds where his grandfather made Emmentaler (see page 275) in 1929. Times have changed since then, and Daniel saw the writing on the wall in the late 1980s. Emmentaler production was heavily subsidized and, anticipating an eventual backlash, Daniel applied to produce Appenzeller (see page 279). At that time, there wasn't enough on the market. When cheese production was deregulated by the Swiss government in 1999, Daniel took his excess milk and began inventing cheeses. The most impressive of these is Der Scharfe Maxx and its long-aged brethren Maxx Extra. Full-fat milk has cream added to it for a target 58 percent butterfat content. Although Scharfe Maxx looks like Appenzeller, it's made with unique cultures bred from skim milk. The same recipe that produces Der Scharfe Maxx can become Maxx Extra. Wheels are tasted at five months, and those with longer-aging potential are separated out for a full twelve months of ripening. You might expect that more time would simply mean a drier, saltier, stronger version of the original. In fact, it's nearly the opposite. With time comes a loss of water, and the presence of extra fat lends a creamier texture. There are little flecks of crisp, amino acid crystals whose formation is proof, says Daniel, that the cheese is ready. The spicy prickle of younger wheels fades to black in Maxx Extra, replaced by voluptuous slow-cooked, cheese-draped French onion soup. His favorite. My favorite.

# DO THE 'DUE

It wasn't until I visited the Gruyère region of Switzerland that I understood how much fondue the Swiss eat. It's not just a winter thing, or a special guest thing. It's the equivalent of frozen pizza night in the American suburbs. And with good reason—any Alpine-style cheese can be shredded; melted down with corn-starch and white wine; and served alongside bread, veggies, and even fruit for dipping.

**A FONDUE POT**

**1 POUND ALPINE (STYLE) CHEESE\***

**1 GARLIC CLOVE, HALVED**

**1 CUP DRY WHITE WINE**

**1 TABLESPOON CORNSTARCH**

**1 TABLESPOON FRESH LEMON JUICE**

**SALT AND PEPPER TO TASTE**

**DIPPERS: CRUSTY BREAD, APPLES, CRISP PEARS, BROCCOLI, AND CAULIFLOWER**

1. Rub a pot down with garlic; a double boiler works best as the cheese won't get too hot.

2. Add white wine and heat over medium-high heat.

3. While wine heats, toss the grated cheese with cornstarch.

4. Add the cheese to the pot one handful at a time, keeping heat below a simmer.

5. Stir until melted and glossy.

6. Add lemon juice, salt, and pepper to taste.

7. Transfer cheese to a fondue pot to keep cheese warm while eating.

8. Dip bread, fruit, and veggies.

SERVES 4

\* The classic blend in Gruyère is 50 percent Gruyère (see page 282) and 50 percent Vacherin Fribourg; here you're likely to be recommended Gruyère, Emmentaler (see page 275), and Appenzeller (see page 279) (the latter two because they're cheaper). Don't favor your wallet over your belly. Buy some better cheese. I also love GrandCru Surchoix (see page 276), Pleasant Ridge Reserve (see page 284), and Scharfe Maxx (see page 286) as possibilities.

UNITED STATES | COW

UNPASTEURIZED

**AROMA:** Juicy yellow fruit

**TEXTURE:** Velvety firm, studded with crystals

**FLAVOR:** Lush, pineapple and papaya

IN SHORT: Tropical

UNITED STATES | COW

UNPASTEURIZED

**AROMA:** Pineapple upside-down cake

**TEXTURE:** Dense, crystalline

**FLAVOR:** From Castelvetrano olive to tropical fruity

IN SHORT: Gruyère mated with Parm

# Tarentaise FROM SPRING BROOK FARM

Tarentaise was inspired by the French mountain classic Beaufort (see page 277) and is the brainchild of John Putnam at Thistle Hill Farm (he still makes an organic Tarentaise today). The recipe and technique were taught to cheese maker Jeremy Stephenson at the nonprofit teaching farm Spring Brook/Farms for City Kids. The cheese had to be made with unpasteurized Jersey cow milk in imported copper vats. Appearance-wise, Tarentaise is a dead ringer for Abondance (see page 272), but the make technique more closely resembles Beaufort. I think of it as a hybrid. Jeremy's long, slow-pressing technique produces a cheese that's firm but velvety, not requiring too much bite and never gummy. His goal is to sell the cheese with a minimum of six months' age. And although every wheel isn't meant to become an eighteen-month reserve, my biggest complaint about Tarentaise is that much of what's available is too young to express the complexity of what this cheese can be, which is neon yellow; rich with ripe, tropical fruit; and finishing with the pleasant prickle of pineapple. It's worth buying less frequently to get a minimum nine- to twelve-month-old cheese.

# Rupert (Reserve)

**FROM CONSIDER BARDWELL FARM**

Like all of the farm's cheeses, this one is named for a nearby Vermont town, although its inspiration originates in the mountains of France and Switzerland. Unlike its European brethren, a well-aged Rupert (that would be, ideally, thirteen to sixteen months) assumes a chewy, crystalline texture that could mistakenly be called waxy. In fact, it's dense; lodging under tooth; and exploding with long, lingering tropical fruit notes. It even boasts the hairy-tongue intensity of fresh pineapple. Younger wheels are subtler, all broth and Castelvetrano olive, but incredibly savory, almost addictively so. The farm sells Rupert at ten to twelve months. Those wheels that are tasted and determined to have the ability to improve with age (rather than degrade into bitter or metallic flavors) are held to my preferred profile, fourteen to sixteen months, when they are sold as Rupert Reserve.

APPROACHABLE

# Adelegger

Driving through the apple-strewn valley around the tip of Lake Constance to get from Austria to southern (Bavarian) Germany, you feel how the Algau region of Germany and Austria have more to do with each other than either has to do with other parts of its own country. Presiding over Käsküche Isny, Evelyn Wild tells me how this land is meant for grassmaking. At 700 meters, it's too high for potatoes or corn. It's ideal for feeding cows. Adelegger is the recipe that Evelyn came to know when making cheese on the alp, a variation of the regional specialty Alpine Algau (or alp cheese). Despite being made in a style that's ubiquitous to the area, Adelegger is simply better than most alp cheese. It unfolds, mouthwatering, with an incredibly long finish anchored by sweet, hay-y milk flavor. It begins like deeply caramelized French onion soup and ends with an intensity nearly tropical. When I asked why her cheese was superior, she demurred. Another visitor posited, "It's because she [Evelyn] laughs so much. If you do it with a happiness, it's better." In an ideal world, the cheese would hit market at eighteen months, but demand is so great you're more likely to find it at fourteen to sixteen months if you can find it at all.

GERMANY | COW
UNPASTEURIZED
**AROMA:** Bouillon and onion
**TEXTURE:** Breaks apart in chunks, flecked with crystals
**FLAVOR:** Sweet French onion soup with a tropical fruit finish
IN SHORT: Revelatory

## FROM THE MOUTHS OF MAKERS

Cheese sits at the intersection of art and science, with, at its best, a bit of mysticism tipped in. When asked about their work, here's what Swiss type makers have to say:

How do you come up with thirty-plus recipes?

"The dreams, the third eye."—Thomas Stadelmann, Käserei Stofel (see page 170)

"Bacteria are the unpaid workers in the dairy."—Martin "Floh" Bienerth, Sennerei Andeer (see page 276)

"This is my calling."—Daniel Studer, Käserei Studer (see page 170)

About cows with horns: "I know the milk is better . . . you must look and talk with re-spect. She [the cow] is proud. . . . You see them without horns and they just look so . . . stu-pid."—Evelyn Wild, Käsküche Isny (see page 289)

On his goal of savory notes in Pleasant Ridge Reserve: "You want to taste that it came from an animal. There's so much sweet cheese out there."—Andy Hatch, Uplands Cheese Company. (see page 284)

Regarding the aging of Gruyère: "At more than fourteen months it . . . [throat clears] it disturbs. You need to drink something."—Gerald Roux, overseer of Fromage Gruyère SA (the only aging facility in Gruyère county, selector of 1655 Gruyère; see page 282)

# Challerhocker

SWITZERLAND | COW

UNPASTEURIZED

**AROMA:** Brown butter, chive

**TEXTURE:** Firm but
intensely creamy

**FLAVOR:** Caramelized onion,
brothy

**IN SHORT:** Succulent

Challerhocker began as an experiment. Cheese maker Walter Rass of Käserei Tufertschwil had been making Appenzeller (see page 279) (a partially skimmed milk cheese) for twenty-seven years. When his brother-in-law imported Jersey cows, celebrated for the glorious fat content of their milk, the question was: could Walter keep the fat and make a magnificent cheese? After four months of age, the answer seemed to be no. The experiment was deemed a failure. Squirreled away, the cheese reappeared nine months later at a housewarming party and it was extraordinary. Challerhocker evolved as an Appenzeller alternative, made of full-fat milk using a yogurt starter culture made weekly by Walter's wife Annalise. After pressing and two to two-and-a-half days of brining, the cheeses age for a month at Walter's before seven to ten more months at a local Appenzeller cellar. Intensely creamy but firm, Challerhocker has broad savory notes, a clear undercurrent of garlic and caramelized onion. The saline, brothy flavors make a bite into a mini-meal: like soup and cheese sandwich all together. The only danger is too-old wheels tasting of salt and allium. The name Challerhocker means "cave sitter." The cheese's label shows a demented-looking little boy, sitting, waiting for the cheese to age. This is depicted from the cheese's perspective: a small face and fingers peek over the edge of a high shelf, contemplating the ripeness of each wheel.

## MEET THE NEW GENERATION OF SWISS CHEESE (MAKER)

Walter Rass appears to be in his early forties, but with a twenty-seven-year career in Appenzeller production he must be older than that. For sixteen of those twenty-seven years, he was named to the top ten best producers, one of only a handful crafting cheese good enough to become six-plus month Appenzeller Extra. Like many of the makers of Switzerland's classic cheeses, Appenzellers' toil in anonymity, their wheels joining thousands of others for aging and grading. Their skill and craft determine how good a wheel can be, but their recipe is predetermined by 700 years of tradition.

These days, there are numerous makers breaking with tradition to venture out and create singular cheeses made from their own invented recipes. Walter is quick to point out that the flavor of his new cheese, Challerhocker, doesn't come from herbal brine or wine washes. It's "my milk, my bacterium. The flavor doesn't come from the outside, it is from the inside." This vision and creativity guides the new generation of Swiss cheese.

## MY PICKS: APPROACHABLE SWISS TYPES

For those with a preference for sweet, milky, and fruity notes, packed into a plump-to-dense but creamy texture, my favorites are:

## Andeerer Schmuggler

Unlikely to be found in all but the best and most adventuresome independent specialty cheese shops, Schmuggler is childhood comfort food, elevated. Dense and fatty, with nuttiness like the leftover milk in the cereal bowl. (see page 276)

## (Gruyère de) Comté PDO (ideally Essex Street)

Firm, yet barely bound together, so moist and yielding is the paste. Warm croissant dough; red fruits; and thick, sweet milk made uniform. (see page 278)

## Holey Cow from Central Coast Creamery

Like better Baby Swiss (see page 272), with a pleasingly plump texture and full, savory flavor faintly reminiscent of beef jerky. (see page 280)

## MY PICKS: INTENSE SWISS TYPES

For the fellow lovers of the savory, the cravers of brothy and beefy things, and those who delight in a tropical fruit encounter, these full-on cheeses are for you.

### Le Gruyère AOP (ideally, 1655 or Alpage Gruyère)

Heading toward smoky, with toasty, hearty intensity, and a dense chew. Fresh-cut wheels have the beginnings of beef stock while remaining balanced and complex. (see page 282)

### Rupert (Reserve) from Consider Bardwell Farm

Dense nubbins lodge under tooth in some fantasy of Gruyère (see page 282) mated with Parmigiano-Reggiano (see page 320), with the hairy-tongue intensity of fresh pineapple and a long finish to match. (see page 286)

### Challerhocker

With broad savory notes and a radical concentration of caramelized allium, eating a piece of Challerhocker delivers the same thrill as the soup-soaked, cheese-crusted bread slab atop a crock of French onion soup. (see page 290)

## TASTING ONE
## THE CLASSICS, FROM SWITZERLAND

These are the most likely to be found in the United States, and also cover the flavor arc from classic Swiss-y with its sweet-feet quality, to progressively nuttier, denser, and more savory.

**1. Emmentaler** (see page 278)

**2. Appenzeller Classic** (see page 279)

**3. Le Gruyère AOP** (see page 282)

## TASTING TWO
## AMERICAN INTERPRETATIONS OF EUROPEAN CLASSICS

Several of the most awarded and highly regarded American cheeses are inspired by Alpine classics. These American makers caution that they have been influenced by the Europeans but have created singular recipes produced in unique environments.

**1. Beaufort** (see page 277) **and Pleasant Ridge Reserve from Uplands Cheese Company** (see page 284)

**2. Abondance** (see page 279) **and Tarentaise from Spring Brook Farm** (see page 288)

**3. Gruyère** (see page 282) **and Alpha Tolman from Jasper Hill Farm** (see page 281)

## PAIRING OVERVIEW

SCALDED MILK

TOASTED NUTS

FERMENTED (CURED) MEAT

BEEF BOUILLON

## BEAR IN MIND

These cheeses exist on a spectrum of sweet rather than sharp. Meaning: these are lower acid than most firm cheeses (not that these are sugary cheeses).

Tartness and acidity balance dense, sweet paste.

Because of that dense texture and low acidity, these cheeses are well suited to bitter pairings: bitter chocolate, bitter greens.

## CLASSIC PAIRINGS

(Whole flavor spectrum) with spice and sour: Ham and Swiss with mustard on rye bread

(Scalded milk/toasted nuts/cured meat) with acidic, nutty wines such as Jura Vin Jaune or Sherry

### 1. PICKLED FRUITS AND VEGGIES

Pickled things are ideal with washed rinds, and many Swiss types are brine washed during their aging. Crunch balances dense, smooth paste while acidity cuts meaty savor and salt. These days there are countless options in a jar, as well as super-quick pickles you can make at home in less than twenty minutes. Pickled fruits, such as raisins, figs, cherries, or apricots (Boat Street Pickles is my favorite brand), are softer and sweeter, whereas pickled vegetables ranging from red onion to okra to the ubiquitous cuke often introduce smoke or heat and do better at the extreme end of the washed-rind flavor spectrum.

FLAVOR SPECTRUM (PICKLED FRUITS): 1–5
FLAVOR SPECTRUM (PICKLED VEGGIES): 6–10

### 2. BITTER FOODS

High-cacao chocolate, espresso, and broccoli rabe all stand in here for high, persistent bitter flavor. The natural sweetness of Swiss types, plus salt and chewy or melted texture, offer a soothing blanket atop bitterness.

FLAVOR SPECTRUM: 1–10

### 3. BELGIAN ALE

With sweetish and toasty malt overtones, yeasty character and, often, natural spice notes anchored in bright acidity Belgian Ales emphasize the natural flavor profile of medium to intense Swiss types. Their similarities push forward the delicate hop and fruit profiles of the ale.

FLAVOR SPECTRUM: 3–10

### 4. CONFIT-STYLE JAMS

Raw and pickled onions are a traditional pairing with Taleggio types and they work here for the same flavor reasons. Other (spreadable) options are slightly sweetened confits and jams made from onions or shallots. On the more intense end of the Swiss spectrum, caramelized and roasted onion flavors prevail. Play them up with a savory smear.

FLAVOR SPECTRUM: 6–10

MERLOT BELLAVITANO

1 YEAR GOUDA

# Parmesan

AGED GOAT GOUDA

PARMIGIANO-REGGIANO

ROOMANO

PAVE DU NORD

## PARMESAN: THE GATEWAY TO . . .

AVAILABILITY SUPERMARKET → SPECIALTY SHOP

FLAVOR APPROACHABLE →

1. BUTTERED TOAST
2. SALTED, CANDIED NUTS
3. CARAMEL
4. BUTTERSCOTCH
5. COTTON CANDY

**Mimolette**
PAGE 308

**Roomano Pradera**
PAGE 311

**Pave du Nord**
PAGE 306

**Aged Goat Gouda**
PAGE 311

**Aged Sheep Gouda**
PAGE 311

**Dry Monterey Jack**
PAGE 306

**BellaVitano**
PAGE 310

**Parmesan**
PAGE 308

**Parrano**
PAGE 310

**Marieke Gouda**
PAGE 316

**Extra Aged Goat**
PAGE 318

**Coolea**
PAGE 314

**Boerenkaas**
PAGE 314

**Podda Classico**
PAGE 316

**Mahón-Menorca PDO**
PAGE 319

**Two- to Four-Year Gouda**
PAGE 315

**Asiago PDO (d'Allevo)**
PAGE 316

**Piave PDO**
PAGE 317

**One- to Two-Year Gouda**
PAGE 314

**Grana Padano PDO**
PAGE 317

**Parmigiano-Reggiano PDO**
PAGE 320

## INTENSE

| 6 | 7 | 8 | 9 | 10 |
|---|---|---|---|---|
| WOODY BOURBON | CARAMELIZED PAN BITS | BALSAMIC VINEGAR | KOMBUCHA | ALL THAT, PLUS SEAWATER |

# It still strikes me as criminal that I worked in cheese for ten years before I made it to northern Italy to experience Parmigiano-Reggiano

production and aging. In the cheese business, everyone is very careful to distinguish between the tongue-tripping mouthful—"Par-me-ja-no Rej-ee-ah-no"—and Parmesan because the latter typically implies an inferior version of the former. To everyone outside of the cheese world, Parmesan simply means a dry cheese that's often used for grating, with a nutty, salty flavor and a crystalline, granular texture that distinguishes it from Cheddar.

Early in my career, I learned the technical differences between name-protected Italian Parmigiano-Reggiano and more generic Parmesan, but my revelations about this grana (grainy) style of cheese evolved from the deeply personal experience of traveling to Milan at a very particular moment in my cheese life. I found myself boarding a flight just three weeks after I'd resigned from Murray's Cheese, the company that had been my home and calling card for a decade. Being without a title, an affiliation, and a business card left me feeling naked. I wondered what my objectives were. What was I doing in Italy? It had been so long since I'd explored cheese for my own pleasure and interest that I feared I'd forgotten how to do it. Luckily, Italy is like balm for my body and soul. There is no region whose food isn't the best I've ever had. I speak enough of the language to feel confident poking into people's lives. Everyone is exceptionally giving and generous.

So it was, in a windowless convention center at an Italian trade show, that I met an old friend who introduced me to his old friend, who suggested we get out of there, drive around the countryside, eat, and go visit Parmigiano-Reggiano producers. He wondered if I'd care to learn about the region's history and the evolution of its farming and animal husbandry practices over a few three-hour lunches? Then we could head into the hills and visit a few small-scale cheese-making couples producing only two or three wheels of Parmigiano-Reggiano a day. Would that be okay?

Because, you know, he didn't want to bore or burden me. Jeez. It was around this moment that the greatness of free agency dawned on me.

Over the next three days, I tasted wheels of Parmigiano-Reggiano ranging in color from straw yellow to amber, each teasing out a tenuous flavor balance between sweet and salt, acid and bitter. The difference between valley cheese and hill cheese was profound. Wheels made in one season rather than another looked and smelled radically different, as small, stocky men drove their almond-shaped knives beneath burnished, waxy rinds to show me the fine, nearly flaking paste. As someone who spent many years regarding Parmigiano-Reggiano as a glorified seasoning, I was bowled over by the range and complexity possible from a single cheese made in only five provinces of northern Italy. The take-away from that trip is that Parmigiano-Reggiano is in fact a very intense cheese. Fresh-cut wheels of two-plus years hint at toasted nuts and syrup, but they are lean and acidic, mouthwateringly so, with a push-pull between sweet, salt, and spice. Maybe this is why we are inclined to shower our food with Parmigiano-Reggiano rather than eat it by the chunk, although that straightforward delivery makes a remarkable meal opener. It is a true *amuse-bouche*, enlivening your mouth, priming you for the food that will follow.

*Parmesan*, meanwhile, is the generic derivative of "Parmigiano-Reggiano." A cheese called Parmesan need not meet the same exacting standards of production, aging, and quality grading (see page 322) as Parmigiano-Reggiano. But of far greater relevance to most cheese eaters are the flavor differences offered up by Parmesan. It is sweeter; its texture moister and mealier; and, ultimately, it has far less acid (sharpness, or piquancy) than Parmigiano-Reggiano. The Italians might argue with me, but I've found that Parmesan isn't strictly inferior Parmigiano-Reggiano (and certainly need not be synonymous with the shelf-stable Stuff in the Green Can). It's a similar-looking cheese that tastes significantly, even radically, different. When I think of the possible flavor spectrum for grana-style cheeses, the mild, approachable end begins with the sweetness of Parmesan and the intense end concludes with the lingering piquancy of Parmigiano-Reggiano. In between are numerous hard cheeses with flavors that are toasty-tasting and evocative of bourbon, melted butter, citrus fruit, and walnuts—and ultimately of aromatic spices like white pepper and nutmeg. Parmesan and many Parm-type cheeses are more like cheese candy than they are like Parmigiano-Reggiano. They are nummy; they go down easy; and in many cases you will impress and horrify yourself with how much you can eat if you're not really thinking about it. That's the approachable end of the spectrum. The intense extreme commands your focus and thoughtful consumption. It awakens your tongue. While you can garnish with it, you'd do better to sit with a bit of wine and a bit of lusciously fatty cured pork and pay close attention. A little goes a long way.

# Chapter Guide

While Parmesan is tossed around as an indiscriminate term to describe hard, often Italian-style cheeses, it is decidedly generic and should not be confused with the specific cheese Parmigiano-Reggiano PDO. That being said, it's the gateway to crunchy, crystalline cheeses that exist at the intersection of sweet, salty, and spicy flavors.

## WHAT TO KNOW

**WHAT'S A GRANA CHEESE?** Grana means "grain" and refers to the size of the curd-cutting during the make process for these cheeses. The smaller the curd cut (and grain-sized is as small as it gets), the more moisture (whey) is expelled. In other words, by cutting the curd into tiny bits, a maker is crafting a drier and more ageable foundation for cheeses that will typically ripen for six to thirty-six months before being eaten.

More generally, grana refers to harder crystalline cheeses native to Italy's Po River Valley. Parmigiano-Reggiano PDO (see page 320) is the best known of these, followed by Grana Padano PDO. (see page 317)

**WHAT ARE THE WHITE SPECKS AND SPOTS?** As a cheese ages, its protein chains break down and amino acid clusters form throughout the interior. Typically, this begins to occur after nine to twelve months. In harder, longer-aged cheeses, these crunchy clusters (known as "tyrosine") become visible as white specks or patches, sometimes as large as a dime. They're most commonly found in the cheeses of this chapter, which as a group are the longest-aged of the cheese world.

**RIND:** In general, these cheeses are aged for one to three years (or more) and they have the thickest, hardest, most shell-like rinds. As such, I don't recommend them for eating, although they won't hurt you, and in some cases are excellent for flavoring soups and stews.

## WHAT TO AVOID

In the world of cheese, the big, brawny, aged cheeses are regarded as durable. And, compared with the limp Brie types and the flaky freshies, they are. They were invented to be. That does not, however, make them indestructible.

➼ **COLOR:** The typical color spectrum in the Parmesan Gateway ranges from pale straw to deep orange (as in aged Gouda, shaded with the plant-derived colorant annatto). When you see a sizable (half-inch) perimeter of browning under the rind, you're looking at an old and dried-out cheese. It's not spoiled, but it's not as good as it should be. The exposed, cut face of these cheeses should not have specks of blue or green mold. This is an indication that the cheese has been sitting, precut in plastic, for too long. The mold won't hurt you and may be scraped off, but the cheese is likely to taste like plastic wrap. To avoid this predicament, especially in a supermarket context, I opt for cheeses wrapped in a waxy parchment-looking paper by the producer. These are vacuum-sealed and are not likely to have off flavors. Or, I go for cheeses that are freshly cut in front of me. You should not see pink streaks or patches of white, blue, or green mold on the cut surface of the cheese.

➼ **FLAVOR:** Extremely bitter or acidic flavors are not typical or desirable.

➼ **RIND:** The rind on many of these cheeses is waxed and should be removed before eating. Additionally, smushy, smearable, or wet cheeses should be avoided.

## STORAGE AND SHELF LIFE

Whole wheels have the ability to age for two or even three years. Once cut, the cheeses of the Parmesan Gateway have a relatively long shelf life. That said, they're not impermeable. Paper wrap alone (unless it's specially designed cheese paper) will shorten shelf life because the cheese will rapidly dry out. My preference is plastic zip-top bags so you can squeeze all the air out and have individual storage units. Plastic wrap becomes a legitimate possibility here because low-moisture cheeses are more durable than any of the Brie types. My trick when wrapping in plastic is to always "face" the cheese before serving. Meaning: run a knife along the cut surface of a cheese to scrape off the paper-thin layer that's been in contact with the plastic. Taking the time to expose the fresh cheese underneath costs you very little and buys you instantly renewed and refreshed flavor.

Ideally, cheeses in the Parmesan Gateway should be eaten within two weeks of being cut, although they can last for three to four weeks with diminished flavor and complexity.

Small spots of blue or green mold may develop on the cut surface of the cheese. These can be easily scraped away and the cheese beneath consumed, although they are a reliable warning sign that you're pushing the limit on storage life.

## PARMESAN TYPES: TEXTURES

### IN A WORD: HARD

### SMOOTH AND/OR SPRINGY

CHEWY  EVEN  PRESSED  SLICEABLE

### HEAVY AND/OR WET

FUDGE

### DENSE AND/OR CRUMBLY

BRITTLE  CHUNKY  CRAYONS
CRUMBLY  CRUNCHY  CRYSTALLINE
DENSE  DRY  FLAKY  GRANULAR
WAXY

### FLAWS

DRIED-OUT  DUSTY  MEALY

# PARMESAN TYPES: FLAVOR & AROMA WHEEL

**ATMOSPHERICS**
SMOKE
WOODSY
BURNT WOOD
BRINE / SEAWATER
(WET) SOIL
POWDER
PETROL
MINERAL
METALLIC
PUTRID
ACETONE (NAIL POLISH REMOVER)
SULFUR (ROTTEN EGG)
AMMONIA
FISHY
PUTRID
BITTER
FISHY

**SPICES**
VANILLA
NUTMEG
ANISE
WHITE PEPPER
BLACK PEPPER
LICORICE
CLOVE

**FLAWS**
ACRID
EXCESSIVE SOURNESS
RANCID

**LACTIC**
FRESH ➤ GOAT MILK  COW MILK  SHEEP MILK
BUFFALO MILK  CREAM  BUTTER
CULTURED ➤ CULTURED BUTTER
YOGURT  BUTTERMILK
GAMY BUTTER  CRÈME FRAÎCHE
SOUR CREAM
COOKED ➤ COOKED MILK / MILK SKIN
MELTED BUTTER
BROWNED BUTTER
CHEESE-Y (MAC-AND-CHEESE POWDER)

**FRUIT**
STONE FRUIT ➤ APRICOT  PEACH  PLUM
GREEN OLIVE  BLACK OLIVE
BERRIES ➤ STRAWBERRY  BLUEBERRY
RED CURRANT
CITRUS ➤ ORANGE  GRAPEFRUIT
LEMON
TROPICAL FRUIT ➤ PAPAYA
PASSION FRUIT  PINEAPPLE
COOKED FRUIT  PICKLED FRUIT
FERMENTED FRUIT

**OTHER FOOD**
BISCUIT  COOKED PASTA
POLENTA
NUTS ➤ NUT SKIN
NUT SKIN  MACADAMIA NUT
PINE NUT  PECAN  (TOASTED) ALMOND
(BOILED) PEANUT
(TOASTED) HAZELNUT  WALNUT
COCONUT (OIL)
SWEETS ➤
CHOCOLATE-
DIPPED ORANGE
LEMON CURD  CARAMEL  BUTTERSCOTCH
WERTHER'S ORIGINALS
(CARAMEL HARD CANDY)
DULCE DE LECHE
FERMENTED FOODS ➤  WHITE WINE
RED WINE  MILK CHOCOLATE  COCOA  BOURBON  COFFEE
DARK CHOCOLATE

(BUTTERED) TOAST

**ANIMAL**
COOKED ➤ CHICKEN BROTH  BEEF BROTH
BEEF BOUILLON  MEATY  GRILLED  OFFAL
PAN DRIPPINGS  LAMB FAT  GAMY  SAUCISSON SEC
FERMENTED / CURED ➤
SERRANO  JERKY  MANURE
BARNYARD ➤ LEATHER
BODILY ➤ (WET) WOOL  MUSK  SWEAT  UNWASHED SOCKS

**HERBS & PLANTS**
HERBS ➤ HERBACEOUS  THYME
MINT  ROSEMARY
PLANT MATTER ➤
(MOWN) GRASS
HAY  FLORAL
TOBACCO  PINE  EUCALYPTUS
WHITE MOLD
BLUE MOLD
MOLD/MILDEW ➤

**FUNGUS**
(COOKED) MUSHROOM ➤
SHIITAKE MUSHROOM
PORCINI MUSHROOM
TRUFFLE
BUTTON MUSHROOM
YEAST  BREAD DOUGH

**VEGETABLE**
AROMATICS ➤ (COOKED) CELERY (ROOT)
(COOKED) TURNIP  (COOKED) LEEK
(CARAMELIZED) ONION
(ROASTED) GARLIC
OTHER ➤  BAKED POTATO
CORN  NORI
CRUCIFEROUS ➤
(COOKED) CABBAGE  (COOKED) CAULIFLOWER
(COOKED) BROCCOLI
SPICY ➤
MUSTARD GREENS  HORSERADISH
BITTER ➤  ENDIVE  ARUGULA
BROCCOLI RABE  DANDELION

# Pave du Nord

Aged for ten-plus months, Pave du Nord (from the North [Nord] of France) is the cobblestone (pave)-shaped alternative to Mimolette's (see page 308) cannonball. Although the crusty brown rind looks like moon rock, the neon-orange interior is smooth and firm, with a moist, waxy texture. I like it as a Mimolette alternative, although it's got a distinctly Cheddar quality as well. Served up by the slab it's like a slice of some bizarre orange bread (that color comes courtesy of the plant-derived coloring annatto and is flavorless). I've found Pave du Nord to taste pretty consistently like aggressively salted macaroni and cheese. It's got a bit of hazelnut and caramel to it, but on the whole is milder and softer in flavor than aged Mimolette.

# Dry Monterey Jack  FROM VELLA CHEESE COMPANY

The Vella Cheese Company is a very important producer in the history of American, and particularly Californian, cheese making. Dating back to 1931, Tom Vella made Italian-style and American original cheeses that were especially popular with the Italian immigrant community settling Sonoma. With residential refrigeration a scarce luxury, Vella developed various aged (dry) versions of Monterey Jack that stored well. His son Ig continued the family tradition and made their Dry Monterey Jack, one of the first nationally available and respected American artisan cheeses. The world lost Ig in 2011, but his no-nonsense candor is present in every bite of this cheese. Covered in a mixture of oil, cocoa, and pepper, Vella Dry Jack is beautifully dense and crumbly, with a richer, mellower flavor than Parm-Reg. I find it's often coconutty, with a fruity finish.

**FRANCE | COW**

**PASTEURIZED**

**RECOMMENDED BRAND:** Herve Mons (Whole Foods exclusive)

**AROMA:** Cheese powder

**TEXTURE:** Moist and waxy

**FLAVOR:** Salty, cheesy, with a hint o' sweet

**IN SHORT:** The crayon cheese

**UNITED STATES | COW**

**PASTEURIZED**

**AROMA:** Minimal

**TEXTURE:** Crumbly and breakable

**FLAVOR:** Round, rich, and coconutty

**IN SHORT:** Munchable

PARMESAN

# Parmesan

UNITED STATES | COW

PASTEURIZED

**RECOMMENDED BRANDS:**
Bel Gioioso, Cello Riserva
Copper Kettle, Sartori
(SarVecchio Parmesan)

**AROMA:** Caramel

**TEXTURE:** Smooth; in
unfortunate cases, gluey
or mealy

**FLAVOR:** Toffee-like

**IN SHORT:** Sweet 'n' easy

You'll notice that I've said "Parmesan" and not "Parmigiano-Reggiano."
I'm talking specifically about American-made imitations of the titan
Parm-Reg; they have a radically different flavor and texture and are not
interchangeable with the import. Domestic Parmesan has a markedly
sweeter flavor than Parmigiano-Reggiano: it's nutty, but caramel, dulce
de leche, and butterscotch dominate, along with buttered Pullman
toast. It's not uncommon that I'll have people taste domestic Parmesan alongside imported Parm-Reg, and they often prefer its candied
approachability to the leaner, acidic, and more layered complexities of
the original. Unlike original Parm-Reg, domestic Parmesans are often
aged for less time and are not open-air aged. They are sealed in airtight
Cryovac, and as a result the texture is always moister, waxier, and occasionally mealy. Here's the thing, though: when I'm in a supermarket
in Somewhere, USA, I often opt for domestic Parm over imported, if
Parm-Reg is even available. The quality is far superior to sad, desiccated
pieces of Parm-Reg that have been poorly wrapped in plastic and left to
dry out. That said, if the import is available in manufacturer packaging
(gas-flushed, usually parchment-looking paper), I snap that up. Domestic Parm isn't Parmigiano-Reggiano, but if you go in expecting a different eating experience, I bet you'll find you like what you encounter.

# Mimolette

FRANCE | COW

PASTEURIZED

**AROMA:** Weirdly, none

**TEXTURE:** Dense, waxy,
and layered but lacking
crystallization

**FLAVOR:** Salty and mildly
caramelly

**IN SHORT:** If the moon
were made of cheese,
this would be it.

Mimolette is a classic, and though I think it's a pretty overrated
cheese, it deserves mention. Mimolette is said to have been invented
in seventeenth-century Normandy as a domestic alternative to Edam
and Gouda (see page 126), the Dutch makers of which were at war with
France. It's a brilliantly orange cheese, the interior paste colored with
annatto, and properly aged wheels (don't bother with young, smooth
ones) are pocked and cratered thanks to the work of microscopic bugs
called "cheese mites." Those mites led to a 2013 import crackdown on
the cheese; supposedly their presence made the cheese unfit for human
consumption, according to the U.S. Food and Drug Administration.
You'd be mad to eat the rind that they help form—it's thick as rock,
although the mites contribute a honeyed, mead scent that's quite beguiling. For all its history, though, I don't get Mimolette. It's expensive.
It's hard to cut. It's vaguely caramelly, a little bit lactic, and often quite
salty. It looks cool. But, for far less than $28 to $35 a pound, you can find
a great aged Gouda.

# WHAT'S GOUDA DOING IN THE PARMESAN GATEWAY?

When it comes to their flavor and texture, young Gouda and aged Gouda might as well be two different cheeses. While younger (less than a year) Gouda is springy and smooth, with sweet-tart flavor, aged Gouda has much more in common with Parm types: there's the hard, crystalline texture and its noticeable crunch. Then there are intense flavors redolent of toast, roasted nuts, and bourbon. Unlike Parmigiano-Reggiano, they're considerably less acidic and less salty (meaning, they taste sweeter).

The Parmesan Gateway includes aged versions of the Netherlands' most famous cheese, Gouda, made of various milks. Here's what you need to know:

- Aged Gouda might be sold by brand, or it might be sold by age profile (one year, eighteen months to two years, three to four years, etc). The theory is that the more aged a Gouda is, the denser, drier, and crunchier its texture—and the more candied and intense its flavor.

- Surprise! That's not always the case.

- Many aged Goudas are made with the starter culture *Proosdij*, which gives an approximation of long aging in a much shorter time. As a result, cheeses may be only a few months old, although they are sold as Gouda aged one-plus years.

- These quick-aging Goudas also rely on starters that deliver a sweet, candied taste, butterscotch and pineapple being the most common flavor profiles.

- The best aged Goudas are made in North Holland, from its milk: thick, luscious clay soil grows great grass. It makes milk that's been fondly described to me as greasy.

- The best aged Goudas can be aged anywhere in Holland: many brands are made by the same facilities. The aging makes a big difference in flavor and texture. Warmer temperature ripening (57°F/14°C to 59°F/15°C) means more moisture loss and more expensive cheese, but arguably more flavor development.

- The best Goudas are dense and crunchy but creamy under tooth—they're not dry or waxy.

- The best aged Goudas aren't just cheese candy, but rich and complex, typically laden with flavors of bourbon, vanilla, toast, dulce de leche, and the savory anchor of browned pan bits.

# Parrano

NETHERLANDS | COW

PASTEURIZED

**AROMA:** Vaguely toasty

**TEXTURE:** Even crunch

**FLAVOR:** Toasty yet sweet

**IN SHORT:** The aged upgrade from Havarti for an always-have-around cheese

Knowing the international renown and popularity of Parmesan (see page 308), and struggling with people's perception of Gouda (see page 126) as a solely moist, wax-bound wheel, several Dutch producers invented cheeses meant to be a cross between the two cheeses. Their goal was a cheese younger, moister, and cheaper than Parmigiano-Reggiano (see page 320)—and also nuttier, sweeter, and more complex than young Gouda. The result is an Italian-style cheese or Parm/Gouda hybrid. While Parrano is the best-known brand, competing (and largely comparable) brands include Paradiso, Prima Donna, and Ravenno. These cheeses manage to walk a line of dense and creamy paste with nutty and brown aromas (bourbon, wood barrels, something savory). Designed to be sliceable yet gratable, meltable yet noshable, they're positioned to become the new all-purpose cheese. Unlike the snackers of my youth, the flavors are complex and delicious, but incredibly egalitarian. They're made to be liked, with age profiles ranging from five months to about one year. I especially love Paradiso's texture: it looks firm yet creamy and is laced with small, evenly round holes. But under tooth it has the fine grit of a Hershey Krackel bar.

# BellaVitano FROM SARTORI

UNITED STATES | COW

PASTEURIZED

**RECOMMENDED FLAVORS:** Black Pepper, Chai, Cognac, Gold, Merlot

**AROMA (INFLUENCED BY FLAVORS):** Melted butter, vaguely fruity

**TEXTURE:** Firm but moist, not crystalline; chunky; some flavors verge on gummy

**FLAVOR:** Nutty, melted butter, sweeter than Parm

**IN SHORT:** The new American Parm

I'm a big fan of Sartori cheese. Their roots as an employee-owned factory in Antigo, Wisconsin, anchor a tradition of hands-on cheese making, even though they operate at a large, national scale of distribution. Their Italian-inspired recipes don't attempt to be Parmigiano-Reggiano—each is universally moister, sweeter and fruitier, with subtle acidity and crowd-pleasing smoothness. BellaVitano Gold is a base recipe that also becomes dozens of reserve and limited-edition flavored cheeses. Sartori takes risks here. They don't always pay off (peppermint cheese? Why?), but when they do they are quite extraordinary. Their Cognac BellaVitano, for instance, smells dark and fruity, all plummy wood, and the cognac has real presence. It's not gimmicky; instead the acidity and oak from the brandy permeates the dense, buttery paste and creates something altogether better than what was there originally. I appreciate that Sartori can be found in almost any supermarket. When I am in Nowheresville, Maine, where my family retreats every summer, I know that I can eat good cheese, thanks to Sartori.

# Aged Goat Gouda

You'll likely find this cheese sold as Aged Goat Gouda, although the Dutch shy away from giving the Gouda moniker to any noncow milk cheese. It is, essentially, an aged Gouda made of goat milk. When tasked with pairing a line of Kentucky bourbons with cheese for the Atlanta Food and Wine Festival, I struggled to find a cheese that could stand up to both the burn of alcohol and the heavy wood and vanilla flavors from oak barrel aging. Most cheeses (delicate goats especially) were mown down by the drink. A one year or so aged Dutch Goat like Brabander was too tropical, too fruity. Balarina, meanwhile, was a remarkable bedfellow. Incredibly dense and crunchy, it brought its own brown-vanilla sweetness, tamping down the sear of 90 Proof. I prefer it to the candied cow milk aged Goudas because the milk adds a layer of complexity.

**NETHERLANDS | GOAT**

**PASTEURIZED**

**RECOMMENDED BRAND:** Balarina

**AROMA:** Goat milk caramel

**TEXTURE:** Dense and crunchy

**FLAVOR:** Candied nuts, caramel

**IN SHORT:** Goat goodness

# Aged Sheep Gouda

First of all, props for a great brand name (Ewephoria). The promise of sheep milk–induced ecstasy is enough to lure even those consumers suspicious of Gouda as boring and predictable. This cheese makes three distinct contributions to a final flavor driven by fat and sweetness: 1) It's a washed curd cheese (less acidic reads as more sweet); 2) its milk has double the fat and protein of cow; and 3) it's aged for a minimum of one year, which concentrates the rich, toffee flavor. In the land of cheese this is a newbie—invented just over a decade ago with the express purpose of annihilating any gamy flavors that might alienate Americans from aged sheep cheese. Ewephoria is made with cultures designed for candied flavors. While you might get a whiff of whiskey, it's all smooth going down.

**NETHERLANDS | SHEEP**

**PASTEURIZED**

**RECOMMENDED BRAND:** Ewephoria Aged

**AROMA:** Butterscotch and whiskey

**TEXTURE:** Firm and dry but fatty in the mouth

**FLAVOR:** Toffee

**IN SHORT:** Engineered for you to like it

# Roomano Pradera

Roomano Pradera claims to be a three-year Gouda (see page 315), but its appearance and flavor are so consistently different from the pack that it deserves its own mention. Perhaps because the wheels are smaller (a petite twelvish pounds, as opposed to twenty to thirty-five pounds), or perhaps because of the recipe and aging, the cheese is intensely dense, dry, and waxy under knife. The saturated russet hue comes from annatto coloring. If you seek cheese candy, look no further. Butterscotch and molasses, for sure, but of late this cheese has taken confection to the next level. It's been pure carnival cotton candy.

**NETHERLANDS | COW**

**PASTEURIZED**

**AROMA:** Shockingly different from the others, candied, light, and fruity

**TEXTURE:** Moist yet dry, creamy under tooth, not all that much crunch

**FLAVOR:** Straight-up cotton candy

**IN SHORT:** Candied

AGED GOAT GOUDA

# One- to Two-Year Gouda

NETHERLANDS | COW

PASTEURIZED

**RECOMMENDED BRANDS:**
Beemster Classic,
Reypenaer 1 Year

**AROMA:** Hinting at beef
bouillon, vanilla, and bourbon

**TEXTURE:** Firm but velvety,
with occasional crunch

**FLAVOR:** Southern praline

**IN SHORT:** Mouthwatery
but rich

The truth is that you really can't know how aged an aged Gouda is. Some producers make age claims, while others select for flavor profile and consistency. The starters and ripening temperatures employed have an enormous impact on the final cheese. What's interesting here is that my recommended brands are actually produced at the same facility in northern Holland but are aged differently. I attribute their recipes to a final flavor profile that isn't just sweet or candied. That Werther's Original/butterscotch quality is present, but it's balanced by an incredible richness and the feeling you have after swallowing brown liquor. The burn is gone, and it's all vanilla and wood essence.

# Coolea

IRELAND | COW

PASTEURIZED

**AROMA:** Vaguely candied

**TEXTURE:** Rough

**FLAVOR:** Brown (bourbon,
honey, hazelnut)

**IN SHORT:** Serious

A relative rarity, Coolea is made following a Dutch Gouda-style recipe by a Dicky Willems, son of a Dutch couple who settled in a remote corner of County Cork, Ireland. While a younger version of Coolea is sold in the United Kingdom, what's exported are the matured wheels made from the sweeter summer milk of neighbor Daniel Lynch's grass-fed herd. I like Coolea because it surprises. It's got the typical waxed rind of a Dutch Gouda and looks young, the paste smooth and pliable. There's a whiff of butterscotch candy about it, so you assume it will be pleasant—mild and sweet. Not so! Its flavor is much deeper and more intense than appearance would suggest, the interior punctuated with wonderful nugget-like crunches. It was one of the first cheeses I encountered in which I could taste bourbon, without the burn of alcohol: dark and smooth, with a complex finish. I've also had Coolea when those dark flavors were sweet, as in brackish chestnut honey. In all cases, it's an intense and serious cheese.

# Boerenkaas

While most Gouda, aged or otherwise, is made of pasteurized milk, Boerenkaas is not. The name means "farmer cheese," or "farmstead cheese," and it is produced on a farm from unpasteurized milk. Be wary of aged Gouda that says "Cheese from the farm." This phrase may be used without any regard for the Boerenkaas tradition of exclusively raw milk usage. While the inconsistency of Boerenkaas drives me crazy, I love it as an indicator of one of the last traditional cheeses in a country of large and centralized cheese and dairy production. If you prefer a handmade cheese, you need to be prepared for it to change throughout the year. I've had this cheese on more than one occasion start off with promising deep, dark, caramelized flavor only to veer sharply into a lingering bitter finish. It can be as if the tyrosine crystals release an unpleasant chemical quality each time you crunch down on one. That's no good. But when the cheese is showing well, it's lightly savory, more delicate than my preferred two- to four-year Goudas but more complex than the younger ones. If you want to play around, it's worth a dice roll.

# Two- to Four-Year Gouda

Long before I spoke with Betty Koster of L'Amuse, I'd come to regard Cheddar as a cheese divided into two camps: the eating person's Cheddar and the thinking person's Cheddar. Imagine my thrill when Betty said of aged Gouda: Let's talk about "eating it with your mouth, or eating it with your mind." Eating aged Gouda with your mouth means scarfing down (delicious, delicious) cheese candy. Eating it with your mind means noticing the evolution that comes with time: the small crunchy bits that appear around the first year have become ghostly rounds the size of a marker tip. The cheese feathers delicately in your mouth but delivers the mouth pucker of tannin. You come across a seriously big but soft crunch. The cheese has become dense, intense and flavorful but not dry. And the taste! The suggestion of savory flavor that some aged Goudas have at one year have become insistent brown sweetnesses, like well-caramelized onions and Woodford Reserve bourbon.

**NETHERLANDS | COW**
**UNPASTEURIZED**

**RECOMMENDED BRAND:** Boorenkaas

**AROMA:** Chicken bouillon

**TEXTURE:** Velvety and smooth on the tongue, laced with pleasant sand grains

**FLAVOR:** Pan drippings and homemade caramel

**IN SHORT:** Inconsistent and so slightly maddening

**NETHERLANDS | COW**
**PASTEURIZED**

**RECOMMENDED BRANDS:** Beemster Extra Aged, L'Amuse Signature, Pittig Gouda, Reypenaer V.S.O.P.

**AROMA:** Intense, like a Carvel store

**TEXTURE:** Chunks of wax, but still velvety in the mouth

**FLAVOR:** Toasted buttered pecans, bourbon, caramelized onion

**IN SHORT:** For eating with your mind

# Marieke Gouda FROM HOLLAND'S FAMILY CHEESE

**UNITED STATES | COW**

**UNPASTEURIZED**

**AROMA:** Baking spice

**TEXTURE:** Nestlé Crunch

**FLAVOR:** Brilliantly woody, bourbon, and butterscotch

**IN SHORT:** Possibly better than Dutch aged Gouda

Wisconsin-by-way-of-Holland cheese maker Marieke Penterman has been making cheese only since 2006 but produces the best aged Gouda outside of the Netherlands (and better, frankly, than many made there). Working exclusively with raw milk from the family's herd of 700 cows, she makes more than a dozen flavored Goudas, but it's her aged recipes that are especially remarkable with nine- to twelve-month aged, flavor coalesces in the toasty, nutty interior. Premium (twelve to eighteen months) and Super Aged (eighteen to twenty-four months) have tons of crunch—big, crystalline hunks that pop under tooth with sweet, woody intensity like a butterscotch chased by a swallow of whiskey. The Overjarige (twenty-four-plus months) is hard to come by; should you find it, the cheese is deep and roasty, all coffee bean and aromatic spice. Point being: they're all good. And since it's so rare to find an imported aged Gouda made from raw milk, this is your chance to do a side-by-side comparison.

# Asiago PDO (d'Allevo)

**ITALY | COW**

**(UN)PASTEURIZED**

**AROMA:** Savory

**TEXTURE:** Flaky and dense

**FLAVOR:** Butter-braised plum

**IN SHORT:** Just a little spicy

Unlike young Asiago (see page 124), ripened (or aged) Asiago is made from partially skimmed milk and must be aged for a minimum of sixty days from the last day of the month of production, or ninety days for cheeses marked as coming from the mountains. Really, though, it's the wheels of six to twelve months that you're likely to encounter. These are hulking, straw-yellow rounds with a waxy, whitish crust and flaking paste. Real Asiago manages to be both fruity and savory, a bit piquant but anchored by deep buttery flavor. It's a cheese that's been handily ripped off, particularly by domestic producers who sell a white, salty, and spicy cheese more akin to Provolone than to actual Asiago. The real deal isn't just a seasoning for your salad. It's better than that and especially noshable with deep-red, fruity, earthy wines.

# Podda Classico

**ITALY | COW AND SHEEP**

**PASTEURIZED**

**AROMA:** Toasted almonds

**TEXTURE:** Fine and flaky but fatty in the mouth

**FLAVOR:** Fleur de sel caramel

**IN SHORT:** The unexpected alternative to Parm

From Sardinian maker Ferrucio Podda comes this mixed-milk flying saucer of a cheese that I am consistently shocked to not see more frequently. It's remarkably well priced and delicious—reaching for Parm-Reg's complexity and delivering briny, grassy flavors but sweeter; hard enough at five-plus months to grate or shave but full and fatty, thanks to the addition of sheep milk.

# Grana Padano PDO

Despite its reputation as a kind of poor man's Parmigiano-Reggiano, Grana Padano is the best-selling PDO cheese worldwide—more than four million wheels are produced annually. Its name means "grain," and grana is often used to describe many of the granular, nutty cheeses in this chapter. Grana is made in the Po River Valley and its recipe and aging process bear great resemblance to Parm-Reg, although the minimum mandatory aging is nine months, and you'll typically find it on the market at sixteen to twenty months. I look for Trentingrana, which is Grana Padano made in the province of Trento from cows that may not be fed silage (as is permitted for regular Grana Padano). The absence of fermented feed contributes to a cleaner flavor with less chance of acidic, fruity, fermented notes. Grana on the whole is subtler and more delicate than Parm-Reg, with a white-to-straw–colored interior and fragrant paste. Devotees attribute this to the corn grown in the Po River Valley, which comprises a large part of the animals' diet.

**ITALY | COW**
**UNPASTEURIZED**
**AROMA:** Toasty corn
**TEXTURE:** Grainy yet moist
**FLAVOR:** Delicate, less acidic and salty than Parm-Reg
**IN SHORT:** Subtle

# Piave PDO

Piave began humbly as the local cheese of Belluno, within the northeastern province of Veneto. It was traditionally made with at least 80 percent milk from local cow breeds including Italian Brown, Holstein, Friesian, and Red Pied, and still is today, under the management of the single producer Agriform. Piave is produced in five age profiles ranging from the rarely seen Fresco (which is not unlike young Asiago, see page 124) to the rarely seen eighteen-plus-month Vecchio Riserva. In the States, you tend to see blue label (more than 180-day) Vecchio or red label (more than twelve-month) Vecchio Selezione Oro. Hold out for red label and discover a Parmigiano-ish cheese that has acidity and lightness, coupled with bright pineapple flavor. Recently, I tasted a piece and found it to be quite vegetal—it reminded me of the Italian cheese crisp *frico*, grated cheese crisped golden in a nonstick pan. Because it lacks the big, crunchy tyrosine patches of aged Parm and Gouda, I prefer it as an eating cheese, although it grates easily and happily.

**ITALY | COW**
**PASTEURIZED**
**RECOMMENDED BRAND:** Piave Vecchio Selezione Oro D.O.P. (red label)
**AROMA:** Tangy, almost juicy
**TEXTURE:** Smooth and dense
**FLAVOR:** Lean, acidic, tropical
**IN SHORT:** The good-for-the-money cheese

# Extra Aged Goat FROM SARTORI

**UNITED STATES | GOAT**

**PASTEURIZED**

**AROMA:** Muted caramel, soft goat

**TEXTURE:** Dry, crumbly, a bit grainy on the finish

**FLAVOR:** Surprisingly goaty and acidic

**IN SHORT:** Goat milk Parmesan

Wisconsin maker Sartori has a number of limited-edition cheeses that are produced seasonally and available only until the batch runs out. Extra Aged Goat is one of them. While it's often described as being mild and sweet, this summation sells the cheese short—it's the closest thing I've found to a goat milk Parmigiano. It's crumbly and grainy, with a surprisingly goaty, acidic flavor. While Dutch goat Goudas are tropical and candied, this is different. It's got white pepper spice and a mouth-watering linger.

# PROTECTED PARMESAN TYPES

In addition to the cheeses noted in this chapter, Europe boasts the following name-protected Parmesan types:

**ITALY**

**BRA PDO:** From the Cuneo province of Piedmont, Tenero (younger, firm, elastic) is made of whole milk, while Duro (aged, hard, savory) or d'Alpeggio (produced in mountain communes) may be whole or semi-skimmed milk. In any of these cases, up to 20 percent goat or sheep milk may be added. Duro has the beginnings of a crystalline texture and is spicy, milky, and savory.

**MONTASIO PDO:** From the northern region of Friulia-Venezia Giulia, Montasio is made from unpasteurized cow milk and aged a minimum of sixty days. Longer-aged wheels are more typical for export, with hard, straw-colored paste. My very first cheese-tasting (March 9, 2002) included this one, and my notes read, "Toffee flavor. Grassy edge. Liked better over time." Montasio is best known for the dish *frico*, where it is grated onto a nonstick pan or mat and baked until golden and crisp. It's the essential cheese crisp and guaranteed gluten-free.

**SWITZERLAND**

**SBRINZ AOP:** It's extremely rare in the United States but worth it if you can find it. Made by only thirty-two dairies in central Switzerland and aged for a minimum of eighteen months (although often as much as thirty-six), Sbrinz is golden and crunchy, redolent of wildflowers and melted butter, and generally as complex as Parm without the spicy notes.

## WHO IS GIORGIO CRAVERO?

Giorgio Cravero is a fifth-generation selector and ager of Parmigiano-Reggiano PDO. The Cravero family have overseen the *stagionatura* (seasoning, or aging) of this cheese since 1855. Ironically, they do so in the town of Bra (Piedmont), which is outside the approved region for Parm-Reg production or conversion. When I visited Giorgio, the wheels stood like silent barrel-chested soldiers, protected by thick, natural stone walls, although the temperature of the maturation room can fluctuate from 41°F/5°C in the winter to 64°F/18°C in the summer.

I often find that people who claim to select and age cheese don't really have any specialized know-how and instead use these claims to create a unique brand. That's not the case at Cravero's. He's the only person I've found who can consistently deliver Parm-Reg that's got a dimension of caramel sweetness and a miraculously creamy texture under tooth.

All of the wheels sent to the United States through importer Essex Street Cheese are made by Modena's Caseificio Sociale San Pietro (#2659).

Cravero Parm-Reg can cost twice the going rate for Parmigiano-Reggiano. If you find it, insist on tasting it because it can be easily ruined by a retailer who lets it sit around in plastic. If you have anything less than mind-blowing cheese, don't blame Giorgio.

# Mahón-Menorca PDO

Produced and aged in Menorca, itself a UNESCO Biosphere Reserve, Mahón is produced in three distinct age profiles: under two months (tender), two to five months (*semicurado*), and five-plus months (*curado*). The latter two are what you're likely to find in the United States. Most Mahón is unimpressive: pasteurized, medium aged, with a neon-orange spray wax coating. If you can find a farmhouse production, or a cheese labeled "artisan," which denotes the use of unpasteurized milk, expect a radical departure into intense flavor complexity. The unpasteurized curd is bagged in a cotton cloth and tied for pressing, leaving a charming knotted impression at the top of the wheel (square, actually). These cheeses have a dusty apricot to rusty orange rind and deliver a briny essence attributed to cows grazing on the sea-sprayed grasses of the island. Aged examples can get serious, attacking the tongue with salt and a burn just this side of unpleasant, but held in check by roasted hazelnut and woody flavors.

**SPAIN | COW**

**(UN)PASTEURIZED**

**RECOMMENDED BRAND:** Mitica

**AROMA:** Cooked, a little rennety

**TEXTURE:** Granular with jagged openings

**FLAVOR:** Intense brine, apricotty to woody

**IN SHORT:** Of the sea

# Parmigiano-Reggiano PDO

ITALY | COW

**UNPASTEURIZED**

**RECOMMENDED BRANDS:**
DiSola Bruna from Forever Cheese, Giorgio Cravero from Essex Street Cheese, Zanetti

**AROMA:** Heady, melted butter, citrus edging into tropical fruit, spice

**TEXTURE:** Granular but malleable

**FLAVOR:** Sweet, salt, and spice with a firm backbone of acid

**IN SHORT:** Thoughtful yet not obvious

The true and original Parmigiano-Reggiano differs greatly from Parmesan (see page 308) and even more so from the shelf-stable green can of saltdust we all scarfed down as kids. Colloquially referred to as the King of Cheese, it's easy for Parm-Reg to disappoint because the expectations are set so high. Despite its rocky, granular texture and relative durability, the cheese loses its complexity when it's cut, wrapped and left to wither under the fluorescent lights of a store. It's necessary to get it cut fresh or, alternatively, vacuum-sealed so that oxygen has been removed and the cheese gas-flushed for stability.

Don't bother with Parm-Reg less than eighteen months, and don't swoon if you're offered Parm-Reg that's five years. Chances are it will be acidic and dry. Two to two and a half years is ideal; look for deep straw yellow to ochre color and broad, expansive white patches throughout the paste. While everyone talks about Parm-Reg for cooking, excellent cheese should always be revelatory to eat. My preferred brands, cheese that has been selected and aged by Giorgio Cravero, or made by one of four farms under the DiSola Bruna name, are heady and aromatic. When I taste their cheese, my initial reaction is that it's too young because the texture is so moist in the mouth. It's not young, it's just not dried out. While Parm-Reg hints at the butterscotch, toasted nuts, and tropical fruit of other cheeses in this chapter, what sets it apart is acidity and nuance. Aged Gouda is like having dark syrup poured over your tongue. Its intensity is what's so impressive about it. Parm-Reg is more thoughtful, layered, a push-pull between sweet, salty, and spicy. That acidity is lean, high, and fruity—mouthwateringly so. A last note: use the whole cheese. The rind is waxy and hard, no good for eating. But add it to vegetable soup. Let it soften over several hours of slow cooking and marvel at the savory complexity that imbues your broth.

APPROACHABLE

PARMIGIANO-REGGIANO PDO

# WHAT DOES IT TAKE TO BE PARMIGIANO-REGGIANO?

The inspiration for the generalized Parmesan is Italian Parmigiano-Reggiano. Its production is strictly regulated, and the following requirements all contribute to a final cheese that is vastly different from, and more intense than, Parmesan.

• Milk and cheese production may occur in the provinces of Parma, Reggio Emilia, Modena, Bologna to the west of the Reno River, and Mantua to the east of the Po River.

• Cows are milked twice each day, and milk is taken to the cheese house within two hours of milking.

• Milk is exclusively grass and hay fed. No silage is permitted.

• Milk may never be pasteurized.

• 363 dairies make cheese from the milk of 3,348 producers.

• Evening milk sits unrefrigerated overnight, allowing the cream to separate, after which it is partially skimmed.

• This partly skimmed milk is then added to full-fat morning milk.

• Parmigiano-Reggiano is made in a copper vat.

• Natural whey starters are used for acidification.

• The curd is coagulated, stirred, and broken into tiny granules before being cooked.

• Each vat produces two wheels of cheese, the curds of which are gathered by hand in cheesecloth.

• Each cheese is immersed in brine for twenty days.

• The curds are never pressed.

• Wheels are open-air aged on wooden boards.

• Wheels are graded at twelve months. Those not suitable for aging to the typical twenty-four months are marked with parallel grooves and classified *mezzano*.

• At the request of a producer, a second inspection may occur at eighteen months for additional certification. Wheels meeting higher standards may be branded "extra" or "export."

• A red seal indicates a wheel matured for over eighteen months.

• A silver seal indicates a wheel matured for over twenty-two months.

• A gold seal indicates a wheel matured for over thirty months.

# MY PICKS: APPROACHABLE PARMESAN TYPES

On the whole, I find the cheeses of the Parmesan Gateway to be among the most universally approachable, even at the intense end of the flavor spectrum. That's due in part to their familiarity and to the fact that intense usually means a concentration of easy-eating flavors such as butterscotch, toasted nuts, and woody bourbon rather than a total departure into new and challenging flavors. That being said, the approachable Parm types capture a beguiling combo of brown butter and yellow candy in a firm texture that's still moist enough to slice easily.

## Paradiso

Although Parrano is the most readily available, this is my favorite of the Parm-Gouda hybrids. Made by Beemster, the only farmer-owned cooperative maker of Dutch Gouda, Paradiso has a fine interior crunch that reminds me of a Nestlé Crunch bar, but the flavor is toasty, nutty, and vaguely savory. (see page 310)

## BellaVitano Gold

Moister and sweeter than domestic Parmesan (see page 308), this is compellingly delicious eating cheese. It's also a rare illustration of flavored cheese done right, with washes of Merlot, balsamic, and Cognac that elevate and improve flavor rather than cloaking it. (see page 310)

## Aged Goat Gouda (ideally, Balarina)

Although many aged cow milk Goudas might as well be cheese confections, wheels made from goat milk keep the candied character with greater complexity. Vanilla and caramel are there, but so is a bit more acidity to lighten things up (and none of the animal tang that people hate about goat cheese). (see page 311)

# MY PICKS: INTENSE PARMESAN TYPES

Moving into intense Parmesan types, you can expect hard, dense, and waxy cheeses with huge, lingering flavor. A small crumb goes a long way, and at the end these cheeses boast a tongue-prickling, mouthwatering acidity reminiscent of tropical fruit and white pepper.

## Coolea

Holland by way of Ireland, and correspondingly darker and more rugged. Nugget-like crunch and true bourbon flavor, without the burn of alcohol. (see page 314)

## Marieke Gouda, Super Aged from Holland's Family Cheese

Because it's raw milk, it's complex and wildly flavorful, with deeper roasty, toasty notes including coffee bean and baking spices. (see page 316)

## Parmigiano-Reggiano PDO (ideally, DiSola Bruna or Giorgio Cravero)

When it's good, it's truly great. Get it fresh-cut, at least twenty-four months, and savor small bits that unravel into lean, high acidity anchored by sweet, salty, and spicy flavor. (see page 320)

# PARMESAN TYPES ↠ VERTICAL TASTINGS

TASTING ONE
## THE GREATNESS OF GRANA

Dig into the differences between Parmesan, on the most approachable end of the flavor spectrum, and Parm-Reg, at its intense conclusion.

**1. Parmesan** (see page 308)

**2. Grana Padano PDO** (see page 317)

**3. Parmigiano-Reggiano PDO** (see page 320)

TASTING TWO
## AGED GOUDA, BY MILK

Here are aged Gouda recipes interpreted through the three basic milk types. Despite the differences in milk, similar cheese-making steps and age profiles produce a flavor gamut that's remarkably similar.

**1. One- to Two-Year Gouda** (see page 314)

**2. Aged Goat Gouda** (see page 311)

**3. Aged Sheep Gouda** (see page 311)

TASTING THREE
## AGED GOUDA, BY AGE

There is an intensification of flavor that comes with age. The question is, how do you take your Gouda?

**1. Parrano** (see page 310)

**2. Roomano Pradera** (see page 311)

**3. Two- to Four-Year Gouda** (see page 314)

## PAIRING OVERVIEW

SCALDED MILK

BUTTERSCOTCH

BOURBON

ACID/SPICE

## BEAR IN MIND:

Hard, waxy, and crunchy texture is the unifier across Parmesan types.

This being said, the way you serve Parmesan types makes a big difference: consider a thin shaving versus a dense chunk.

Approachable cheeses are quite sweet (low acid), and intense cheeses are quite sharp (high acid).

## CLASSIC PAIRINGS

(Whole flavor spectrum) with red fruit and effervescence: Grana cheeses with Lambrusco (dry, sparkling red wine)

(Butterscotch/bourbon) with wood, vanilla, and alcohol: aged Gouda and bourbon

(Acid/spice) with sweet and either fatty or viscous: Parmigiano-Reggiano and Prosciutto di Parma or aceto balsamico (syrupy, aged balsamic vinegar)

### 1. SMEARABLE FRUIT PASTES/SPREADS

I avoid smearable condiments with creamy, buttery cheeses because I want to avoid a mouthful of goo. Firm cheeses can act as cracker or bread slice, and a favorite (incredibly easy) appetizer of mine is one of these cheeses smeared with fruit paste.

(Lighter fruit pastes such as pear, apricot, and pomegranate):
**FLAVOR SPECTRUM (DELICATE FRUIT): 1–5**

(More intense/tart fruit pastes such as plum, cherry, fig, and quince):
**FLAVOR SPECTRUM (TART FRUIT): 6–10**

### 2. SWEET(ISH) VISCOUS OR SYRUPY THINGS

Parm-Reg is classically drizzled with local balsamic that's barrel-aged, thick, brackish syrup with mellow tartness, woody flavor, and dark fruit sweetness (fig, cherry, plum). Other possibilities are saba (aka vincotto), an unaged syrup made from spent grape skins, seeds, and sticks after wine production (*must*), molasses, and buckwheat or chestnut honey.

**FLAVOR SPECTRUM: 1–10**

### 3. BIG RED WINE

High alcohol and candied black and red fruit flavor, as found in New World Malbec and Zinfandel, mow down most cheese. They are juicy and jammy, with more alcohol, which means oily texture and big body. Parm types can take it and nestle in comfortably: dark fruit complements woody, nutty flavor; smooth, full body softens crunchy-rough edges.

**FLAVOR SPECTRUM: 1–10**

### 4. CARAMELIZED NUTS

The inherent flavor of the nuts is trumped by a slick overlay of deeply caramelized sugar, which balances lean, salty, and acidic flavors. Crunch is a welcome counterpoint to waxy nubbins of cheese.

**FLAVOR SPECTRUM: 6–10**

### 5. (FRIED) MARCONA ALMONDS

Spain's indigenous almond, best purchased fried and sea-salted, is traditionally served with Manchego types. I find its silken, buttery crunch and salty sweetness better suited to intense Parm types.

**FLAVOR SPECTRUM: 7–10**

STICHELTON

SHROPSHIRE BLUE

PERSILLÉ DU
BEAUJOLAIS

BAYLEY HAZEN BLUE

MOODY BLUE

CAMBOZOLA
BLACK LABEL

BAY BLUE

BLU DI BUFALA

# Blue

SPECIALTY SHOP

**VerdeCapra**
PAGE 342

**Chiriboga Blue**
PAGE 343

**Beenleigh Blue**
PAGE 344

**Bleu de Berger**
PAGE 344

**Dunbarton Blue**
PAGE 345

**Blu di Bufala**
PAGE 339

**Shropshire Blue**
PAGE 346

**Cambozola Black Label**
PAGE 339

**Mycella Blue**
PAGE 344

**Persillé du Beaujolais**
PAGE 346

**Gorgonzola PDO (Dolce or Cremificato)**
PAGE 342

**Fourme d'Ambert PDO**
PAGE 345

**Bayley Hazen Blue**
PAGE 348

AVAILABILITY   SUPERMARKET ➤➤

**Saint Agur**
PAGE 338

**Saga**
PAGE 338

**FLAVOR** APPROACHABLE ➤➤

**1** SALTY CREAM  **2** BLUE BRIE  **3** PUNGENT YOGURT  **4** COCONUT  **5** ANISE

**Blau de Cabra**
PAGE 351

**Stichelton**
PAGE 350

**Tilston Point**
PAGE 351

**Shaker Blue and Ewe's Blue**
PAGE 354

**Rogue River Blue**
PAGE 352

**Cabrales PDO**
PAGE 358

**Echo Mountain**
PAGE 356

**Stilton PDO**
PAGE 349

**Bay Blue**
PAGE 348

**Bleu d'Auvergne PDO**
PAGE 351

**Gorgonzola PDO (Naturale, Mountain, or Piccante)**
PAGE 352

**Queso de Valdeón**
PAGE 355

**AmaBlu St. Pete's Select**
PAGE 353

**Buttermilk Blue (Affine)**
PAGE 354

**Maytag Blue**
PAGE 354

**Smokey Blue**
PAGE 356

**Moody Blue**
PAGE 355

**Roquefort PDO**
PAGE 356

INTENSE

**6**
MEATY

**7**
UNSWEETENED CHOCOLATE

**8**
FERMENTED FRUIT

**9**
SMOKED OR SMOKY

**10**
ALL THAT, PLUS BLACK PEPPER

# Perhaps more than any other cheese style, Blue types suffer from a case of mistaken identity. For Blue, you see, is not just one cheese. It's a whole

crazy family of cheeses bonded by the visible thread of mold. And bleu, BTW, is just "blue" in French, so the same rules apply. Back in my cheese counter days, many of my customers dismissed Blue as a viable category because they'd had one Blue cheese that they didn't care for and assumed all the rest would be the same. Even today this is true, as with my friend Jenny who, when I arrived at her gorgeous San Francisco home with a bag of cheese, semiapologetically explained, "Sorry. I don't like Blue." I told her the one in my bag would convince her otherwise. She tried it and grudgingly acknowledged it was better than most but that it still wasn't her thing. I'm going to keep trying.

Here's why: While Blue cheeses have some commonalities—namely, they all have blue mold and elevated salt levels—their variety is nothing less than stagger- ing. Sometimes that mold appears in little blips and bits, and sometimes it's in big, thick, coursing rivers. While as a group the blues are saltier than other groups, they need not be salt licks, all crumbly, metallic, and harsh. If the cheese doesn't have a name beyond "blue," it's likely, however, to be all of those things. The Blues I'd known before I worked in food were interchangeable—a seasoning rather than a cheese, the food equivalent of a frat boy challenge: prove that you could handle something that made your mouth pucker and your throat burn.

I met Blue-cheese-with-a-name in a small, hilly hamlet of northern Italy. I was dazed with equal parts jet lag and the bright sparkle of Lake Como, my first-ever gelato, the fact that everyone ordered either wine or Coca Light with lunch. I'd been to Europe only once before, and this was my inaugural visit for cheese. It came with the dim awareness that seeing a place, smelling the air, and experiencing a food as its makers intend it is the difference between knowing something in your soul and watching it on TV.

At one meal, the final dessert course was presented. A single plate, bestowed upon a single diner. And on that plate sat a fat, glistening, ever-so-wobbly slab of

Gorgonzola Cremificato. I don't use the word "slab" merely figuratively. This probably was a quarter-pound slice of Blue cheese. A spoon was brought. My hosts watched amusedly to see what I would do. So I ate it. I didn't want to be rude. I ate the whole thing. And while I ate it, I thought: oh God, I didn't know Blue could be like this. I didn't know I could eat it with a spoon and find it more delicious than any chocolate thing or cake thing I'd ever encountered. I didn't know it could be sweet-yet-yogurty, gelatinous and smearable, immaculate on its own but oddly equipped to be eaten with a whole slew of unexpected foods (at that meal: bitter, roasted espresso; small jellied wobbles of quince candy; sweetly benign milk chocolate).

It was the first time I experienced what my buddy Aaron Foster bestows as his supreme compliment to this style: "Cheese first. Blue second." Sure, it's got mold and salt: those are dimensions of the cheese. But there's a foundational layer of complexity and flavor that exists first and whose presence can be tasted throughout. This is what I'm looking for: a Blue with its own identity and not just a nameless, faceless salt alternative to be sprinkled on salad. After that inaugural trip to Europe, I began eating different Blues as cheeses unto themselves. The high moisture, minimally blue ones that could be lobbed into bowls of steaming pasta for an instant cheesemonger's cream sauce. The deeply pocked, marine Blue ones popping with fruity intensity were smeared atop well-buttered, jammed toast for something akin to but far greater than PB&J. The fudgy ones with coarse brown rinds replaced meat at my solo dinner table, best enjoyed with fruit, or fruit paste, or fruity barley wine, earthy and substantial.

Eating across this family of cheese inspired my mission to talk about Blue cheeses rather than Blue cheese. It's not one, it's many. Chances are, at least one of them is for you.

# Chapter Guide

Just like your family has tall ones and short ones, fat ones and thin ones, mousy ones and acerbic ones, so too do the Blues. Blue is the gateway to the tribe of cheeses that have some type of blue/green/gray mold growing inside the cheese. That mold differs from the foggy gray coat some cheeses wear, or the wavering lines of ash that decorate cheeses like Humboldt Fog (see page 88) and Morbier (see page 135). Blue mold might be pockmarks or flecks, delicate veining or intense rivers, but the blueing traverses and defines the cheese's interior.

## WHAT TO KNOW

**SO, HOW DOES BLUE CHEESE GET BLUE?** The story I learned on the cheese counter was that a young shepherd (origins unknown, let's say southern France) left behind his lunchtime hunks of bread and cheese in a cool cave (pick the variation you like: he was tired and fell asleep; he was drunk and forgot the cheese; he was focused on a buxom young shepherdess and ran off). When he returned some days later (it must have been a great piece of cheese, or a near-starving shepherd), he discovered that his bread and cheese were riddled with mold. Shockingly, the cheese tasted even more delicious than it had before. And so, Blue cheese was born!

The truth is, there are very few Blue cheeses that develop their veining without focused efforts on the part of the cheese maker; unlike our shepherd's, today's Blue cheeses are made, not born:

➤ Powdered mold spores are added to the vat of milk during cheese making, or liquid mold may be added to curds before wheels are formed.

➤ The most common strains are *Penicillium roqueforti* and *Penicillium glaucum*.

➤ Blue cheese mold requires specific acidity, moisture, salt, and oxygen conditions to flourish. This is distinct from blue mold that grows spontaneously on old bits of food in your refrigerator.

➤ During aging, the mold grows upon contact with oxygen, so young wheels of Blue cheese quickly become coated in gray/blue/black mottling.

➤ In order to develop veining, the wheels are pierced to introduce oxygen to the cheese's interior.

➤ Blue mold speeds proteolysis (the breakdown of proteins, which contributes increasingly creamy texture) and lipolysis (the breakdown of fats, which contributes pungent, spicy, and metallic flavors). Proteolysis is arrested by cold temperatures, but lipolysis continues, which means a cheese can leave its maker tasting great and reach a customer tasting like razors on the tongue. A good maker understands this evolution and produces cheese that will improve, rather than degrade, over time in the supply chain.

➤ Blue cheeses are often wrapped to continue aging while keeping oxygen at bay and impeding rampant blue mold growth.

**MEET THE MEMBERS OF THE BLUE CHEESE FAMILY** Presented in order from generally more approachable to generally more intense:

➡ **SOFT-RIPENED, OR BRIE-LIKE:** Soft and creamy in texture with an edible skin that might be white or blue gray. These guys are butter-like with the occasional fleck of blue mold, as in Cambozola Black Label (see page 339).

➡ **NATURAL RIND:** Lower moisture Blues on which a drier, sandier, or dusty-textured rind develops. The cheese's interior tends toward fudgy, its flavors nutty and earthy. You can crumble it, but it's more inclined to chunk up. Stilton (see page 349) is the poster child for this type of Blue.

➡ **RINDLESS, OR FOIL-WRAPPED:** You may well know these as the Blue cheeses sold in triangular foil-wrapped wedges, or featured on menus as gracing your spinach salad. There are cheap, salty, metallic versions and well-crafted, layered, and complex versions. My best advice is to start to learn cheese and brand names because these guys look alike, and it's entirely possible that you'll like Maytag Blue (see page 354) but not Roquefort (see page 356); both fall into this camp.

➡ **LEAF-WRAPPED:** Essentially a rindless Blue that is wrapped in leaves during aging or before transport. The leaves are typically dry and not meant for eating; also, weird-looking molds may grow underneath them.

## WHAT TO AVOID

➡ **COLOR:** Blue cheeses should have a regular interior pattern of mold. If the cut surface of the cheese is covered in fine patches of white or pale green mold (like a fog, or a scum), it's sporting mold from somewhere else. You can scrape this off and the cheese underneath won't hurt you, but know that the surface mold is not an intentional part of the cheese. Blue cheeses with pink or red (especially the Brie-like Blues) patches should not be eaten. A significant perimeter of brown discoloration under the rind is a sign the cheese has been sitting around.

➡ **AROMA:** The smell of ammonia, if it doesn't dissipate after the cheese is unwrapped.

➤ **FLAVOR:** A strong ammonia smell is a warning with all Blue cheeses. If it smells like Windex, it's going to taste like Windex. Moldy Windex, in this case.

➤ **RIND:** The natural rind Blues may have a dusty white or knobby brown rind, but it should be dry. A sticky, smearing, or wet rind is a sign the cheese has been suffocating in plastic wrapping and is likely to be ammoniated.

## STORAGE AND SHELF LIFE

Blues are higher in moisture than many types of cheese, and are accordingly more delicate than drier, aged cheeses. While most Blues lack the bloomy rind of Brie types, they suffer similarly from plastic wrapping, which allows liquid to pool around the cheese, causing disintegration and spicy flavors. Blues are the only cheeses I don't store in plastic bags. Foil wrap, instead, is the reliable best option.

Once cut, Blues are best consumed in varying amounts of time, depending on the style: seven days (Brie-like); ten to fourteen days (natural rind); two to three weeks (rindless).

Scum-like patches of blue or green mold may develop on the cut surface of the cheese. These can be easily scraped away or a paper-thin slice cut off to remove it, although they are a reliable warning sign that you're pushing the limit on storage life.

---

## BLUE TYPES: TEXTURES

### IN A WORD: VARIED

### LIGHT AND AIRY
AIRY  CREAMY  CRUMBLY  FLUFFY
SLIPPERY  VELVETY

### SMOOTH AND/OR SPRINGY
GELATINOUS  PLUMP  SLICEABLE
SMOOTH  SMUSHABLE  SUPPLE
TENDER

### HEAVY AND/OR WET
BEATEN BUTTER  CHALKY
CHEESECAKEY  CLAY  COLD BUTTER
FUDGE  MOIST  PUDDING  SPONGY
TEMPERED BUTTER  YIELDING

### LIQUESCENT
SCOOPABLE  SMEARABLE

### DENSE AND/OR CRUMBLY
CHUNKY  CRUMBLY  DENSE

### FLAWS
GLUEY  GRAINY  MUSHY

# BLUE TYPES: FLAVOR & AROMA WHEEL

# Saint Agur

**FRANCE | COW**

**PASTEURIZED**

**AROMA:** Not much

**TEXTURE:** Tempered butter that dissolves on the tongue

**FLAVOR:** Luscious saltsweet balance

**IN SHORT:** The Ikea or H&M of Blue

Developed in 1988 by the (relatively large) company Bongrain, this cheese is proof of the greatness of mass-produced French cheese. While the largest and most industrial American cheese makers crank out cheese food, the French crank out incredibly consistent and widely likable cheeses that characterize a certain type. Saint Agur is one of these: a sexy, sticky Blue with muted sweet-salt flavor. To ensure your attention, the cheese is cream-enriched and thus 60 percent butterfat, hence its nearly whipped texture and mild succulence. I wouldn't call this an especially complex cheese, but it's really, really tasty and a gentle gatekeeper to a style of cheese many associate with a salty, metallic edge.

# Saga

**DENMARK | COW**

**PASTEURIZED**

**AROMA:** White mold, a whiff of mushroom

**TEXTURE:** Thick 'n' sticky

**FLAVOR:** Buttery with a bitter green finish

**IN SHORT:** Blue Brie

The French are known to eat bread slathered with butter and piquant, peppery Blue cheeses like Roquefort (see page 356). The idea is that the soothing spread of the former tempers the bite of the latter. Danish producer Castello takes this concept and puts it into practice within a single cheese. This is essentially a triple crème Brie, laced with very occasional, concentrated pockets of blue mold. The texture is thick and sticky, to the point of being almost chewy, and the persistent flavors of blue mold are extended by a sharper, edging-on-bitter note from the white molded rind. Although this would certainly be considered a milder Blue for its buttery dedication, don't expect a sweet or bland bite.

APPROACHABLE

# Cambozola Black Label

This is the twenty-first-century evolution of the classic triple crème Blue Cambozola. The primary differences are the rind and the aging. The exterior is blanketed in a fine, even coat of edible gray mold (as opposed to the original's thick, rather chewy Brie-like rind), and the cheese is aged for a longer period of time in cold cellars, where it develops a creamier texture and stronger flavor. The texture is what makes this cheese. It's not springy or sticky, but decadently silken, like butter. Being more intense in flavor than regular Cambozola isn't saying much, as the original is the ultimate almost-tastes-like-nothing-so-people-will-eat-it Blue. But it's good to know that the type of flavor intensity Black Label develops is of the leathery, earthy sort rather than the salty, peppery sort, which makes it a great step up from very little taste to measured and satisfying taste.

**GERMANY | COW**
**PASTEURIZED**
**AROMA:** Butter and leather
**TEXTURE:** Slightly gelatinous but insanely buttery
**FLAVOR:** Salt and slightly meaty
**IN SHORT:** Luscious

# Blu di Bufala

Like the mushroomy wonder Salva Cremasco, Blu di Bufala is a tall, hefty square with a stunningly rustic rind. Despite an occasionally orange, mold-dappled gray rind suggesting a washed rind (see page 152) or tomme (see page 123), very little aroma wafts off a cut piece. This is a weird and special cheese. While water buffalo milk is very common in Campagna, the southern Italian region known for Mozzarella di Bufala, it is basically nonexistent everywhere else. Up north in Bergamo, brothers Bruno and Alfio Gritti of Caseficio Quattro Portoni were struggling to support the family dairy farm, and so they took the radical step of buying forty water buffalo and branching out into original (but regionally inspired) recipes. So you've got two youngish guys working with very traditional milk in very untraditional ways. With nearly twice the fat of cow milk, buffalo milk presents special challenges in a Blue. The mold accelerates lipolysis, the breakdown of fats, and the by-product of this breakdown is spicy-hedging-on-bitter flavor. With double the fat you've got the potential for double the badness. Remarkably, then, well-kept Blu di Bufala tends only toward the lush, slightly gamy richness of buffalo milk. Salting is judicious, so you get to experience the rarity of aged buffalo cheese followed by a white peppery finish. Do be warned, however, that with too much time and lack of turnover on a cheese counter Blu di Bufala becomes hyper-spicy and intensely salty, quickly turning it into a 9 or 10 in flavor intensity. It's such a rarity that I encourage you to give it multiple opportunities to show you how great it can be.

**ITALY | BUFFALO**
**PASTEURIZED**
**AROMA:** Minimal
**TEXTURE:** Even, dense, pliable
**FLAVOR:** Buffalo milk, like slightly gamy butter
**IN SHORT:** Hella rich

BLU DI BUFALA

GORGONZOLA PDO

# Gorgonzola PDO (Dolce or Cremificato)

ITALY | COW

PASTEURIZED

**RECOMMENDED BRAND:**
Ciresa (Gorgonzola DOP
Marca Oro)

**AROMA:** Sour yogurt/milk

**TEXTURE:** Limpid and
scoopable

**FLAVOR:** Not as sweet as
you'd expect. Pungent, with a
lightly spicy finish

**IN SHORT:** Cream sauce
with attitude

The cursive G stamped on both sides of the moist rind and the name "Gorgonzola" denote a protected Blue cheese exclusively produced in the regions of Piedmont and Lombardy. Trickily, Gorgonzola is made in two distinctive styles and typically sold as either dolce (or *cremificato*) or *piccante* (aka mountain or *naturale*, see page 352). Dolce is so-called because it's sweeter due to less salt and less blueing than the piccante style. Cremificato is dolce as it's eaten in Italy, much higher in water content, and oozily dripping. Lovely stories are told of tired cows making their autumn return to the valleys in and around the town of Gorgonzola, but production today is quite modernized and limited to factories. There is no truly small, farmstead tradition behind this cheese; as a result, the cheese is consistent, generally okay, occasionally remarkable. In Italy, both styles of Gorgonzola are used regularly, but primarily as ingredients rather than stand-alone cheeses.

Dolce is especially vulnerable to mishandling, and cremificato is often sold from unrefrigerated dishes atop cheese counters. This makes for great presentation, but risks a soured wedge of cheese should you not get it within a few days of opening. Gorgonzola Dolce is mild for a Blue, but tends toward yogurt notes, often with a slightly spicy finish. These warnings aside, a fresh slab is a wondrous thing indeed: gelatinous and wobbly, almost liquescent, and pockmarked with fruity eyes of pale green mold. In my early counter days, when money was tight but I got a discount on cheese, dinner was often steaming al dente spaghetti tossed with glistening blobs of Gorgonzola Dolce. The cheese softened into a heady cream sauce that required nothing, although I'd add a sprinkling of fresh parsley for color.

## VerdeCapra

ITALY | GOAT

PASTEURIZED

**AROMA:** Buttermilk

**TEXTURE:** Panna cotta

**FLAVOR:** Piquant, mouthwatery, fermented fruit

**IN SHORT:** Slatherable

From Lombardian Taleggio (see page 159) producer Ca De Ambros comes this panna cotta wobble of a Blue. Heavy, wet curd collapses instantly when pierced, meaning you may find traces of lines but little if any actual blue or green mold. If otherwise uninstructed, you'd be likely to guess this cheese a piece of Gorgonzola PDO (above) made in the dolce style. The substitution of goat milk for traditional cow can be seen in the fine, snowy white paste, and tasted in the amped-up fermented fruity notes that a Gorgonzola might not otherwise display. This is first and foremost a textural marvel, silken and squishy in a way that makes you want to grab it by the handful.

APPROACHABLE

# Chiriboga Blue

Crisscrossing the grounds of the fairy tale inn/restaurant/creamery compound where this cheese is made, there's a fast-running canal reminiscent of the log flume ride at childhood amusement parks. In this protected wonderland, Ecuadorian Arturo Chiriboga makes his ethereal Blue. Trained in western Switzerland with the intention of running a cheese operation for his family's cattle business, Arturo and his wife (of German descent) relocated to Bavaria when Ecuador politically destabilized in the 1980s. He makes sixteen different cheeses, and they're all about texture. Plump, shiny, bulging, plush texture that you want to lie down on and squash into again and again. What's remarkable about Chiriboga Blue is that no mold is added to the milk during cheese making. The cream-enriched curd (minimum 60 percent butterfat) is cut three times and heated, then ladled into forms but not pressed. After twenty-four hours of resting (and four rounds of flipping), followed by another twenty-four hours of brining, the cheese is pierced with needles that have been dipped in *P. roqueforti* mold. I have never heard of another maker using this approach, and the result is minimal striations of blue penetrating a tall, fluffy, briny-sweet paste of unbelievable butteriness. During and after each bite, expect a cloud of subtle, floral perfume.

GERMANY | COW

UNPASTEURIZED

**AROMA:** Violets

**TEXTURE:** Flakily buttery

**FLAVOR:** Floral dark chocolate

IN SHORT: Sophisticated and heavenly

# Beenleigh Blue

ENGLAND | SHEEP
PASTEURIZED

**AROMA:** Very little

**TEXTURE:** Tempered butter

**FLAVOR:** Pure coconut oil

**IN SHORT:** Fatty, with an edge

The best-known sheep Blue in the world is Roquefort (see page 356), and even those of the highest quality have a layered and formidable spiciness that puts them at the intense end of what Blue cheese can be. How remarkable, then, that this apparently comparable recipe tastes radically different: incredibly gentle, and focused on the sweet, lush fat of sheep milk. Robin Congden created Beenleigh initially in an effort to replicate Roquefort on his farm in Devon. From pastures of French herbs to managed humidification in the aging caves to mold spores scraped and ferried away from the famed caves in Combalou, Robin's efforts delivered a brilliant cheese, but one that is wholly its own food. Ben Harris has joined on as cheese maker, and Robin now buys the sheep milk from a farm in Cornwall. This has allowed the focus to remain solely on the making, and what a result there is. With a texture so moist as to be nearly wet, each hunk dissolves lazily on the tongue, like some miraculous dairy cough drop.

# Mycella Blue

DENMARK | COW
PASTEURIZED

**AROMA:** Mineral milk

**TEXTURE:** Cool pat o' butter

**FLAVOR:** Hint of smoke, dried cherry, mellow salt

**IN SHORT:** The reclaimer of Danish Blue

A response to the industrialization of Danish cheese making, Mycella was invented in 2010 by Denmark's Tradition and is made exclusively from the milk of Bornholm Island's dairy cooperative. Wheels are aged for a minimum of four months, ensuring a thickly creamy paste and rich, mellow, judiciously salted flavor. I've tasted wheels with smoky undertones and know of one retailer (St. James Cheese Co. in New Orleans) who capitalizes on this inclination and smokes the cheese before using it in a sandwich recipe (Mycella and roast beef with horseradish hits some ancient flavor center in the brain programmed to hoard a sweet/salt/fat/spicy-food combination). The milky approachability and lack of bite are inspiring reasons to seek the cheese out, if farming philosophy alone doesn't compel you. This is especially true for people who've eaten only the brittle, crumbly, and intensely metallic Danish Blue that dominates the market.

# Bleu de Berger

With a name translating to "Blue of sheep," there are multiple options, from different makers, on the market. The one I'm plugging is made in the French Pyrenees. Most milder Blues maintain their broad appeal with relatively higher moisture. The wetter texture means that when wheels are pierced, the curds collapse, preventing deep, regular veining of mold and limiting it to little blips and bits (and thus less Blue flavor). To find, then, a mellow, nearly sweet Blue with a firm texture is a rarity indeed. Made near the Spanish border, in the region best known for the classic sheep wheel Ossau-Iraty (see page 201), this is the most delicious failure of a cheese I've encountered. The initial goal was to produce a Roquefort-type Blue (see page 356); the creamery instead wound up, thankfully, with this dense, natural-rinded wheel. My favorite qualities of the Pyrenees sheep cheeses are their fatty chew and caramel undertone. Add to that the barest lines of Blue, and a texture so moist as to nearly cave in at the center, and you get something special.

FRANCE | SHEEP

UNPASTEURIZED

**RECOMMENDED BRAND:** Fromagerie Mont Royal Tradition

**AROMA:** Fresh hay and dulce de leche

**TEXTURE:** Smushable

**FLAVOR:** Almost sweet

IN SHORT: Unexpected

# Fourme d'Ambert PDO

This is one of life's most underrated Blues, and I struggle to understand why it's not sold on every cheese counter across the land. A good cheese department has Blues for every taste, and Fourme d'Ambert is mild, to be sure. But it's a more delicious and complex upgrade for folks who might otherwise go with the blandest Blue around. High in moisture (and thus perceptibly less salty or spicy), this cylindrical form sometimes cracks under its own weight—moist, buttery insides pushing out through the powdery, gray-rinded cracks. As is true with most European PDOs, the animals' diet is strictly regulated, in this case to ensure a minimum of five months' grass grazing and non-GMO grain for supplemental feed. All hay must come from the PDO region of the Massif Central in Auvergne. If the merits of provenance don't sway you, the cheese itself will. Good Fourme d'Ambert is velvety, and although the bone-white paste is punctuated with large and developed pockets of Blue, the flavor is subtle, with anise qualities and a mildly bitter finish. It's a rare Blue that can be enjoyed straight up, not alongside a smear of butter or chunked on a salad, but unadulterated—with baguette or water cracker only if you need something crunchy.

FRANCE | COW

(UN)PASTEURIZED

**AROMA:** Mushroom

**TEXTURE:** Velvety

**FLAVOR:** Subtle licorice

IN SHORT: Sexy

# Dunbarton Blue FROM ROELLI CHEESE HAUS

Is it a Blue? Is it a Cheddar? It's both, technically. A hybrid recipe invented by Wisconsin's fourth-generation cheese maker Chris Roelli, Dunbarton is made from unpasteurized milk from April to October when the cows are on pasture (the rest of the year it's pasteurized). Although the milk is inoculated, like most Blues, with *P. roqueforti*, the curds are pressed, which makes a dense, compact paste and fewer air passages for the mold to flourish in after piercing. Dense and sturdy, the golden paste is abundantly meaty rather than peppery or Bluey. Unusually, its Cheddar qualities make it a solid red wine partner, although I like the malty sweetness of brown ale to play with the cheese's lingering umami.

UNITED STATES | COW

(UN)PASTEURIZED

**AROMA:** Earth

**TEXTURE:** Dense and compact

**FLAVOR:** Bacony

IN SHORT: Blue Cheddar

# Persillé du Beaujolais

FRANCE | COW

PASTEURIZED

**AROMA:** Leather, cooked portobello mushroom

**TEXTURE:** Dense and gluey

**FLAVOR:** Salt, yes, but sweeter blue mold and hints of anise

**IN SHORT:** Thoughtfully earthy

Persillé means "parsleyed" and refers to the greenish frond-like veining that can characterize French Blue cheeses. This one, created by the Lapierre family outside of Lyon in the Rhone-Alps and aged primarily for Whole Foods by affineur Hervé Mons, reminds me of a denser, more complex Fourme d'Ambert (see page 345). (Keep a particular eye out for cheeses that are pinkish red or dark brown beneath the rind—dried out and thus ammoniated wheels are not uncommon and will quickly swamp the delicacy of flavor that makes this Blue great.) The story goes that Monsieur Lapierre invented the recipe to show up Italian truck drivers who arrived at his farm for veal calves, claiming Gorgonzola was the greatest Blue cheese in the world. I wouldn't say Persillé du Beaujolais is anything like Gorgonzola , either the dolce (see page 342) or the piccante (see page 352) style, and this is to its credit. It's uniquely French, at once mushroomy and leathery, with the warming tingle of pink peppercorn.

# Shropshire Blue

ENGLAND | COW

PASTEURIZED

**RECOMMENDED BRANDS:** Colston Bassett (exported by Neal's Yard Dairy), Long Clawson

**AROMA:** Toasted nuts

**TEXTURE:** Cool butter

**FLAVOR:** Salty, savory

**IN SHORT:** Good presentation

I still recall the first time I read about this cheese, in Steve Jenkins's seminal *Cheese Primer*. He basically said you'd be an idiot to buy Stilton (see page 349) if you could buy Shropshire instead, and since that day I've been waiting for the magic with this cheese. It hasn't come yet, perhaps because most Shropshire is made by the more industrial Stilton producers, and so it doesn't compare to the best Stiltons available. To say Shropshire is Stilton-esque is an understatement of epic proportions. It basically is Stilton, colored orange with annatto, which imparts the barest spiciness but otherwise makes no appreciable flavor impact. Invented by Cheshire (see page 234) grader Dennis Biggins in the 1930s. Shropshire is a beautiful cheese: sunny, sherbet orange with deep, insistent, denim-blue veins snaking throughout. Minerally and savory, the most likely flaw you'll encounter is cheese that is over-aged and thus overly salted.

UNITED STATES | COW
UNPASTEURIZED

**AROMA:** Somewhere between biscuits and crème brûlée

**TEXTURE:** Heavy and moist

**FLAVOR:** Sweet and savory, with blue mold held in balance by excellent milk

**IN SHORT:** Because it's worth it (and you are too)

# Bayley Hazen Blue   FROM JASPER HILL FARM/ CELLARS AT JASPER HILL

The story I tell about Bayley Hazen (so named for the Revolutionary War–era road that first brought settlers to Greensboro, Vermont) is this: when Mateo Kehler and I were the new kids on the block, he made a fluffy dreamboat of a cheese that I wanted to buy. And he told me I could, if I bought the Blue. The Blue, he said, was the thing that would keep his and his brother Andy's farm in business. So I bought the Blue. I liked that it was a natural rind Blue—denser and drier, subtle, and quite unlike most of the rindless, foil-wrapped Blues American makers were producing. It was inconsistent—sometimes too salty, sometimes too moist—but when it was good, it was brilliant. Fast-forward thirteen years, and Bayley Hazen was awarded Best Unpasteurized Cheese in the World (2014) at the World Cheese Awards. Bayley is still a core of Jasper Hill's growth plan: made with single-source milk, either from Jasper Hill Farm or a recently purchased second farm, produced in one of two facilities within Greensboro. Because the wheels are still hand-salted, there is variation in salinity from wheel to wheel. It might remind you of Stilton (see page 349), but there is far less veining and an open, creamier texture. Every time, this cheese walks the line between sweet and savory, smelling like crème brûlée with a taste reminiscent of a griddled hamburger: buttery, meaty, and easy to eat. Anise notes are extremely typical, but in each case the flavors of the blueing are checked by clean, grassy milkiness.

UNITED STATES | COW
PASTEURIZED

**AROMA:** Subdued, caramel

**TEXTURE:** Fudgy

**FLAVOR:** Dark chocolate, pronounced Blue finish

**IN SHORT:** Hybrid

# Bay Blue   FROM POINT REYES FARMSTEAD CHEESE CO.

While the Giacomini family has anchored their farm's name and reputation on the unpasteurized Original Blue they launched in 2000, it's their newer Bay Blue that's got my attention. I've admired Original Blue's moist, almost mousse-like texture, and the shockingly white paste laced with verdant blue-green veining that evokes the hills of Point Reyes, California, rolling to meet the Pacific Ocean. It's always been a solid Blue cheese. But Bay Blue is a great one. The farm likens it to Stilton. The rind is far less developed or crusty than its English inspiration; although by comparison to Original Blue, Blue Bay is certainly fudgier. What's special about it is how not Stilton-y the mold is. The cheese is mellow, with a caramel sweetness. But the veining, which is marbled and well integrated, has a much more assertive zing than the English types. It's, well, more American. I like a cherry picking of cheese traditions in the interests of new invention.

## STILTON: NAMED AFTER A TOWN WHERE IT CAN'T BE MADE

Stilton is named after the village that was a market and travel crossroads for travelers heading north from London and is anchored by the popular Bell Inn, which promoted and sold the cheese of the region. It's been found that a specific cheese was produced in the town of Stilton as early as the 1720s: cylindrical in shape and comparable in size to modern Stilton, this early cheese was a pressed, cooked cream cheese. It appears that some blue vein versions may have existed, and over time the specialty of the region evolved into its current recipe of an unpressed, blue-veined cheese. The Bell Inn still exists in Stilton, and is a lovely pub still serving "The King of Cheeses." Ironically, the village of Stilton is located in the county of Cambridgeshire; thus, due to the PDO restrictions on Stilton cheese production, any cheese produced in the village of Stilton cannot actually be called Stilton.

# Stilton PDO

Like Cheddar type English territorial cheeses including Cheshire (see page 234), Lancashire (see page 244), and Double Gloucester (see page 241), Stilton begins its life as a firm, crumbly cheese. Only after the wheels are pierced does it become a Blue, and the length of time a maker waits before piercing has a profound impact on the final flavor and quality of the wheel. There are white Stiltons, essentially the same recipe that has not be inoculated with mold or pierced but instead flavored with studs of fruit, like blueberry. For our purposes, let's presume that Stilton refers to the Blue cheese. All Stilton is produced in the counties of Derbyshire, Nottinghamshire, and Leicestershire. It is always made of pasteurized milk, a conscious choice on the part of the Stilton Cheesemakers' Association, who adopted this restriction in 1989 after a food-poisoning incident threatened to taint the public's perception of raw milk. Given the strict production guidelines, there are few major opportunities for a maker to differentiate their cheese. This is where Colston Bassett Stilton, produced for Neal's Yard Dairy, separates itself from the pack. While all Colston Bassett wheels are hand-ladled, those for Neal's Yard are coagulated with traditional animal rennet and aged an extra five weeks before piercing. Then it's an additional three months before the wheels are sold, resulting in a cheese far more complex and layered in flavor than other brands. For these reasons, I think of Colston Bassett Stilton as a cheese first and

**ENGLAND | COW**

**PASTEURIZED**

**RECOMMENDED BRANDS:** Colston Bassett (exported by Neal's Yard Dairy), Cropwell Bishop, Long Clawson, and Tuxford & Tebbutt

**AROMA:** Milk chocolate rolled in butter

**TEXTURE:** Cold butter

**FLAVOR:** Peanuts and chocolate with a bite

**IN SHORT:** The Dairy Queen Buster Bar of Blues

a Blue second. Qualities of Blue—persistent salt, the bite of *roqueforti* mold, chocolately undertones—these are all present, but harmonized with the dense, buttery paste. And a finish like the Energizer Bunny. It keeps going. And going. And going. Because all Stilton is relatively lower in moisture than, say, Roquefort (see page 356) and Gorgonzola (see page 342), it is a more durable cheese. Even the most ill-treated Stiltons avoid the nail polish burn of other overaged Blues.

# Stichelton

**ENGLAND | COW**

**UNPASTEURIZED**

**AROMA:** Diacetyl (intense butter)

**TEXTURE:** Butter fifteen minutes out of the fridge

**FLAVOR:** Cool yet bright, papaya

**IN SHORT:** One for the ages

In Nottinghamshire, one of the three approved counties for Stilton (see page 349) production, a farm is doing what no Stilton maker has done since the 1930s: making raw milk Blue cheese with the (organic) milk of their own herd of cows. Pronounced "stitch-il-tun" after the Anglo-Saxon word for the town of Stilton, this is the closest you can get to what Stilton once was before pasteurization became mandatory, back when a single farm produced a few dozen wheels of Blue a day. In this case, Joe Schneider, working on Collingthwaite Farm, crafts thirty wheels daily. He begins with a scant twenty milliliters of starter bacteria for a 600-gallon vat of milk and minimal rennet, undertaking a creepingly slow acidification that straddles the line between a lactic and a rennet set. Translation: quiveringly delicate curd that acidifies and drains overnight. "Traditional rennet," he says, "makes traditional cheese." Only Colston Bassett employs animal rennet for a select subset of its Stilton wheels; with Stichelton it's the norm. The curd is milled and salted one wheel at a time; its texture is too fine to grind up the entire vat's worth of curd at once. Pierced at seven weeks, and with only two piercings, the bone-white paste beautifully balances limited and erratic zips and blips of spicy blue mold. There's no shortage of Stilton available, so I guess one might ask why it's worth the bother to re-create a cheese that died seventy-five years ago. I'd ask, "Why isn't it worth it?" Tasting Stichelton next to even the finest PDO Stilton is to experience a miraculous difference in flavor complexity: the cool, buttery paste holds on to a caramelly sweet edge and finishes with a pop of bright intensity, like tropical fruit. Stichelton is a continual work in progress, and with each passing year it gets more profound.

# Blau de Cabra

From the Catalan maker Oriol Antunez, who is experimenting with buffalo milk in a region known for goat and sheep cheeses, comes one of the more unusual goat milk Blues I've encountered. Oriol's roots at his parents' farm are in goat cheeses, although this recipe is more akin to Italian Blu di Bufala (see page 339) than any goat Blue I've tasted. Tall and pliable, the cheese's interior has squiggly fissures of blue-edging-on-green mold. The texture feels almost processed in its creamy slipperiness, but the flavor is anything but manufactured: earthy, with the delicate savory perfume of cured serrano ham.

**SPAIN | GOAT**
PASTEURIZED

**AROMA:** Toast, hazelnuts

**TEXTURE:** A little processed, creamy, but holds together

**FLAVOR:** Earthy, salty like cured meat, very subdued mold

IN SHORT: Cheese first, Blue second

# Bleu d'Auvergne PDO

Why is Bleu d'Auvergne better than most foil-wrapped Blues? Its PDO regulations require only four weeks of aging (Roquefort, see page 356, by comparison sees a minimum of four months' aging). It looks like nothing special. Perhaps, then, the limited pool of ten producers (four of whom are farm producers) has something to do with it. Maybe it's the volcanic soil of the Puy-de-Dôme and Cantal departments of Auvergne? Every PDO has its geographic specializations, but Bleu d'Auvergne never fails to impress me as being eminently better than I think it's going to be. The salt is there, but it's held in perfect balance. The cheese is moist and smeary, so if you tried to crumble it atop bitter greens you'd happily wind up with big, irregular chunks. It manages to have a griddled hamburger essence while reminding me of carefully pan-roasted mushrooms. Mild enough to eat straight, but stalwart enough to balance meat or sherry. You can't lose.

**FRANCE | COW**
(UN)PASTEURIZED

**RECOMMENDED BRANDS:** Hervé Mons (Whole Foods exclusive), La Mémée

**AROMA:** Quite a lot—horsey, leathery

**TEXTURE:** Fat cap

**FLAVOR:** Salt-sweet perfect balance

IN SHORT: Seriously underrated

# Tilston Point FROM HOOK'S CHEESE COMPANY

The name "Tilston" is an anagram of Stilton (see page 349), the cheese that inspired Tony and Julie Hook to make this one-year aged hybrid mash-up in Mineral Point, Wisconsin. A cross section of the wheel looks like an accident: individual curds pressed together in a cohesive mass, dense and uniform on the inside but bulbous and brain-like on the outside, painted the telltale neon orange of a washed rind. That brine washing imparts an entirely new layer of flavor to what might be called Cheddar-like, or earthy Blue, depending on where the critic bit. A few dusty gray lines of mold punctuate the paste, and tasting around those is to confront the wet soil authenticity of English clothbound Cheddars (see page 250). With the mold comes the toasty, savory smack of caramelized pan bits. It's bizarre but neat.

**UNITED STATES | COW**
PASTEURIZED

**AROMA:** Washed rind fruity

**TEXTURE:** Medium-aged Cheddar

**FLAVOR:** Like actual dirt, toasty pan bits near the rind

IN SHORT: Novel

# Gorgonzola PDO (Naturale, Mountain, or Piccante)

**ITALY** | **COW**

**PASTEURIZED**

**RECOMMENDED BRAND:**
Ciresa

**AROMA:** Buttery biscuit

**TEXTURE:** Crumbly and smooth but with sandy/gritty mold

**FLAVOR:** A bit of salt and a bit of astringency but sweet milk and balance

**IN SHORT:** Solid

You can read about the basics of the PDO in the Gorgonzola Dolce (see page 342) entry, so I will limit my musings here to the spicier, crumbly style of Gorgonzola, more akin to what most of us think of as Blue. Mountain Gorg is a divisive cheese indeed. When tasting recently with a number of cheese friends, one sniped, "If I had the choice I would never eat this again. Not that it's so bad, it just has no redeeming qualities." Damning praise, indeed. A cheese newbie (but food enthusiast) was gentler if not terribly more generous: "It's not offensive. It's just . . . Blue." Truth is, the world of Blue has become crammed with options, and Gorgonzola is old hat these days. If you desire a middle-of-the-road, crowd-friendly option or a solid Blue for crumbling, this classic is classic for a reason. That said, if you have to pick one style of Gorg, go for the Cremificato (see page 342). There are also some long-aged Gorgonzolas out there, marketed as 300-plus days. I've found them to be consistently oversalted and unbalanced, often pretty harsh on the tongue.

## Rogue River Blue FROM ROGUE CREAMERY

**UNITED STATES** | **COW**

**UNPASTEURIZED**

**AROMA:** Smoke and cider

**TEXTURE:** Packed wet clay

**FLAVOR:** Pear brandy, cured meat

**IN SHORT:** Flavor cascade

There are a rare few cheeses that sell out before they're made. Rogue River Blue is one of them. Made seasonally, the batches are generally presold to retailers in the know. There's a big hoopla around the cheese's production, but it's not just marketing BS. Because it is made annually on the fall equinox when the farm's cows are late in their lactation cycle, this cheese comes from fattier, richer milk than at any other time of year. The wheels are wrapped in Syrah grape leaves, picked the previous spring from Carpenter Hill Vineyards, that have been washed and macerated in pear brandy from Clear Creek Distillery. After months of aging, the leaf-wrapped wheels are released beginning on the one-year anniversary of their production. Contrary to what you'd expect, a year of aging does not make a brutally intense Blue. Instead, the cheese is packed with small crystalline crunches throughout the paste. The high, clear notes of pear brandy are evident even in the wheel's dead center as is a vegetal, earthy essence that I attribute to the leaves. What I love about this cheese is that is always throws off a smoked, meaty flavor as well. Somehow, these disparate tastes meld into a bite that's like eating a crumble of cheese, a sliver of saucisson, and a swallow of wine, all at once. It's just incredibly elegant and layered, and curious to taste. New elements unfold. For all this, it's worth the $45 per pound price you're likely to encounter should you find it between September and January.

APPROACHABLE

# AmaBlu St. Pete's Select
### FROM CAVES OF FARIBAULT

The name means "I love blue" in Latin, and when I entered the caves just outside of Minneapolis on a snowy early winter day, I fell in love with the intensely floral perfume of aging Blue cheese. The limestone caves are dug into the hillside, a former site of beer lagering and then Blue cheese production and aging. Now St. Pete's Select spends a minimum of 100 days aging in the open air. Until I went to the source, I thought of St. Pete's Select as a perfectly fine, run-of-the-mill foil-wrapped Blue. It's much better than that. Many Blues have lipase added to the milk to speed the ripening process, which imparts spicy and prickly flavors. St. Pete's is creamily damp, with easy layers of sweet milk, salt, mushroomy savor, and then a flowery finish. It's superbly clean, which is saying a lot. No throat tickle, no itch.

**UNITED STATES | COW**
**UNPASTEURIZED**
**AROMA:** Perfumed
**TEXTURE:** Packed and creamy
**FLAVOR:** Complex
**IN SHORT:** Traditional and supremely well done

## PROTECTED BLUES

In addition to the Blues noted in this chapter, Europe boasts the following name-protected blues:

**DENMARK**
**DANABLU:** A foil-wrapped Blue (aka Danish Blue) made of full-fat cow milk and cream. The recipe dates to the 1920s when homogenized cream could be added to an existing Danish recipe riff on Roquefort. There are three producers of Danablu; its production is now very commercialized.

**ENGLAND**
**BUXTON BLUE PDO:** A Stilton-esque cylindrical Blue that looks like Shropshire, the cheese was made by a single creamery that has closed and is no longer produced.

**FRANCE**
**BLEU DES CAUSSES PDO:** A cows' milk Blue as old as Roquefort (see page 356), made in Rouergue and parts of Aveyron, Lot, Lozère, Gard, and Héraut. The cheese must be aged for a minimum of seventy days in the natural caves of Causses.

**BLEU DE GEX HAUT-JURA PDO AND BLEU DE SEPTMONCEL PDO:** Large, flat wheels of raw cow milk (French Simmental or Montbeliarde breeds only) Blue produced in the Ain or Jura. Although unpressed, the texture of the Blue is creamy and dense with minimal, pale-green veining that may be developed with *P. glaucum* or *P. roqueforti* mold.

**SPAIN**
**PICÓN BEJES-TRESVISO PDO:** A Cantabrian Blue of cow, goat, and sheep milk like a cross between Valdeón (see page 355) and Cabrales (see page 358).

# Buttermilk Blue (Affine) FROM ROTH CHEESE

UNITED STATES | COW

UNPASTEURIZED

**AROMA:** Curing meat

**TEXTURE:** Fudgy

**FLAVOR:** Red currants

IN SHORT: Foil-wrapped done right

The hallmark Blue of this Wisconsin producer (now owned by Swiss dairy cooperative Emmi) is available in an at least two-month version and an affine, or six-month-or-more, version. The recipe and presentation are the same, and although the affine is marketed as being spicier, I prefer it for its greater creaminess and mellower balance. Good American foil-wrapped Blues have a porky smell, like legs of prosciutto hanging to cure. Often, though, the ensuing bite is harsher and sharper than the initial enticing smell. By six-plus months, this Blue is damp and dense with the pronounced acidity of fresh red fruit. The paste is snow white, with delicately lacy blueing that gets greener and deeper with age. An excellent house standard from which one could make an insanely good Blue cheese dressing.

# Maytag Blue

UNITED STATES | COW

UNPASTEURIZED

**AROMA:** Blue mold and salt water

**TEXTURE:** Wet crumble

**FLAVOR:** Classic Blue cheese

IN SHORT: America's sweetheart

You can't talk about Blue cheese in the United States without mentioning Maytag. Begun by Fred Maytag II in 1940, Maytag Dairy Farms used the milk of their prize-winning herd of Holstein cows to adapt a Blue cheese recipe developed by Iowa State University. That cheese hit the market in 1941 and has held pride of place as America's Blue cheese ever since. It's still the most commonly cited domestic Blue in recipes and on restaurant menus: rindless, moist-yet-crumbly, and piquant. It's what we as a country have come to understand Blue to be. With all due respect to Maytag's storied history, it's not one of my top-list American Blues—not because it's bad, but because it's only fine. Consistent and readily available, with a reliable sweet/salty/spicy balance, it's the consummate crumbler.

# Shaker Blue and Ewe's Blue

FROM OLD CHATHAM SHEEPHERDING CO.

UNITED STATES | COW

(UN)PASTEURIZED

**AROMA:** Cocoa nibs, mushroom

**TEXTURE:** Crumbly, smearable, little worms of Blue mold

**FLAVOR:** Currant chocolate

IN SHORT: Hudson Valley Roquefort

The debate over the merits of raw versus pasteurized milk rages daily but rarely is there an opportunity to remove nearly all the other variables associated with flavor and isolate pasteurization. Old Chatham gives us that opportunity with their Ewe's Blue and Shaker Blue. Same farm, same milk, same Roquefort-style recipe (again, Old Chatham is a pioneering American maker whose origins date to a time when invoking the European greats was a savvy marketing strategy likely to succeed in getting consumers to pay upwards of $15 for a chunk of American cheese). The two Blues look the same, smell the same, and share a crumbly yet smearable texture that is sturdier than their

APPROACHABLE

French namesake. But then there is the flavor, markedly different and more complex in the raw milk Shaker. The vaguely Hershey-ish notes and whiff of mushroom in Ewe's Blue are honed and improved upon: all cocoa nibby, with a ripe red fruitiness and acidity that lightens the load. My gut tells me that, given the option, raw is better. These two prove the case.

# Queso de Valdeón

Commonly found on the U.S. market, but often misrepresented as Cabrales (see page 358), you once knew Valdeón by the dusty brown maple sycamore leaves that encased each wheel. As of 2014, the cheese began arriving on American shores in leaf-colored camouflage foil due to import restrictions on the leaves. Underneath, that gray mottled rind may boast smears of yellow or reddish yeast that protect an even, bone-white paste and irregular pockets of blueing. While the flavor is mellower than Cabrales, it is by no means a mild Blue—creamy, yes, but with lingering white pepper heat and a generous dose of salt. The bit near the rind boasts earthy notes that deliver my favorite kind of rusticity. While Valdeón is also cave aged, the caverns of the Picos de Europas in Castilla León, where it is housed before sale, are drier than those used for Cabrales.

SPAIN

COW OR COW/GOAT

PASTEURIZED

**RECOMMENDED BRANDS:** (all brands are made by Queserías Picos de Europa) El Rebeco Queso Azul, La Casería Blue Cheese, Queso Azul, Queso Azul Picos de Europas

**AROMA:** October leaf pile

**TEXTURE:** Moist and flaky

**FLAVOR:** White pepper

IN SHORT: Au naturel

# Moody Blue FROM ROTH CHEESE

When I have this cheese in my fridge, the entire box smells like a damply smoldering fire. So much so that I can't believe every other piece of food I own isn't going to reek of sleepaway camp. Moody Blue has a drier, flakier texture than Roth's Buttermilk Blue (see page 354), and although the fire pit essence permeates to the center of the cheese, it's far subtler than the smell would suggest. Under the salt, there's a caramel note and lightness that I chalk up to its smoking over fruit-wood rather than hickory. Most amazingly, the essence of this cheese is pure coffee ice cream, minus the sugar. A warning: don't eat the rind/unblued perimeter, which is akin to the newspaper tatters at the bottom of that fire pit.

UNITED STATES | COW

PASTEURIZED

**AROMA:** Nearby, smoldering fire pit

**TEXTURE:** Dry and flaky

**FLAVOR:** Coffee ice cream

IN SHORT: Proof that smoke can be subtle

# Smokey Blue FROM ROGUE CREAMERY

Rogue likens Smokey Blue to candied bacon, and it manages to capture that food's great satisfaction without the actual sugar. Sixteen hours of cold-smoking over Oregon hazelnut shells softens the sharp edge of their base Oregon Blue recipe and, I would argue, improves it. The bold, peppery essence of the cheese remains, but it's made more complex with the roasty, toasty whiff of smoke, which somehow pushes the natural sweetness of good milk to the fore. This was the first smoked Blue I ever tasted, and the moment I did it seemed so obvious. For anyone who enjoys a Blue cheese burger, now you can have one without the meat patty.

# Echo Mountain FROM ROGUE CREAMERY

Bucking the cow milk dominance of American Blues, Echo Mountain includes in its blend seasonally available goat milk from animals grazing along the Rogue River, before wheels are aged for a minimum of six months. The whiter paste is the first tip-off that goat milk is present, followed by the vaguely goaty aroma of the paste. The addition of goat milk and time takes Rogue's standard foil-wrapped recipe and turns it into a screamingly intense Blue, full of high, fruity, acidic notes that linger long after you swallow. Goat milk Blues are relatively rare, and much of the time they are incredibly subdued—minimal veining and drier paste with mellow hay and grass aroma. Not this guy. Think unapologetically fermenting pear, with a dose of salt to even it out.

# Roquefort PDO

Cheese folk tend to fight about Roquefort. "Why buy this cheese?" one asks. (It is, consistently, one of the most expensive cheeses on any counter because it is subject to a 100 percent import tax that effectively doubles the price as it crosses into U.S. territory.) Another answers, wisely, "It's the Champagne of Cheese. You could buy Cava or Prosecco, but if it matters you buy Champagne." People get Champagne: it means Fancy! Special! You're worth it! Roquefort sends a similar message. As with Champagne, there are a few big name brands that are very pleasant, and many more lesser known brands that can be downright life changing. A defining characteristic of the cheese is its raw material: only unpasteurized sheep milk. With a significantly higher fat content than cow or goat milk, exceptional sheep milk cheeses should capture

# WHAT DOES IT TAKE TO BE ROQUEFORT?

In 1925, Roquefort was the first cheese awarded AOC protection in France. Its unique production has made it a target in more ways than one—stories exist of American producers stealing mold spores from the aging caves in the 1950s and 1960s to try and imitate the cheese back home. These days, Roquefort is subject to grossly inflated tariffs when the United States wants to punish the European Union for refusing to import, say, our hormone-laced beef. It's not easy being Roquefort.

Its PDO specifications are extensive and require the following guidelines be met:

• Whole, raw sheep milk.

• Height and weight is dictated; mold spores may only be *Penicillium roqueforti.*

• Milk must come from the rayon, comprising 560 departments in Aveyron, Aude, Lozre, Gard, Herault, and Tarn, south of the Massif Central.

• The sheep must be of the Lacaune breed.

• Mold may be added in liquid form during coagulation, or in powder form when curds are placed in the mold.

• Cheese making is specified: highlights include a prohibition on pressing the curd during draining and a requirement that pierced wheels must arrive at the aging caves within two days of production. While the *P. roqueforti* is ambient in the caves, all wheels are inoculated before their arrival.

• There is a minimum of ninety days of aging.

• Every wheel must age, exposed, for a minimum of two weeks in the caves of Roquefort-sur-Soulzon.

• All aging, wrapping, and cutting of the cheese must occur in the municipality of Roquefort-sur-Soulzon.

There are seven producers of Roquefort. The largest is Société des Caves de Roquefort (maker of Roquefort Société). Others include Roquefort Papillon, Roquefort Carles, Roquefort Gabriel Coulet, Les Fromageries Occitanes, Vernières Frères, and Yves Combes (Roquefort Le Vieux Berger).

and capitalize on this fat. Great Roquefort vanishes instantly on your warm tongue. It shouldn't leave little strings of mold, or grainy bits, or salty crystals. It shouldn't be gamy, like rare lamb chops. It should creamify on contact. It should also be in balance. It should tease you to the moment of thinking it's too salty, and just then, at the very second you're about to diss it, the salt should quiet down so that you taste sweet cream, and then the mouthwatering pop of the mold. Hanging over this whole moment is the first bite of well-browned mushrooms straight from a cast iron pan. You're left with a whole that is far greater than the sum of its parts.

# Cabrales PDO

SPAIN

COW OR COW/GOAT/SHEEP

UNPASTEURIZED

**AROMA:** Clean, nutty

**TEXTURE:** Sticky—it lodges under tooth

**FLAVOR:** Black pepper

IN SHORT: Ass-whooper

Just by looking you can tell this cheese wants to kick your ass. The blueing is tiny and totally integrated into the paste, mapping out like an invasive vine you'd fear in the Plant Kingdom. As a result, the paste becomes grayish rather than white and blue. I've seen wheels that look like Yoda. For some reason, "Cabrales" became the name associated with Spanish Blue cheese, and in the aughts everything was sold under that name. True Cabrales is a peculiar and regulated cheese, made in multiple villages of eastern Asturias, and aged for a minimum of two months in natural caves. It is never wrapped in leaves (although this used to be permissible). It is usually cow milk but in summer months may be made from a blend of cow, goat, and sheep milk. The typical rennet used is kid (goat) rather than calf. In terms of its flavor, the Spanish talk about it having medium piquancy. I shudder to think what strong piquancy would entail. This is simply the spiciest Blue out there, especially when made from blended milk. It's not so much about salt as it is about the burn on your tongue tip and the back of the throat. It's about acid, your mouth watering relentlessly after a bite. Yet in its own way it maintains balance. Its aroma is clean, and redolent of toasted hazelnut. The finish is persistent, tingly, but somehow makes you want to try again and see what the experience will be like a second or third time. Chefs often cook with it, and stuffed within a piquillo pepper its spice becomes a welcome seasoning.

APPROACHABLE

## MY PICKS: APPROACHABLE BLUES

Mild Blues are most likely (but not always) to be higher moisture Blues: creamier and spreadable in texture with fine veining or only occasional pockets of blue. As a result, flavors of milk, cream, and butter are dominant; salt balances their sweetness; and the blue mold reads like a blip of fruity acid.

## Chiriboga Blue

Bavaria, known for its very large-scale, industrial Blue cheese makers, brings the world what might be the greatest Blue cheese ever. Cream-enriched, fluffy, and unbelievably buttery. (see page 343)

## Gorgonzola PDO, Dolce style (ideally Marca Oro from Ciresa)

From Italy, the most wobbly type of Gorgonzola Dolce is often bumpy in texture with striations of barely blue mold overlaid with white. It can't be prepacked and it sours quickly, so get it from a service store that you can trust to tell you when it's arrived fresh. Then: luscious, slippery, sweet-yet-pungent blobs you can eat with a spoon. (see page 342)

## Beenleigh Blue

For everyone who thought the only English Blue was Stilton (see page 349), try this. The hefty fat of sheep milk is ever present, and the cheese tastes like coconut oil. With a splash of sea water. It's like eating a day at the beach. (see page 344)

## Bayley Hazen Blue from Jasper Hill Farm:

The Best Unpasteurized Cheese in the World isn't a bad ending place for approachable Blues. Bayley was that, and continues to get better with each passing year. Sometimes anise-y, other times grilled burger-y, always shining from clean, sweet milk. (see page 348)

## MY PICKS: INTENSE BLUES

Intense Blue need not be synonymous with salt or spicy burn. For me, the intense Blues deliver unfolding layers of flavor and longer finishes that stay with you well after you've swallowed. In particular, this includes the better natural rind Blues with their earthen edge and biscuity rinds, those I'm most likely to call cheese first, Blue second.

## Stichelton

This is cheese brought back from the dead. The classic English Blue Stilton (see page 349), reimagined as it once was. It feels like a wedge of barely room-temperature butter and tastes bright yet layered: caramelly, toast, and then tropical fruit. (see page 350)

## Bleu d'Auvergne PDO (ideally, La Mémée)

It looks like what most people think of as Blue. Rindless, wrapped in foil, yet it tastes like eating a mushroom Blue -cheese burger without the beef or fungus. (see page 351)

## Rogue River Blue from Rogue Creamery

The pairing wisdom on Blues advocates for sweet wines. Here, you can have both in one with the lingering suggestion of pear brandy that skims the exterior of each bite. The cheese itself is stalwart and meaty, a whiff of smoke. Together they are just brilliantly good. (see page 352)

## Roquefort PDO (ideally, Carles, Gabriel Coulet or Le Vieux Berger)

The distinction between great and mediocre brands is nowhere more apparent than in strong cheeses. Here, mediocre equates to salt and bitter (strong, but not in a good way) and great equates to meltingly creamy balanced by fruity pop. (see page 356)

### TASTING ONE
## BLUES BY TYPE

Texture, salt, and mold content vary dramatically over the three basic types of Blue cheese. This may be the key to finding the type you like best.

**1. Soft-ripened: Saga**
(see page 338)

**2. Natural Rind: Stilton PDO**
(see page 351)

**3. Rindless/Foil-Wrapped: AmaBlu St. Pete's Select** (see page 353)

### TASTING TWO
## BLUES BY MILK

Tasting a selection of relatively intense Blues of varying milk types is a chance to see how goat and sheep milk impact the flavor and texture of what you assume Blue cheese to be.

**1. Cow: Bleu d'Auvergne PDO**
(see page 351)

**2. Goat: Echo Mountain from Rogue Creamery** (see page 356)

**3. Sheep: Roquefort PDO**
(see page 356)

### TASTING THREE
## COUSINS OF THE BLUE CHEESE WORLD

Spanning Old World and New World recipes, this tasting is an opportunity to see how cheese makers are inspired and influenced by one another, and how key regions of the cheese world interpret Blue in various ways. You can taste just one or two pairs, or go whole hog and do all 12 cheeses at once.

**1. Cambozola Black Label** (see page 339) **and Chiriboga Blue** (see page 343)

**2. Gorgonzola Dolce** (see page 342) **and Gorgonzola Mountain** (see page 352)

**3. Stilton** (see page 349) **and Stichelton** (see page 350)

**4. Buttermilk Blue** (see page 354) **and Maytag Blue** (see page 354)

**5. Shaker Blue** (see page 354) **and Roquefort** (see page 356)

**6. Valdeón** (see page 355) **and Cabrales** (see page 358)

# PAIRINGS WITH BLUES

## PAIRING OVERVIEW

BUTTON MUSHROOM

SALTY YOGURT

TOASTED NUTS/EARTHY

BLACK PEPPER/METALLIC

## CLASSIC PAIRINGS

(Whole flavor spectrum): Dense or crumbly Blue with sweet, viscous wine: Stilton and port; Roquefort and Sauternes

(Toasted nuts/earthy/black pepper/metallic) with watery crunch and smoke: iceberg wedge salad

(Black pepper/metallic) with butter: Roquefort and butter

### 1. CHOCOLATE

Gritty or slightly bitter dark chocolate offers a textural and flavor contrast to salty, spreadable, approachable Blues; sweeter, milder milk chocolate soothes fierce Blues.

FLAVOR SPECTRUM: 1–10

### 2. FRESH, CRUNCHY VEG

Blue cheese is probably best known in the United States as a salad topper, where its inherent saltiness stands in as a seasoning and the watery crunch of lettuce wipes away any residual intensity from the cheese. Celery, cucumber, endive, and jicama all stand in as worthy upgrades.

FLAVOR SPECTRUM: 1–10

### 3. CANDIED NUTS

Pecans and almonds are the most common choices, and can be easily candied at home with butter, brown sugar, and patience, although more exotic options abound at the market (Bobbysue's Nuts! is a fave of mine). Crunch, a hint of sweet, a bit of butter, and undertones of toast or smoke hit the perfect storm of Blue-balancing power.

FLAVOR SPECTRUM: 1–10

### 4. DRIED (MEDJOOL) DATES

My second take on Devils on Horseback (see page 180 on Taleggio pairings for the first take) involves pitting a dried date, stuffing it with Blue, wrapping it in half a slice of thick bacon, and securing the package with a toothpick. Five to ten minutes at 400°F and you've got a sweet, salty, smoky, and compulsively edible treat for friends.

FLAVOR SPECTRUM: 1–10

## 5. BUTTERY, OFF-DRY, OR SWEET WHITE WINES, LIKE CHARDONNAY, VIOGNIER, MOSCATO, RIESLING, OR GEWÜRZTRAMINER

Round, fruity, floral white wines with some oak or sugar deliver a drinking experience similar to eating slices of ripe yellow pear with your Blue.

**FLAVOR SPECTRUM: 1–10**

## 6. BISCUITS OR OATCAKES

Thick, coarse biscuits or cakes with a hint of sweetness are especially well suited to slatherable Blues. Carr's Whole Wheat Crackers are ubiquitous; Effie's Homemade Oatcakes, Corncakes, or Nutcakes can cover cheese or tea time. Also, consider very judiciously sweetened crackers or cookies using aromatic baking spices, like gingerbread.

**FLAVOR SPECTRUM: 1–4**

## 7. STOUT

Thick dark beer with big, roasted flavors of dark chocolate, plums, figs, dates, and malt. I find stout especially transformative with the drier-pasted fudgy Blues and their nut, toast, and earthy flavors.

**FLAVOR SPECTRUM: 4–7**

## 8. HONEY

It's not just for toast. Blue cheeses are probably the only group on which thick, sticky, sweet honey enhances the eating rather than smothering it. This is especially true for the moist, crumbly types at the intense end of the flavor spectrum. Honeycomb is a particularly beautiful option, but you need to be willing to eat the wax of the comb.

**FLAVOR SPECTRUM: 7–10**

## BEAR IN MIND

Salt! Saltiness is a prominent component of all Blues, approachable to intense.

Mold! Even approachable Blues are influenced by the presence of mold. This can read as fungal, metallic, and potentially bitter.

Sweetness balances salt and mold most easily.

Acid can be tricky, and is most likely to bring out bitterness, as is tannin (making red wines a dicier choice).

PROVOLONE

FORMAGGIO DI FOSSA

(SO-CALLED) VALENÇAY

LE CHEVROT

# Misfits

COUPOLE

TRUFFLE TREMOR

MONTE ENEBRO

GJETOST

TORTA DEL CASAR

# Once or twice a year I hear from a press outlet that's writing an article on weird food. Inevitably, they call me to ask about the maggot cheese.

Before I go any further, let me clarify that the maggot cheese (official name: *casu marzu*) isn't in this book. And not just because you can't get it in the States, but because I think it's gross. Why would you want to eat a cheese teeming with maggots? Probably you wouldn't. Most Sardinians don't keep a hunk of larvae-infested cheese in their fridges even though they can get their hands on the stuff.

Inevitably, when confronted with the weird food inquiry, I gently steer journalists away from the maggot cheese and toward one of the cheeses in this chapter. Part of what I love about cheese is that it's ALL weird! It depends on bacteria, yeast, and controlled spoilage for its very existence. It smells bad but tastes good. It's moldy but on purpose. And then there are the cheeses whose recipe is so different, or whose flavor is so singular, that they defy easy categorization. My former colleague Nathan Aldridge fondly called these cheeses "the misfits." They're the punks that don't neatly fall into any other gateway, and they don't really want to.

The only quality these cheeses share in common is their uncommonness. They run the textural gamut from soupy to solid, with flavors that might be delicate, sour, or beefy. They're hard to generalize because what they most taste like is themselves. And that's not a terribly helpful reference point if you've never eaten them.

Ever heard of a goaty cheese? That's the first group of misfits. While there are goat cheeses aplenty throughout this book, spanning the Mozzarella, Brie, and Manchego Gateways, I've studiously avoided most of the soft but mold- and yeast-ripened goat cheeses, until now. While fresh goat cheeses taste like lemony, hay-ey goat milk—and firm, aged goat cheeses taste softly herbaceous or approachably caramelly—many soft but ripened goat cheeses taste goaty. The best point of reference I can give you is the smell of a billy goat during mating season, when their natural musk is complemented by the urine they let loose on themselves. These goaty cheeses don't taste like musk, or pee—they're far more delicious than that. But if you've spent time with goats, there's a lingering association. A little sharp-edged and of that particular animal. They're too bucky to be Brie-like and not earthy or firm enough to be Manchego-like. They also happen to encompass the most famous small-format goat cheeses of the cheese world, those classics from France's Loire Valley. They stand alone, like a lone buck surveying a field of lady goats.

Then there are thistle-renneted cheeses. In a single valley of Extremadura, Spain, two name-protected cheeses are produced from unpasteurized sheep milk. These, along with a smattering of offerings from Portugal, are made using plant coagulant. In order to make the proteins of sheep milk knit together in solid curd form, dried thistle flower is used. The resulting style, called *torta* or *amanteigado*, is texturally remarkable. Imagine a loose, silken pudding. Then imagine spooning this pudding onto your tongue, only to find a shiver-inducing combination of fatty sheep milk and a pleasantly sour flavor somewhere between lemon-sprayed artichoke and asparagus. It doesn't taste like any other food you've eaten, although all the amanteigado cheeses have some echo of this bitter green edge cutting through the panna cotta cloud of their insides. I've searched far and wide for an explanation as to why this style is so geographically specific. Somewhere in my research I encountered the theory that Sephardic Jews migrating northward from Africa into Spain adopted plant matter to use as a coagulant in an effort to avoid combining milk and meat (rennet), prohibited by kosher laws. But I've never found any proof of this theory. So we are left with this small tribe of exceptional if bizarre cheeses.

Finally, I give you the WTF Cheeses. Or, as I fondly think of them, the misfits of the Misfits Gateway. True one-offs, these include a block more like caramel candy than like cheese; a cheese buried and ripened in deep, subterranean holes; and a cheese with a name that nine in ten Americans has heard but only one in ten Americans has really experienced.

Cheese first attracted me, and has held my attention for so many years, because it exists at the crossroads of sustenance and cultural history. Different styles evolved under very specific geographic and cultural conditions, and these cheeses begin to explain why and how milk, salt, and coagulant can and were turned into so many diverse foods. The misfits, more than perhaps any other cheeses, insist on historical exploration. Their traditions are a great part of their appeal. In short, they are as much cheeses to talk about as they are cheeses to eat.

# GROUP 1:
# SOFT-RIPENED GOAT CHEESES

Traditionally hailing from France's Loire Valley or its southwestern neighbor Poitou (although now being made with great results in the United States), soft-ripened goat cheeses are sort of Brie-ish. They have a mold-/yeast-ripened exterior, the growth of which may be supported by a sprinkling of black vegetable ash that changes the surface acidity and helps the rind grow. This can lead to a foggy gray cheese that may look like small, wrinkled brain thanks to *Geotrichum candidum* (see page 23). Soft-ripened goat cheeses are distinguished from Brie types in two key ways:

    **1. TEXTURE:** While high moisture and relatively soft, these tend to be cakey or clay-like rather than sticky or runny.

    **2. FLAVOR:** While the Brie types are united by their buttery character, these cheeses hold fast to their goat origins. With flavors described broadly as grassy, hay-like, tangy, goaty, or "of the animal," the soft-ripened goats are likely to strike a lover of mild, salt-butter Brie types as too strong or too weird. With increased age, the ashed goat cheeses develop flavors that are nuttier, piquant, and mushroomy while the unashed cheeses remain sweeter, yeastier, and milder.

Do note that the ashed goat cheeses may also be sold fresh or un-aged. In this case, you'll be buying a round or log of fresh goat cheese sprinkled with black ash. The cheese will be similar to the fresh chèvre described in the Mozzarella Gateway (see page 32): wet, creamy, tart, and lactic. What I'm focused on instead are the ripened or aged goat cheeses, where that sprinkling of ash has become a soft, foggy gray or blueish skin; the cheese underneath smooth, compact, and mostly flaky; the flavors layered, complex, and several steps away from pure goat milk.

## UNASHED, SOFT-RIPENED GOAT CHEESES

# Coupole FROM VERMONT CREAMERY

Named for its likeness to a snow-covered dome, Coupole is most akin to France's Le Chevrot (below) and Chabichou du Poitou (see page 371). While those cheeses are densely clay-like, Coupole has a moister center and more lactic flavors: goat milk and yogurt freshness burst from beneath the downy, paper-thin rind that has often just begun to look ridged and brainy. That edible skin remains mellow and nutty, and the cheese's full flavor spectrum is remarkably light and easy, without being terribly goaty or acidic. As a good cheese friend of mine says, "The French have a stranglehold on our collective consciousness when it comes to the benchmark we hold for goat cheese. Fortunately there is Vermont Creamery." He goes on to point out that the condition of Vermont Creamery cheeses across the United States is reliably excellent, and that you often get to choose the state of ripeness you prefer. It's a compelling reason to consider an American-made cheese when the alternative may be a dried -out, soapy, or bitter import.

**UNITED STATES | GOAT**
**PASTEURIZED**

**AROMA:** Wet hay, goaty, almond

**TEXTURE:** Sticky cheesecake

**FLAVOR:** Yogurt, melted butter, almond skin

**IN SHORT:** Sweet, mellow

# Le Chevrot

Europe inspires me for its "factory" producers that still prioritize tradition and handmade cheese. In this case, Sèvre & Belle Cooperative has the sixth-largest production of goat cheese in France, but still hand-ladles all its curd into teeny tiny molds and works only with fresh goat milk (rather than frozen curd). Based in the Poitou-Charentes town of Celles-sur-Belle, they make pasteurized cheeses for the States, but from the same facility that produces raw milk versions for the home market. (Le) Chevrot was a door-opening cheese for me, proving that a mold-/yeast-ripened goat cheese could be an entirely different animal from a fresh, lactic, lemony chèvre. Its consistency is remarkable. Nearly every cheese you find is a beautiful little drum the color of almond milk, covered in the wrinkly, brain-like rind that is the calling card of the yeast *Geotrichum candidum*. Accordingly, its flavor is sweet and mellow, with nutty undertones, while the snow-white center of the cheese has a mouthwatering tang. The combo becomes addictive, driving you back for another trilayer bite until the whole round vanishes. The biggest danger is that the cheese dries out; its brainy ridges deflate and shrink; and it takes on a piquant, potentially soapy edge.

**FRANCE | GOAT**
**PASTEURIZED**

**AROMA:** Hay and goat milk

**TEXTURE:** Dense but creamy

**FLAVOR:** Sweet 'n' tart

**IN SHORT:** The fresh chèvre upgrade

# MEET THE REAL FRENCH GOATS

The most famous soft-ripened French goat cheeses are named for their towns of origin; they are PDO cheeses; and most must be made of unpasteurized milk. They are also aged for less than sixty days. Accordingly, the real deals are not legal (and not available) in the United States. This being said, the pasteurized adaptations made for the U.S. market are nearly always sold under the PDO name. Buy them, because what choice have you got, but know that the cheese you will eat in France is radically different and, I would argue, a lot more complex and mind-blowing.

### CHABICHOU DU POITOU PDO:
The only PDO soft-ripened goat that may be made of pasteurized milk (although it's more likely to be found from raw milk in Europe). Made in the limestone areas of the Vienne, Deux-Sèvres, and Charente départements and characterized by a moist, yellowy, brain-like rind. It's mellow and faintly nutty, most akin to Le Chevrot (see page 369)

### POULIGNY-SAINT-PIERRE PDO:
Pyramid produced in the département of Indre from unpasteurized goat milk. It's got the nutty angle of all *Geotrichum*-rinded goats but tends toward stronger minerality and smoky undertones.

### CROTTIN DE CHAVIGNOL OR CHAVIGNOL PDO:
Produced in the départements of Cher, Loiret, and Nièvre—and centered around the Pays-Fort farming region known for its clay and clay-chalk soils—Crottin de Chavignol is made in a squared-off golf ball shape with an ivory rind. Blue mold patches aren't unusual, and its texture is denser and drier than other small-format goat cheeses. A well-aged version is piquant and walnutty.

### VALENÇAY PDO:
Ash-coated truncated pyramid made exclusively from the unpasteurized milk of Alpine and Saanen goats in the départements of Cher, Indre, Loir-et-Cher, and Indre-et-Loire.

### SELLES-SUR-CHER PDO:
Ash-coated disc made exclusively from the unpasteurized milk of Alpine and Saanen goats in the départements of Cher, Indre, and Loir-et-Cher.

### SAINTE-MAURE DE TOURAINE PDO:
Ash-coated log with a straw traversing its interior made exclusively from unpasteurized goat milk in the département of Indre-et-Loire and some parts of Loir-et-Cher, Indre, and Vienne.

# Chabichou du Poitou PDO

Chabichou is the only soft-ripened goat cheese whose PDO regulations permit production from pasteurized milk. Meaning: what's sold in the United States is technically the real deal, although the flavors of the pasteurized cheese are softer and more muted than the raw milk version. Shaped like a small, truncated cone, Chabichou looks like a brainy spark plug. Its name comes from the Arabic *chebli*, meaning "goat," and is a testament to the long history of east to west migration in this area of Poitou. The Saracens were making Chabichou in the Middle Ages; goat herding was conducive to a migrant, semi-nomadic lifestyle that helped spread cheese-making traditions around northwestern France. The designated regions of Chabichou production are known for their limestone soil, and I'm convinced this impacts the cheese's character and flavor. *Geotrichum* means a sweeter, yeastier rind; but the dense, moist paste of the cheese has a soft, minerally flavor not unlike wines made from limestone-grown grapes. It's an earthier, even slightly smoky alternative to the more common Le Chevrot (see page 369).

**FRANCE | GOAT**
**(UN)PASTEURIZED**

**AROMA:** Powdery goat milk and wet stone

**TEXTURE:** Dense, moist clay

**FLAVOR:** Soft and minerally

**IN SHORT:** Elegant and restrained

**UNITED STATES | GOAT**

**PASTEURIZED**

**AROMA:** Wet hay, goaty

**TEXTURE:** Smooth, sticky, thin creamline

**FLAVOR:** Yogurt (goat), seawater

**IN SHORT:** Tart, tangy

**FRANCE | GOAT**

**PASTEURIZED**

**AROMA:** Goat milk to roasted hazelnut

**TEXTURE:** Dry and a bit chewy

**FLAVOR:** Salt, goat milk, toasted hazelnut

**IN SHORT:** Bracing

# Bijou FROM VERMONT CREAMERY

Those familiar with the French classics will be reminded of a young Crottin de Chavignol (below), the inspiration for this little jewel. The cheese curds are coagulated overnight, allowing many hours for acidity to develop slowly and gradually before each gumdrop is aged for a week. Accordingly, the cheese is tangier and more intense than its fat, creamy brother Coupole(see page 369), and especially impressive after thirty to forty-five days, when it becomes drier and spunkier, with a toasted nuttiness that pushes to the fore. Like Crottin de Chavignol, Bijou's small size (about three ounces) makes it ideal for two (or one, the way I eat), sliced into little wedges on a side salad.

# (so-called) Crottin de Chavignol or Chavignol

Crottin are small (two- to three-ounce) drums of goat cheese, and there are few cheese rumors more persistent than the one that Crottin is so-called because, as it ages, it becomes drier and darker, resembling a turd. While *crottin* does translate to "dung," the cheese's name has more rarefied historical roots. It is thought to come from the Berrichon word *crot* (hole) and referred to the riverbanks where farmer women washed clothes in the Pays-Fort region of France, where the province of Berry is located. From this clay soil, farmers made pottery, including small cheese molds. Crottin de Chavignol is a cheese traditional to the poor farming regions of Cher, Loiret, and Nièvre; it was made by women for food and supplemental income, and the curds were predrained before being shaped in pottery molds. The predraining meant that women could continue with their day's work and not have to stop to deal with the cheese. It also meant a uniquely dense and dry curd prior to aging, which characterizes the cheese to this day. Typically it has a thin, ivory-colored rind that may have blue mold spots on it. Older versions become darker, turning brown, and actually get softer rather than harder in texture. These cheeses are known as *repassé* and are unlikely to be found outside of Europe. The pasteurized imitations exported to the United States are younger and tamer than is desirable, although that predrained curd is evident in the dense, teeth-sticking texture. This cheese becomes great as a dry, flaky nubbin with concentrated salt, toasted nut flavor, and a dose of piquant acidity.

## ASHED, SOFT-RIPENED GOAT CHEESES

# Wabash Cannonball FROM CAPRIOLE GOAT CHEESE

In the winter of 2001, I tasted my first Wabash Cannonball at the New York restaurant Artisanal. I had just become interested in cheese, although I was more than a year away from making it my career. It was one of several choices I checked off a long yellow menu of several dozen. It was a fortunate selection: tasting it made me want to quit my job and work in cheese. It was such a revelation that I bought myself a piece to take home. Back then, Indiana-based Capriole was selling to the New York market because there just wasn't much local demand. These days, Judy Schad's cheese is more likely to be found in her local region than on far-flung cheese plates, and that is a testament to the market she helped build. A three-ounce golf ball of goat milk, Wabash Cannonball is ashed and relies on *Geotrichum* for its rind. Accordingly, the cheese is fog-gray and brainy, with a dense, slightly flaky, snow-white interior. Its flavor is somewhere between the sweeter, mellower unashed goats (above) and the increasingly tart, citrusy ashed versions (below). I picked Wabash Cannonball up and ate it like a lady apple, forever cementing my passion for cheese.

**UNITED STATES** | **GOAT**
**PASTEURIZED**
**AROMA:** Fresh hay and goat milk
**TEXTURE:** Dense, moistly crumbling
**FLAVOR:** Lactic, citrus, mineral
**IN SHORT:** Bite-sized

# Truffle Tremor FROM CYPRESS GROVE

Truffle Tremor is essentially a smaller-sized wheel of Humboldt Fog Grande (see page 88), without the center line of ash and with the critical addition of Italian summer black truffle to its paste. Because it's practically half the size of Humboldt Fog, the thin white *candidum* rind breaks down the first quarter-inch of paste into creamy liquescence, contributing lactic and vaguely goaty notes. The one-pound size of newly released Truffle Tremor Mini only amplifies the concentrated flavors of the creamline. This piquancy is offset by the sexy, fungal haze of truffle, which manages to be musky and mushroomy rather than artificial or flavored. When I first tasted Truffle Tremor, I wrote that it "made me want to snuffle under the leaves." Today, I would modify this sentiment and say that the cheese makes me think of a rogue goat, browsing over a forgotten forest floor.

**UNITED STATES** | **GOAT**
**PASTEURIZED**
**AROMA:** Goat milk and truffle
**TEXTURE:** Iced cake
**FLAVOR:** Lactic, fungal
**IN SHORT:** Worth foraging

# (so-called) Valençay

FRANCE | GOAT

PASTEURIZED

**AROMA:** Lemon milk

**TEXTURE:** Moist and crumbly

**FLAVOR:** Crisp, lactic, lemony

**IN SHORT:** Lemon (goat) cheesecake

The pasteurized cheese sold under the name Valençay is often accompanied by Valençay's origin story: originally made in a pyramid shape, but following Napoleon's military losses in Egypt, he ordered that the top be struck from the cheese lest he be reminded of the Great Pyramids. I'm pretty sure that's another cheese rumor, but it makes good cocktail party chatter. Because there is relatively little rind to interior paste, Valençay breaks down more slowly than other ashed goats. Its texture remains fluffier and moister; its flavors milder. It tends to be the least goaty, despite the blue mold spots that can develop on the light gray to blue-gray rind. For this reason, I recommend it as a transition from fresh chèvre but find it less interesting than so-called Selles-sur-Cher (below) and Sainte-Maure (below).

# (so-called) Selles-sur-Cher

FRANCE | GOAT

PASTEURIZED

**AROMA:** Moist mushroom

**TEXTURE:** Smooth and chalky

**FLAVOR:** Black walnut, seawater

**IN SHORT:** Supremely balanced

I've noticed that ashed rounds of goat cheese (sold as Selles-sur-Cher though they're pasteurized) are more commonly found than their pyramid or log-shaped brothers. While Valençay (above) remains relatively unchanged as its rind ages, and Sainte-Maure (below) can become downright runny, Selles-sur-Cher exhibits some nice evolution without getting too crazy. The rind develops into a uniform gray, while the ivory-white interior becomes smooth and chalky with a modest creamline under the rind. Aromas of fresh goat milk give way to a more fungal quality over time, and the flavor is a good balance of salt, acid, and bitter (as in black walnut or bitter greens).

# (so-called) Sainte-Maure de Touraine

FRANCE | GOAT

PASTEURIZED

**AROMA:** Salty goat

**TEXTURE:** Smooth to flaky

**FLAVOR:** Piquant and salty

**IN SHORT:** Goaty

If you like your cheese soft and runny, with a persistent animal character and lingering bitter-green notes, then this is the ashed goat cheese for you even when made from pasteurized milk. The log-shaped cheese has quite a bit of rind relative to the interior paste, and as a result it breaks down more quickly and dramatically. This ripening is aided by the straw that traverses the cheese's interior, providing structure to increasingly droopy paste and allowing air to get inside the cheese. Well-ripened examples have a moist, gray-black rind and thick, yellowish creamline just beneath. The interior core evolves from smooth fondant to dense and flaking, with correspondingly intense flavors of salt and black walnut and aromas of goat.

(SO-CALLED) VALENÇAY

# GROUP 2: THE THISTLE-RENNETED CHEESES

To make cheese, one must transform (liquid) milk into (solid) curd, and for that a coagulant must be added to knit the milk proteins into a web that traps fat and water (see page 23). The traditional coagulant is the enzyme rennin, derived from an animal. The nouveau coagulant is microbial rennet, derived from a mold or yeast. From a consumer's perspective, neither has an appreciable impact on flavor or texture. You wouldn't be able to guess that a cheese was made with one or the other, although many cheese makers have a particular rationale for choosing traditional or vegetarian. Where you can taste and feel the coagulant every time is in a few very special cheeses made in Spain and Portugal, which are made with a plant-derived coagulant: thistle or cardoon flower. Collectively, they are known as *torta* or *amanteigado* cheeses. While cheese makers in Italy, France, and the United States are now experimenting with thistle rennet, I'm focused here on the traditional rounds made of unpasteurized sheep milk that exhibit a thick, gelatinous texture and bizarre, confusing flavor that is at once fruity, sour, bitter, and creamy. A cheese friend describes it thusly: "It's very loud."

The thistle-renneted cheeses have loud flavor and beguiling texture and are important to try and know, even if they're not your favorite. There's just nothing like them.

# Zimbro

Somewhere between an Azeitão (see page 377) and a Serra da Estrella (see page 377), but without PDO status, Zimbro is a remarkably mild intro to the thistle-renneted cheeses. Although you can expect a scary-looking package—mold-speckled cloth encircling a wobbly yellow round—the scoopable cheese inside is fatty and yeasty, with the bitter edge of thistle a mere undercurrent. The first bite of Zimbro often reminds me of apple Jolly Ranchers, but then comes the lanolin of sheep milk and a bracing smack of salinity. It's never too sour, which its PDO inspirations can often be.

**PORTUGAL | SHEEP**

**UNPASTEURIZED**

**AROMA:** Green

**TEXTURE:** Overcooked soft-boiled egg

**FLAVOR:** Herbaceous and lightly acidic

**IN SHORT:** Gently bitter

# Queso de la Serena PDO

As its name suggests, Extremadura is a land of extremes, and although agriculture is still one of the region's main means of sustenance, the summers can be so punishingly hot and dry that only (Merino) sheep would flourish. Although they make a scant third of a liter of milk each day, this milk is spun into one of the most special cheeses on the planet. Coagulated not with rennet but with the thistle-like cardoon, curdled at a low temperature and hand salted, the resulting cheese is a golden, bulging Frisbee about three inches tall. When properly ripe, the cheese's texture ranges from spoonable to liquid. My preferred serving method is to buy an entire 2.5-pound wheel; cut the thin, crusty top off; and dunk chorizo and bread directly into the torta. The cardoon imparts a bizarre, vegetal, slightly sour flavor at shocking odds with the puddingy texture. It's tart and green-tasting, and lush with fat.

**SPAIN | SHEEP**
**UNPASTEURIZED**
**AROMA:** Vaguely woolly, sour
**TEXTURE:** Panna cotta
**FLAVOR:** Vegetal, pleasantly bitter
**IN SHORT:** Popeye's pudding

# Queso Torta del Casar PDO

The other thistle-renneted cheese from Extremadura, Torta del Casar, more closely resembles a washed-rind cheese like Epoisses (see page 172) or Soumaintrain (see page 174) and is smaller than La Serena (above). Its wrinkled, pinkish rind bulges over the top of its confining wood box, but it tends to be springier and more compact than La Serena. Nine out of ten times, Torta del Casar is more intense than its valley neighbor, with woody, acidic bite up-front and a clean, milky finish.

**SPAIN | SHEEP**
**UNPASTEURIZED**
**AROMA:** Fruity, bready
**TEXTURE:** Gummy and thick under the rind and loose pudding at the center
**FLAVOR:** Green and floral
**IN SHORT:** Cheese custard

## FOR THE THISTLE LOVERS

If you're especially taken with thistle-renneted cheeses you're bound to find more varieties on your next trip to Portugal, or possibly in the country's best cheese shops. They're increasingly difficult to find stateside but offer an astonishing range of floral, vegetal, and acidic flavors worth seeking out abroad. Cheeses to look for include:

**OVELHA AMANTEIGADO:** Creamy and buttery, essentially a non-PDO Serra da Estrella.

**QUIEJO DE AZEITÃO PDO:** From spongy to still curdy, with a rough bark-like rind.

**QUIEJO DE NISA PDO:** The most cured and thus semifirm texture, floral and restrained.

**QUIEJO SERRA DA ESTRELLA PDO:** Closed, buttery texture with smooth, clean, slightly acidic flavor.

**QUIEJO SERPA PDO:** Semisoft texture and wilder flavor—fermented, bitter, wild yeast.

(AGED) PROVOLONE

## GROUP 3: THE WTF CHEESES

The misfits of the Misfits Gateway. These are bizarre cheeses whose flavor is singular and defies categorization.

# Gjetost

While not technically a cheese because it's made from whey rather than milk, *Yay-toast* is made, sold, and eaten like a cheese. A weird, stiff, smooth peanut-butter-colored block of candy cheese, that is. To make it, residual whey from traditional cheese making is boiled down, stirred, and condensed to a quarter of its original volume—in the process becoming thick and pourable as the lactose in the whey caramelizes. The name comes from the required goat whey (*gje* means "goat"), which I'm convinced contributes enough tang to prevent the cheese from otherwise becoming an eight-ounce block of salty caramel. It won't win any awards for complexity or nuance, but its tooth-sealing stick and sweet-salty appeal are strong enough that you might find yourself sneaking some well beyond the traditional Scandinavian cross-country ski trip. Because Gjetost can be cut into firm squares, I tend to slather them up with tart jams, like those made from sour cherry, and serve the pairing as utensil-free dessert.

# (Aged) Provolone

Not to be confused with the mild Provolone (see page 41) that is sold for slicing at deli counters across America, aged Provolone is typically aged for six to twelve months and can be shaped like an enormous torpedo missile or a hulking, rope-wrapped gourd. Thanks in good part to its large format, even aged cheeses maintain a soft, moist interior. The rind is a waxy, yellowish crust that darkens with age. The stretched, kneaded paste is elastic, compact, and uniform, possibly with small holes. What you don't want in an aged Provolone is a dry, mealy cheese that separates into dusty bits on the tongue. Provolone's characteristic spicy taste is the work of the enzyme lipase, which breaks down fat molecules in aging cheese over time. Depending on the producer and age profile, you're likely to encounter a high, fermented, spicy quality most akin to bile. Bad Provolone is like a throw-up burp; good Provolone hits you with the hairy tongue prickle balanced by beefy savor and salt such that you keep going back for more (even as you

**NORWAY**

GOAT AND COW WHEY

PASTEURIZED

**AROMA:** Cooked milk and sugar

**TEXTURE:** Thick, chewy, caramel block

**FLAVOR:** Salted caramel

**IN SHORT:** Dessert

**ITALY | COW**

(UN)PASTEURIZED

**RECOMMENDED BRAND:** Auricchio, Pondini Imports

**AROMA:** Beefy

**TEXTURE:** Elastic, compact and uniform, firm but moist

**FLAVOR:** Beef bouillon and fruit acid

**IN SHORT:** I've gotta say it—sharp

compulsively rub your tongue on the roof of your mouth). Provolone and other aged pasta filata cheeses are traditional to southern Italy; I've been told that the hot climate played a role in the accelerated work of lipase and the resultantly spicy flavor profile. There are two PDO Provolones: Monaco, which is from Naples; and Valpadana, which is from several northern Italian municipalities around Verona. Should you get the chance, they offer a perfect comparative tasting opportunity. With either, the juicy red wines of southern Italy balance the cheese's beefy, salty intensity especially well. I like Aglianico for its cooked plumminess, but any moderate tannin, high-acid, fruit-forward red does the trick.

# Formaggio di Fossa di Sogliano PDO

This "cheese of the pit" is the result of seasonal, laborious work to produce a sheep, cow, or mixed milk cheese that is subsequently aged for 80 to 100 days in subterranean pits found along the ridges of the Appenine Mountains, between the Romagna and Marche regions. The use of these pits dates back to the Middle Ages, both for food preservation and for hiding food during tribal raids. These days, before cheeses are buried in August, the pits are sanitized with wheat-straw fires and lined with wheat straw. They are then filled with irregular loaves of cheeses that emerge with dents and bumps, often smattered with mold, and anywhere from ivory to amber in color. Traditionally, the cheese is removed during the holiday of Santa Caterina on November 25. Because the cheese is wrapped and buried, it doesn't develop a distinct rind like other aged cheeses. The exterior and the hard, crumbly interior (both of which are often wet and greasy) are edible. It's often described as having a truffly or woodland aroma; I find it more pungent and gamy than that, with a pronounced fermented funk. The sheep milk version is most common and has a surprisingly fragrant, even floral, flavor with a lean, acidic finish. While I often avoid honey with cheese because the pairing can be cloying and sticky-mouthed, I love it here. Raw honey retains the essence of its botanical origins, playing up the floral qualities of Fossa while softening its acidic bite.

**ITALY** | **SHEEP/COW/MIX**

**(UN)PASTEURIZED**
*Da latte crudo* on the label signifies unpasteurized milk

**AROMA:** Damp stone and sheep

**TEXTURE:** Wet crumble

**FLAVOR:** Floral but acidic

**IN SHORT:** Spicy

# Monte Enebro

SPAIN | GOAT
PASTEURIZED

**AROMA:** Caves and blue mold

**TEXTURE:** Chalky to wet flakes

**FLAVOR:** Spicy yet milky

**IN SHORT:** The goat cheese for Blue lovers

In a cheese tasting or party spread, I often include Monte Enebro in lieu of Blue cheese, even though it lacks interior mold and isn't technically Blue. It can hold pride of place, however, because it has an ashed, molded exterior brimming with metallic, mushroom intensity. The snow-white interior is a giveaway that the cheese is made from goat milk, but otherwise you might not know, so layered is the flavor. It is produced in Avila, near Madrid, by Paloma Baez. The recipe for Monte Enebro was for years known only to Paloma's father Rafael. There was concern that should he die, the cheese would die along with him, so unique was its recipe. Monte Enebro develops a thin creamline after thirty to forty-five days, while the loaf-shaped interior remains moistly flaky and lactic. The more aged the cheese, the more intense it becomes: salt concentrates; the creamline thickens into a translucent, spicy goo; and the interior takes on dark, piquant, walnutty flavor. Monte Enebro manages to smell cave-like—all minerally, wet rock, while tasting brightly acidic with a racy, white pepper finish. There are a few pairings I've experienced in the past fifteen years that were so profoundly and immediately delicious that they remain lodged in my memory as near perfect. The sweet, often-scoffed-at sparkler Moscato d'Asti, with its lush peach and nectarine quaffability, alongside slivers of Monte Enbero, was one of my pairing game changers.

The misfits' weirdness is best understood alongside the more familiar and conventional flavor profiles of the preceding gateways. For this reason, and the fact that I've avoided cross-chapter tastings thus far, the following vertical tastings span the entire *Book of Cheese*.

TASTING ONE
## DISCOVERING "GOATY"

Tasting soft-ripened goat cheeses next to fresh, cream-enriched, and aged versions drives home the minerally, edging-on-animally quality that cheese people call goaty.

**1. Fresh (unaged) goat cheese: Fresh goat cheese, or Chèvre** (see page 56)

**2. Cream-enriched (Brie-like) goat cheese: Cremont from Vermont Creamery** (see page 93)

**3. Aged (Havarti-, Manchego-, or Parm-like) goat cheese: Young Goat Gouda** (see page 131)**, Garrotxa** (see page 193)**, or Aged Goat Gouda** (see page 298)

**4. Unashed, soft-ripened (goaty) goat cheese: Le Chevrot** (see page 369)

**5. Ashed, soft-ripened (even more goaty) goat cheese: (so-called) Sainte-Maure de Touraine** (see page 374)

TASTING TWO

## THISTLE, THE ONLY COAGULANT YOU CAN TASTE

People often ask me if they will taste a difference between cheeses coagulated with animal rennet and vegetarian rennet (see page 23). My answer is no, except with the thistle-renneted cheeses. Here, the flavor is a direct result of the coagulant, as this comparative tasting of sheep milk cheeses demonstrates. I've chosen soft sheep milk cheeses so texture doesn't become another variable, but you can pick any sheep milk cheeses you'd like.

**1. Vegetarian (microbial) rennet: Kinderhook Creek from Old Chatham Sheepherding Company** (see page 86)

**2. Animal rennet: Brebisrousse d'Argental** (see page 98)

**3. Thistle rennet: Zimbro** (see page 376)**, Queso de la Serena** (see page 377)**, or Queso Torta del Casar** (see page 377)

TASTING THREE

## LOOKS (AND NAMES) CAN BE DECEIVING

The misfits of the Misfits Gateway may look and sound like other cheeses, but they march to the beat of their own drum, as revealed by a comparative tasting with their apparently closest relatives. These couplings can be tasted alone, or as a group.

**1. Young Provolone** (see page 41) **and aged Provolone** (see page 380)

**2. Pecorino Toscano (Stagionato)** (see page 197) **and Formaggio di Fossa di Sogliano** (see page 381)

**3. A rindless Blue such as Bleu d'Auvergne** (see page 351)**, Buttermilk Blue (Affine) from Roth Cheese** (see page 354)**, or Roquefort** (see page 356) **and Monte Enebro** (see page 382)

# Pairings to Try

### SOFT-RIPENED GOAT CHEESES
FLAVORS: GRASS/HAY, NUT SKIN, YOGURT, SALT
TEXTURES: MOIST, DENSE, CLAY-LIKE

### (WHOLE FLAVOR SPECTRUM) WITH SAUVIGNON BLANC

If what grows together goes together, then the Loire's characteristic Sauvignon Blanc grape and its traditional small-format goat cheeses should be a slam-dunk match made in heaven. And you know, they are. Sauvignon Blanc makes green, herbaceous wines with great acidity and citrus fruit flavors. The grassy acidity is matched by similar characteristics in the cheese, causing these flavors to recede so your wine becomes fruitier and your cheese becomes nuttier and earthier.

### THISTLE-RENNETED CHEESES
FLAVORS: HERBACEOUS, FRUITY, SOUR, BITTER
TEXTURES: FATTY, SCOOPABLE

### (WHOLE FLAVOR SPECTRUM) WITH SMOKY, SPICY CURED MEAT LIKE CHORIZO

These are intensely challenging cheeses to pair with because the flavors are acidic, sour, and not unlike that most-impossible-to-pair vegetable, artichoke. Add to that the thick, palate-coating texture of sheep fat and pairing becomes a real conundrum. Something acidic or tannic to cut the fat amplifies the sourness. Something sweet or fruity to balance the sour feels heavy with the fat. Enter coin-shaped discs of chewy, smoky, spicy meat. Although the cheese is incredibly rich, it feels lean because of the sourness and acidity. Smoke and heat temper those, and you wind up with a pleasantly bitter, vegetal dip.

# APPENDIX 1: THE NITTY-GRITTY ON PASTEURIZATION

Named for Louis Pasteur, pasteurization is the process of heat-treating milk prior to cheese making, with the express intention of destroying potentially harmful pathogens that may be present.

**HIGH-TEMPERATURE SHORT-TERM (HTST)** uses metal plates and hot water to raise milk's temperature to at least 161°F for not less than fifteen seconds, followed by rapid cooling.

**HIGH-HEAT SHORT-TERM (HHST)** is similar, but uses different equipment and higher temperatures for shorter periods of time.

**ULTRAPASTEURIZED** milk is heated to no less than 280°F for two seconds.

**ULTRAHIGH TEMPERATURE (UHT)** heats milk until sterile and shelf stable.

The latter two methods are most commonly used for drinking milk.

**THERMALIZATION** (or *thermisation*) is a lower, slower process of heat treatment that does not destroy as many organisms as HTST and HHST pasteurization. Many European producers are quick to point out that they thermalize rather than pasteurize their milk before making cheese. Thermalization does not, however, meet the U.S. Food and Drug Administration's criteria for pasteurization. Thus, thermalized cheeses are legally considered raw, or unpasteurized, and are subject to minimum aging requirements.

# APPENDIX 2: THE STEPS OF CHEESE MAKING

### 1. BEGIN WITH FRESH MILK
This may be cow, sheep, goat, water buffalo, nak (female yak), or some combination thereof.

### 2. PASTEURIZATION, IF APPLICABLE

**3. ACIDIFICATION:** The process by which lactose (milk sugar) is partially or entirely converted to lactic acid, making milk thicker in texture and more acidic in flavor. Long, slow acidification yields a more crumbly texture (as in unaged goat cheese). Brief acidification followed by stronger coagulation yields a smooth, pliable texture (as in Gruyère). During this time, milk may be heated to speed acidification. Mold may be added to create a Brie-style or Blue cheese.

**4. COAGULATION:** A coagulating agent (rennet, microbial, or vegetable) is added to the milk, breaking down protein chains into a web that traps liquid and fat. Liquid milk becomes gelatinous, solid curd. Milk may be heated during coagulation for a firmer set.

**5. CUTTING:** Curd may not be cut at all but simply scooped into draining molds, or it may be cut into pieces as large as a bread slice or as small as a rice grain. The smaller the curd, the more water released, and the drier and firmer the final cheese.

**6. STIRRING:** The curd may be stirred during cutting.

**7. COOKING:** During cutting and stirring, the curd may be heated as high as 130°F. Heating forces the explosion of moisture and results in a drier, firmer final cheese.

**8. (A) DRAINING:** Whey is drained from curd. This may happen simultaneously with hooping; curds and whey are poured into perforated hoops or molds for draining. (Some cheeses are salted in the vat, meaning that whey is drained and curd is salted before being hooped.)

**(B) CHEDDARING:** If a cheese is Cheddared, whey is drained and the curd is allowed to form mats. These are then cut into blocks, which are stacked and restacked atop each other.

**9. MILLING:** If a cheese is milled, the drained curd is run through a machine that chops it into strips or bits the size of popcorn.

**10. HOOPING:** Drained curd is scooped into perforated hoops or molds that will define the cheese's final shape. Many cheeses are drained and hooped simultaneously, skipping steps 8a and 9.

**11. PRESSING:** The drained curd may be pressed, by hand or mechanically, to further expel moisture. Pressing may happen as briefly as a few minutes or as long as overnight.

**12. SALTING:** Wheels are submerged in brine or rubbed by hand or machine with dry salt.

**13. RIPENING OR AGING:** Wheels are transported to temperature- and humidity-controlled rooms (cellars or caves) for open-air ripening of several days or several years. Some cheeses are encased in plastic; oxygen is removed; and they ripen in a refrigerator.

Cheese is a living organism that continues to change over time. Most notably, the following processes are ongoing:

**LIPOLYSIS:** The breakdown of fats. During ripening, lipolysis releases free fatty acids (FFAs) that may have a significant impact on flavor. Also, FFAs may be metabolized to other highly flavored compounds.

**PROTEOLYSIS:** The breakdown of proteins. During coagulation, this enables the conversion of liquid milk to solid curd. During ripening, proteolysis impacts texture, making the creamy layer under the rind of a Brie, for example.

# APPENDIX 3: FLAVOR ACROSS GATEWAYS

Each gateway cheese in this book introduces you to a spectrum of flavor ranging from approachable (1 on a scale of 1 to 10) to intense (10 on the same scale). My goal is to help you understand the world of cheese from the perspective of your flavor preferences rather than with some mandate about what flavors are supposed to be good.

| | GATEWAY | | | |
| AROMA FLAVOR PROFILE | MOZZARELLA | BRIE | HAVARTI | TALEGGIO |
|---|---|---|---|---|
| MILK, CREAM, BUTTER | 1–4 | 1–3 | 1–2 | |
| COOKED MILK | | | | |
| TANGY DAIRY: YOGURT, CRÈME FRAÎCHE, CITRUS | 5–7 | 4–5 | 3–5 | |
| HERBACEOUS, FLORAL, GRASSY | | | | |
| YEASTY, DOUGH, SEA SALT | | | | 1–2 |
| STONE FRUIT, STRAWBERRY | | | | 3–4 |
| RAW NUTS, NUT SKIN | | | | |
| TOAST, TOASTED NUTS | | | | |
| CARAMEL, BUTTERSCOTCH | | | 6 | |
| EARTHY, VEGETAL, MUSHROOM, TRUFFLE | | 6–8 | 7–10 | 5 |
| CURED MEAT, BRINE | | | 8–9 | 6–8 |
| CRUCIFEROUS VEGETABLE | | 8–10 | | |
| PIQUANT, FERMENTED FRUIT (KOMBUCHA) ACIDIC | | | | |
| ALLIUM, BEEFY | | | | 9–10 |
| INTENSE SALT, GAMY | 8–10 | | | |
| BITTER GREENS | | 10 | 10 | |

One of the cool things about cheese is that flavors are shared across gateways. For example, many of the qualities that land a cheese at the intense end of the Mozzarella Gateway reappear at the intense end of the Manchego Gateway. Below, I've mapped out overlapping flavor characteristics so you can begin to explore beyond the confines of the safe and reliable cheeses you've been buying for years.

| MANCHEGO | CHEDDAR | SWISS | PARMESAN | BLUE |
|----------|---------|-------|----------|------|
|          | 1–3     |       |          |      |
|          |         | 1–2   | 1–3      |      |
| 2        | 4–5     |       |          |      |
| 1–2      |         |       |          |      |
| 3        |         |       |          |      |
|          |         | 3–5   | 1–7      | 4–5  |
| 6–7      | 6–8     | 8     | 1–7      |      |
|          | 8–9     |       |          | 1–3  |
| 4–5      |         | 6–7   |          | 6    |
| 8–9      | 8–9     | 9     | 8–10     | 7–10 |
|          |         | 10    |          |      |
| 10       | 10      |       |          |      |

# ACKNOWLEDGMENTS

If it takes a village to raise a child, then it's taken a small nation to bring up this book. Our story begins back in 2012. My agent (and Consider Bardwell cheese steward), Angela Miller, introduced me to the writer, cook and generally wonderful woman Suzanne Lenzer. Suzanne and I wanted to do a cheese cookbook, a good one that was contemporary and seasonal and free from the constraints of grilled cheese, mac and cheese, and fondue. Sadly, no one wanted to publish it. But through this I met the legendary editor Leslie Stoker, who connected me to the visionary Will Schwalbe and Bob Miller at Flatiron Books and suddenly it was Cheese Game On.

Angela, for hearing me out on my weird dreams and gut instincts and little voices, and believing in them too (or not telling me if you didn't), thank you.

Suzanne, for reminding me that working with people you like is the most important criterion of all, thank you.

Leslie, for thinking this thing up and shepherding the project in its initial phase.

Bob, for seeing my vision and believing in it from Day 1, thank you.

Will, for doing all of the above, for pushing my writing, and for your genuine enthusiasm for cheese and making this book, thank you.

Throughout the text I mention the friends, colleagues, and cheese geeks who helped and inspired me. They tasted with me, let me steal some of their best one-liners, and supported me through a very. Long. Writing process. My Cheese Advisory Group: Aaron Foster, Carey Polis, Elizabeth Chubbuck, Laure Dubouloz, Matt Spiegler, and Tia Keenan. My friends at St. James Cheese Company in New Orleans, who welcomed me to sit, taste, and, often, drink: James Gentry, Justin Trosclair, Richard and Danielle Sutton. Nathan Aldridge, who invented the Misfits. Adam Moskowitz, who made it possible for me (and my family) to spend a month in Switzerland, Austria, and Bavaria, where I met some of the most inspirational makers I have ever known and reconnected with my joy for cheese.

Capturing the sensual, organic, communal, tactile greatness of cheese, in the context of a 400-plus-page reference book, ain't easy. And without the brilliance of Ellen Silverman it would not have been possible. I'm so grateful not only for her enormous talent as a photographer, but for her friendship and humor.

William van Roden, designer extraordinaire, translated dozens of ideas about charts and wheels and graphs and sidebars into a book that is truly beautiful and not just functional.

Prop stylist Bette Blau brought her impeccable taste and instinct, plus her formidable collection of cool stuff to take pictures on. Food stylist Eugene Jho gently heard out my ideas for food presentation and then (blessedly) took us in the other direction.

Photographing more than a hundred cheeses from all over the world simply would not have been possible without the generosity and support of dozens of makers and importers. Heartfelt thanks to Ancient Heritage Dairy, Arthur Schuman, Beemster, Bellwether Farm, Carr Valley Cheese Company, Castello, Cato Corner Farm, Caves of Faribault, Cellars at Jasper Hill, Chalet Cheese Cooperative, Columbia Cheese, Cowgirl Creamery, Cypress Grove, Emmi USA, Essex Street Cheese, Goat Cheeses of France, Gourmino, Hook's Cheese Company, Interval, Laura Chenel's Chèvre, Lioni Latticini, Maison Mons, Many Fold Farm, Marin French Cheese Company, Meadow Creek Dairy, Neal's Yard Dairy, Nettle Meadow, Pondini Imports, Point Reyes Farmstead Cheese, Quicke's Traditional Ltd., Rogue Creamery, Roth Cellars, Sartori, Sequatchie Cove Creamery, Spring Brook Farm, Sprout Creek Farm, Sweet Grass Dairy, Swiss Valley Farms, Uplands Cheese Company, Vermont Creamery, Widmer's Cheese Cellars, and Wisconsin Milk Marketing Board.

Particular appreciation and thanks to Michele Buster with Forever Cheese and Brian Scott with Gourmet Foods International for their enormous contributions.

Once a book is written and photographed and designed, the often thankless tasks of editing and copyediting ensure that the author doesn't look like a fool. Kara Rota talked me off multiple editing cliffs and made this book so much better for her questions and ideas. Alda Trabucchi made literally thousands of small changes, the result of which is one hugely improved text. Bryn Clark kindly and sagely shepherded me and the manuscript through it all.

Which brings me to the end of the small nation that made this book possible, and to the smaller nation who make everything I do possible. David, at some point in every day I say a small prayer of thanks that I get to be your wife. Heron and Esme, being your mother is the greatest honor and privilege I will ever know. Thank God you're both good eaters.

# INDEX

Page numbers in *italics* refer to photographs.